MW01036983

PSYCHIANA
THE ADVANCED LESSONS

PSYCHIANA
THE ADVANCED LESSONS

FRANK B. ROBINSON

WILDSIDE PRESS

PSYCHIANA: THE ADVANCED LESSONS

This edition published in 2007 by Wildside Press, LLC.
www.wildsidebooks.com

Dear friend,

Thanks very much for your enrollment in this Course of Instruction. I appreciate your confidence and value it very highly.

I shall not say very much to you now because I much prefer to let these Lessons speak for themselves, which they usually do. Whenever possible, I personally read every letter coming to me from students, and in my absence they are read and answered by very capable assistants. In your individual case I want to help you if I can.

As these marvelous Lessons come to you, study them carefully, and as you apply the great Spiritual Law to your own life, you will find that this Law is a very vital Power, which can bring to you the things you need.

If there is anything about the Lessons you do not understand, you may feel perfectly free to write me.

Sincerely yours,
Frank B. Robinson

At the beginning of our studies together I have one regret and that is that it is not possible for me to be seated in your home with you and talking with you face to face. You must realize that in a course of instruction such as this course is, and which is going all over the civilized world, I am talking to people in every occupation of life and in every walk of life. Who you personally are, I have, of course, no way of knowing as I write this. Perhaps you are a professional man or woman. Perhaps you are a mail carrier working for Uncle Sam. Or it may be you are an auto mechanic, school teacher, minister, priest, or possibly you may be one of the unemployed. It makes no difference, however, for the great fundamental Law governing and controlling HEALTH, HAPPINESS and MATERIAL ABUNDANCE is no respecter of persons, and operates with perfect precision in every human life.

This mighty Law takes no cognizance of a person's circumstances but it operates with remarkable precision whenever and wherever it is used. So, no matter who you may be, and no matter what your circumstances are, be prepared to receive some of the greatest Spiritual Truths which have ever been called to your attention. In fact, I am positive this startling revelation never has been brought to your attention before. If your circumstances are such that you have an abundance of wealth, perfect health and perfect domestic happiness, then the Law can bring to you an increased measure of these things without which no life can be normal, for it never was meant to be that you and I should be born on this earth, and go down to the tomb fighting against failure, disease and unhappiness. Such a thing is foreign to the eternal principle behind this scheme of things as it exists, and furthermore, it is not necessary that such a condition of affairs exist. Really there is no need for such undesirable conditions of life, and these conditions only manifest through ignorance of a Motivating Principle which can and does absolutely operate to bring into existence conditions of a far different nature.

It may be, however, that you are one of those engaged in one continuous struggle with unhappiness, ill health, lack of money, and business failure. And the world is full of such. There are millions living in this Country today whose predominating thought is one of failure. They see men and women all around them making a success of life and they marvel at the ability these fortunate ones seem to possess. But in their own case, failure and neglect of everything good manifests, and they consider the finest things of life far beyond their reach. They are dissatisfied with this and they are dissatisfied with that. First they try this and then they try that. But ever they are found to be chasing the elusive rainbow. Success does not come to them, nor does perfect health come to them. And as far as domestic happiness goes they do not know what it is. The entire human race seems to be in the grip of what some psychologists call an inferiority complex and there seems to be no possible way out of it.

It is to such people as this that my message is directed more than to any other class; and if you are unfortunate enough to be a person from whom success, health and happiness seems to steer clear, then I have a very vital message of hope for you.

There is far more possibility of the Law governing success, health and happiness operating where there is no success, health and happiness, than there can be of this Law operating in the lives of those who are already successful happy, and enjoying perfect health. True it is that those now enjoying these blessings of life may enjoy them to a far greater degree as they understand this mighty spiritual Law; but you will readily see there is far more possibility of success, health and happiness manifesting through the application of this mighty Law, where there never has been either success, happiness or health. I drive along one of the beautiful California highways and my car just glides along as if it had wings. The road is in perfect condition and it would be absolute foolishness to send steam shovels, scrapers and a crew of men out to repair a road of that kind. But what a different question on one of the bumpy side roads on which I sometimes get. On this road there is need of repair. And so in the human life, for only in the life which lacks success, health and happiness can these things be manifested and only in such a life can they be appreciated.

I am not an old man by any means but to the contrary I am in the very prime of life and never before could I do the volume of work I am doing today. And yet, for over forty years I was tossed hither and thither like a piece of driftwood on the bosom of the stormy ocean of life, vainly trying to achieve something worth while. First I tried this, and then I tried that—and tried hard too.

But ever it seemed I was relentlessly pursued by this demon of poverty. I usually had good health but never was really happy and I do not think it is possible for people to be happy when they are denied the very things which tend to happiness.

So I know whereof I speak when I say to you that there is a Law operating here and now, which Law is abundantly able to provide you with everything you can possibly need to make your life abundantly happy, abundantly healthy, and abundantly successful. I am going to show you in this course of instruction just exactly what that Law is and then, naturally, you will apply this Law to your own life problems and you should be able to drive poverty, ill health and unhappiness completely out of your life as fast and as effectively as I did. So again I say that my only regret is that I cannot be talking to you in your own home or from the lecture platform, in which case you would see me and I would probably be able to express myself much more forcibly than I can in writing. However, in less than one year's time this teaching went all over the civilized globe, and my files are literally teeming with hundreds of letters which have come to me from all over the world, telling in unmistakable language of the benefits and changed circumstances brought about through the study of these lessons.

There comes to my mind at this moment a letter I recently received from a lady in Oakland, California. This lady had been struggling consistently with several problems and never had been able to master them. Shortly after enrolling with us, however, we received one of the most remarkable letters of them all. The woman was gloriously happy and she had discovered that the Law worked, and to use her own words she said, "Not only does this Law work for happiness but it brings results in a very MATERIAL WAY." Back in St. Joseph, Michigan, is the head of a business. This person for years had been tortured with varicose veins in the leg. After having received our fourth Lesson, however, this business executive received one of the most remarkable manifestations of instant healing through the LAW that has ever been called to my attention as the result of this study. This party stated that practically instantaneously the soreness and the pain left, and in two days all signs of swelling were gone and he has never been bothered since. I merely mention these two cases in passing but have hundreds of them in my files and I know whereof I speak when I say to you that such a Law exists.

This course of instruction is entirely different from anything ever put in to print before. Probably that is the reason for its remarkable success. It is complete in itself and the person finishing these studies with me does not need to search elsewhere for the secret of health, happiness and success, for this mighty Law I teach is a complete Law. Deep down somewhere in your nature there is a longing and a desire to know what it is all about. I do not care what your religious experience or teachings have been, nor do I care whether you are living a life filled with the good things of life and are abundantly happy or not. I do not care whether you have a million dollars in the bank or nothing at all, for there is still that unsatisfied longing to know the truth not only of success, but the truth of life itself. I think it is safe to say that fear rules ninety nine per cent of the lives in this country. This course of instruction will take that out, for when you and I understand this Spiritual Law, then fear will have no place in your makeup. We do not regret the past nor do we fear the future, but we live moment by moment in the conscious realization of the actual presence of a Power or Law or Spirit which is abundantly able to work with us for success, health and happiness in the very moment in which we work with the Law.

You will discover that these Lessons deal with the very fundamentals of life, for there can be no such thing as perfect health, domestic happiness or success until men and women realize their relationship to the overruling Law which Law is responsible for this created scheme of things as it exists.

Some night when the stars are shining brightly, get outside and look up in to the heavens. You will see like a silver band girdling the celestial sphere, the Milky Way. Try and realize that the light from some of those myriads of stars comprising that Milky Way was on its way to this earth long before the earth was created. Look up at the sun some day through a smoked glass and try to realize the thought that the flames from that ball of fire are leaping into the atmosphere in all directions as high as 150,000 miles or five times the circumference of this earth. Then if you can, let your imagination roll still farther and realize that every one of those glowing diamonds of the heavens is but an other such sun, many of them countless millions of light years away. As you are standing there looking at this celestial dome, try to imagine the earth suddenly cut from under your feet and then look down where you will see in your mind's eye the other half of the celestial sphere. Then realize, if you can, that you, standing there, are infinitely more intricate a physical system than are those entire heavens. Not one of those stars, satellites, or planets can make a mistake and swing out of its orbit bringing destruction and disaster to the rest of the marvelous scheme. For behind them all and spreading through them all is the Law I am here speaking to you about. You will admit with me that it is almost impossible to comprehend such a magnificent scheme as the heavens disclose; but it is not hard to understand that an eternal Law is responsible for this.

This same Law is responsible for every success and every failure. Many successful men and women comply with the Law unconsciously and naturally success follows. It is much more satisfactory, however, to intelligently work with and use this Law than it is to use it unconsciously, and where it is consciously used, then it may be directed to whatever object is desired and surely you will agree with me that if you and I can utilize the mighty Law behind this universe for the things we need, then in that case there cannot possibly be any lack, can there?

I think I can safely say to you, whoever you may be, that when you realize what a dynamic power is placed into your hands by the knowledge of this Law, you too, like hundreds of others will write me expressing your happiness in words of wonder and joy. Raised in a very religious family, son of a prominent Baptist minister, for many years I suspected that those who were attempting to enlighten the rest of the world spiritually were off at a tangent. I don't think their motives can be questioned at all but any thinking man or woman knows that these good brethren who have attempted to teach us something about God, have made a miserable failure of their job. They cannot explain Him, nor are they able to demonstrate any spiritual power of any kind either in their own lives or in the lives of others. Many of them make a lot of noise, many of them are specialists in religious emotion, and many more have amassed a fortune in an attempt to tell you and me something about the Spiritual Law or Power responsible in its entirety for yonder heavens, this earth, and every created object both animate and inanimate in existence. There lies on my desk at the present moment a letter from the Reverend "Billy" Sunday.

This good brother is conducting a revival campaign in Canton, Ohio. This letter came to me a few days ago and in it Sunday attempts to take me to task for denying some of the things he preaches. Yesterday morning in reply to that letter I sent "Billy" Sunday the following telegram:

> "Letter received stop I challenge you to debate authenticity of Bible or Christian religion anywhere anytime anyplace stop consider you to be teaching pagan superstition and blinding minds of people to truth of God through your ignorance of Bible and Christian history stop will put actual results of my teachings for past two years up against yours and if I cannot show more results achieved by my students in two years than you can in twenty years will quit the game stop play your own game but don't attempt to interfere with me or I might call your bluff." (Signed) Frank B. Robinson.

I have hardly had time to receive a reply from Brother Sunday yet and the chances are many to one that he will steer clear of any public debate with me on this subject. Not for worlds would I attempt to undermine anyone's religious faith. I went through Theological School and know just about what the orthodox religionists have to offer. I know just how much evidence they have in proof of their unusual story, and I also know how much evidence they have not.

It will be sufficient to say here that I do not believe many of the fundamental truths of God are contained in any system of theology offered today. We have hundreds of them and most of them fighting among themselves and none of them having any basic truth on which they are all agreed. When I discovered the way the Spiritual Law of God really works, the teachings and practices of most of the present day religionists seemed very foolish to me as they will to you when you discover something of the real Power at your disposal. Under the old teachings, for almost forty years I struggled with adversity and got nowhere. I was told, of course, that being a "Christian," everything would be all right "up yonder." But I began to wonder why it should be that the Power so mighty that it could cause me to live forever in the sky, could not do something tangible and material for me NOW. I reasoned that if all the Power and manifestations of God together with eternal life and perfect happiness were reserved until after death, why would it not be a good thing to shoot myself and begin enjoying all this happiness and bliss right away. I do not see the logic of struggling along trying to make both ends meet, with all the good things of life reserved for some future period in some far removed country to which we might go after death.

I just simply could not see any sense or reason in such teachings, so being in earnest about this matter, and believing that nothing about God was really known, I formulated a philosophy of life and of God and immediately put it to the test. This philosophy of life while quite revolutionary, was formulated by me only after having absorbed everything the church had to offer, and practically everything the scientists and psychologists had to offer. It seemed to me that I caught a faint glimpse of a vital Law running through these creeds, discoveries and philosophies which Law might very easily answer the entire problem of life.

I knew that it would hardly be possible for any of the many various teachings about God to be true and the whole world not know of it; for you may depend upon it that if any one body of people possesses the divine truth of the mighty Creator of this universe, it would not take very long for all the rest of them to die by the weight of their own error. For you will discover on your journey with me that the Creative Power behind this universe is a Law and not a personality of any kind. You will also discover that the Spiritual Law which is as free as the air we breathe, and quite as readily accessible, is no respecter of persons. You will find that the divine Law would not secretly whisper its truths to the head of some religious organization, barring all who did not believe that way from ever knowing those truths. In fact, how foolish it is to consider for one moment that such might be the case. There is no religion higher than truth, and this you will discover also. You will find further that there need be no long waiting for actual results to be manifested by you through the power of the Law I shall show you. So get ready to learn immediately how to throw off the shackles of ill health, poverty and unhappiness if it be that you are bound down by them.

You say, "Well did the Law work for you?" and in answer to that question let me say that within eighteen months of the day I decided to put this mighty God Law to work in my life, the picture had so changed that my success today is classed as one of the most outstanding transitions from poverty to affluence that this country has seen in many a year. Eighteen months ago I had a job at a very mediocre salary. I lived in a rented apartment. I had no money, no life insurance, no car, and nothing between me and the poorhouse but this job. This was before I had decided to put myself in tune with the God-Law I believed to exist. The picture today, however, is entirely changed. I own a beautiful home, one of the finest homes in the city of Moscow. In this home is a wonderful pipe organ from which I derive lots of enjoyment. I drive one of the best cars in this city and my life is covered by sixty-five thousand dollars worth of life insurance. In addition to that I own the controlling stock in this corporation which inside of eighteen months had put some part or other of my teachings into sixty-seven different countries. My articles have appeared in some of the leading national magazines in the realm of psychology. My three books are well known and in addition to that I edit a magazine of national distribution. This is what the Law did for me in only EIGHTEEN MONTHS' TIME. Perhaps it would be better to say that this is what I was enabled to do, through a knowledge of the Law. My home surroundings are perfectly happy and I have a standing credit at a bank in this county and I assure you that I am no genius of any kind. In fact, for forty years I was one of the most complete failures the world has ever seen, but when a human being finds something of the workings of the Spiritual God-Law, then let me assure you things sometimes happen very fast.

This Law, being a Law, is immutable in its workings. It does not change its operation to suit the needs of any one person but is more than sufficient to supply every need. You may depend upon it that if there is any lack in your life it is because the mighty Spiritual God-Law is not being used by you. I understand that perfectly well, and the chances are many to one that you have never suspected that such a Power existed. Certainly you never hoped that you might be able to use it for the manifestation of the things YOU desired, and therefore, the revelations of this course of instruction will probably knock you off your feet and open your eyes wide to the dynamic possibilities at your disposal. I am now going to give you a simple little exercise to do. Before I give it to you, however, let me warn you that although this little exercise might seem simple and to some probably foolish, the principle involved is the most dynamic principle in existence. So do not make the mistake of thinking that on account of the simplicity of this little exercise it has no value. That is exactly the trouble with the religious structure of the world today. It would not be satisfied with an every day Power close at hand, but it had to manufacture one, surround it with mystery, put it millions of miles away and put its rewards in the future. Such a thing is a million miles from the truth and you will find this out before you have traveled very far along the road with me. It is only natural is it not, that if there be in existence a dynamic Power such as I claim, that the workings of this Power must be so simple and so universal that it can be found and used by any normal man or woman? It is a pity that you and I had to be born under the shadow of a teaching which told us that we were born in sin and shaped in iniquity—that we should never know until we stood before a judgment throne in the sky, whether we were doomed to eternal death or whether we had been found worthy of eternal life.

No wonder fear predominates ninety-nine and nine-tenths per cent of the people of this country in the face of such a teaching as that. "PSYCHIANA," however, very effectively relegates that sort of a teaching and that sort of a god into the dark ages from whence it came. We of "PSYCHIANA" know, and we know beyond the shadow of a doubt that the mighty dynamic Power responsible for this Creation does not operate according to such principles and beliefs, and never did. Herein lies my discovery, which discovery I am now passing on to you. This discovery and the Power it teaches is a Spiritual discovery and a Spiritual Power, consequently whatever exercises I prescribe for you to do will be designed to enable you to touch or to become acquainted with this same Spiritual Power. It may be therefore, that some people may think that the simple little things which I shall ask you to do have no value and cannot possibly be instrumental in changing your life from one of illness, poverty and unhappiness into one of overwhelming victory. Let me assure you, however, that such is not the case. In doing these exercises I shall ask you to temporarily lay aside what ever ideas you may have of God. I don't say discard them entirely at this point but just discard them for the time being and as long as you are studying with me. Then go back to them if you can or if you want to. You will not travel very far along this road though, until your eyes will begin to open to what I am talking about and what I have proven to exist. You will know before many weeks have passed that your previous thoughts and ideas of God are being revolutionized, and the smile of hope and anticipation will light your countenance, and for the first time you will begin to grasp something of the astounding possibilities lying in a correct understanding and use of the God-Law behind this universe and particularly behind you.

Little is this Power understood, for if it were fully understood there certainly would not be misery within and poverty all around us that there now is. The time is at hand, however, when the knowledge of the potent dynamic force about which you are to learn will be common knowledge, and the facts as you are to learn them will be universally known and used. You will receive from us one Lesson every two weeks and the exercises prescribed in each Lesson must be continued until the next Lesson arrives. These little exercises will cause you no inconvenience whatever. In fact, it will not be very long until you are more than willing to do them as many times as you possibly can. Furthermore, these exercises being mostly mental, may be done either walking to work, eating, riding on the street car, or wherever you may be. It is advisable, if you possibly can, to have some definite hour and definite place in which you can give full attention to these studies without interruption from the outside. This is not absolutely necessary but it is advisable. Had not the truths I am passing on to you been abundantly proven in my own life you would never have heard of me. These truths, however, have proven to be true in the vast majority of cases studying with me. These truths are Spiritual Truths, they deal with the Spiritual Law, and they go right into the very heart of the subject of man and his relation to the greatest Power this world has ever known, the Power of the God-Law. Hence you need have no hesitation in doing as I ask you to do, for you must remember that I am the teacher and you are the student.

I may know nothing about railroad engineering; I may know nothing about radio; I may know nothing about mixing explosives; and I may know nothing about physics. But I do know something about Spiritual Law and its effect upon a human life. I know that there is an unseen Power in this universe, which Power can do what is usually looked upon as supernatural. As a matter of fact, however, there is nothing supernatural in the universe and those things which may seem supernatural only seem so because of a lack of recognition or understanding of the Law involved.

As you become acquainted with this Law and as you demonstrate a little of its power in your own life you will find that the petty annoyances of life as well as the major struggles will begin to worry you a whole lot less. You will probably not be able to explain just how or why this is so, but you will know beyond any shadow of a reasonable doubt that something is happening in your mental makeup which is changing you for the better. There will probably be a marked and noticeable feeling of better health generally.

If it should be that you are suffering from some functional or organic disease, you will find that the utilization of the Life Principle you are now dealing with will have a tendency to alleviate such conditions. I am personally convinced that if you and I understood the Law I am teaching you now as Jesus understood it every authentic work He did would be possible for you and me for the great God-Law is no respecter of persons. In Billy Sunday's letter, which I hold in my hand, he says, "I challenge you or your followers to raise the dead, open the eyes of the blind, cast cut devils, heal diseases, still the tempests, and forgive sinners." I am afraid, however, that I will have to check Brother Sunday on those statements. As far as raising the dead, no one to date has ever been known to have raised a dead man, but neither can "Brother Sunday" nor any other preacher or theological professor prove that Jesus raised the dead either. There has never been known to exist one original manuscript covering this Bible story, nor was there ever known to exist one single eyewitness to any of the supposed miracles of Christ, nor was there ever known to exist any one ever having seen such an eye witness. As a matter of fact, belief in the divinity of Jesus Christ did not come into existence until hundreds of years after He died. It was not believed then, and nowhere did Jesus claim to be God, or to have any Power to the exclusion of everybody else. On the contrary, He very specifically stated, "The things that I do shall ye do also." And as far as raising the dead goes let me say this; if Jesus ever raised a dead man to life through his understanding of Spiritual Law then, it is my candid opinion that when you and I understand Spiritual Law as He must have understood it, we shall be able to duplicate every authentic work that this man did, but "Billy" Sunday and the rest of them will have to prove to my satisfaction a good many things they are asking us to believe on faith, before I shall believe them.

If Brother Sunday were sitting in my office here with me now instead of being on that platform in Canton, Ohio, I should show him letters and telegrams which would convince him beyond the shadow of a doubt that disease of every kind is powerless before the mighty Law of God. As far as casting out devils goes, in those days everyone suffering from any disease or illness was supposed to be "possessed of a devil," and hundreds of thousands of innocent men, women and children were burned alive at the stake by "Christians," because they were presumed to be practicing witchcraft. Today, instead of "casting out devils," we of "PSYCHIANA" are applying the Spiritual Law as Jesus did. As far as "forgiving sins" goes, the only sin I know anything about is the sin of living in poverty, unhappiness and ill health, when there is at the disposal of all the same mighty God-Law that Jesus used. They did not believe Him then, and they do not believe Him now. Instead of trying to understand the simplicity of the Law He taught, certain religious fanatics conceived the bright idea of making a God out of Him, and then telling those who would not accept that story that if they did not believe that, they would all go to Hell. Thousands of years before the time of Christ many more millions of people than there are Christians had the same story in a slightly different form, and before the time of Christ this world had seen at least sixteen other crucified Saviors. They all had a miraculous birth; they all came to save the world. Most of them were crucified and they all rose from the dead, and they all were a combination of God and man. So there is nothing original at all in the story given us today by those posing as agents of God, nor after two thousand years of teaching can we say that such a doctrine is much more than a failure. However, those wishing to follow those teachings are at perfect liberty to do so as far as I am concerned, and I have no quarrel with them at all; they will reap the benefit of such beliefs while we of "PSYCHIANA" will reap the benefit of our teachings here and now, and in a material, substantial way. The other folks get theirs in the future after they die.

Now, to come back to our little mental exercise which I shall ask you to do faithfully. The very fact that you sent an inquiry in to me regarding "PSYCHIANA" is evidence that you were interested, and the fact that you have enrolled for this course of instruction, is further evidence to me that you really do want to be successful, healthy and happy. This is the point at which you will have to do your part and cooperate by actually doing the simple little things I ask you to. I am not asking very much, and on the very start of our studies together I want to impress upon you the necessity of playing ball with me throughout all our studies together. I will show you this mighty God-Law which is abundantly able to place you in circumstances in which you have happiness, health, and success. I want to teach you that Law. I want to help you. And I believe that you want to help me help you, so shall we get together here and now and you do the little things I want you to do? As I said, after awhile when you have demonstrated something of this God-Law you will be only too anxious to do it, but now is the time when you need to do them most, right at the very start.

It is a Law of the Spiritual Realm that the outstanding predominating desire of a human heart be gratified. The fact that the desire is there is absolute assurance that the object of the desire is somewhere also. In other words, the Creative Law of this universe, being responsible for all things created, and for all things which ever will be created, is quite capable of creating for you, or to cause to be created for you, the very thing you desire the most. This is probably what Jesus meant when He said, "According to your faith be it unto you." But a heart faith is absolutely useless in this matter. The only sort of faith or the only sort of belief which is effective in the Spiritual Realm is the belief which will actually work for the desired things. Grasp the picture here that the Spiritual Realm is an unseen realm, and the Power of the Spiritual Realm is an unseen Power. But, although unseen, it is a very living, vital, potent, dynamic Power. You cannot see radio waves—you can see the manifestation in the radio. You can not see electricity, but you can see the manifestation of electricity in a light globe or in the electric chair. You cannot see the Power of the creative Life Spirit, but you can see its manifestation in the human life. So do not try to understand the "hows" and the "whys" of this mighty Law at this point, but do as I tell you to for a little while until you demonstrate to your own satisfaction that such a Power exists.

At the present moment you suspect that such a Law as I am talking about exists. I KNOW THAT IT DOES. I have PROVEN that it does. You suspect it does, but have never found or experimented with it. It is necessary therefore, at this point for me to help you believe literally in the existence of this living God-Law. My little Alfred has just started to take Lessons on the pipe organ in my home. When he comes home from school every night he must practice for one hour. He has weeks and months and years of such practicing ahead of him. Now, what will be the final result? Three years from today Alfred will probably be able to play rings around me on the pipe-organ whereas today he cannot play a note. All this little fellow is doing is impressing on the Creative principle behind the universe, the thing he wants to manifest in his own life, and the first thing you know he will walk to that organ and sit down with no music in front of him at all and play anything he has learned to play. The same methods exactly will be employed by me on the start of these Lessons in your case. After one month there will be so much of those music lessons in Alfred. He will positively know so much about playing an organ; not much, 'tis true, but he will be able to actually go and do certain things which he cannot do now. This is a crude illustration but it will put over to you what I mean and will give you an inkling of the methods of securing the help of the mighty God-Law of the universe in your own life.

On awakening I would like to have you take several long, deep breaths for a few moments, not because this has any effect on the Spiritual Realm but it has a mighty good effect on your physical body and as you are going to enjoy increased life with its blessings from now on, it will do no harm for you to keep your physical body in good shape. If you want to make it a habit to breathe slowly and deeply, filling the lungs to their utmost capacity without straining and then slowly exhaling, it will be a mighty fine thing. As you know, the blood is purified by the lungs through the process of breathing and the deeper the breath you take the purer will your blood be. Now, for the other part of these exercises. When you come home at night or no matter what period of the day you have chosen to be alone with your lessons from me, I should like to have you rest in an easy chair, or lie on the bed or on the davenport, and physically relax. There need be no unnatural straining of any kind but give your body a chance to rest. Breathe slowly and deeply and then lay your Lesson down, close your eyes and repeat as many times as you care to, slowly and very quietly, the following sentence "I BELIEVE IN THE POWER OF THE LIVING GOD." Repeat this slowly anywhere from thirty to one hundred times according to your own inclinations. Then get on your feet and, standing erect if feasible, say the same sentence three or four times out loud if there is no one around to annoy you. If this would bother anyone else or for any reason would be inconvenient, you may omit doing this. On your way to work in the mornings or whenever you have unoccupied moments, I want you to repeat this sentence mentally as many times as you can. The more times you repeat it the more definite the results I am after will be.

There is a physiological Law governing this simple little exercise which I will explain briefly. When a thought goes through the human head, it slips through and is gone making no impression of any kind; but if the same thought be repeated a sufficient number of times a definite thought channel in the neurons of the cerebro-spinal system is created and that repeated thought becomes a very definite part of your mental makeup. In this course of instruction I shall not attempt to make any psychological explanation other than this. I only mention this here to show you that this little exercise is scientifically correct from a psychological standpoint. If your work calls for concentration, you need not repeat this exercise while you are concentrating on your work, but in every leisure moment that you have until you receive the next Lesson, I want you to do this little thing faithfully. You will get a lot of pleasure out of it, and the first thing you know there will come to you an entirely "different" feeling from any you have ever experienced before, and the chances are many to one, that two weeks of this exercise will work a revolution in the spiritual part of you for you certainly are a spiritual being much more so than you are a physical being.

This is as far as it is advisable to take you now. Do this exercise very faithfully and remember that you are the one who will reap the benefits and not me. I went through this a couple of years ago and I have told you what the material results have been to date; and I am not through yet. Let me say to you at this point that when you get to the place where belief in this God-Law is a material part of you, there will be no right thing you desire which you cannot get. You have a wonderful future ahead of you whoever you may be, and will thank me a good many times for ever having called this work to your attention.

In the next Lesson we shall deal with the subject of the Subconscious Mind. This mythical mind is what many would have us believe exists as ninety percent of a man's mentality. I do not believe in the existence of the subconscious mind for I have proven the Power involved to be far greater and more easily accessible Power than that is. The next Lesson will probably open your eyes a little wider and I am anxious to send it to you as you are to receive it but we will progress faster if we do not make haste along the way. A good many of my students have been failures a good many years, so they can well afford to spend the few months time necessary to complete my instructions.

I would esteem it a special favor if you have a snapshot or photograph of yourself which you could send me. If you have one and wish to send it to me I shall send you a picture of myself. If any question arises, or if there should be any point on which you are not quite clear concerning this Lesson, please feel free to write me and I shall give the letter personal attention. If I should be away one of my assistants will answer the letter probably quite as capably as I could. Ninety-five percent, however, of all the letters coming to me from students are answered personally. Don't forget "I BELIEVE IN THE POWER OF THE LIVING GOD," and if you will do this faithfully. it will not be long before you begin to realize that there is in existence, this dynamic LAW of which I am telling you, which LAW can operate for YOUR OWN Success, Health and abundant Happiness and Prosperity.

POINTS TO NOTE
ESPECIALLY IN LESSON NO. 1.

(1) You are now receiving instruction in finding and using the God-Law which heretofore has been unknown to you. Bear this fact well in mind. Anticipate it. Be happy in this knowledge as it is unfolded to you. For the first time in history, scientific information regarding the literal Power of the God Law, operating HERE and NOW is being given to the world by me.

(2) You must be ready to discard whatever preconceived notions of God you may have, if those notions clash with the revelation of this God-Power as I shall explain it to you. I shall take nothing out of your life which is beneficial to you. And whatever I do take out. I shall replace with a more powerful and reasonable truth. All I shall do is to remove religious superstition regarding any "God" who operates "in the future" and "after death," and replace it with a living vital faith in a Living Vital God-Law which operates HERE and NOW.

(3) Ninety-nine per cent of the human race is walking the streets today only HALF ALIVE. This probably applies to you. You have not the faintest suspicion of the mighty dynamic God-Law behind you, and at your disposal. You live in a limited physical sphere. You are afraid of

death. You know nothing of the existence of the God-Law I shall teach you about. You have seen superstition passing itself off as "God" and you probably are at a place where you are about to admit there is nothing in religion and nothing to this "God" proposition after all. You are right in one sense, but you are wrong in another sense.

(4) Prepare yourself to make up your mind definitely what it is that you need to make you happy, successful, and healthy. Be sure you know what this thin is at this point. Fix it definitely in your mind—you will need it a little later.

(5) Don't forget—over and above any monetary consideration involved in this course, I WANT TO HELP YOU. I will if you will let me.

Cordially your friend,
FRANK B. ROBINSON

LESSON 2

Dear friend and student:

In this Lesson I am going to show you just a few of the things possible to YOU, and possible to YOU—NOW. The chances are many to one, that to date you have never even suspected that many of the good things of life might be yours. You found yourself placed on this earth some years ago, and you accepted life as it was given to you. You were handed certain cards when you first came into being, and, to the best of your ability, you played those cards in this game called LIFE. It probably has never dawned on you that if you did not hold a WINNING HAND, you could draw other cards. It is my happy privilege, however, to tell you that such is the case.

For life is a card game. You draw when you enter the game. And you play accordingly. Most of us, however, seem to be laboring under the delusion that what ever cards were first dealt us, are the only cards we can ever draw. Such, however, is NOT the case. You may say that heredity enters into the playing of this game of life. The "heredity" card may have been dealt you, and you may not like it. Then perhaps the "circumstance" card was also dealt you. Perhaps you don't like that card either. The card of "poor education" may also have fallen in front of you, and you don't like that card either. Perhaps, through no fault of your own, a "college" education was denied you. Well I'm not so sure that you have missed too much through that—for "college-bred" men are in every breadline, and if you trace history back, you are very apt to find that those who have forged ahead to the greatest heights, were either men of no "college" education, or men who achieved in spite of their "college education. "

Many are the cards which may have been dealt you when you first entered this game of life. You had nothing to say about these cards either. You did not deal. You could do nothing else than accept the cards as the "dealer" gave them to you. And to date, the chances are, you are highly dissatisfied with this game. The "other fellow" seems to be having all the "luck" while you seem to be always holding the "losing" hand. Well, in this Lesson my friend, let me just point out to you a few of the things which may be accomplished by YOU. And I mean YOU—whoever you are that is reading this Lesson. For never was a truer word spoken than this. You ARE the MASTER of your fate. You ARE the captain of your soul. And if you go on in this game of life, playing with inferior cards, it is simply because you want to. For THE CARDS MAY BE CHANGED— remember that. And I have contracted with you to show you how to change them.

I know how to show you that. And I do not know it just in an abstract way, but I have PROVEN TO MYSELF FIRST THAT I DO KNOW THE WAY. I KNOW THE LAW INVOLVED. And let me say to you with all the earnestness at my command, that this great God-Law is no respector of persons. Have I made that clear? The mighty Creative God-Law of the universe, IS NO RESPECTOR OF PERSONS. Nor is the Power of that Law limited. The only thing that keeps you from having an abundance of health, wealth, and happiness, is your ignorance of this mighty LAW. Its not the fault of the Law—but the fault of YOU. I am not blaming you, for I did not know how the Law worked until I was 40 years of age. But I know now. And so will you before you finish this course of instruction with me.

Now just a word about your religious persuasions, for I don't want to hurt your feelings nor tread on your religious toes. I may do so, but if I do it will only be because your religious "persuasion" clashes with the truth as I know it to exist. I think, however, that you are a broad enough man or woman to see that no matter what system of religion you have had thrust upon you, or have knowingly embraced, it has come far short of providing you with the happiness, health, and wealth, which things you so much desire. For most of our present systems of religion are based on fear. This is not our fault at all, for they were built on fear. They all originated away back ages ago, when the human race was a very fearful and superstitious race. Our forefathers were brought up to "fear" God. They were told that unless they "feared" God they would either roast and fry in "hell-fire" or go through a session in "purgatory." And millions of good honest souls who could not accept that theory, were burned alive at the stake—millions of them. That could not be done today however. For the human race is progressing, in fact it has made more progress the last 25 years than it had made in the previous 1000 years. And as the race progresses, this rotten thing called "fear" is being taken by the throat and laid on its back, where it cannot do any more harm to humans.

"Fear" of God, is now out of the question. For any God that you need to be afraid of, is no God for you. There is no such God in the first place, and even if there were, you wouldn't want him—would you? Most of that "fear" proposition, however, is a relic of the dark ages, and is not believed in any more. People are progressing past that stage. If you could put all fear out of your life my friend, there would be absolutely no limit to the heights to which you could climb—none at all. But as long as that snake is lurking in your makeup, you probably will be handicapped in your fight for the best things in life. Let me tell you something else here, which is of vital importance to your whole future. The very moment in which you are able to discard all FEAR, in that moment you will find a "something" which will open up to you an entirely new vista of life. It will thrill you. It will raise your hopes a million miles in the sky. For you will begin to faintly realize the magnitude, not of any Power within you, but of the CREATIVE GOD-LAW OF THE UNIVERSE WHICH IS ALL AROUND YOU, AND IN EXISTENCE FOR THE FULFILLING OF YOUR EVERY RIGHT DESIRE.

Think that over for a little while, my friend—for that is EXACTLY the fact governing all success and happiness. These blessings of life do not lie in the fear realm at all. They lie in the realm in which man finds himself, when he dismisses fear, and begins to learn who and what he really is. They are found when a man or woman first realizes his or her VITAL CONNECTION WITH THE GOD-LAW existing here and now. That's where these good things come from, and the law itself is the Power which brings them into manifestation. For when a human soul gets that first faint glimpse of the God-Power at his disposal, a strange new consciousness will take complete possession of that soul. A Power he heretofore knew nothing about will possess him, and he will begin to realize that he is MASTER OF HIS OWN DESTINY—CAPTAIN OF HIS OWN SOUL. I have on file many telegrams from students who have awakened to that Power in their own lives. Last week the mails delayed one of our Lessons to a student in Switzerland, and we received a cable from him asking what had become of the Lesson. Telegrams have come to us from many different places, telling us that a certain Lesson has not arrived there on time—probably delayed in the mail. So anxious are these good students of mine to learn more of this mighty Power, that MONEY SEEMS TO BE NO OBJECT AND THEY DO NOT HESITATE ONE MOMENT ABOUT SENDING US A CABLE, EVEN FROM HALF WAY AROUND THE GLOBE. That is what a man or woman experiences when the God-Law of health, success, and prosperity begins to make its Power known in the life.

And these things, my friend, are for you. All I ask is that you play the game with ms, and play it fairly and squarely. If you will do that, I promise to show you the existence of the greatest Power this world has ever seen or ever will see. And I promise further to show you how to apply this mighty God-Law for success, happiness and health, in your own circumstances. Isn't that worth working for? Don't you think that's worth playing the game for? I do.

You have heard the story of the two brothers who were riding along a country lane in a small car. They were on a visit to their mother who was staying at a neighboring ranch. There was little traffic on that road, and they did not expect to meet any other car. But flashing around a corner came a big truck, upsetting the little car, and pinning the younger of the two brothers under it. This little fellow was only 11 years old. The brother with him was 14. Unheeding the truck did not even stop to see what damage it had done, and the elder brother found himself there, miles from help and with his little brother pinned under the car.

What could he do?—there was no one near to help him lift the car off little Bennie. He tore his hair—he cried, and agony was written all over the poor boy's face at the thought of his little brother's helplessness. Finally, despair creeping over the face of the little fellow pinned under the car, he said, "Billie, why don't you try to lift the car off me?" "Oh, but I can't lift that whole car." said Billie. "But you haven't tried yet," moaned little Bennie. This seemed to bring Billie to his senses, and he said,

"Bennie—I've just GOT TO GET THAT CAR OFF YOU," and, an agony of despair creeping over him, he seized the car, and with a strength that seemed superhuman, he lifted. And he LIFTED THAT CAR OFF LITTLE BENNIE. Where the strength came from he did not know. But it came.

And this crude illustration will help to show you what I mean when I say to you that the Great God-Law in existence here and now, is abundantly powerful enough to put you where you should be, and will do so, IN THE VERY MOMENT YOU ARE IN EARNEST ENOUGH TO COMPLY WITH THE SIMPLE EASY CONDITIONS GOVERNING THAT LAW. For the first time in Billie's life, he realized that there was a strange Power at his disposal which he had known nothing about before. Something awakened him, and in the stress of need, he did what he thought was impossible. And to you, sitting around the table of life, and playing the game the best you know how, I say that this same "something" can also awaken you to your vast possibilities. I say more than that. I say it WILL awaken you to your vast possibilities and will begin doing that in the moment you WANT TO BE AWAKENED. So in these Lessons, my friend, be sure that you are in earnest. Be sure that you mean business. Be sure that you are playing the game fairly and squarely with me. And I promise you, your eyes will be opened, and you will thank me from the bottom of your heart for ever calling this course of instruction to your attention.

Let me remind you that this course of instruction is entirely different from anything you have ever before read in your life. You have heard a lot about "this" Power "within" and "that" Power "within", and so I don't want you to make the mistake of thinking that I am going to tell you to look within for help, for I am going to do no such a thing. There is no Power "within" you that can help you to climb to the top. Many thousands have thought there was, but on trying to find this Power, they find it conspicuous by its absence. The theory is a beautiful one, the only trouble with it being that it does not work. For the Power DOES NOT LIE WITHIN, at all. IT LIES WITHOUT. It's in what I choose to call "THE GREAT WITHOUT", and as we travel along this little road together for a few months, you will know full well that what I am saying to you is the truth.

You will also know before we have traveled very far together that the very best things in life are for YOU, if you want them. I am sure of my ground when I say to you that there is no height too great to be climbed, if you will learn the secret of the Power of the God-Law operating for your benefit. What is it you want to do? Just where do you want to climb? Just how happy do you want to be? Well, Brother or Sister—it lies in your own hands, through the knowledge and use of this mighty God-Law I am here telling you about.

So at this point it will be well to suggest that you make up your mind that you are going to be and do just exactly what you want to be and do. It will be a good idea here to get your backbone all polished up, and get it ready for action. For you are going to need it. My backbone won't help you—neither will yours unless you use it. So shake yourself together and get ready to start on the road which leads to health, wealth, and happiness. For this road lies just a little bit ahead of you. And you will need your spine and your muscle and your head all working together, to help you use the God-Law I shall show you.

Don't make the mistake of thinking that you can just lie easily on your oars, trusting to some power or other to transport you on flowery beds of ease to realms of health, wealth and happiness. If you think that, you are going to be badly fooled—I promise you that. But if you really mean business, and if you really want to DO, then come along, for I can show you how to utilize the greatest Power or Law the world has ever seen to help you do what you want to do. For it takes men and women to achieve. There is no place in life for a laggard. There is no place in life for a lazy man or woman. There is no place in life for the shiftless. They never get anywhere and never will. And if it should be that you have been just a little bit on the "lazy" order to date, then get down to brass tacks, clench your fist, grit your teeth, and say, "By God. I'm going to do it." I do not mean this phrase in any slangy or profane manner at all. For if you do it—if you do achieve—it will be certainly by the God-Law and no other way. Remember this.

In other words, mere wishing will get you nowhere. The God-Law always works where it is needed to work. But how can it work in your life if you do not want it to? You can take a magnet and try to make it pick up sawdust until the crack of doom. And when it cracks you will never have made that magnet lift one grain of sawdust. But put some iron filings near that magnet and see how quickly it will get busy. The Law of magnetism is in that magnet. You cannot see it—but it's there just the same. It means nothing to the sawdust, however, for the law of magnetism DOES NOT WORK IN THE CASE OF A MAGNET AND SAWDUST. NEITHER DOES THE LAW OF SUCCESS WORK IN THE LIFE OF A MAN WHO IS NOT ANXIOUS ENOUGH TO BE HELPED TO TRY AND HELP HIMSELF. Such a man must first have the desire to be helped. He MUST FIRST COME TO THE LAW AND RECOGNIZE ITS PRESENCE. Then—when that has been done and when the desire to be helped is there the LAW WILL WORK, because it CAN work. Do you see that? The conditions have been complied with, and there is then no limit to the future of the man who so complies with those simple conditions. For the only condition the God-Law requires, is the one condition that you really WANT THE LAW TO HELP YOU. And that's probably your normal condition, isn't it?

There are very few men and women in the world who do not want to get ahead. There are mighty few who do not really desire to achieve things. There are some, of course, but the chances are that you are not one of those; otherwise you never would have enrolled for this course of instruction. So I am taking it for granted that you really do desire and want to get ahead. You really want health, you really want perfect happiness, and you really want perfect success. All right—the conditions under which this God-Law works have been met, so from now on we shall begin our climb up the road that brings, at the end of it, the realization of these things. You probably wondered a little at the little affirmation I had you repeat in the first Lesson. You might have thought, well what good can that do me? If such a thought entered your head, let me say to you here that in making that little affirmation, you were beginning to use the most dynamic power you have ever tried to use. You know absolutely nothing of the power behind that little exercise. You know nothing of the power of such a thought. And I cannot blame you. You have had no experience with such a thought, and you also look upon a thought as just something that comes and goes through your head meaning nothing.

But say brother—if you only knew now, what I know about the power of a thought, or about the power of many thoughts, you would look with amazement on these little exercises I assure you. If you could but faintly realize what a thought really is—say—you would be liable to be up half the night doing the little exercises I asked you to do. For let me say to you here that a thought is one of the most dynamic things you have ever experimented with. A thought is a thing, an actual thing. It can be weighed—you did not know that, did you? But thoughts can be weighed, and that fact certainly proves them to be things. BUT—and listen well to me here—THOUGHTS ARE MORE THAN THINGS—THEY ARE PART OF THE DYNAMIC GOD-LAW I AM SHOWING YOU. Did you grasp that? Read it again. Now read it again. Now lay this Lesson down for five minutes and think about what I have just said to you. Go ahead— lay the Lesson down on your knees, close your eyes, and try to realize that THOUGHTS ARE PART OF THE MIGHTY GOD-LAW WHICH CREATED THIS UNIVERSE MILLIONS OF YEARS AGO AND WHICH SUSTAINS IT EVERY MOMENT AND MORE THAN THAT, WHICH SUSTAINS YOU WITH IT.

Now you have the Lesson in your hand again, and perhaps the thing I have just told you has opened your eyes a little. They will be opened many times in this course, my friend, I promise you that, for never before has this God-Law been described and told about as I am dealing with it here. And you probably can see now why it is that my Lessons went around the world into 67 countries inside of a year. Just think of it—a thought—is a spiritual power, and a part of the Creative God-Law responsible for every created thing. In fact, if you can grasp this, let me tell you that THOUGHT IS THE MANIFESTATION OF THE GOD-LAW IN YOUR OWN LIFE. In fact, there is NO OTHER WAY THE SPIRITUAL GOD-LAW CAN OPERATE AND COMMUNE WITH

YOU, IN YOUR WAKING MOMENTS, EXCEPT THROUGH THE POWER OF WHAT YOU CALL A THOUGHT. We shall see later that thoughts are not what we have to date supposed them to be. They are something far more potent than that. To date, not much attention has been paid to "thoughts" but I assure you, my friend, that we shall pay lots of attention to them from now on.

I shall show you a little later, the existence of a thinking "something" in the atmosphere all around you. I shall show you that this "thinking something" comes from millions and probably billions of miles away from here. So please accept this statement at face value and go accordingly. I want you to check every thought from this moment on that ever enters your mind. And more than that, I want you to EXERCISE A STRICT CENSORSHIP OVER EVERY THOUGHT YOU EVER THINK. You say, "But Doctor Robinson—can I do that?" You bet you can. You will HAVE TO if you go very far with me, and if you get very many of this world's "best things." But you will be glad to do it, for as you will see, there is no work entailed at all in governing your thoughts. Not any. Some may say, "Yes—but Doctor—thoughts come into my head and I can't help that—how about that?" No—you cannot help thoughts coming into your head, BUT YOU CAN PREVENT THEIR STAYING IN YOUR HEAD—can't you?

Of course you can. And this is something you must do. I strongly suspect that if you have not so much success in life, it is because you have never thought "success." You have had no reason to. You just naturally have been playing the cards you were dealt when you sat in on the game, and so have never even faintly suspected that you, by the exercise of any known Law, could ever achieve success. So you never let any thought of success enter into your head—did you? Well, we'll change that from now on, for from this moment I want you to exercise the very strictest censorship over EVERY THOUGHT THAT EVER ATTEMPTS TO BUILD A NEST IN YOUR HEAD. A bird can light on your doorstep, but it doesn't take you very long to "shoo" it away, does it?

The same thing with a thought. In your last Lesson, which was the first in this course, I gave you certain little things to do on retiring. You did not know then just why I was doing that did you? But you begin to see now—don't you? Now listen to me—tonight when you retire, I want you to relax every muscle. Lie as limp as a log in bed. Close your eyes. There always is, in every man's closed eyes, a certain area which, when you learn how to find it, is the very thin veil between you and the God-Law of the Universe. I may show you later how to penetrate that veil. This veil it was that Edison penetrated a little, just before he died. You will remember that he exclaimed, "It's very beautiful over there." This man, and incidentally hundreds of others, have caught a faint glimpse of beyond the veil. And while it may take you some time to get used to absolutely relaxing your body and just lying limp as a log, when you do learn to do that, you will not have so much trouble in finding that "bright spot" I spoke to you about. Sometimes I think I should call it a "white spot." At any rate, it won't be very long before you know what it is, although if you have never attempted anything like this before, it may be some time be fore you get that "white spot." There is nothing mysterious about this at all; nothing mystic, nothing "supernatural", it is perfectly natural. In fact one of the most natural things I know of is for a man to begin to realize that the Living God-Law is an actual thing which can be contacted here and now by every normal man and woman.

Would you wish me to believe that this great God-Power has thrown this universe with you and me on it, into space, and left us all here to shift for our selves? Would you ask me to believe that? No—my friend—that did not happen. And this mighty Creative God-Law, not only put us here, BUT STAYED HERE ITSELF WITH US. And more than that, IT IS STILL HERE WITH US, WAITING FOR A CHANCE TO DO FOR US WHATEVER RIGHT AND PROPER THING WE NEED. Do you need wealth?—the God-Law can give it to you. Do you need health?—the God-Law can give it to you. Do you need happiness?—the God-Law can give it to you. You would not attempt to tell me that it could not—would you? You would not ask me to believe that the Intelligence, capable of making such a scheme of things as this beautiful world and yon beautiful heavens, could not give you and me wealth, health and happiness —would you? It would be useless for you to tell me that, for my experience has been different. I KNOW BETTER. And besides, if this mighty sustaining Intelligence—this mighty Creative God-Law is SO CLOSE TO YOU THAT YOU COULD NOT GET AWAY FROM IT IF YOU WANTED TO, do you not think it can more than give you these things. You have never suspected before that such a power was at your right hand—have you? Well it is brother, and before we get through with these Lessons you will know that it is. And what a difference that will make to you.

You are at this point beginning to get a faint glimpse of the True Light as it exists, and you can already see that it is more than likely that you yourself will be able to use this mighty God-Law. There is also coming to you as you read this, renewed hope, as you begin to faintly grasp the staggering possibilities which are yours, as you realize that it is possible for you to instantly contact this mighty God-Law as it is. There is also coming to you now the impression that I know how to lead you aright and you have mentally said to your self, "This fellow knows what he's talking about." And I assure you I do. There is not one single thing that can keep you from either health, wealth or happiness, if you use this mighty Creative God-Law as it may be used. Now that should make you certainly hopeful and should inspire you to say, "I'll play with Dr. Robinson in this course of instruction—I believe he can help me." And that is exactly what I want you to do. It's all so wonderful when one begins to realize that poverty and ill-health—and failure are about to be kicked out of the door, isn't is? It doesn't seem possible—does it? And how happy it makes one feel to know that no matter who they are, they can use, for their own health, wealth and happiness, THE VERY SAME GOD-LAW THAT CREATED THEM AND GET IN TOUCH WITH THIS GOD-LAW INSTANTLY.

Now about these thoughts and the pre-retiring exercise. Remember—absolutely at rest. Every muscle lax. Just like a log of wood. Then—the thoughts turned to the white area on the field of vision through the closed eyes and a simple resting in that position. Keep your eyes on that "white spot", and over and over again, mentally repeat, "I AM FINDING THE POWER OF THE LIVING GOD." Direct that sentence into the very depths of your mentality and right into the "white spot." There is a scientific reason for all this, but you just do it, remembering all the while that A THOUGHT IS PART OF THE CREATIVE GOD-LAW, and you yourself are now using THIS MIGHTY GOD-LAW FOR THE FIRST TIME IN YOUR LIFE. In the morning, on awakening take your deep long breaths, and right away, start this same line of thought going and KEEP IT UP. Do not say it out loud, but just simply KEEP ALL NEGATIVE THOUGHTS OUT OF YOUR HEAD BY KEEPING IT FILLED WITH THIS THOUGHT. Do you see what I am doing now? I don't want you to ever let one single thought of failure, ill-health or poverty enter your head. Never mind how sick you are, never mind how poor you are, never mind how unhappy you are, and never mind how big a failure you are. KEEP THIS ONE THOUGHT IN YOUR MIND TO THE EXCLUSION OF ALL OTHER THOUGHTS FOR THE NEXT TWO WEEKS.

REMEMBER, you are beginning to put into operation the spiritual GOD-LAW which can change all those things for you, and every day you keep this one thought upper most in your mind, you are ONE DAY NEARER THE REALIZATION OF YOUR DESIRES. Remember that. As you walk down the street, throw out your chest, fill your lungs and keep the thought in your head "I AM FINDING THE POWER OF THE LIVING GOD." Don't bother your head at this time with who and what God is, you will find that out later. Just now, keep this thought uppermost all the time, for it is a fact. If there comes a time when you have the chance in your business hours, get alone, close your eyes and with a relaxed body, look directly into the center of your being and say this same affirmation of truth. Then, not only say it, but realize it. And I'm here to say to you, my friend, that the power that is to come into your life will knock you off your feet when you look back and see the change which has taken place. REALIZE THAT IT IS A FACT THAT YOU ARE, EVEN NOW, VERY CLOSE TO THE POWER OF THE LIVING GOD.

This realization will grow and grow and grow upon you as you progress and with the realization will come into your life a Power, the God Power, which can over ride every obstacle, can thrust aside every want and can heal every condition of ill-health. There has never been known to exist a Power which could even faintly begin to approach this Power of the Living God. So do your study well, I know the same God-Law lifted me from out of the quagmire of failure to brilliant success, and it didn't take very long to do it either. And the very methods you are using are the same ones I used. Remember that. And I am happy as I leave you at the end of this second Lesson, for I know that after you have read it and after you have begun to realize your closeness to the greatest Power the world has ever seen, you will be as happy as I am, for you will begin to see the actual realization of your hopes and desires. For years perhaps you thought it could not be, and NOW you know it can be.

It's your happiness and success I'm after, not mine. I have mine already, you have yours to get, and through my teachings the way is to be shown you and that makes me very happy for there is no more noble work in the world than to show men and women their relationship to the Creative Law, at work now as ever throughout the whole universe. For when men and women begin to get a faint glimpse of that Power, their lives are revolutionized and their hearts' desires fulfilled.

At this point I must leave you till you receive the next Lesson. In the next Lesson we shall deal with the story of the creation of man. It is astonishing what a lot of light comes to a man when he begins to realize who and what he actually is. And this you have never known yet. To date not a single soul has put into print the story of the creation of man as you will learn it in your next Lesson. All of these Lessons are charged with a dynamic spiritual power and the next one I consider perhaps one of the most interesting and important of them all. It has caused more comment than any other Lesson I have ever written, so look forward to it. In the meantime, let the simple little exercises become a part of your mental life. You can't even faintly conceive at this point, what can be done through the power of concentrated thought. Nor can you conceive of the dynamic power of the God-Law. And all I am asking you here is that you do as I ask you to and begin to put this mighty spiritual God-Law into action in your own life.

Don't waste any time in foolish conversations. Don't be vulgar or rude. Let the best instincts and impulses in you come to the surface. Perhaps you are a profane man and if you are let me suggest that this is very foolish and unnecessary. Don't do it. I am not speaking to you now as any "sky-pilot" for I assure you I am not on that order. I am talking common sense and decency to you and besides, the cleaner you are, both physically and mentally, the more surely will the God-Law work in your life. As you progress, you will find that this mighty producing LAW is becoming very real to you and at that time you are not very apt to waste much time or many words in useless and foolish conversation. Don't try to sprout any wings on your shoulder blades, for wings were meant to grow on a duck, not on a man. And you will never have any wings growing on you either here or "hereafter." Just be decent while you are studying with me. Be clean, be honest and in two weeks time I shall be with you again and take you one more step into this intensely interesting and profitable study.

POINTS OF SPECIAL INTEREST
IN LESSON 2.

(1) If you are not satisfied with the cards dealt you in the game of life, you may change them.

(2) There is at your disposal, through the inherent God-Law, a wealth of unseen and hitherto unrecognized power. You have never suspected that power there, but under the stress of some emergency you have seen flashes of it. THAT UNSEEN POWER IS THERE FOR YOUR DAILY USE. It is a "sleeping giant" and is in existence for YOUR ETERNAL SUCCESS AND HAPPINESS, IF YOU USE IT FOR THOSE THINGS.

(3) Before the God-Law can work, the conditions governing its operation must be met BY YOU, if it is to operate in YOUR life. Remember that. What is the one condition governing the operation of that God-Law?—desire for these good things and a belief in the Law itself. You believe in the Intelligence that created this world, do you not? Then recognize the fact that this same power is STILL HERE AND STILL OPERATING wherever given a chance to operate.

(4) A thought is a "thing" and a very powerful "thing" too. Let no negative thoughts ever roost in your hair. Shove them out as fast as they come in. No harm can be done by their just flitting through your mind, for you cannot stop thinking if you want to. The harm comes from LETTING THESE NEGATIVE FEAR THOUGHTS STAY THERE. So don't allow them to roost in your mind for one second. If you are faithfully doing the little mental exercises I prescribe there will be no room for the fear thoughts, for TWO THOUGHTS CANNOT OCCUPY THE SAME MIND AT THE SAME TIME. No two things can occupy the same place at the same time you were taught in school. That works in the thought realm. If you don't believe it, try it some time. Try to think of two things at the same time.

SPECIAL NOTE

This is a course of religious instruction. I am not a politician, nor is it my intention to allow politics to enter into "PSYCHIANA." Since this course of instruction was written, we have had given to us a "new deal" in America. The people made a mandate on President Roosevelt to give them a deal, and, to the very best of his ability he is doing just that. Without adding to, or detracting from the truths contained in "PSYCHIANA" I respectfully make the suggestion to my students that each one of them cooperate to the very full with the President of the United States. I am not a Democrat and never have been a Democrat. Nevertheless, I have supported that party and will continue to support it so long as it functions under its present leadership. I make this suggestion because I believe it to be incumbent upon every citizen to give to the present administration, whole-hearted support.—F.B.R.

LESSON 3

In our search for the LAW which controls health, wealth, and happiness, it is necessary at this point that we turn our attention to the creation of this universe and man. It might occur to you that it is passing strange that a consideration of creation is necessary when all we are attempting to do is to find the LAW which is responsible for success, health, and happiness. You may say, "Well what has the story of creation to do with either health, success, or happiness?" And my answer to you is that it has a whole lot to do with it. In fact you cannot obtain any of these blessings intelligently until you have a true picture of creation, For behind that picture of creation lies a POWER. And what a Power it is.

Were it not for that mighty Power or Law, you and I would not be here, neither could we possibly stay here another second of time. The fact that there is a creation presupposes, in fact proves that there is a Creator. It would be utter foolishness to think for one moment that yon heavens, decked in all their glory and splendor, together with their millions of satellites, planets, suns, stars, etc.—just haphazardly happened. To think that would be utter foolishness. For the remarkable precision with which yon starry spheres revolve in their orbits, and travel along their respective paths, through infinite space, is proof beyond shadow of doubt that an intelligent Power, or Law is in control. And not only is this Force, or Power, or Law in control every second of time, but this same Power or Law was the causing factor in the first place. This same POWER, this same LAW, this same FORCE, no matter what it may be called, (and we will not concern ourselves with that yet) this same LAW, IS THE VERY SAME LAW THAT CAUSED THEM TO BE IN THE FIRST PLACE. I do not care when the creation was. I do not care so much how it happened. I DO know that whether it be a Power, a Law or a Force, it must needs be AN INTELLIGENT POWER OR LAW OR FORCE.

By no mere chance could such an elaborate scheme of things ever come into existence without some controlling Power overlooking and controlling this brilliant scheme of things—for in reality it is a very brilliant scheme when we only faintly begin to understand something of the Power operating. And YOU are going to be given a glimpse of this very Power, so study earnestly and intently, and drink in every word I say to you. I can assure you that this course of instruction has not sprung into existence overnight, I promise you that. It has involved a lifetime's study and thought along this line and in this realm. At times I have had to be rather daring. At other times I have had to do lots of experimenting in this remarkable realm. But in being able to point you direct to THE LAW as it exists, I think my efforts have been more than justified. I think my reward is great. So realize, my friend, that I am putting into your hands a weapon which you can use against all the enemies of life, and if you will use this weapon as I direct you to use it, you will be an absolutely overcoming warrior in life's battle.

For life is a battle to those who do not know it as it is. Of course it's a fight when one does not understand the mighty Law waiting to be used for either success, health, or happiness. But let me say to you here and now that life lost its fight when I began to realize the magnitude of the staggering truths I am revealing to you. Now—instead of fighting, I know a far better way—and I use it. And success follows everything I do. I am perfectly healthy, and I am supremely happy also. And it is all because I learned something of the existence of this mighty Creative Life Principle I am teaching you about. Now—instead of being defeated at every turn of the road, I win all around. Now—instead of spending half my time in a sick bed, I hardly ever see one. Now—instead of moping around, disgruntled with myself and with everybody else, you will generally find a smile on my face and a joke on my lips. And that's much better than the other way, is it not? This success and this happiness is for you also, if you obey me, so study carefully and if you are not quite clear on any point, read it again, and then, if still not clear, drop me a line—I will answer it.

Now to get back to our story of creation and the marvelous realm it opens up. I have stated that it is absolutely necessary for you to understand a little about this scheme of creation, and also about your relationship to both the creation and the Creative Life Principle. Although perhaps not quite in the way in which you have been taught to believe in that mighty Power. If you were raised in the type of "Christian" home that I was, you were probably told that "God" was a very wonderful person, having his dwelling place "far beyond the starry sky". You were probably led to believe that some day this "god" who is a personality, would stand you up before a "judgment bar" and would reward you according to the deeds done by you while here on the earth. In other words like myself, you were probably told that 'god' was a PERSON of some sort, which PERSON was responsible for your being here. I have no quarrel with anyone holding that theory, however, I just don't believe it—that's all.

And I don't think you believe it either. However that's beside the point here. The thought I want you to grasp here is that this same Intelligence that created the earth, and the heavens, and their firmament is the very same Power that created YOU. And in passing did it ever occur to you what a marvelous Power or Law this must be? Did you ever stop to think of the marvels of the creation of a human body? YOU—no matter who you are at this moment—one hundred years ago did not exist. At some time or other, your parents complied with the LAW governing the birth of a child, and YOU WERE BORN. It sounds simple does it not? But have you ever stopped to think of the marvelous intelligence of the Creative Life Principle in doing that seemingly simple little thing? Try and catch this point—and catch it well: when your two parents had complied with the Law governing the birth of a child, THAT WAS AS FAR AS THEY COULD GO. They could do positively nothing more. The building of the body from those two tiny little germs, the ovum of the female and the spermatozoa of the male, was an operation entirely removed from the power of your parents. But it was done just the same. And in due time came forth YOU—and without any help of any sort. After the first operation of joining those two germs together was done by your parents nothing more could be done by any human agency.

Did you ever stop to think of that? Did it ever occur to you that whatever power or intelligence, law, or force did the building, must be a mighty powerful and intelligent one? Did that ever occur to you? And did it ever occur to you that if this creative Life Principle (for that's what I call it) could supervise with unerring precision the building of a human body from two tiny germ cells. It also might be expected to sustain the same body that it had built? Never thought of that did you? And you never once thought that such almost inexplicable intelligence as that could ever be called upon to bring you health, wealth, and happiness, did you? Of course you didn't—for it has never been called to your attention before that I am aware of. This one point, my friend, opens up a realm which will stagger you when you quietly think of it in the light of what I have just told you.

Here I sit at this typewriter, a marvelous piece of human mechanism. Yet, 46 years ago I was absolutely unborn. Today I am able to influence the lives of tens of thousands, and yet, 46 years ago I just simply wasn't in existence. And it is the Power or Law of this Life Spirit which caused me to be, that I am talking about. I have no use for any system of philosophy or religion which relegates its God to the far regions and which promises its reward beyond Jordan. Nor have I any use for any system that holds over one's head the threat of eternal damnation unless the particular brand of theology is believed in. That stuff is all pagan superstition and should be relegated to the dark ages of faith from whence it came. For the theory does not stand up under intelligent investigation. I am not concerned with that sort of a god at all, my friend, for there is no such a being. But I am vitally concerned with this ever-present Life Spirit, which, only 46 years ago, went to work on the building of my human body. I have a right to be interested in that Power. I have a right to know that Law. For we should be very intimate seeing that it brought me here. And along this very line have been conducted all the experiments, and all my thoughts for the past forty years have been given to understanding something of the application of this mighty God-Law—this Life Spirit for the obtaining of the things I needed most, and that was what I was interested in—that was what I wanted to find out. I wanted to know whether or not the mighty dynamic power—intelligent power if you please—which created this universe, especially, could be brought into play for the achieving of the things I wanted and needed here and now. My parents told me that we never could understand God. My father, still a good old Baptist preacher, often said to me in answer to my questionings, "Well son—the Finite can never grasp the Infinite—that is reserved for the angels." Dad, maybe so—and then again maybe not so. At any rate there was no law that I knew of which prohibited me from trying to find out, or from thinking for myself. Nor was there any law which prohibited me from trying to find out whether or not God, as we call Him, could be understood. Just because my old father and the other preachers told me that it was not meant for me to know, was no reason for my believing them at all., Not that Dad or the preachers were dishonest, not that, but one must remember that those old beliefs had their origin in an age of religious superstition and intolerance. It's not so long ago since the Christians' fires were burning all over Europe, torturing to death hundreds of thousands of "heretics." And all a "heretic" ever was, was one who would not believe the story these religionists asked him or her to believe. All that is history now, however, but in passing it is well to remember that the statement that we cannot know God until we die originated at the same source as these burnings. You cannot burn people alive today for their religious beliefs—can you? Perhaps it is a good job too, for maybe there might be some who would want to fry me up a little.

But to progress; I doubted the statement that God could not be known till after death. I analyzed the stories and theories told to me, and I also ran down the "sacred book" telling the story. It may appeal to some people, and if it does they are welcome to it. It did not and does not appeal to me especially as I now KNOW that the story is not true. For right now I know that the mighty Life Spirit CAN BE USED FOR HEALTH, SUCCESS, AND HAPPINESS BY EVERY SOUL KNOWING THE LAW OF THIS MIGHTY LIFE SPIRIT. I did it and so can you. It would be absolutely false to state that this Life Spirit, which could take two germs and make a human body out of them could not do a single thing towards making that body happy after it had made it in the first place. This is a very revolutionary theory, but it's a true theory as you will find out before you finish your studies with me. Can it actually be done?—you ask. Wait and see, but for your information let me say to you right here that it certainly CAN be done. The same Great Power, the same great Law, the same great Force which created you and me in the first place, can do for us NOW whatever right thing is necessary to be done.

It displayed superhuman intelligence in making us in the first place and can do for you and for me whatever is necessary to be done, and more than that, it will display the same superhuman intelligence in providing for us that it displayed in making us. Who said the mighty power of this Life Creating Spirit was limited to the manufacture of a human body from a two-germ cell? Who said so? I deny it, and deny it with all the power I have. And more than that I will prove to you, my friend, before you finish your studies that the power of this mighty Creative Life Spirit, IS JUST AS POTENT TODAY AS IT EVER WAS. If, 46 years ago this power could start building ME, don't tell me that 46 years later it has lost all power over me. Not by a long shot. It's all a matter of knowing the secret of invoking this power—that's all. The story of creation as told me by my parents was the usual one given out by religious people. God created the world, the sun, the moon, and the stars, and Adam and Eve in six literal days. That's the story I was told as a youth. I have had lots of arguments with ministers over that story of creation. They try to tell me now that the "days" were "periods of time." But that argument will not hold water for the writer distinctly states, "and the morning and the evening were the first day" etc. The word used in those passages means a literal day of 24 hours, so this theory will have to be discarded as we know by scientific facts that the earth was in existence long before 6000 years ago. At the very least reckoning it is at least 500,000 years old, and probably many millions of years old. I mention this six-day story in order to deal with the two stories of creation given to us—one by religionists, and the other by scientists. For the benefit of those who still take the six-day story to be true, but to mean "periods of time", let me say that the Westminster Confession of Faith is in full force today, and that "confession" makes belief in the LITERAL six-day creation mandatory to "salvation", whatever that may be.

Then we have the scientific theory. This is the theory of evolution, and is universally accepted by thinking people today. It is taught in nearly every University in America, and is accepted by almost every reasoning mind. According to this theory, the first known cell having LIFE and INTELLIGENCE, was the humble Algae, a jellylike mass that floated on top of stagnant water. Then came the equally humble Amoebae, a one-celled piece of protoplasm and having LIFE and intelligence. We are told that this little one-celled piece of protoplasm had ability enough to float to the top of the water, or sink as needs be. And from this little amoebae, millions and millions of ages ago, are you and I presumed to be sprung. There is a lot of reason and truth in that story. It was probably away back when it happened, but those knowing the story of evolution know by its unmistakable evidences that quite likely the theory is correct. At any rate, it is far more reasonable and far more scientific than is the six day theory, which theory by the way, although all the rage 100 years ago, is practically extinct today.

It goes to show how intelligence increases, and how, as intelligence increases, ideas change, and always for the better. One cannot say with certainty that all life sprang from the tiny amoebae, but one can say with absolute assurance that behind the human race and behind LIFE itself, are ever-growing and evolutionary processes. There was no instantaneous creation. Nor did any supreme being say, "Let there be light" or anything on that order. It is pretty well established today that this story is but old Chaldean allegory. And, of course, it is treated as such. True, there are still those to be found who say they believe that the mighty Creative Intelligence had an argument with a talking snake in the Garden of Eden one day, and, of course, they MAY be right. At any rate I grant them the right to believe that if they want to. That's their business. It's my business also not to believe it if I want to. And I certainly don't want to. NOW—which ever story is correct or incorrect is quite beside the point here, so we shall not quibble and quarrel as to whether evolution is the answer or whether instantaneous creation is the answer. For it makes no difference at all in our search for this mighty Law which did the creating in the first place. What you and I are trying to do is to get a clear-cut picture of the Creative Life Spirit, which Life Spirit can and does manifest in the life of everyone, not only as their physical creator, but as their sustainer and provider of all things needed, whether success, health, or happiness. That is what we are after, and I say it is quite immaterial by what means the first creation sprang into existence. The fact that there is a creation is enough to warrant the existence of a Creative Living Spirit. There are at least 50 stories in existence of "gods" who created the earth, and while, of course, they are all more or less allegorical in their origin, I'm not so sure that they all do not carry a hidden truth in them.

Take the Bible story of creation for instance. The story is not accepted as written; in that story you find this passage: "and the spirit of God moved upon the face of the waters." Now if the findings of science regarding the floating of the little amoebae on the waters is correct, then you see there is no clash at all. So in all these systems of religion, as I study them, I do not, of course, believe them literally, but perhaps they all contain a truth under their clothing of words. If there ever is a clash between any religious book, or any religious history, and science, then science must come first, for what science knows, it KNOWS. Scientific facts are known facts, and all the religious history of the world cannot refute one scientific fact of truth. There is no question in my mind that some of these old timers of Bible history had inspirations from the Creative Life Spirit, no question at all. But at the same time we believe the "spit and mud" story of creation to be false. We do not believe the "God and talking snake" yarn either. There is no question in my mind that John Greenleaf Whittier had a revelation from the Life Spirit when he penned his beautiful lines.

"I know not where His islands reach, Their fronded palms in air, I only know I cannot drift, Beyond His love and care."

Nor is there any doubt in my mind that the beautiful old soul Cardinal Newman knew something of the power of the Creative Intelligence when he wrote that marvelous old hymn, "LEAD KINDLY LIGHT." No question at all is there in my mind about that. The trouble with those old fellows was that they starved the body and pinched the soul, lived as "pilgrims" here on earth, denying themselves this and denying themselves that, in order that they might "go to heaven." They taught that a rich man could not enter into heaven. They gave not a second thought to this life, but concentrated on heaven without even knowing whether or not there was such a place. Consequently the Life Spirit could do nothing for them for the simple reason that they did not expect it to. They thought that every good thing was for the other side, and not for here and now.

And that is where they have all missed the point. I claim, and will prove to you that this same mighty Creative Life Spirit is as active now as it ever was, and is abundantly able to bring into being in your life, all the success you can ever need, all the health you can ever need, and all the happiness you can ever need. I found it. I was transformed from poverty to plenty and in 18 months too, so you would have a hard time trying to convince me that this mighty God-Law is for use only on "the other side." It may be for "the other side" all right, but it is also for this side. Now here I want to take a look at the creation story as told in the Bible. Of course you will realize that I am not taking it literally at all. What I am doing is taking from the allegorical story the truth as it exists, for the truth is certainly told in that allegory and told very plainly too. As you progress with me you will find that the unseen, or shall I say the spiritual part of man and of creation is by far the most important part. Remember that, for the power you are using and are to use further is an unseen Power. You will see the manifestations of it certainly in a material way, BUT THE POWER ITSELF IS UNSEEN. Don't forget that. It HAS to be an invisible Power. There could be no power controlling the material and the physical unless it were an UNSEEN SPIRITUAL POWER. Do you follow me? Now let us look at the story for a moment briefly, and I think you will see ,just what I am driving at. I am sure you will see the mighty Law at work. Read this Lesson over and over again, and try and grasp a little of the truth as I am giving it to you.

I cannot give you much at a Lesson for you might miss it, but you see that what little I am giving you is dynamic, don't you. Right here, and in fact all through this course of instruction, you and I are dealing with the most dynamic and important Law in the universe. And this Law is to be used in your case to manifest plenty of every good thing you desire. So follow me closely from now on, for it will pay you to do so. Here we go: The Scriptures inform us that no man has ever seen God at any time—nor indeed could he, so whatever inspiration or revelation Moses had, was received in the very same manner in which you and I may receive our revelations or our inspirations. Moses DID NOT see God, and neither has anyone else at any time nor in any place. You can bank on that. Were I to go to the leaders of our great religious denominations, existing by the way for the express purpose of teaching the truths about God (so they say), and were I to say to those leaders, "Sirs—I want you to tell me how your God made the world," I wonder what sort of an answer I should get. I should, in all probability be told that they did not know. I should also be told in all probability that no one else knew either, and that it has not been given man to know just how this created world came to be. I might also be told that the scriptures were silent on that point, giving us no information at all. Ever since our present systems of religion sprang into existence, we have been taught that it was a mystery just how God did this.

But wait a minute, for IF EVER A STORY WAS PLAINLY TOLD IN ANY BOOK, THEN THE STORY OF CREATION IS PLAINLY TOLD IN THE BIBLE. Why it should be considered such a mystery or so hard to understand, is a greater mystery by far to me. Read and re-read a million times by ministers throughout all Christian countries, and by those supposed to be teaching Bible truths, the story seems to be clothed in impenetrable mystery to this day. And the plain simple truth of it all seems to have been missed in its entirety. Here we find the key lying on top of the puzzle where it usually lies, and if Moses could have put it any plainer, then I do not see how he could have done it. LISTEN CAREFULLY. It's so wonderfully simple—yet so wonderfully profound. The first two verses in the Bible give us the story of creation as it actually happened. Now read carefully as I unfold it to you. Genesis reads as follows: "In the beginning God created the heavens and the earth." Here we have a definite statement to the effect that God (and we shall not concern ourselves here with what God is) did a certain thing. He performed a certain act. He accomplished a certain piece of work. The statement is in the past tense and speaks of the deed as having been done. It had been actually accomplished. IN THE BEGINNING GOD CREATED THE HEAVENS AND THE EARTH. There can be no question as to what that means, can there. A certain person or power or something or other, which was God, DID A CERTAIN DEED. It was DONE. Past tense. This great power or spirit or force or whatever it might be, HAD CREATED THE HEAVENS AND THE EARTH. Nothing so very hard to understand about THAT, is there?

In this sense the statement is no harder to understand than if I said to you: "My little boy Alfred built a toy house out of blocks today." It would only signify that SOMETHING HAD BEEN DONE. That is the point I want to get across to you here. This earth HAD ALREADY BEEN CREATED, for this is what that statement of Brother Moses signifies and means. And it means nothing else. It was finished. The heavens and the earth had been created. I believe you will grasp that, but if not, then please READ IT AGAIN UNTIL YOU DO GRASP IT FOR IT IS VERY IMPORTANT. Your understanding of this entire course rests upon your properly grasping this one point here. Now watch the next statement. And mark well here that we have no way of knowing just how long a time elapsed between the first statement and this next one. Furthermore, it makes no difference whether it was ONE SECOND or TEN BILLION YEARS. The fact as stated, stands. The heavens and the earth had been created. NOW, grasp this next statement to the very full because it is mighty important—"AND THE EARTH WAS WITHOUT FORM AND VOID."

Now I ask you as a man or woman of common sense, what sort of a being would you be if you had already been created, and still were WITHOUT FORM AND VOID? Answer that and you have the answer to the question, "How did God make the earth, and what sort of a creation was it?" If you and I, created beings, were without form and void, then certainly we should be invisible or spiritual beings, would we not? If we were without form then we were not visible, were we? You cannot see anything that has not a form, can you? And if the creation of this earth and man was, as Brother Moses says, THEN IT COULD NOT HAVE BEEN A VISIBLE CREATION, could it. And if it were not a visible creation, then WHAT SORT OF A CREATION WAS IT? My friend and student, THERE IS ONLY ONE SORT OF A CREATION THAT IT POSSIBLY COULD HAVE BEEN, if the story of the Bible is correct, and that is A SPIRITUAL CREATION or, AN INVISIBLE CREATION. This fact is entirely foreign to the views that have been held for so long by the exponents of the Christian religion, but it is the story of the first creation just the same, AND TOLD EXACTLY AS THE BIBLE TELLS IT. The actual materialization of this spiritual or invisible creation did not take place for a long time (millions of years) after the original invisible creation was an accomplished fact.

If you read a little farther into the Genesis account of it, you will find that it was at a later date that the herbs, trees, etc., were called into being. You will also note that an entirely different method was used by "God" in manifesting physically the things that he had already created. Now mark me well, this point I am trying to make here is that the creation of the earth and the actual manifestation of it were two entirely separate and different creations, each requiring a different method of operation on the part of the Creative Life Principle. And now I am going to leave you for a couple of weeks when we shall go into the other part of the creation. It's mighty interesting I know, and it is necessary for you to grasp it in full, and understand the workings and the relationship between you and the Power that created you. For remember, that very same Creative Life Principle which went to work on those two little germs nine months before you were born, IS STILL AT WORK IN YOUR LIFE TODAY AND JUST AS EFFECTIVELY CAN IT ADJUST YOUR AFFAIRS IN EVERYDAY LIFE. Remember that. It did not place you on this earth a crying squalling baby, and then say:—"Well good-bye baby, shift for yourself now." Not that. It did not say: "I've made you and put you here and you can paddle your own canoe from now on." Not at all.

Now remember what I am saying to you please, for it's mighty important. THAT SAME MIGHTY CREATIVE GOD-LAW IS STILL HERE AND IS STILL OVERSEEING EVERY MOVEMENT OF YOUR LIFE. It is still a very vital part of you although not connected with your physical system in any way shape or form. And don't you forget it either. Now listen to me some more, whoever you may be. THIS SAME

CREATIVE LIFE SPIRIT CAN DO FOR YOU NOW, AND IN A MATERIAL WAY, WITH YOUR COOPERATION, WHATEVER IS NECESSARY FOR YOUR COMPLETE HAPPINESS HERE ON EARTH. And you will find out as you continue your studies with me that there is no personality of any kind connected with this Creative Life Principle or Spirit. You will find that it is a LAW, and, as such, it CANNOT FAIL when the conditions are complied with. I think I have plainly put across to you the fact that you still are IN VERY VITAL ASSOCIATION WITH THE CREATIVE INTELLIGENCE BEHIND THIS CREATED UNIVERSE. If you do not see it quite plainly yet, you will as we journey along together during the next few months.

Let me tell you a little advance secret at this point; if it were not for such an existing connection, YOU WOULD NOT EXIST ANOTHER SECOND. I think you can see though, that the very same Intelligence which began to manifest when you were a combination of two tiny germ-cells, is STILL MANIFESTING in your own individual life. You will admit that, and right away you will want to know if it is possible for you to get acquainted with this mighty Creative God-Law. And my advance answer to your question is yes, a thousand times YES. What do you think of that? Are your hopes rising a little higher now? You are really beginning at this point to believe that what I claim might possibly be true, are you not? Well, if you are, let me say to you that you can raise your hopes just as big as you want to, for there are no limitations that I have ever been able to find, to the Power of this mighty God-Law. If there are limitations in your own life, then that is because you, through ignorance of the God-Law probably, IMPOSE SUCH LIMITATIONS YOURSELF. And from now on I know that you are not going to do this. In your last Lesson I gave you a few bedtime exercises and some few instructions, not many, but enough to give you a little start on the road with me. I want these instructions to be carried out faithfully while you are studying with me. They are dynamic I assure you, for, whether you know it or not, your thought life is by far the most important part of you. You are what you are now because of what someone else and you, yourself have thought. In other words you are DIRECTLY a result of thought on the part of someone, and certainly on the part of yourself. In years gone by, say one hundred years ago, the Caucasian race was far different from what it is now. In those days, not so far back, people's thoughts were very different from what they are now. AND THEY WERE LIMITED BY THOSE THOUGHTS. It is not the one who sees limitations who gets anywhere, it is the one who can think ABOVE all limitations, for there never was a single thing created yet, that was not created in THOUGHT FIRST. Take the building in which I am sitting while writing this. There was a time, and not so far back either, when no building stood here. I want to trace the actual happenings in the construction of this, and every other building for that matter. FIRST: an architect was engaged and he was told what sort of a building was wanted and how much it was to cost.

Then, this architect, SAT DOWN AND VISUALIZED THIS BUILDING IN HIS OWN THOUGHT REALM. He drew a thought-picture of what the building should look like. But the entire operation was performed ENTIRELY IN THE REALM OF THOUGHT. Remember this. After the architect had drawn his thought-picture of what the finished building should look like, THEN, AND NOT BEFORE THEN, did he transfer his "thought results" to paper, in order that they might be Permanent, and in order that the actual builder might build the building. NOW—which was the more important operation of the two? The thinking out of the building in the thought realm of the architect, or the actual mechanical work by the builder? Certainly not the latter, for this man worked mechanically, and ENTIRELY ACCORDING TO THE BLUE PRINT WHICH ORIGINATED IN THE THOUGHT REALM OF THE ARCHITECT. In our office there is a very intricate electrical machine. It seems almost human. As fast as one of our operators can write a letter on a typewriter, this machine sets that type into pages, and actually does the work of ten people setting the type single handed.

I happen to know that the development of this machine took years and years of WHAT? Why of THOUGHT, of course. The men responsible for this marvelous piece of mechanism, thought, and thought, and thought. Then, when they had the correct THOUGHTS, they put down on paper a drawing of THE RESULT OF THEIR THOUGHT. And this machine, which but a few years ago did not exist, NOW IS AN ACTUAL THING AND IS BEING USED BY US IN THE PRINTING OF MILLIONS OF SHEETS OF PAPER. But the all important thing for you to grasp is the fact that the ACTUAL MAKING OF THIS MACHINE WAS DONE IN THE UNSEEN REALM. It was done in the THOUGHT REALM. And you cannot get around that, can you? Had there been no thought realm, and had there been no "thought creation," there would have been no electrical typesetting machine in my offices, I assure you. Take the radio. There would be no such a thing in existence as radio, had not Mr. Marconi spent hours and days and weeks and months and years of intensive THOUGHT. As a thought would crystallize, he would put it down on paper, and it would be turned into an actual thing ere long. The actual mechanical manufacture of the parts of a radio, is entirely secondary to the THOUGHT FORCE which brought radio into being. You may take any created thing you care to, and if you investigate it carefully, you will find that its first cause lies nowhere else than in the unseen realm of THOUGHT. Let that sink in please. It's vital to your finding the LAW underlying success, health and happiness. We think all too little of such simple things as THOUGHTS. We don't pay much attention to them. And yet—they are the most dynamic things in existence. For there never was a man or woman yet that could or ever did rise higher than he or she could think. And when I say think I mean THINK, not dream. And the chances are, many to one, that if you are a failure, the reason why you are a failure is because FAILURE thoughts have been the predominating thoughts of your life. You cannot continually think "failure" without being a failure. Nor can you continually think success without being a success. Ofttimes one must FORCE HIMSELF TO THINK SUCCESS THOUGHTS, but that makes no difference for the results are sure, for the Law of God is immutable. IT NEVER FAILS. IT NEVER CHANGES. And just as sure as day follows night, if the preponderance of your thought is SUCCESS THOUGHT, the preponderance of your life will lie in the realm of success.

You may make up your mind here also, that the God-Law is sure and inviolate and any failure to manifest success or happiness, must and will be a failure on your part to comply with this mighty LAW. By no possible means can this Law fail. And so, by no possible means can you ever manifest either health, success, or happiness, if your mind is full of thoughts of failure, unhappiness, and disease. That cannot be. It is not the God-Law that it should be. And this God-Law cannot work on your everyday life unless the conditions governing it are complied with. So I say to you, whoever you may be, give me the benefit of the doubt at this point, for I assure you I know the way and I shall not mislead you one step. I know whereof I speak, and every thinking man and woman will know, from the angle from which I am approaching this subject, that I do know whereof I speak. I realize that this course of instruction will be read and studied by as many different sorts of people as there are different trades and professions, for I have students in every walk of life. Grand opera singers. Government Officials. Editors. Nationally known columnists. Scientists. Catholic Priests. Preachers. Butchers. In fact I think I may safely say that every walk of life is represented in my student files.

But it makes no difference, for, as previously stated, THE GOD-LAW IS NO RESPECTER OF PERSONS. It works the same way for all. So do these simple little exercises. Most people in this day and age go along at breakneck speed, and at the highest nervous, tension. They do not know what relaxation means. They gulp down their meals, rush here, rush there, and even when they go to bed they toss and roll most of the night. These exercises of mine will do at least one thing. But it's an important thing though. They will teach you how to positively rest every muscle in your body. And if they never do more than that, they are worth alone many times the cost of this course. For when absolute physical relaxation is indulged in every night, I will tell you that it isn't very long until one knows that they are being benefitted through such relaxation. But these exercises will do far more than teach you how to relax. They are designed by me to do far more than that. For they deal directly with the thought realm, which, of course, is the unseen realm. After a while you will probably change your ideas about thoughts. Today, you may probably think: "Oh well, a thought is just something or other that keeps going through my head. Everybody thinks, and they can't help it." That may be what you think now. But I have an idea that before you and I get through with each other, you will have a far different opinion of your thoughts. What I am after at this stage of our journey, is to get you every night into a state of absolute relaxation. Then too, I am doing something else. I am directing your thoughts into the unseen thought realm. You will recall that we have seen that every manifested thing FIRST HAD ITS ORIGIN IN THE THOUGHT REALM. Well, that is exactly where I am leading you, into the thought realm, or, to be more precise and exact, into the realm of MANIFESTATION. Or, to be still more correct, into the Realm of the God-Law. Here you are beginning to see a little more clearly I think, just what I am trying to do. But don't be impatient. Take your time. You probably have been dissatisfied and unhappy a long time now, and you can afford to spend the next few months studying with me I think.

Here we are then, in bed, and we are utterly relaxed. Every muscle is at ease. We are breathing slowly, and filling the lungs to the full with fresh breath. We are slowly exhaling. We are very quiet. All clocks and other ticking things are out of the room. We are prepared to drop off into a natural quiet sleep. We close our eyes. We don't move a muscle, and the first thing we know, we do not even feel the physical body at all. First the toes go to sleep. Then our hands get numb and they are asleep. Then, sleep slowly and almost unconsciously creeps up our legs and into our arms. (We are still awake remember.) We do not move a muscle but just lie there like a log of wood. And now comes the important part of the exercises. We are still conscious, and our eyes are directed into the field of vision as we see it. KEEP THE EYES CLOSED. There is always one certain part of the field of vision which is lighter than any other part. It moves with the eyes. This is true even though our eyes are shut tight, and even though the room be pitch dark. There is ALWAYS that one area in which it seems lighter than any other area in this field of "closed eye vision."

You will probably find this bright area very easily, but by way of warning let me say that you will not find it until you are relaxed as fully as you possibly can. To those who have not found it yet let me say that you must keep on until you do find it. It isn't hard to find, for this white or bright area is the part of you which is very close to the Realm of the God-Law. The idea now is to take the little affirmation I shall give from time to time, and. WITHOUT ANY ATTEMPT ON YOUR PART TO CARRY THEM INTO YOUR SLEEP, LET THE AFFIRMATION YOU ARE WORKING ON BE CARRIED BY YOUR THOUGHT, RIGHT INTO THAT BRIGHT AREA, AND TO THE EXCLUSION OF EVERY OTHER THOUGHT. For instance, last Lesson gave you the affirmation, "I AM FINDING THE POWER OF THE LIVING GOD". Now for the next two weeks, use this affirmation carefully and faithfully: "MY THOUGHTS ARE PART OF THE LIVING GOD." I don't want you to try and force anything at all at this time. You should be in a condition of semi-sleep, utterly relaxed, lying there in bed as motionless as a log, and with part of you half asleep as it were. And then, direct this above affirmation into the very depths of your being, and you will be doing this by directing it right into that brighter area in your field of vision.

Shortly, you will drop off to sleep without knowing it, and A DEFINITE STEP ALONG THE ROAD OF YOUR UNDERSTANDING OF THE MIGHTY UNSEEN POWER OF GOD WILL HAVE BEEN ACCOMPLISHED. You probably will not know it. but it won't be very long now until you begin to realize that something is happening in you. For these thoughts are powerful things, and THEY COME DIRECT FROM THE MIGHTY LIFE SPIRIT, AND, MORE IMPORTANT THAN ALL. THEY GO BACK TO THIS SAME CREATIVE LIFE PRINCIPLE. Remember this well. Every thought you think under these circumstances, GOES DIRECT TO THE ORIGINATOR OF ALL LIFE, AND THE ORIGINATOR OF WHAT WE NOW CALL THOUGHT. We may see a little later that thought is a far more potent and dynamic thing than we have ever suspected, I don't want to anticipate however. All I want you to do is to follow me closely through every move I suggest and advise, I shall probably open your eyes before you have finished this course of instruction.

Don't forget, on awakening, fill your lungs with pure air. Open your windows and get down to the very bottom of those lungs of yours. Chances are you only use a fraction of them when you should be using them to their full capacity. Many people write me asking if calisthenics are a good thing. Yes, they are a fine thing for the physical body, and there is, of course, a very vital connection between the physical and the spiritual, and as long as too much stress is not laid on calisthenics, and as long as they are not overdone, they are good, for the time being at any rate. Through the day, whenever opportunity occurs, let this same thought I have given you be in your mind TO THE EXCLUSION OF EVERY OTHER THOUGHT. You will notice that in these exercises, I very seldom use the word "mind" and where I do use it, it is only because the use of it is handy. I have a very definite reason for not doing so, and as you progress, you will have a very revolutionary definition of "mind" given to you. You do as I ask though, and hold this one thought every moment in which you comfortably can do so, and remember above all, the most important part of this work is the relaxation exercises at night, and the impressing of the affirmation into the very center of your being. And perhaps, FARTHER THAN THAT.

Our next Lesson will go into the subject of who and what God actually is. This next Lesson has brought more favorable comment than anything I have ever written. This present Lesson, No. 3 has brought many, many favorable letters to me, but the next Lesson is a very vital one, as you will know when it reaches you. You have never had before such an explanation of God given to you as the next Lesson will give you. And the thought will probably revolutionize all your previous ideas of this great Power. It will also throw a flood of light on the Lessons you have received to date. In fact, it will throw a flood of light into your whole life itself. It has been said many times that I was inspired when I wrote that Lesson. Perhaps so. But every soul, living in touch with the God-Law, is inspired to just the extent he or she can assimilate that marvelous LAW. For truly marvelous it is. We will not anticipate however, but will do the work in our hands well, so that we shall be ready for Lesson 4 when it comes in two weeks.

POINTS TO REMEMBER IN LESSON NUMBER THREE

(1) The very same Power responsible for creation, and especially responsible for YOU, IS STILL HERE WITH YOU, WAITING TO BE USED BY YOU for the achievement of every good and right thing you can desire. This Power did not put you here and go away, leaving you to your own resources, but STAYED RIGHT HERE WITH YOU.

(2) You are now, through this course and my exercises, LAYING THE FOUNDATION of the things you desire to manifest in your life in the future. LAY THAT FOUNDATION EXACTLY AS I TELL YOU TO. What you are today is the result of what you and others thought years ago. What you will be in the future depends largely on what you think today. Think the thought given in the Lesson and think it to the exclusion of other thoughts.

(3) Adopt the mental attitude that the things you desire ARE ALREADY IN EXISTENCE SOMEWHERE, and the actual manifestation of them is begun. This is absolutely a fact. As the architect first plans in his thought realm, the building he is to build, so you are now planning the future you are to enjoy—or not to enjoy. There is in this world or in this creation somewhere, more than sufficient of everything to satisfy your needs, and do it without robbing someone else. So keep an expectant attitude—expect the best—and be ready for it when it comes. Don't do these exercises nor go ahead with this course, unless you PREPARE YOURSELF TO EXPECT, AND REALLY DO EXPECT BETTER THINGS TO COME TO PASS IN YOUR LIFE. It would be a pity if the GOD-LAW had been complied with, and you, through you own attitude of non-expectancy, were to MISS THE GOAL, would it not? Well that can happen. So be expectant—and the more expectant you are, the surer will the manifestation be.

(4) Be absolutely on the level with me, with yourself, and with your fellow men and women. Downright crookedness will invariably defeat the Law, and there is no need for it in the first place. So, as a matter of

business alone, if for no other reason, be on the level with everyone for YOUR OWN GOOD. Every wrong deed brings its own reward, and may hinder the workings of the God-Law. When you know this mighty LAW better, automatically you will never bother your head with anything that does not comply with the God-Law. I'm not preaching now, for I quit preaching a long time ago. I'm merely telling you that you will get along faster playing the game on the square with everybody.

Sincerely your friend and teacher,
FRANK B. ROBINSON

LESSON 4

Now we come to Lesson number Four. It is an intensely interesting Lesson, and is of vital importance to you in your studies. It is one of the most important Lessons of them all, for the profound truths it contains are the most fundamental you have ever studied or dealt with. This is the Lesson which has brought the amazing number of complimentary letters to us from all over the world. It has revolutionized the thought and life of a good many of our students, and has been the cause of an entirely new vision of the Creative Spirit behind this universe. So study it very carefully and very thoughtfully, and very earnestly. Read it over and over again. Drive home into the very core of your being the mighty truths this fourth Lesson discloses. There are other Lessons equally as interesting as this one is, and also as dynamic, but I especially want you to grasp this one please. For it contains the key to the others which follow later.

You have come to me in your search for health, success, and happiness, and you believe that I know the way. I KNOW that I know the way, and am now, through these Lessons showing it to you. You, of course, are in earnest in these studies. You actually want the good things of life, don't you? There are hundreds of thousands trotting around this old globe who are not in the slightest degree interested in either financial success, good health, or happiness. Some of them have never tasted happiness. They do not know what it means. Others there are who don't seem to care whether they ever amount to anything or not. They live their lives, or rather, they exist out their lives, and thoughts of the higher, nobler, better things of life never seem to come to them. They just simply are not interested at all. As long as they have a JOB which keeps them in eats and sleeps, they seem to be abundantly satisfied. But I don't think you are that sort of a person. I know you are not.

You would not have put yourself in my hands if you had been, and now that you are in my hands for this unusual teaching, I earnestly want to show you the LAW which CAN and WILL, and MUST bring whatever right and needed things you desire into your life when this mighty Creative God-LAW is complied with. And when that happens there can be no failure. And right here let me say to you that if there is no desire, no real desire in the life for the better things, the chances are many to one against any of these better things ever manifesting. In fact, it is practically an impossibility for life's finer things to come, where the earnest intense desire for them is absent. It is a part of the LAW that first of all the DESIRE MUST BE THERE. In your individual case I KNOW it is there or you would not have enrolled with me. I do not know what in your particular case the particular need may be. Nor do I care. All I am asking at this point is that you remember that you are in earnest in your search for the LAW controlling every good thing life has to offer. If I thought the students who will read this would not be in earnest, then I promise you it never would have been written. But it has been written, and it HAS gripped thousands of people all over the world, and we have not gotten off to a good start yet.

For the day is coming when the truths of the GOD-LAW as this course of instruction reveals them to you, will be known all over the world. What a change will there be then. What a difference that will make. This ceaseless and ofttimes useless struggle against poverty, ill health, unhappiness, will be a thing of the past in the life of the one knowing how to utilize the GOD-LAW as Jesus understood and used it. He had no monopoly on this LAW. This was the message He came to preach, the universality of the GOD-LAW. But the people wouldn't have it then. It has taken two thousand years for the people to get the first faint inkling of what this mighty GOD-LAW actually is. And mighty few of them know yet. And in the meantime thousands of men and women have turned in disgust from what has been offered to them in the name of God, knowing that such ridiculous doctrines and dogmas never could do any thing material and lasting in life. Perhaps after death, but not in LIFE.

All that is changing, however, and as this teaching goes on its way around the world, the eyes of men and women are being opened to the actual TRUTHS of GOD and as ever when natural or Spiritual Law is complied with, THE RESULTS ARE SURE. I have purposely stopped here for a moment on our journey together, and have reconnoitered for a few moments, just to look the land over and see just where we stand to date. I am to show you the workings of the GOD-LAW behind the universe, and show you how to apply it in your own life for health, success, and happiness. You, in turn, are deeply in earnest in this entire matter. You really want to be a success. You really DO want to get out of the rut and away from the "don't-cares" and you actually WANT and DESIRE to find the better things of life. If you are a married man or woman, you want that home. You want that car. You want that account in the bank. You want that life insurance, and, above all, it may be that you want that domestic happiness. In other words, you want to be an all-round success with the needs of your individual life supplied (the proper needs of course). So at this point we are agreed as to where we stand. You have done the little exercises I have prescribed for you, faithfully. That is exactly what I want you to do. Perhaps you have not understood them at all, but that is perfectly all right at this point, if you have done them as I directed you to. A little later on you will understand just what these exercises are designed to do. You will know what they really are, and for what purpose I prescribed them. Jut now, however, you just DO them exactly as I ask you to. Remember, you are the student and I am the teacher. I know what I am doing and talking about, and you want to know. All right then, faithfully follow me and remember as you follow me in this marvelous Lesson that we are not studying a fairy story in any sense of the word. We are studying the story of THIS WORLD and ITS CREATOR.

We are also to study something else. We are to study the most marvelous creation God ever made—YOU—man or woman. Let me interpolate here long enough to suggest that you be very sure of your ground before we progress any farther along the line of these studies. If you are not so clear on any point, or if for some reason or other you have not done the exercises, then may I suggest that you start at the beginning again, and this time do them. Those of my students who are the most earnest will be the most anxious to do these things. But, no matter how intensely interesting these Lessons are from a historical and literary standpoint, I am afraid that it will take much more than just a reading of them to achieve many results. SO, being in earnest, you want the TRUTH, and I will give it to you.

In dealing with this immense subject of this world's Creator, and its created marvel man and woman, I realize, of course, the utter impossibility of doing it the justice I should like to. I could probably write year in and year out on this subject but it is necessary now that I condense as much as possible, and put the vital truths of this course of religious instruction into as few words as possible. You will at once recognize their dynamic power, however, and on applying the principles as I give them to you, you will find that they work. So follow me closely, for it has taken me a lifetime of study and thought to formulate and prove the facts that I am now writing down on a piece of paper for you to read. I am not attempting to write these mighty facts in a scholarly manner at all, nor shall I introduce scientific terms. I am writing for the man on the street—the man who needs them most. I want THAT fellow to grasp what I am talking about. Hence, the use of highbrow terms will never be found in anything coming from my pen, no matter where it appears.

The big business man in his swell office probably has not the same need for these truths that you have, and as many of my students will be just ordinary everyday fellows like I am, my wording and expressions will be understood by them. In fact this whole course of instruction is written so that even a child can understand it. I have been asked many times to analyze the power and grip my writings exert, and I think my answer to that question and request has always been to the effect that the reason why these Lessons grip is because they contain the truths of GOD, written so that anyone can comprehend them. And in passing once more let me say to you that wherever and whenever you find a TRUTH of GOD, you will instantly recognize it for such, and you will invariably find that such TRUTH is so plain that even a child can understand it. I have always claimed that the Creative God-Law behind the universe has been lost sight of on account of the simplicity of its operation. The greatest truths in life come from the mouths of little children, and the great underlying truths of God are unmistakably plain when the attention of the earnest seeker is directed into the proper channel. So in this entire course of Lessons please remember that I am writing them very plainly, and am giving you the very best that is in me. And as I pass these mighty truths along to you, I want you to rise to them, and, line up your life with the great fundamental GOD-LAW. I want you to know for the first time in your life perhaps, what true success, true health, and true happiness really are. And man will never know any of these things until the GOD-LAW operates in his life. When it does so operate, no heights are too great to be attained. In your own case, there is not much limit to what may be done, REMEMBER THIS.

These Lessons, as you will very shortly see, have come to me through the Great Source of all truth; therefore they cannot be wrong. They MUST and DO contain the truth. Had they not contained the living vital truth, both myself and "PSYCHIANA" would never have found even public attention. As it is, this teaching will probably be one of the greatest forward religious movements this world has seen for a good many years. Now in this fourth Lesson, don't attempt to read or study it if you are liable to be disturbed. I should like you to have at least one hour in which your time is absolutely your own. Get into a quiet restful and relaxed mood, and get into an expectant mood too, for this Lesson contains lots of spiritual power for those who can recognize it. In preparing your mind for the beginning of the understanding of the mighty dynamic GOD-LAW, let me say to you here that the idea of God which I shall give you will, in all probability upset your previous ideas of who and what God or this GOD-LAW actually is. Instead of it being some distant Power which MIGHT do something for you AFTER YOU DIE, you will find a very present and self-existent POWER which can do something real for you HERE and NOW.

Which, of course, is much better than having it in the future. You are sure of the life you are living now, and you are also sure that had you the many benefits and blessings of life, you could enjoy them. But you are not at all sure of the future. Not a single soul can prove that there is any future. Many try to tell us of a home of bliss to be enjoyed after we die, and in some future life, but that cannot be proven. It is only what they think. So shall we confine our operations of the GOD-LAW to the here and now, letting the future take care of itself? I think that will be better. Don't you? Now just a word of explanation as to your religious beliefs, which, by the way, I know nothing of. Probably most of my students have long since discarded the old orthodox idea of God, which is a good thing. For if one were to try and get a definite explanation of who and what God really is from the many differing sects etc., claiming to know God, I am afraid one would have a wonderful time doing it. For every preacher in the world there is a different definition of God. There are over 3000 differing sects and denominations operating in our land today, and each is convinced that the rest of them are all wrong.

They have the truth, and no one else has it. Unless you find their "god" in their own prescribed manner, you can't find Him at all. In my mind, however, there is a mighty big question as to whether any of them have seen the Light as it exists. You can form your own opinion, however, when these Lessons are finished. You will then have a pretty good idea of who is right, the differing religious organizations or I. It's pretty hard to reconcile the differing conceptions of God with the truth as it exists, and sometimes I wonder how it could have possibly been that religious idolatry has taken the place of the dynamic GOD-LAW. But such seems to be the case. However, no matter what your religious persuasion is, remember, you have agreed to lay it to one side for the time being. Running through all the systems of religious instruction the world has ever seen, there is like a silver thread, the TRUTH. The system may be ninety-nine percent error, and it probably is, but there is some truth in every system of religion, no matter where it originated and who originated it. The world has been to date many crucified "saviors." Long before the Christian "savior" appeared there had been many others. And their followers, of course, all considered THEIR OWN "savior" the only one who really was a combination of God and a man.

I won't spend any time discussing all these other "saviors" at this point any more than to say that they were all supposed to be a mysterious combination of GOD with some man. They were all supposed to have done miraculous things; most of them were crucified, they all rose from the dead, and they all came into the world to save people from their sins. There have been enough divine "saviors" down through history to save a dozen worlds including this one. That is of course, if their claims were true. Unfortunately however, their claims were NOT true, as history also shows. The point I want to make, however, is that the man who was considered to be "god" and a man in combination, was usually a very bright thinker, and a man with a deep insight into Spiritual Law. Not always, but usually so. Some of the most brilliant and elevating of sayings came from the mouth of Confucius. In the case of the Christian religion, its prophet, one Jesus was no more than a man. If I had the time I could convince you that this statement is a fact, and could convince you beyond any shadow of a doubt. But at the same time, that man Jesus knew what Spiritual LAW was, and to a wonderful degree. He had a grasp on the truths of the GOD-LAW that very few have ever had either before or since that time, so I am going to take that man and use him, because you are probably more familiar with that story than you are with the story of any of the other world's "crucified saviors." And in dealing with this man I shall show you the staggering import of the truths He saw and used.

And mighty truths they are too. It is interesting here to note that never did Jesus Christ say He was God. At no time did He ever make such a claim. To the contrary, He claimed the very opposite. Did He not say that the things He did you and I should do also? Did He not say that? Did He not ask why anyone should call Him God? Many, many times He specifically claimed NOT TO BE GOD, to the exclusion of the rest of the human race. The church is the organization which tacked divinity on to Christ, and by so doing, they absolutely killed His message. Had the church left Him as a man, as HE claimed to be, and not tacked onto Him the nonsensical resurrection from the dead, and the equally nonsensical and unprovable ascension into a place called heaven, what a difference it would have made—wouldn't it? But by introducing a story that He was God, and therefore possessing a power which no one else can possess, they just simply took Him away out of reach of the common folks like you and me, and placed Him on a pedestal where He never belonged. And further than that, they robbed mankind of every chance of ever doing the things that He did. If Christ were God, then there can be no possible chance of you or I ever duplicating his words. If He were but a man, however, in full tune with the GOD-LAW, which I claim then there is every chance of every man using the same God Law as He used, to do whatever is needed in life. And what a different light this throws on things does it not?

Just think for a moment—suppose there were, existing now, a great Spiritual Law more than sufficient to make possible every proper desire of the human heart, wouldn't that be a very welcome Power? Well friend, that is the message of the Christ. That is the message He came to bring. That—and nothing more. His message was totally one telling of the Power of the GOD-LAW. His message was completely limited to the telling of the actual literal physical and spiritual results to be obtained through the application of this mighty GOD-LAW. And He proved that He knew how to call into play, this self same Law that I am telling you of. Diseases disappeared, the blind received their sight again. The deaf had their hearing restored, the lame walked, the hungry were fed, we are told.

And it is my contention that this same Power exists today and FOR THAT VERY PURPOSE. True it is, the religiously inclined will laugh at that. They tell us that we cannot know the Spiritual God-Law until we die. NO? They cannot tell me that though, for I know better, and before you have gone very far on your way with me you will know better also. But just suppose that I DO know what I am talking about. Just suppose that there IS such a POWER as that, easily available HERE and NOW. Do you think such a POWER would make any difference in your life? I think it would. And take it from me whoever you are, that is the fact of life as it exists today. That was the truth Jesus proclaimed, and for which, we are told, they killed Him. Never did He take any credit to Himself. It was ever, first, last, and all the time, GOD. And that is the way it is with "PSYCHIANA" today. FIRST, LAST, and all the time——GOD. To us however, GOD is a Spiritual LAW. It operates here and now and is the greatest operating LAW or POWER this world has ever seen or known. And it hasn't known much about this Power to date either. It's learning though, and as this teaching of mine and its accompanying power continues to go around the world, so will men and women begin to learn something about this self-existent present, immutable, dynamic God-Law, and, knowing the operations of that Law, their every want will be supplied, and their every right desire will be fulfilled, by and through the operations and existence of this mighty GOD-LAW—which is GOD.

So shall we look for a little while now at what Jesus said about this mighty God-Law. I shall ask you to go back to the story of the woman of Samaria at the well of Jacob. You will remember that this Carpenter Man had asked her for a drink of water. In the conversation which followed, He made a Positive and definite assertion that GOD IS SPIRIT. He did NOT say "God is A spirit" at all. A search of the oldest text here will disclose the fact that the article "a" is not in there at all. It was interpolated or added to make sense out of the statement, according to the ideas of the translators of this chapter. Instead of making sense out of the statement, however, they made complete nonsense and destroyed the entire meaning of the verse. More than that, they destroyed the definition of God as Jesus gave it. As a matter of fact no one can tell the harm these translators did through the interpolation of their own ideas as to just how these scriptures should read. While passing, it might be as well to call attention to the fact that there has never been known to exist, one single original manuscript covering this Bible story. This fact is not published by the church folks and many of them may question this statement. But it is a fact.

NOT ONE SINGLE ORIGINAL MANUSCRIPT COVERING THIS BIBLE STORY HAS EVER BEEN KNOWN TO EXIST. Even the authorship of the four gospels is absolutely unknown. It IS known that at least three of them were NOT written by the men whose titles they bear, and it is a further fact that no one knows who actually did the writing of them, if they were not written by the church itself. All that has ever existed on the New Testament, are "copies" and copies of "copies." But of original manuscripts, there are none. Nor have there ever been any known to exist. In view of this fact, I am of the opinion that too much dogmatism concerning the "divinity" of the scriptures is certainly quite out of the order. The story may be taken on "faith" but there certainly is no evidence of its truth as far as authentic proof of the existence of any original manuscripts goes. I shall not enlarge upon this subject here though, as my magazine "PSYCHIANA" QUARTERLY goes into this phase very fully. Let me say a word or two to the warring church factions here though, and here it is —if you would only understand that the men who translated this Bible were ordinary everyday human beings just like you and me—if you would only understand that they were only educated up to the light of their time, then it seems to me that you would not care what interpretation were placed on the story Or the creation of man, provided, of course, that this interpretation were reasonable. We know, and we know full well that the mighty Creative Intelligence behind this universe DID NOT make a man from a mixture of spit and earth. We KNOW that, and all the religiously inclined could not make us believe that it did. We also know that no "god" caused a deep sleep to come upon a man, and then, while fast asleep, removed one rib and made a woman out of it. WE KNOW THAT DID NOT HAPPEN. But what difference does it make whether man's creation took one second of time or ten million years? What difference does it make whether man began his existence as a humble amoebae, progressing through the millions of ages until his present stage was reached, or whether he was instantly made in one second of time? That is not what matters my friends. What actually matters is this—WHAT MESSAGE HAVE YOU FROM YOUR GOD TO THE MAN ON THE STREET HERE AND NOW? If you and your brethren cannot agree as to whether the story you depend on is true or not, THEN HOW DO YOU EXPECT TO CONVINCE THE MAN ON THE STREET THAT IT IS TRUE? If you continue to war and fight between yourselves as to whether or not Jesus Christ was God, and if you cannot agree on the subject, then WHAT LIGHT IS THE MAN ON THE STREET GOING TO GET FROM YOU? HOW IS HE GOING TO KNOW?

You may depend upon one thing though, and that thing is that the men who deciphered these old anonymous manuscripts you call the Word of God were one hundred percent human men. And you may depend upon another thing also—you may depend up on it that the men who wrote them were one hundred percent human also. And this being a fact, these men, whoever they were, were certainly subject to human limitations. So if I were you, I believe I should quit squabbling amongst yourselves, and try and get down to basic fundamental facts concerning the LIVING GOD as He exists and operates here and now. For unless the church does quit its squabbling and get down to actual facts concerning God, you will find that the revelations which should come through you, will come through men and women WHO MAKE NO PROFESSION OF RELIGION AT ALL. And this is exactly what is now happening, and the church has no one to blame but itself.

I have digressed here a little. Please excuse it—and we shall go back to where we were. To say "a" spirit would have been implying the existence of more than one spirit and JESUS DID NOT DO THIS. So then we have the plain statement from One who certainly knew, that GOD IS SPIRIT. A very plain and definite statement and one that is quite understandable I am sure. And how that statement opens up like a rose, the entire scriptures when fully grasped. The next thing incumbent upon us then, in order to have an intelligent explanation of what GOD is, is to find out what "spirit" is. Now if you wanted to know the meaning of any word, where would you go to get the definition of it? To the dictionary I believe. So there is exactly where we shall go. I think perhaps Webster is the accepted authority today, so we shall quote him. His definition is, in effect, that "spirit" is LIFE or INTELLIGENCE conceived of entirely apart from physical embodiment. What is that? Let me repeat the statement, for it is very dynamic. Webster said that "spirit" was LIFE or INTELLIGENCE conceived of, or capable of existence of being WITHOUT PHYSICAL FORM. Here we are getting down to something definite about God. We have a definition of terms. We are not accepting that someone else told us, neither are we accepting some theory or other—we are getting down to bed-rock as it were. We have then, the statement that God is "LIFE" or "INTELLIGENCE" capable of existence without bodily or physical form. And that is the very best definition possible. THAT definition is corroborated throughout the entire scriptures, so for the purpose here I shall take it as it stands. There are, of course, many other things that GOD is, BUT BEFORE HE COULD HAVE BEEN ANY OF THESE OTHER THINGS HE MUST NEEDS HAVE BEEN LIFE FIRST. I wish I could drive that statement home to you. Let me repeat it once more. BEFORE GOD COULD HAVE BEEN ANY OF THE OTHER THINGS THAT HE IS, HE MUST NEEDS HAVE BEEN LIFE FIRST. And without LIFE, all of the other things that He is would be as naught. HAD HE NOT BEEN LIFE, HE NEVER COULD HAVE BEEN ANYTHING-ELSE. So for a while here I shall concentrate on the accepted fact that GOD IS SPIRIT, and that SPIRIT IS LIFE CAPABLE OF EXISTENCE WITHOUT PHYSICAL FORM. In other words, God is INVISIBLE LIFE.

It will take you a long time to fully grasp that statement, my friend. You will not grasp it overnight. But when you DO grasp it to the full, you will begin to understand a little bit, just what God really is, and more than that, just WHERE HE IS. Try and imagine this Living God, the most dynamic Power in the universe, being all around you in the air so to speak, in the very room in which you are reading this—BUT INDISCERNIBLE TO YOU IN YOUR PRESENT STATE OF CONSCIOUSNESS. That is the EXACT FACT of the presence of God. He is not hidden away "in the sky" somewhere, nor does He hide and operate from some remote portion of your brain, through your "subconscious mind" either. Nor are His manifestations made known through the medium of your sympathetic nervous system, or anything on that order. Never believe such twaddle as that is. THIS LIVING DYNAMIC POWER, THIS MIGHTY LIVING GOD IS IN THE VERY AIR YOU BREATHE—not, of course, as one of the chemical constituents of the air, but LIVING IN IT—AND YET NOT PART OF IT. Can you grasp what I mean? I am sure you can. Many scientists on the verge of this mighty truth have stated that "there is thinking substance in the ether all around us." It is MORE THAN THAT.

This statement completely revolutionizes the entire understanding of God as we have it today. You must make a clean cut distinction here though between God's actually living in any part of your physical body, and His actual presence there. To say that God dwells in you, as a body, would be grossly wrong. For as "spirit" He could not inhabit a material body. But to say that God dwells within you, and at the same time has positively no physical connection with you at all, is stating the TRUTH as it ACTUALLY EXISTS. Many Psychologists find it hard to do this, so they immediately go on the assumption that God Himself, or some attribute of Himself, actually lives and operates through the brain and spinal column or some other part of the human mechanism. Such a statement, however, is grossly misleading, and is false in its entirety. Furthermore, God has no attributes which might so operate. He has no mind—He cannot have. Nor is there any such thing as a "god-mind" or a "god-consciousness" or a "god" any thing else. There cannot be because GOD IS—not God HAS. Do you see THAT? There is a little book published by the Unity School of Christianity at Kansas City, Mo. and written by H. Emilie Cady. The book is called "Lessons in Truth." I should like to have every student of mine, when he has finished these Lessons, send for that book. It gave me a lot of help in my early metaphysical studies, and while I do not agree with Mrs. Cady in many things she teaches, I can and do agree with her on many other points.

When I saw the flock of geese flying high in the sky and filling the air below with their honks, I saw GOD IN ACTUAL OPERATION THROUGH AN IMMUTABLE LAW, WHICH LAW IS GOD, THAT GEESE SHOULD FLY. And when I saw the little robins building their nests, I SAW GOD IN OPERATION THROUGH AN IMMUTABLE LAW MADE AGES AGO WHICH LAW REQUIRED THAT LITTLE ROBINS MATE—BUILD THEIR NESTS—AND PRODUCE MORE LITTLE ROBINS. And when I went into the bedroom and looked upon the sleeping form of my little Alfred, I SAW GOD IN ACTUAL OPERATION THROUGH AN IMMUTABLE LAW HE MADE AGES AGO, WHICH LAW ORDAINED THAT THE HUMAN RACE SHOULD PROPAGATE THEIR OWN KIND. AND IN THE SLEEPING FORM OF MY LITTLE ALFRED I SAW THE RESULTS OF THAT SAME LAW STILL OPERATING, THOUSANDS AND PERHAPS MILLIONS OF YEARS LATER. But it would be the rankest kind of folly and untruth were I to state to you that either the Living Creative God himself, or any of His supposed attributes, were actually living in, or operating through the brain and spinal column of either the boy, the geese, or the little robins. Man's brain was given to him to control the functions of the physical body only. The same thing applies to the brains of the geese, the robins, and the little boy, and you may depend upon it, no God, as such, operates personally through any flesh of any kind. Nor did the creative LIFE or INTELLIGENCE or GOD ever come down to this earth, and occupy the body of any human being to the exclusion of all others. As spirit, he could not possibly have done that. In the body—but not of it.

The common idea of God held by the church people of today, seems to be that of some personality who dwells in a home in "heaven," and who is now up there, checking and perhaps rechecking on us and making notes of all of our actions down here. At some future time, we are told, we shall come back to life again, and shall stand in a court of judgment, and those of us who do not measure up to a certain standard will be everlastingly punished. Those who do, however, will be everlastingly rewarded. Well—I have no quarrel at all with those who care to hold such a theory as that. Their outlook on life and their future must of necessity be very stunted though, and certain it is that with such prospects ahead of them, they can never attain very much happiness in THIS life. The statement, however, to put it mildly, is erroneous—but all that will appear later. The point I want to send home to you now is that GOD IS INVISIBLE LIFE. In "Him" we live and move and have our being, and that would be manifestly impossible if "god" were in "heaven" or any other place removed from his creation.

The stunning fact is that you could not take another breath without God. Not without God's help but without this mighty Creative Life Spirit. A sparrow can't fall to the ground without Him. The wild geese would get lost without Him. The lily on the mountainside could not grow without Him. The little robins might raise baby scorpions without Him—not without the "subconscious mind," but without HIM. Do you begin to see what I mean? This mighty LIFE SPIRIT, this supreme Intelligence is everywhere. Right here in the room in which I am writing this and so close to me that in Him I press down these typewriter keys and send this message to you. And if I were to leave the room I should not take Him with me out of the room, he would still be here after I had gone. It is very important that you grasp the fact of the nearness and actual presence of the most dynamic Power and Intelligence and Life, all around you, at your call, and more than able to provide for you whatever may be necessary to your complete health, success and happiness. In the room next to the one in which I am writing this, lies my eight-year-old son little Alfred. I have just gone in and kissed the little fellow for I love him more than I do my life. There lies that little body, and to all intents and purposes, and as far as he is concerned, he is as one dead. He does not even know that he is asleep. And as I stood there watching that little breast heave and contract—just what did I see? I call the little physical form lying there, Alfred. But is that what it really is? No. For "ALFRED" is only a name, and you cannot see a name. So what is it that I actually saw lying there in that little bed? Shall I tell you? Lying there in that little bed, my friend, I saw, not Alfred, but the mighty immutable GOD-LAW IN ACTUAL OPERATION. This—and nothing more. Some Psychologists would have us believe that every tree, every blade of grass, every piece of rock, every piece of metal—in fact, everything in the universe is what they call a manifestation of the "universal mind" whatever that may be. I have explained once that "mind" has nothing to do with it, and again I must ask you to disabuse yourself of the idea, if you hold it, that any "mind" of any sort manifests in any animate or inanimate object on this earth. That is NOT the explanation.

The reason the trees grow is because, AWAY BACK YONDER IN THE BEGINNING, THE GOD-LAW ORDAINED THAT THEY SHOULD GROW? AND AS A MATTER OF FACT? IT CAUSED THEM TO GROW. And they can no more refuse to grow in violation of the immutable GOD-LAW than can you—or myself. And the reason that the beautiful white lily blooms and grows on the hillside, is because, AWAY BACK YONDER IN THE BEGINNING, BEFORE LILIES EVER GREW BEFORE, THIS SAME ETERNAL AND EVER-PRESENT GOD-LAW COMMANDED THEM TO GROW. Not because the power of "mind" had anything to do with it, BUT BECAUSE THIS GREAT IMMUTABLE NEVER-CHANGING LIFE SPIRIT, CAPABLE OF EXISTENCE WITHOUT BODILY FORM, CAUSED IT TO SO BE——that is the reason. In other words, this great Life Spirit made an absolutely inviolable LAW, that out of the single ear of wheat should grow hundred of ears. And that is the reason the farmer KNOWS that when he plants grain he will reap grain, and not jack pines nor cactus. When the first wild goose was placed here upon this earth, the mighty Creative Life Spirit that created the goose, implanted within that goose, or caused it to react to an IMMUTABLE GOD-LAW, which immutable Law guides it from one part of the earth to another. And THAT is the reason it CANNOT be "fooled."

And when the very first pair of red-breasted robins was placed by this mighty Creative Life Spirit on this earth, they were ordered to comply with the God-Law covering their existence, and to mate—AND PRODUCE OTHER ROBINS—and THAT is the reason they cannot produce scorpions. I said they CANNOT. For the LAW is immutable. And when the first pair of the human race, away back yonder in the beginning, lost whatever spiritual estate they once had—if they had one, they were commanded to exist as physical beings, reproducing their kind and were commanded to grow as we are growing today. And THAT is the reason we are as we are—and that is the reason we exist at all. Not because of "god" spitting in the earth and making a man, but because IT IS THE IMMUTABLE GOD-LAW THAT WE SHOULD BE. In other words, as Alfred, so are we, a DIRECT ACTION PRODUCT OF THIS MIGHTY LIFE SPIRIT. Yes, and more than that, my friend; we are the very greatest manifestation this God-Power ever had or made. Think that over. Living in the midst of this mighty GOD-LAW, and yet separated from IT, that is the situation as it exists in the human race today. So you see the matter of finding the God-Law is not going to be as hard as you may have imagined it might be. The fact of the matter is that it is harder to GET AWAY from this mighty LAW than it is to find it. Please try to grasp the fact of this LIVING CREATIVE GOD POWER being all around you, and at your disposal, and directly available to you for the actual manifestation of whatever proper things you may need, no matter what they may be. Try I say, to grasp this mighty fact, for that is exactly the condition in which you live. There is, at your disposal, all the power of the God-Head for the manifestation of whatever it may be that you must stand in need of, whether wealth, health, or happiness. You would not attempt to tell me that the mighty God-Law which caused this created scheme of things to be in the first place, and which momentarily sustains them, could not, or would not lend its aid to one of its created beings—would you? It would be useless for you to try to tell me that. I know better. Had you been taught this fact when you were a child, you would have accepted it without question, and the chances are many to one that you would have been far more prosperous, healthy, and happy than you now are. But you were not taught that. You were taught that God was some great power living up in the sky, and that not until after you were dead could you know anything about Him. You were taught that you came into this world as a lost, guilty and hell-deserving sinner, and that unless a certain thing happened to you, you would go down to a terrible doom. What the doom would be, and what would save you from it depended, of course, on whatever system of "supernaturally-revealed" religion you were brought up amongst.

But suppose that from your earliest childhood you had been given the picture of God that I am giving you now? Suppose that you had been raised to know that instead of this mighty Creator only operating "after you die," He actually lived and operated for your benefit here and now—how much better would your life have been? This is the point at which I clash with a good many of the differing systems of religion. I have no use for the theory that God has left His creation alone until "after we die." I don't believe it, and I KNOW BETTER. I have again digressed here a little bit and I shall ask you to excuse it, please. Now where were we? Well—we find ourselves surrounded on every hand with a Power, an omnipotent Power, so creative and so dynamic, that in the beginning, and you may place it where you will, this Power was of sufficient intelligence, and wisdom and ability, and omniscience, to create the very first LIFE-GERM, if there ever were a first life germ. Personally I don't think there was for it is my own personal opinion that this Great GOD-LAW is self-existent and has been before the beginning of time. Here you are then, surrounded by an intelligent LAW or Intelligence, capable of stepping into the picture before you were a fetus, and, in nine month's time, making a complete human being out of you. Don't you think that is some power? Don't you think that such an intelligence is capable of taking complete charge of your future, and providing you with whatever it is you need?

Don't you think such an intelligence can provide you with that car, or that home, or that bank account, or perhaps, that domestic happiness you so much crave? I think it can. Yes—I KNOW IT CAN. And if it be that this revelation of God is upsetting your previous views and ideas of Him, then I ask you which is most valuable to a man today, a God who only does things after you die—or a God who is a personal entity, and who does things for one HERE and NOW, when you KNOW you can appreciate them. WHICH? And I know your answer.

At this very moment my secretary has just walked into my office with a letter. "Did you read this letter?" she asked. I replied "No, let me see it." Here is the letter and I am going to quote it in full for it just fits in beautifully with the thought you are getting now. Furthermore, the very last Lesson you read last week was the one which evidently did the trick. "Does this Power actually exist," you ask. Well, here is the letter word for word. It comes from Philadelphia and is dated November 24th 1931. Not so very long ago—is it?

> Dear Doctor Robinson,
> What a change—only the third Lesson and here I am, changed from a living death of inactivity to an office full of men. Plenty of work that a man needs.
> Do I believe in the power of the Living God? I should say I do. Please hold Lessons until I get over the dizziness of it all and get a proper address.
> Very sincerely your student,
> J.A. T_____d."

This and many similar letters come to me in the course of a week, and they all tell the same story. Wherever this mighty ever-present Power, this God-Law is used, IT BRINGS RESULTS. Sometimes the first Lesson does the trick. Other times it takes the whole course before the student grasps something of the operation of this mighty Power. And please remember here that this Power is NO personality. It never was a personality and it never will be a personality. It has, however, a PERSONAL EXISTENCE FOR YOU AND ME. BUT IT IS A LAW. IT IS THE GOD-LAW I AM NOW TEACHING YOU HOW TO FIND AND USE.

Now just a word about your mental attitude. I will explain fully a little later all about the exercises before you go to sleep. In the meantime, keep on your relaxing exercise at night. Put all clocks and other noisy things from the room if you can. Lie as limp as a log, for this is the very best way to rest the body and restore it. Have no thoughts in your mind except one. Stay in that limp condition, looking at the inside of your eyelids, and absolutely motionless until you see the "bright area" in your range of vision. Keep looking at that spot until you go to sleep. There will automatically come to you in these moments of resting and relaxation, the thought that is uppermost in your nature. Mind you, I do not say "in your mind" but in YOU as you really are. I want you now to think about the thing you need in life more than anything else. Just let that thing center on the "bright area." Lie there absolutely like a log, and think about the needed thing that you want the mighty God-Law to bring to you. Then, still absolutely motionless, linger your thought on this one thing. No effort is required at all, for you are resting and will soon be asleep. Then, after you have dwelt on this one thing you need more than anything else, let this little sentence run through your mind and KEEP YOUR VISION ON THE BRIGHT SPOT.

Here is the little sentence I want you to use, and remember, only let it be a thought, don't whisper or utter a syllable, for I want you to forget that you have a physical body at all for the time being. Then let this thought run through you—"I AM FINDING THE POWER OF THE LIVING GOD-LAW." Let this thought continually run through you and the first thing you know you will be asleep. Then, through the day, in earnestness, do the same thing. Whenever and wherever you have the opportunity, let your predominating thought be this same sentence and then KEEP ETERNALLY AT IT. It takes no effort at all, and it may seem simple BUT THE POWER BEHIND IT IS DYNAMIC. Don't question this or any other exercises that I prescribe. I know what I am talking about, and you will know that I do pretty quick. I will say, however, that you are getting to the place where you will begin to understand a little bit, how this mighty God-Law works, and what it is.

Remember, you are a physical being, and you are trying to find the Creative GOD-LAW, and this Law, being a spiritual Law, WILL BE CONTACTED BY SPIRITUAL MEANS. It lies in an unseen realm. Remember that, please. Its manifestations will be made physically to you, but your initial contact with this God-Law will be made in and through the spiritual realm. Don't forget this, and DO THESE EXERCISES. In the next Lesson we will go deeper into this mighty subject and you will learn some things that may possibly open your eyes a little wider. It will be a good thing to read this Lesson every night before retiring, and then go right to your good night exercises in finding this mighty Power which is to bring to you the things you need. Whenever you know how to supply the Law in your own life, remember, there is no limit to this mighty Power. And remember also, THE POWER IS FOR YOU.

SPECIAL NOTE TO MY STUDENTS.

The first course in "PSYCHIANA" made what I think is a world record, for in the first year it went into 67 different countries. This present course, however, seems destined to make a better record than did the first one. If letters came to me thick and fast on the initial course, they certainly are coming to me faster on this one. The great fact to remember here, my friend, is the fact that there is in existence, a God Power so dynamic that it almost staggers one when one thinks about it. I cannot give you everything I should like to all at once, for this is a mighty big subject. It is also quite a revolutionary teaching. But you may take it from me that I am convinced beyond any shadow of doubt that this question of God is the most misunderstood subject in existence. We are living evolutionary lives. We are a product of evolution. And that evolution is not ended yet. We are at the point of transition. We are to change our conception of the spiritual part of men and things quite materially. That is not strange at all. A few years ago the radio would not have been believed. But the radio is here. Every honest man and woman will admit that what has been given to us concerning God and religion does not satisfy. People don't believe the stories told to them by professional religionists any more. They question their truth. And if these varying stories were true, the world would soon know it. So would those professing these things. But a new day is dawning, and these old stories of men being "lost souls" are on their way to the bone-pile where they belong. And to you I say at this point in your studies, get ready for a new revelation of truth for you are going to get one.

FRANK B. ROBINSON

LESSON 5

Here is Lesson five. It is one of the most intensely interesting Lessons you have ever read and I want you to read it many times over and then quietly lay it to one side and try and imagine some of the enormous truths this Lesson teaches. There are distances and planets so far away that the human mind cannot begin to grasp these distances. But no matter how far away we get from this globe we find still existing and operating with unerring precision, the same mighty LAW that we are trying to find here. The study of the "Heavens" and the stars is a very fascinating study so learn this Lesson well and be sure to notify me of the progress you are making. especially if you experience any difficulty in grasping these Lessons.

More than anything else I want you to absolutely understand the workings of the God-Law which can and will and does provide every material thing necessary for one's happiness once it is understood and correctly used.

Sincerely your friend,
FRANK B. ROBINSON

At this point in our studies I am going to take you with me on a little trip into the marvelous realm of the sky. We are going to discover some staggering facts in this realm of astronomy. You may wonder what astronomy has to do with your understanding of the GOD-LAW and I shall tell you, for it has very much to do with it. There is no realm or part of the universe which offers to men and women such a vision of the CREATIVE INTELLIGENCE that this celestial dome above us called "The Heavens" does. And it is quite necessary that you get a glimpse of the magnitude of the handiwork of the Creator before you can understand to the very full just how mighty a Power you have working with you. Before we go into this realm, however, let us look back, for a moment or two, over the road traveled together so far. It is an interesting road and one that is full of surprises. Practically every Lesson you receive will contain some new glimpses or some new facts of the Creative Spirit which is responsible for the entire creation including you and me.

Better than all, however, you will discover to be a fact that as you learn of this mighty God-Law, you will find yourself automatically putting it into practice. You will find yourself almost unconsciously grasping and using the principles that I lay before you, which principles are part of this mighty Law; after awhile, and when you have progressed further, it will become second nature to you to live your life day by day, month by month with the consciousness of the fact that you are throwing into action in your daily life and affairs the most potent and dynamic power in creation. At this stage of our journey I do not expect, of course, that you will be able to grasp this law in its entirety nor can I show you all at once. I must take it up step by step along the way and you, of course, will intelligently follow me and will, to the best of your ability, meet me more than half way and help me to help you to be complete master over every circumstance of life, and to so shape circumstances and conditions that instead of them mastering you, you master them.

In Lesson One you saw that there existed an unseen dynamic power or force known by the name of the God-Law. You had never known anything about the existence of this God-Law before because it had never been called to your attention by anyone. Then you saw that it was necessary to discard whatever preconceived notions of God you may have had, if those notions clashed with the revelations of this God-Law which I am explaining to you. I told you also in Lesson One to make up your mind very definitely what it is that you need to make you happy, successful and healthy. If you have not settled your mind definitely on this point let me urge you right here to be sure and fix definitely right now in your mind one specific thing that you need. Place an objective before you, a reasonable objective, and never forget what this one specific thing is. I gave you a little mental exercise to do at night and told you to utterly relax, filling the lungs to their utmost capacity without straining them, and then slowly exhale, I told you to close your eyes and repeat many times a certain sentence. In the next Lesson I showed you that whatever cards had been dealt you in the game of life, might be changed by you if you did not like them. Furthermore, in Lesson Two, I reiterated the statement that the greatest unseen power in existence is here for your daily use. You will remember too, I called it a "Sleeping Giant" and I told you that once this "Sleeping Giant" were harnessed to your life, nothing would be impossible for you.

You will remember that I spent some time on a thought. I told you that a thought was actually a literal thing, an entity. I told you that thoughts were the most powerful and dynamic things in existence and I showed you also that a thought is part of the great spiritual law we are trying to find in these Lessons. I explained to you that you cannot think of two things at the same time and you understood that whatever thought it is which occupies your mind more than any other thought will be the predominating and molding influence in your life. Then again you will remember that I told you that you were the general manager of your own brain, having absolute say as to what thoughts you should not entertain. I showed you very clearly and asked you never to allow any negative or fear thoughts to roost in your hair. They will, like little sparrows, probably light there once in a while, but you can prevent them from building a nest there.

Then in Lesson Three I emphasized the fact that this mighty God-Law was responsible for all creation including you; it did not make you and then leave you alone to shift for yourself, but is staying right here with you, waiting to be used by you for the achievement of every good and right thing you can desire. Then again you will remember I told you that you were LAYING THE FOUNDATION OF THE THINGS YOU DESIRE TO MANIFEST IN YOUR LIFE IN THE FUTURE. I told you that you are what you are today as the result of what you and others thought years ago. And furthermore informed you, and you know it yourself for that matter, that what you will be in the future depends almost entirely on what you are thinking today. So you see how vitally important it is for me to direct your thoughts into the proper channels.

You will remember I painted a picture of an architect first thinking a building into existence in his own thought realm. And I showed you furthermore, that by far the most important realm in life is the unseen spiritual thought realm. I called your attention to the fact that in this building for the future you should hold an attitude of expectancy because it would be too bad if you MISSED THE GOAL just simply because you did not expect to happen the thing you wanted to happen. Most of the world's leading scientists today have gone on record and stated that the unseen forces of nature, instead of material atoms, govern all nature; this being a fact, we find that immaterialism has replaced materialism as a scientific concept. I think I can safely say to you that the thinking minds of the universe are entirely agreed on the fact that there is in existence some kind of a spiritual power or other which has far more to do with the manifesting of material things than we have ever dreamed of today.

The religionist claims this power to be his peculiar God and he tells us that no other system of religion can possibly know anything about God at all. You and I know however, that present day religionists know very little if anything of any unseen spiritual power which can really do, actually here and now whatever is necessary for the physical comforts of man. These religionists are experts in telling what this great power of theirs can do after you die, but they are not so sure that this power has any ability to do anything for us now. But at the same time the feeling seems to be there that some outside power of some sort is the great controlling factor in life. And they are perfectly correct. The trouble is that they have made the mistake of thinking that this mighty power was disclosed by supernatural relation to some man or group of men ages ago. But this is not a fact; you will remember that Shakespeare stated that "More things are wrought by prayer than this world dreams of." I think it was Shakespeare who said that, at any rate someone said it and there probably is a lot of truth to it.

The point I am leading up to is that no matter in what realm of research we engage, back of it all we find the suspicion that the unseen spiritual realm may be responsible for the material realm. This is a fact, and it has fallen to my lot to be the man to call attention nationally and internationally to the fact that this potent dynamic God-Law is, not in the sky, and not for the future, BUT FOR US HERE AND NOW. The world's greatest physicists, men who like Mr. Oliver Lang, have gone into the physical realm as far as it is humanly possible to go and they are being forced to the conclusion that away beyond, far past the physical realm SOMETHING UNKNOWN IS GOING ON AND THEY DON'T KNOW WHAT IT IS. A little later we shall go to quite some depth into this fascinating subject of the connection between the material and the unseen realm.

Then in Lesson Four you will remember I told you the story of the creation of this universe according to the bible book used by the Christians. Practically every so called superhuman or divine book tells the same story, and as a matter of fact they all contain a human understanding of the spiritual law as it operated in the creation of the universe. You will recall that you saw very plainly that God is spirit, and furthermore, we saw that spirit is Life capable of existence without physical form, or, invisible Life. Be sure and grasp these statements one after another for we are beginning to get now to the realm in which we shall learn the secret of this marvelous invisible Life. I do so wish every student of mine could instantaneously grasp the fact of invisible Life. A great many of you will do that and there are others who will require quite some time before they fully grasp that statement. But that is the fact of existence and the fact of God just the same. And furthermore, in the manifestation by you of the things you need to make you healthy, happy, and successful, you will have to realize the facts or you will never get to first base in your studies with me.

Let me explain here a little bit why I ask you to center your vision on a light area which everyone sees when their eyes are closed and when they are looking through their eyelids so to speak. We have seen that thoughts are spiritual unseen things. We have also seen that there is invisible life throughout the entire universe, millions of light years away and yet so close to you and to me that we could not get away from this invisible life even if we wanted to. Now if a thought is an invisible spiritual thing and a part of the invisible spiritual LIFE, which it is, then do you not see that through your thought realm you will be able to contact this invisible Life spirit that I am talking about. Now once more, if this theory is correct that the greatest forces in the world are spiritual forces, are unseen forces, and if it be a fact that nothing was created in the material form without first being created in the thought realm, then do you not see that by building your future in your thought realm you are actually building it in a realm which will shortly change into the material realm? This is absolutely a scientific fact and a scientific spiritual law.

I do not think I have ever seen the power of thought more strongly manifested than I saw it manifested last week. In Spokane, Washington, a certain theater showed a certain picture. I went in to see the picture and it was one of the most gruesome things that I have ever looked upon. Outside of that theater were patrol wagons and ambulances taking people to the emergency hospitals for treatment. Some of them fainted while others became hysterical and fell limp on the floor. Now let us analyze this a little before we go into our realm of stars.

All those people who fainted knew perfectly well that they were only looking at a picture. They knew that this thing was not happening in real life. In other words it was entirely through their thought realm that this picture was grasped. And yet, that thought realm and the thoughts entering it were sufficient to absolutely lay their bodies cold on the floor. If you receive a telegram informing you that a certain loved one has been found guilty of first degree murder and sentenced to be hanged, on receipt of that telegram you turn white. Your physical body is absolutely changed. Yet it was through the medium of your thought realm that this physical effect was caused. You probably became quite ill and had to go to bed as a result of receiving that telegram. But the telegram may have been untrue as far as you know and someone may be playing a practical joke on you. You have positively no way of knowing whether your friend was found guilty of murder or not. And yet through the medium of what is commonly called your mind, your physical body has been made ill. So then I say it is a fact that the thought realm is by far the most important realm known to man. Probably the future will disclose the fact that it is the only realm there is, the material realm being but a very minor and unimportant part of it.

Now before we go into our study of the marvelous realm of astronomy let me impress upon you once more the importance of following me earnestly and closely in these studies. I am going to show you absolutely, the existence of the God-Law, and I am going to show you that it can be used in the life of every individual who is earnest enough for success and happiness, to use it. So keep busy on this course of instruction and don't be afraid to do the things I ask you to do. They are very simple little things and yet are fraught with dynamic power, and it is the actual doing of these things that brings the material results. There is no question that these Lessons are interesting from a literary standpoint but it will take more than that to obtain anything of the spiritual realm. It will take an active desire, an active will and an active intelligence which means business before actual material results will be seen. But the little effort required is very much worth while and I think you will agree with me that if you desire the good things of life you certainly should be in earnest to at least put yourself so in tune with the spiritual law that these good things can actually come to you. For I want to repeat here that there are positively no limitations of any sort or kind to the power of the creative life spirit or God-Law responsible for this universe.

Our trip into this realm will be very interesting, and highly enlightening. I shall give you facts and figures that your mind cannot possibly grasp. But you will be able to glean from these facts and figures, something of the magnitude of the God-Law which is even now, as you read this, waiting to be applied in your own life for the purpose of bringing into manifestation for you and yours, those things which are needed in order that you be a complete and all-around success. This is my only reason for showing you a few of the marvels of the skies, and truly wonderful marvels they are. You must never attempt to tell me that the Creative Intelligence which was responsible for the vastness of yonder heavens and its millions and perhaps billions of stars, planets, satellites etc., is not able to bring into your little life the things you need. For compared with that starry vault with its celestial treasures, you and I are mighty small fry, brother and sister. And yet—we are really greater than them all. For these marvels are all perfectly inanimate. They possess no intelligence of their own. They cannot think. They cannot create. They can only revolve in their orbits in accordance with the Creative Law which placed them there and which ordained their actions since the beginning of time.

They do, however, give us a faint glimmer perhaps of the very magnitude of both creation and the Creator, and this magnitude should be enough to make you and me wonder what it's all about. Remember here however, that throughout all this marvelous interstellar space, and surrounding all these mighty suns and stars and planets, there is, like a belt of living electricity, the famous "cosmic ray." Don't forget that, and as I paint you this picture of the starry heavens, and take you on a little trip through that realm, don't forget that the existence of these rays is an absolutely proven fact. As we travel together through this marvelous realm of the "heavens" you will see how foolish was the old "Christian" idea of both God and the heavens. In olden days the heavens were supposed to be a solid dome with "lights" suspended from it. This solid dome had windows in it. When it rained, God opened the windows of heaven and let the water through. This is the method we are told He used when He suddenly discovered that He had made a mistake when He created man, and drowned them all out by a flood, leaving only one man and a few animals here on the earth.

These good old "Christians" believed that the sun, which they alluded to as the "greater light" and which was hung in the heavens to light this earth in the daytime, was the only sun in existence. Then they told us that their good book said that the moon, the "lesser light" was put up there hanging in the sky to give us light at night. They told us also that the earth had four corners and was flat. They told us also that over this earth was an immense body of water, which water it was that came down when God opened the windows of heaven, or decided to drown the inhabitants from off the face of the earth. I mention these facts here only to show how ideas of God change. No idea of God can ever be a permanent and lasting idea, for the human race is evolving from its past into its glorious future. There never was any "fall of man" in the accepted sense of the word. Quite to the contrary there has been a steady RISE of man.

And the end is certainly not yet. For only now are men and women beginning to get a faint glimpse of the mighty power this Creative Spirit has for them. Only now are many of the good "Christians" beginning to suspect that what they have been accepting as "gospel truth" is no more than fable and allegory. It has taken a long time for that knowledge to break upon them, and it has not yet broken to the full. But they are suspecting it. They see this, and other works going all over the world, and they see reason, and sense, and results in them, and they begin to analyze their story a little. I think it safe in passing to say that if those teaching this "fall of man, and resurrection, and ascension" story, would analyze it one-tenth as well as they pick flaws in the arguments against it—IT WOULD NOT LAST TWELVE MONTHS. This they will not do however—they are right, and everyone else is wrong. If you don't find "salvation" their way, you never find it.

Let me leave another thought with you here, student, and let this thought take hold of you and grip you. If you will do that, you will never again fear "hell-fire" or the loss of your poor soul, I promise you that. This thought is right in line with our studies, and will give you a lot of comfort, as it has given me just that. Here is the thought: IF THE GOD-LAW IS RESPONSIBLE FOR A MAN'S EXISTENCE, IT IS ALSO RESPONSIBLE FOR HIS ACTIONS, AND FOR EVERYTHING ELSE THAT HAPPENS TO HIM. Think that over carefully. As I hinted a few Lessons back, this Great GOD-LAW brought you into being. It did it in its own way. It required none to help. And it did a perfect job too. NOW—that being the case, this God-Law equipped you as you are equipped, and that also being the case, THIS GOD-LAW IS ENTIRELY RESPONSIBLE FOR YOU AND YOUR PRESENT AND YOUR FUTURE—DON'T FORGET THAT. I shall come to it again. Just here however, let me leave the thought that this mighty God-Law is able and willing to do, and should normally do just that. More of this later, however, for I want to take you with me now onto our little trip through the heavens, and when you return, you will probably have a far different conception of the God-Law than you have had previous to your beginning your studies with me.

Instead of this earth being the entire creation, and instead of the heavens being a solid inverted bowl, with water on the other side of it, we find that this earth is but one of a series of planets which is revolving around the sun. The ancients told us the sun revolved around the earth, because, they said, "Joshua Commanded the sun to stand still," and therefore, the sun must move around the earth, and so they held. Science, however, has very effectively proven that such is not the case. Many of the world's heroes however, were put to death and tortured by those professing to be "God's agents," for stating that the earth moved around the sun, which it does. Remember, Copernicus, Galileo etc., and how they were tortured for their absolutely scientific findings which are now proven to be so boundlessly correct? They were right however, even though their theories were antagonistic to "supernaturally-revealed religion."

If you were to take an orange, and stick in it several toothpicks around the diameter, and at the end of each toothpick stick a pea, and then revolve the whole on its axis you would have a picture of this earth in comparison to this one sun of ours. If you look up into the heavens however, you will find there not only a few other suns, but over twenty million of them, and each sun probably the center of a planetary system as is ours. So let's get away from the theory that this earth is the center of the universe. It isn't as much as a grain of sand on the seashore when compared with the immense distances which are known to exist in the heavens. Every single star you see is a sun, and the light from many of them took millions of years to even reach this old globe of ours. And you must remember that light travels at the rate of 186,000 miles a second. So try to conceive, if you can, (which you can't) of a distance so great that the light from that star, traveling at the rate of 186,000 miles a second, took many millions of light years to reach this earth. Then remember that a light year is the distance a ray of light, traveling at this rate of 186,000 miles a second, could cover in one year. Such distances as that are inconceivable to you. Then again, when looking up into our solar system, we are apt to make the mistake that it is the only solar system there is. But this also is not a fact. For even as far as the mightiest telescope will reach, we see millions of such suns. And then, when a more powerful telescope is manufactured, we find still more millions of suns beyond those we saw before. And so on through this immense canopy of heaven.

Shall we spend a few moments examining this sun of ours. Then let us remember that there are, in yon starry vault, many millions of such suns, many times as large as ours are. Then one even faintly begins to realize the fact that there is a controlling Law or Intelligence behind such a stupendous scheme of creation, it makes one wonder certainly what can happen to the human life, fortunate enough to find and use the Law responsible for such a vast creation. Our sun is a sphere of fire. The flames from it are leaping into space for a distance of 150,000 miles in places. This is five times the circumference of this earth. Can you imagine such a creation as that? And yet it was created FOR YOUR BENEFIT—IT WAS CREATED TO MAKE LIFE POSSIBLE FOR YOU, AND REALIZE THAT SOME INTELLIGENCE OR LAW MADE THIS REMARKABLE BODY OF FIRE, TO PROTECT YOU AND MAKE IT POSSIBLE FOR YOU TO LIVE. For you could not exist one minute were there no sun in yonder heavens.

This sun of ours is approximately one and one-quarter million times as big as this earth in volume. If you take the eight planets, of which this earth of ours is only one, and put them all together, the sun would outweigh them all about 750 times. Imagine such a globe of fire as that is. The circumference around the sun is about two and one half millions of miles, and it takes it about 26 days to revolve on its axis. This means that its revolution is at the rate of about 4000 miles an hour. Picture that in your mind's eye if you can. Were there no sun, it would be absolutely impossible for life of any sort to exist on this earth or on any of the other planets which this sun heats. Incidentally, you might remember here that one of these planets, Mercury, is forty million miles from the sun, and this is the NEAREST of these planets. The farthest away is Neptune, whose distance from the sun is only three thousand million miles—that's all. This puts Neptune seventy times farther away from the sun than is Mercury. It only takes Mercury three months to make a trip around the sun. It takes Neptune one hundred and sixty years to make his little trip around the sun.

These eight planets, which form our immediate planetary sphere, are divided into two groups of four each. There is an inner group and an outer group and the inner group is by far the smaller of the two groups. In between these groups we have our galaxies of asteroids. These asteroids are about three times as far from the sun as the earth is. Then, still comprising a part of our solar system, is another system of moons or satellites as we call them, and these revolve around some of the smaller planets. Its interesting to note here that roundness seems to be the one outstanding characteristic of " nature." Everything in nature seems to either be round, or go around. For those who might think that this earth with its planetary system is all of the eternal scheme of things, I might say that with the exception of Mercury, and Venus, everyone of these eight planets has its own solar system. We call them the Martian system, the Jovian system, the Saturnian system, comprising Saturn and his rings and satellites.

Then we run into another class of celestial visitor known as comets. These fellows are very eccentric gentlemen, and their orbits are very eccentric orbits. We can only see them as they approach the sun. Some few years ago I received a call from a gentleman in Tucson, Arizona, where I was living at that time, inviting me to visit the observatory that evening after dark. I was happy to do so, and shall never forget the sight I saw. It gave me an understanding of God that I have never had before. I saw something of His magnitude, something of His power, and as I left that university building, I felt serenely safe in trusting my whole life into the hands of such a God-Law—for that is what it is in reality. It never was a personality, and it never can be a personality. You cannot compass such creations in terms of personality—they are too big. At any rate, stepping to the objective of the huge telescope, Dr. Douglas directed my view to a certain part of the field of vision, asking me if I saw there a tiny pinhead of light. I saw it and advised him to that effect.

"Do you know what that is?" the good astronomer asked me. I replied in the negative whereat he informed me that it was the planet Uranus. Then followed some interesting facts about Uranus. Here I was, looking through a piece of glass, and was enabled to actually see a planet, the diameter of which is nearly thirty-one thousand miles, and the volume of which is sixty times that of this earth. The distance I was covering that night with my eyes, was seventeen hundred and eighty two million miles. And yet, with the aid of the telescope, I was able to actually see that distance. Think of that. Here I was, looking at an object 1,782,000,000 miles away, and SEEING IT. In case any student questions the measurements of the distances etc., of these planets, let me say that their distances are measured with scientific accuracy. The speed of them can also be measured accurately as is necessary. Also the speed with which they travel can be measured.

Recently a new planet was discovered, a hitherto unknown nebula, existing at a greater distance from the earth than any heavenly body heretofore recorded. The discovery was announced by the observatory on Mt. Wilson just outside of Los Angeles, California. The nebula was discovered on a photograph taken by the 100 inch reflector on that mountain. I have seen that instrument many times. This photograph by the way broke all records for long-distance photography known to science to date, for it fixed the distance of this nebula at 120 million light years from the earth. Think of that my friend—120,000,000 light years, not miles, away and still we can see it on a photographic plate. In addition to having photographed an object farther away from the earth than any other object yet photographed, this telescope achieved a second honor in that it photographed an object that is traveling through space at a velocity 60% greater than anything ever before measured by speed.

Dr. Adams, director of the observatory, states that this newly found nebula is flying through space at the rate of 11,000 miles a second. Think that over some of you people who think that the God-Law which created the very things I am talking about cannot help you to either health, wealth, or happiness. At this velocity it is traveling at the rate of 6,000,000,000 miles a year, and were it traveling earthward, it would require 120,000,000 years to reach this world—And yet the old "Christian believers" thought that the sky was an inverted solid bowl with windows in it through which the rain came. I think you will agree with me that there certainly is an upward evolution in man, instead of any "fall." The most interesting thing about this new nebula however, is that it is a great universe of stars—millions and billions of them—infinitely great in size. The speed of the nebula was measured by means of the spectroscope. Professor Humason found that its spectrum lines were red, so that a recession of 11,000 miles a second was indicated. To show such a shifting of the lines would require a velocity greater by 60% than any so-called velocity yet noted.

Information of this find was cabled to Dr. J. C. Merriam. President of the Carnegie Institute at Washington, D. C., who said, "It is of special interest at this time because of the bearing it will have on Dr. Einstein's conception of the universe."

You know folks, somehow or other, in the face of statements like these, I just simply can't imagine the mighty Creative Power, sitting in "heaven" with Jesus Christ at his right hand, "making intercession for us with groanings that cannot be uttered." Somehow or other I just don't seem to be able to get that. And yet it is what is being taught today in this land as the truth of God. And maybe it is. Maybe God is seated up there somewhere with His son at His right hand, pleading for us mortals down here. I am not saying that He is not. I may be counted an infidel and everything like that, but I JUST SIMPLY DON'T BELIEVE IT, THAT'S ALL. I have no quarrel with those good folks who say they do believe it—no quarrel at all, and the only reason I am calling attention to it here is because before men and women ever can see anything of the marvels and the glories of the creative God Law behind this universe, it will be absolutely essential that untrue stories about Him be discarded.

This old world is trembling, even as I write this, on the brink of a volcano. We do not know what moment it will blow us into a terrible conflagration. And by way if one should come now, don't make any mistake brethren—it will be a dandy.

And it is my contention that as long as you and I are asked to believe anything foolish or unreasonable about God, then just so long will men and women miss the power of the God-Law. Let's get our eyes away from such stories as the "six-day creation—the spit and dirt story—the wholesale drowning story, the fall of man story, the resurrection story etc.," and let's get our eyes on the power that IS. Let's recognize a little bit just what sort of a Law we have working with us. Then, when men and women grasp the larger picture, they won't lack for anything, for they will have learned, as you are to learn, how this mighty God-Law can be used for every right desire in life.

But to get back again to the skies for a moment. I should like here, to try and give you an idea as clearly as I can of what these distances mean. You will never comprehend them because you cannot grasp such immensities. We are dealing with facts of the God-Law now, and it will be a long time before you can ever absorb mentally such distances and such powers as are these celestial distances and powers. I think I can however, give you a faint inkling as to what I mean. I want you to imagine a chart, perfectly round and made of white paper. Imagine that chart being three hundred yards in diameter. You can imagine three hundred yards all right whereas you cannot imagine one light year. Here we have then this big chart three hundred yards across it. It is circular. Now, on this chart of ours we make a spot about half an inch in diameter, and we paint it black. That's half an inch on a round chart three hundred yards in diameter. Pretty small, isn't it? That black spot, half an inch in diameter, we shall call our sun. You can grasp that easily I think.

Now, take the point of a pin and make a tiny prick on that chart near the half-inch black spot. And you have the EARTH. This is a crude illustration, but it brings within your understanding, a faint picture of what the visible heavenly sphere is. That isn't all however. It's only the beginning of the picture. If we started out today in an airplane, traveling at the rate of 120 miles an hour, and put that airplane out in the earth's orbit, it would take it over 500 years to make the complete circle of the orbit. If the earth did not move any faster than that, our winters would last nearly 200 years. So you can imagine from this the speed at which this old ball of ours is traveling. When we get into the solar system, however, we run into vastly more staggering facts. For instance, this earth turns on its axis at 1000 miles an hour and travels in its orbit around the sun at the rate of 1000 miles a minute, or 60,000 miles an hour. The distance from our sun to the nearest (fixed) star, is more than 20,000,000,000,000 miles. Can you grasp that? Twenty millions of millions of miles? Of course you can't grasp it. But the God-Law I am here teaching you about, can grasp it. In fact that mighty Law, which you are to use in your daily affairs, CAUSED THIS CREATED SCHEME OF THINGS I AM EXPLAINING TO COME INTO EXISTENCE.

Take our chart again. This time we make one on the scale of half an inch to one million miles. In the other chart we grasped a little about the size of our sun, but in this chart, it would take one over 500 miles in diameter in order to give us the distance to the nearest star. And then, we have not even begun to really get into space at all. Twenty millions of suns floating around above, and beneath us. Can you conceive of it? They are there. You can see thousands of them with the naked eye any clear night. Is it any wonder I like to get out alone under the stars? I am near God then, and many a time I do it.

There never was a fairy tale ever invented which could be as marvelous as this solar system of ours. Think of the Milky Way. Let me quote from R. A. Proctor's, THE EXPOSURE OF HEAVEN:—

> "There are stars in all orders of brightness, from those which (seen with the telescope) resemble in luster the leading glories of the firmament, down to tiny points of light only caught by momentary twinklings. Every variety of arrangement is seen. Here the stars are scattered as over the skies at night; there they cluster in groups, as though drawn together by some irresistible power; in one region they seem to form sprays of stars like diamonds sprinkled over fern leaves; elsewhere they lie in streams and rows, in coronets and loops and festoons, resembling the star festoon which, in the constellation Perseus, garlands the black robe of night. Nor are varieties of color wanting to render the display more wonderful and more beautiful. Many of the stars which crowd upon the view are red, orange, and yellow. Among them are groups of two and three and four (multiple stars as they are called), amongst which blue and green and lilac and purple stars appear, forming the most charming contrast to the ruddy and yellow orbs near which they are commonly seen."

And yet you and I look at that Milky Way—and see nothing wonderful about it. I have ofttimes made the statement that the literal power of the God-Law is missed by countless millions on account of its simplicity. In making this revelation to you I will be as careful as I can, and you on your part must follow me, closely, carefully, and above all you must be in earnest. For the least you can do is to actually desire or want these good things of life—isn't it? I think thus far however, you have followed me closely, and while right here there is a great temptation to go into the depths in this realm of astronomy, I shall refrain, for I think I have made my point by showing you that the great Creator-Law is a bigger power For I shall show you a little later that this same God-Law, which directs the geese, which turns the robins eggs into a robin instead of a scorpion, reacts with the same remarkable precision in your life. You are the one who sets the objective—the God-Law brings it into actual manifestation. So be prepared as we travel along together for what I shall show you. This same Law—this same Life Spirit, is operating here and now, right on this earth, and right in our midst, as it operated millions of years ago when the very first tiny germ of life appeared on the earth. It is capable of making the fish swim away from the shark. It is capable of teaching the little ant to "hole-up" for the winter. It is day by day manifesting its marvelous intelligence in a myriad ways, and it is here for the express purpose of manifesting its intelligence in your own life. The bee that flits from flower to flower gathering its honey does not starve to death. The nightingale that floods the moonlit nights with melody is well taken care of. The tiny house sparrow—not one of them falls to the ground without this mighty God Law, and YOU—YOU—YOU—the most marvelous of all created things—do you think for one moment that this God-Law cannot give YOU the things you need?

Probably you have never looked at it this way. Probably you have never thought of it like this. Probably you have just bemoaned your fate, and rested in the assurance that you would "get by" somehow and some way. Well—a little glimmer of light is coming to you now, and before you finish your studies with me, if you do not win from life the very best things it holds for you, it will be because you do not want to, and NOT because there is no God-Law governing your success.

This is as far as I am going to take you in this Lesson and I think you will admit that it is quite far enough for one Lesson. I find it is a good idea in the studying of these Lessons to read them some every day and then do the exercise prescribed, faithfully until you receive the next Lesson. You have made up your mind what it is you need more than anything else in life. It may be health, it may be money, it may be domestic happiness. But you have made up your mind what it is. You are doing your deep breathing exercises. Better than all however, you are relaxing and allowing this Cosmic God-Law to take the desires from you and bring them into existence. Your whole thought, every moment is that the God-Law is bringing to pass that which you need. You may now use whatever affirmation of truth best fits your case. Make the statements as if what you want is being brought to pass NOW. For instance, before I had received the actual physical realization of my desires, I used this affirmation, hundreds of thousands of times; "I AM MORE AND MORE SUCCESSFUL." Never did I let up on that one statement. But in a future Lesson, I shall tell you, step by step, just how I manifested from the God-Law everything I now have. Be earnest in your affirmation. Make it dynamic, for you are dealing with a dynamic Law here and the intense, earnest attitude is very effective.

POINTS TO REMEMBER
IN LESSON FIVE

(1) You know what it is you want to do or to be.

(2) You know that if you ever achieve these things they will first be achieved in the realm of your own thought.

(3) Your own thought you now know to be a little tiny part of creative invisible Life-Spirit responsible for creation.

(4) If this be a fact then you also know that though you are only a very tiny little piece of humanity now as far as you go physically, the thought realm of you is part of an immense Spiritual world fully capable of manifesting whatever few little things you may need on this earth to make you abundantly happy, healthy and successful.

(5) You will call this Spiritual Law into practice in your own life by the exercising in the thought realm. The little dynamic exercises I am giving you to do are actually and literally giving you experience in contesting the greatest force the world has ever seen, THE POWER OF THE GOD-LAW.

(6) The more your thoughts dwell upon the thing you want to be, the faster will the manifestation be and the greater will be Your hold on, and your connection with, the realm of God.

(7) I want to hear from students personally and every letter sent is held in the strictest confidence by me. Under no consideration will their contents be divulged and it may be that I shall be able to help you some. Don't be backward about writing to me while you are studying with me. I am not infallible nor do I possess any supernatural powers of any kind but I do know a little about the operation of the God-Law in the lives of humans. Live a clean life, be absolutely on the level with everyone, and if there is anything that needs cleaning up in your life get it cleaned up. You will find the God-Law works more effectively when the thoughts are undiluted and free than it can if these thoughts are not that way.

Sincerely your friend and teacher,
FRANK B. ROBINSON.

EXAMINATION QUESTIONS
FOR LESSON NO. 5

These examination questions are for your benefit and you should know the answers to them all. If they are not clear to you, read your Lesson again and again until they are clear.

1. What have the facts of astronomy to do with one's under standing of the God-Law?

2. Why is it vitally important for you to direct your thoughts into the proper channels?

3. How does it come that immaterialism has replaced materialism as a scientific concept?

4. Give some illustrations of the influence of one's thought realm upon the physical body?

5. It will take more than a literary interest in the Lessons to obtain anything from the Spiritual realm?

6. What is the reason for your being shown, in Lesson 5, a few of the marvels of the skies?

7. Mention some of the beliefs, founded on statements made in the Bible, which have been proved to be wholly erroneous?

8. What is a light year?

9. For what purpose are you asked, in Lesson 5, to imagine a chart three hundred yards in diameter?

10. What should be the character of your affirmations?

11. Of what realm is your own thought realm a part?

12. Why should your thoughts dwell constantly upon the thing you want to be?

LESSON 6

It was the commonly accepted fact amongst the ancient thinkers and philosophers, that everything in existence had been developed from a beginning which was quite primitive. Through all their writings we find this thought prominent. St. Augustine, one of the greatest of all the "church fathers," held this same view. And, as a matter of fact, this view is now known to be scientifically correct. There is no question about it at all now.

But, sad to relate, this old world went through a period of night—the blackest kind of night. It was black spiritually. It was black mentally. It was black intellectually. For religious superstition reigned supreme, and whenever and wherever religious superstition reigns supreme, then you may depend upon it, is a period of black night. In such periods—and there have not been many of them, thank heaven—reason and science are completely buried. Nothing matters except the black pall of religious superstition covering that period.

This was what we call the "Dark Ages." And truly dark they were. In the name of God, those under the spell of religious superstition cruelly tore the limb from the body—they applied the torch to the fagot—they gouged eyes out—they slit tongues—they used the thumbscrew—they threw little babies up into the air and caught them coming down on the cruel prongs of a pitchfork. Nothing mattered to those who cherished their insane belief in a superstitious "god" and these same religionists, throughout the dark ages, stopped at nothing in an attempt to foist their ungodly superstition on others.

In such times, the earth was flat. It had four corners. There was water in the "heavens" and when it rained, "god" was opening the windows of these "heavens" to let a little moisture down to the earth. The stars were lights suspended in the firmament, and the sun was the "big light" while the moon was the "little light," and both were suspended in the sky, hung there by "god" to give light to the earth. And for one thousand ghastly years, this condition existed right here on this old globe as we know it. It hasn't all gone yet by any means—but it's going—and going fast too. But it cannot go too fast no matter how fast it disappears. But as I say, a "remnant remains," and it is part of my other work outside of this course, to hasten the last remnant of such pagan superstition on its way to its inevitable doom. And I am happy in that work, of course.

The thousand years came to a close however, and with the passing of this Dark-age nightmare, men of reason began to appear on the horizon again. Many of them were brutally murdered by these religious superstitionists, but the fires of reason, kindled by these men, were fanned into one great flame of reason and intelligence, which has never been put out and which never will be put out. Came first the Brunos. They were burnt alive at the stake. Then came the Keplers and the

Galileos, and the Copernicuses, and many others.

Sweeping the sky with his little telescope, Galileo and Copernicus both had moral courage enough to state that the sky was not flat. They said that the stars were not suspended in the sky at all, but were other suns, probably giving light to other worlds. You know what they suffered for making such statements. Regardless of whether their theories were true or not, they did not jibe with the teachings of those in power during this thousand years of religious blackness, and so the originators of these theories, (now proven facts) were either tortured or brutally murdered. However—one may bury truth to the earth—one may crush it—but sooner or later, grandly triumphant, it will rise from the earth and shine once more. It may be buried for such periods as this ghastly one thousand years but, sometime or other, IT WILL RISE AGAIN IN SPITE OF ALL THE RELIGIOUS SUPERSTITION IN THE WORLD.

And that is exactly what it did. It took over 1000 years to resurrect it and rescue it from the holy hands of the religious superstitionist, but it was rescued. It was resurrected. And today, it is here with us, glorious in itself. Religious superstition stands aghast at its revelations. Religious superstition wonders where the end will be, and it sees in this TRUTH which is sweeping the world, its own end. And it cannot come too soon for the welfare of every created thing. For, mark me well please, the day is here when people WILL NOT accept religious superstition, no matter what man or what organization gives it to them. They don't want it and they won't have it. And all over the civilized world today, even as I write this, almost every country that has been in the grip of religious superstition is throwing it away.

That is significant—very significant. It has taken them a long time to wake up—but they are awake for sure, and for good. This means much to the intellectual, mental, and spiritual future of such nations, for the moment the black and terrible pall of religious superstition is ended, then can these same nations see the marvelous stunning facts behind this mighty scheme of life. And truly marvelous facts they are. Far too marvelous to be buried under the shroud of any system of religious superstition, where they have been buried for so long now. What a joy comes to me when I think of my part in the disseminating of these new and mighty truths of God. What a happiness fills my soul. What an intense love for all is manifested, and how very careful I am in my efforts to tell you of the existence of this mighty dynamic GOD-LAW, hitherto unknown and unsuspected by the differing religious organizations in existence today.

And you should be happy, also, my friend that you are, for the first time, being given the truths of the mighty Creative GOD-LAW as they exist. For the one who uses this mighty LAW, knows, and he knows full well that a proper application of this spiritual GOD-LAW to his own conditions and circumstances, will very effectively make such circumstances what he or she desires. So get ready my friend—don't think for one moment that I am fooling you. I have neither the time nor the inclination to do that. The very vastness and greatness of the GOD-LAW, though makes me overly enthusiastic to tell you about it, so that you may begin to put it into operation in your own life, and by so doing, obtain the things from God that you need so badly, some of you.

I wish it were possible to unfold these mighty truths all at once. But that is not possible. I don't care what your mentality is, nor do I care what your education along spiritual lines has been; the truths I shall give you are so revolutionary that you absolutely cannot grasp them in one reading. Nor could you grasp them all at once. I have tried it and I know, and in the case in which I have tried it, the truth I have been trying to teach has been invariably missed.

So step by step along the way let me lead you. Let me take your hand and walk slowly into this great God-realm, for to make haste might be perilous to your future. You might miss the goal. You might not find the GOD-LAW. I know better than you do what is the best way to make known this startling revelation of GOD, I think, so all I shall ask you to do is to play the game—fair and square—do as I ask you to do, and follow me very closely. For remember, we are dealing with spiritual things. We are dealing with spiritual LAW, and spiritual things are ALWAYS UNSEEN THINGS. Remember that.

Now to get back again to where I left off. Out of the black night of the dark ages came the torch-bearers of truth. They did not believe in the religious superstition vaunting itself on the earth those days, and masquerading as an agent of God. They saw further than that. They saw beyond the black night. They saw beyond the superstition. They suspected that God did not lie in the teachings of these religious superstitionists who were holding the world in mental and intellectual and spiritual blackness and night. They suspected that God was far removed from such teachings. They saw the cruel flames sear and destroy the bodies of those who would not believe the stories told by these superstitionists, and they used their reason —they wondered what sort of a God it could be who produced such a murdering mob of followers.

They wanted nothing to do with such a "god" and they frankly said so. Lamarck came to France, and Kant to Germany, Spinoza appeared in Holland and Locke in England. They disputed. They thought. And they sowed the seed and made the first move in the removing of the terrible black robe of religious superstition which had so effectively buried the truth for over a thousand years. Then came Darwin who gave to the world his "ORIGIN of SPECIES, and on this work was founded evolution, which today, is being taught in almost every university in Christendom. The religious superstitionists fought this teaching as bitterly as they knew how to fight it. But to no avail. TRUTH TRIUMPHED. IT RAISED ITS HEAD AGAIN. And today the fact of evolution is as firmly established as is the fact of gravitation.

Only the "remnant" which remains of the "religious superstitionists" do not believe it. It is universally accepted by the intellectual class the wide world over. It was accepted as truth when it was first given to the world, and in 73 years it is known to be the truth. But hundreds of thousands perished during the "thousand years of the dark ages" because they would not accept the teachings of religious superstition. But those teachings were all wrong as is now well known.

The superstitionist told us very solemnly and very fearfully that their "god" created the whole universe at once, and in six days. They told us the stories I have once referred to in this Lesson about the "lights" being suspended in the sky by "god" —their god that is. They told us of the creation of man. They said that this "god" of theirs, after making the entire creation in six literal days, spit in the ground, made a man, caused a deep sleep to come on the man, opened up his side and took a rib out, and made a woman—the first woman from this rib. This is what those who were in authority during the "dark ages" and before, told us.

They knew nothing of natural law. They knew nothing of science. They knew nothing of evolution. For the religious superstitionists were in full control. They killed at once, and very brutally too, every soul who would dare doubt their teachings. The Auto-da-fe was in vogue in that day and age, and the only way they were able to get "converts" to their superstition, was to threaten them with either death or torture. They knew nothing whatsoever of geology, and they knew nothing of the other sciences which have opened this whole subject up like a rose, and have subjected it to the sunlight of reason and intelligence. And the dirty little bugs of religious superstition have vanished as they always do, when the sunshine of men's God-given reason shines on them.

All those superstitionists knew in that day was "gods." It was an age of "gods." They knew every "god" but the real one. For as long as the ghastly pall of religious superstition overhung the world, by no possible means could it know anything about GOD as this Spirit actually exists HERE and NOW. If a storm raged, destroying villages and homes and human lives—"god" did it. If a fire was quite naturally kindled in a huge forest, destroying more lives and lots of trees, then "god" did it. No matter what it might be. IF THESE RELIGIOUS SUPERSTITIONISTS DID NOT UNDERSTAND IT, THEY BLAME IT ALL ON "GOD." And never forget here, my friend, that the present systems of religion we have with us today, ALL OF THEM, WITHOUT EXCEPTION, WERE BORN INTO EXISTENCE IN THIS DARK AGE REASONING.

The "remnant" remaining today, is truly JUST AS SUPERSTITIOUS IN ITS ORIGIN AS WAS THE ORIGINAL THING IN THE DARK AGES. It cannot be otherwise for it is part and parcel of that unholy thing, and as such, it is inherently the same. True—reason and intelligence is demanding and has demanded that they throw away a lot of their "dark-age" teachings, but this does NOT change the fact that the whole thing originated in, and is a direct result of, DARK AGE RELIGIOUS SUPERSTITIOUS TEACHINGS. Don't forget that.

SIX DAYS—"GOD" MADE THE WORLD IN SIX DAYS. He made it in stages of twenty four hours each. Think of it. And just because the Bible said so, we have been asked to believe it. That is the Bible story. That is the story of the religious superstitionist. But thank heaven that story is passed now, and taking its place, we find science occupying the field. We find reality taking the place of religious superstition. We find FACTS taking the place of religious superstition. And a great change is coming over the world as this happens.

It is a universally admitted fact that this "dark-age" story of the creation of the universe is not true. And in a former Lesson I showed you the fact that GOD, being Spirit—or INVISIBLE LIFE—could never adopt such methods of making any thing. I showed you that the first creation was an invisible creation. And at this point I shall show you how this invisible creation is absolutely in accord with the very latest scientific findings. And let me add here that there is no religious superstition higher than science. Nor is there any religion of any sort higher than science. For science means TRUTH. And TRUTH is higher than any religious superstition certainly. A scientific fact is a fact that is KNOWN to be true. WE KNOW IT IS TRUE. And up against one known scientific fact, you may pile all the religious theories you care to, and they will all be false if they are against that one known PROVEN scientific FACT.

So let us get along here, and see, if we can, just what is the fact of creation scientifically, and then when we see this, we shall see how marvelously it is in accord with what I told you of the creation in a previous Lesson. In that Lesson I tackled the problem from the religious angle. Here I am tackling it from the scientific angle. And we shall soon see that there is no clash at all. One TRUTH can never clash with another TRUTH. And we shall perhaps find here in this teaching, before we finish—the startling fact that ONLY TRUTH MATTERS, AND THAT ALL IS TRUTH IN THE FINAL ANALYSIS. Perhaps I should not have said that here at this initial stage of our journey together, but I will let it stand as it is, and if some of my students do not understand it, then pass over it for the time being. I know that I have many students who will understand it.

I should like to be fair at this point with the religious superstitionists of the "dark ages," however, to the extent of admitting that they had no way of finding out the truth of creation and its Creator. Whatever theory they evolved must have been sheer guess work. True, they had a book called the bible, but had they known as much of the origin of that book as we know today, they would have known just exactly what the book was and what it was not. And certainly they would never have accepted it as being even in the slightest degree divine, for we who have taken the time to investigate, know that it is no such a thing. It was on the teachings of this superstitious book, however, that these old dark-age religionists depended for their teachings and their inspiration, and, considering that fact, I am not so sure that they are too much to blame for their actions.

But their theory of god was, I repeat, entirely guess work. There were many gods in existence far older than theirs, and the same story they held to and told had been told by other supernatural religious superstitionists, thousands of years before they had ever lived. I think it in order to state here that every supernaturally revealed system of religion the world has seen to date, and there have been many of them, have all had the same story to tell, in a more or less changed or modified manner. In essence it is the same thing. I shall not go into detail here though, as it is aside from the purpose of these Lessons, but I mention it in passing to show that even this ghastly "dark-age" religious superstition was only a copy of a far older system, and was founded in its entirety on similar stories held many thousands of years before by other "supernaturally-revealed" systems of religion. So once and for all we can very profitably discard any story and any religion that informs us that its "god" made the world in six days and by the "spit and earth" method. That is pure guess work and surmise. And the chances are many to one it is very untrue. At least we do not believe it today, for the simple reason that the facts as we do know them, very effectively give the lie to the other story. And it is in the realm of FACT where we shall find GOD—and nowhere else. He will never be found in any individual system of religion at all. Nor will he ever be found in any realm of superstition at all. He will be found, and he has been found in the realm of FACT and TRUTH.

As these thinkers came into existence, fossil remains were studied. Astronomy was studied, and scientists gradually came to accept the theory that the creation had occupied many billions of years of time. (Personally I question the existence of time as we understand it). As their great telescopes swept the heavens, they disclosed unmistakable evidence of other planets than ours, sweeping their way with unerring precision and remarkable accuracy through the heavens. They saw these things, and, shorn of the old superstition that some supreme being had made all this in a moment of time, they began to look for the scientific explanation of it all. Religion did not, and does not answer the question. So they looked to science. It has not all happened in a day, or a year, or anything like that, but it is a well accepted fact that this world has progressed farther, both mentally, intellectually, and spiritually in the past one hundred years than it has ever progressed before.

More of the truths of God have been learned during the past twenty-five years than were ever learned throughout the entire thousand years of "bacchanalian darkness" during which period the superstitious religionists were at the height of their temporary power. (And moral degradation incidentally). Professor Millikan, that giant of the scientific realm, and a man to whom I shall again refer in a future Lesson said:

"DO YOU REALIZE THAT WITHIN THE LIFETIME OF MEN NOW LIVING WITHIN ONE HUNDRED YEARS, OR ONE HUNDRED AND THIRTY YEARS AT THE MOST, ALL THE MATERIAL CONDITIONS UNDER WHICH MAN LIVES HIS LIFE ON THIS EARTH HAVE BEEN MORE COMPLETELY REVOLUTIONIZED THAN DURING ALL THE AGES OF RECORDED HISTORY WHICH PRECEDED. "MY GREAT GRANDFATHER LIVED ESSENTIALLY THE SAME SORT OF LIFE, SO FAR AS EXTERNAL CONDITIONS WERE CONCERNED, AS DID HIS ASSYRIAN PROTOTYPE 6000 YEARS AGO."

And Dr. Millikan is quite correct. And at this point may I remind my students that the end is not yet even in sight. There are fearless men, men of brilliant intellect, who are tackling this great unseen realm and this equally great seen realm, and we have only just begun to find out something of the magnitude of the mighty LAWS in existence. Practically every scientific mind today admits that the answer to the problem of the universe and its Creator, lies in the unseen or spiritual realm. They are recognizing the stupendous fact that UNSEEN FORCES are responsible for material things. It has taken a long time to arrive at this conclusion, but now that it has been reached, watch the progress from now on. I do not want the religious superstitionists to take any heart from this statement, for I assure them that in the last analysis, and when spiritual truth is known as it really exists, there will be mighty little ground for the superstitious of any field of endeavor to take refuge on. None at all. For all spiritual and all natural law, is part of the GOD-LAW. And no sort of superstition, not even religious, can ever enter that sacred portal of the GOD-REALM. Remember that.

Away out yonder in space, millions and billions of miles away, are to be seen great nebulae. These nebulae are vast and immense bodies of cloudlike material, and all of them are quite irregular in form. I have seen many of them through the great telescope on Mt. Wilson and again in Tucson, Arizona, through the glass of the University of Arizona. Chief among these vast bodies, if we can rightly call them bodies, is the great Spiral Nebula and the Nebula of Orion. I question very much whether or not the human mind can grasp the enormous distances these cloudy like bodies are from this earth. The planets are far enough away, and they are of much greater density than are these fleecy looking nebulae.

One evening I stood at the objective of the great scope on Mt. Wilson, looking at the planet Uranus. This structure is only about seventeen hundred million miles away, and yet there I stood looking at it through this wonderful glass, the world's largest. It is accepted that these nebulae consist of the substance from which our suns and planets are made, and there are about 250,000 of them which may be seen through the Mt. Wilson telescope. These bodies are of immense size, and a nebula only as large as our solar system, could not be seen even through the most powerful of all telescopes. Those we do know of, are probably thousands of times as large as our entire solar system.

The most beautiful of all these known nebulae is the one in Orion, and it is perhaps the most beautiful object ever revealed by the telescope. It is more than ONE MILLION TIMES LARGER THAN OUR ENTIRE SOLAR SYSTEM. The Great Spiral Nebula, we are told, represents a mighty sun and a series or system of planets in the process of formation. In passing may I mention the fact that our Moon is but a dead star. It has no light nor heat on it. Nor is there atmosphere either.

It is universally admitted among scientists, that these nebulae are the primary cause of planets such as the one we live on. Just how this happens is more or less obscure, but it is an accepted fact that it has happened, and is still happening every day. Some nebulae are more dense than others. Some are in the nebulous state, whilst others shine as suns. It would take far too 'much' time to explain to you the theories given and as far as these theories go while it is a universally accepted fact that planets are throw-off's from some sun or other and while it is a further fact that a sun is a "completed" nebula we may not at this time give the exact method by which this remarkable transformation takes place. It is not necessary either that we do so. If the fact is accepted that these nebulae are the cause of suns and other planets then that is quite sufficient for our purpose here and now. For further study along this line I recommend a book written by Mr. Marshal Gauvin entitled "THE ILLUSTRATED STORY OF EVOLUTION." The book is published and copyrighted by the Peter Eckle Publishing Company of New York City and is one of the best of the condensed works dealing with evolution I have ever read. Mr. Gauvin has one little paragraph in that book dealing with this subject of nebulae which I should like to have you read so I reproduce it here and suggest that you obtain this book at your earliest convenience. Says Mr. Gauvin:

"HOW IS THE NEBULA FORMED? THE CLUSTER IN THE CONSTELLATION HERCULES, IF IT IS NOT IN FACT A COLOSSAL NEBULA, SHOWS THAT SOME OF THE STARS ARE VERY CLOSE TOGETHER. NOW, THESE IMMENSE OBJECTS, THAT IN BLIND FURY DASH THROUGH SPACE, MAY COME IN COLLISION WITH EACH OTHER AND EXPLODE IN A NEBULOUS CLOUD; OR THEY MAY PLOUGH THROUGH DENSE SWARMS OF METEORITES, WITH A RESULTANT EXPLOSION ON A SMALLER SCALE; OR, TORN BY INTERNAL CONVULSIONS, THEY MAY BURST INTO FRAGMENTS AND SCATTER THEIR DEAD DUST OVER THE ABYSS OF SPACE. IN ONE OR ALL OF THESE WAYS THE NEBULA IS BORN, TO BEGIN AGAIN THE RECURRING CYCLE OF NATURE'S LIFE."

This I think is about the most accepted scientific finding I have run across to date. It explains very simply the process by which these nebulae are existent. This is not the important thing however, but it IS the exact findings of science along this particular line. You may be sure of one thing, and that is that this old globe upon which you and I are living today, at some time or other must have been part of a nebulous substance floating somewhere in the ether. Its formation probably took millions if not billions of years. It was NOT created in six days, nor was it created at once, and by an act of a PERSONALITY called God. Such is NOT the case. For the thing called god by the superstitious, does not exist. And what they would like to term "god" DOES EXIST BUT only exists as a GOD-LAW. And a LAW has no personality of any sort—it cannot have. Neither has it any "mind" of any sort—it cannot have.

This GOD-LAW is infinite. It is omnipotent. It is omniscient. It is all creative. It is impartial. It is NOT a personality—it IS A LAW. It is more than that. It is THE LAW if you please. Now mark me carefully here, IT IS THE ONLY LAW THERE IS IN THE UNIVERSE. Try and think that out and grasp it well. Perhaps you won't understand that statement to the full now, but you will later on in your studies. Remember here though, that there is only ONE LAW in the universe, and that is the GOD-LAW. It is NOT a personality. IT CAN ACCOMPLISH ANYTHING AND EVERYTHING. It is responsible for every created thing, and there can be no creation of any sort or kind without the operation of this mighty LAW. It operates in the flight of the nebula, and it operates in and through me as I write this to you, and it operates through you as you read it. It is responsible for yon clusters of stars and it is responsible for the fish at the bottom of the sea. Had there been no such GOD-LAW there would never have been any created thing at all. And it is this same GOD-LAW operating in and through the intelligence of men, that has given to the world in the past hundred years, the remarkable discoveries that have been made. Now listen to me a moment please. If you ever obtain the things you need in life, THOSE THINGS WILL BE BROUGHT INTO BEING THROUGH THE OPERATIONS OF THIS MIGHTY GOD-LAW. THIS LAW you are learning about now, will be the means of bringing to you, either health, wealth, happiness, peace or whatever it is you need, and THESE THINGS CAN COME NO OTHER WAY.

I have a very specific reason for desiring that you learn well the picture as this Lesson has given it to you. Forget about any PERSONALITY OF ANY SORT BEING RESPONSIBLE FOR THIS UNIVERSE AND FOR YOU. Realize here that a Great Creative GOD LAW is alone responsible. Try and imagine the vastness of space, and try also to imagine that the creative processes which have brought man to his present state of development, have been going on for millions of years. Learn the fact of the great ethereal bodies called nebula floating around in the ether, for ether pervades all space. I shall have a very startling statement to make regarding this in the next Lesson. But realize that a mighty Creative GOD-LAW is the controlling factor and sole and supreme CREATIVE POWER.

I shall not take you any farther into the subject in this Lesson for I want you to grasp carefully every thing I say to you now. Remember that GOD is INVISIBLE LIFE. Remember too, that a thought is an INVISIBLE THING. Remember also, that YOUR THOUGHTS ARE PART OF THE GREAT INVISIBLE LIFE PRINCIPLE RESPONSIBLE FOR EVERYTHING—ESPECIALLY LIFE ITSELF. For where LIFE is, the other things can always be. But where LIFE is NOT, then nothing else can be. I want to get the thought home to you, that YOU are a LIVING VITAL MANIFESTATION OF THE MOST POWERFUL LAW IN THE WORLD. I want you to see that YOU ARE A VITAL PART AND A MANIFESTATION OF THE ONLY LAW THERE IS IN THE WORLD. I want you to grasp the fact that you, through the part of you called your "thoughts" are IN DIRECT CONTACT WITH THIS MIGHTY GOD-LAW WHICH CAN PRODUCE EVERYTHING, INCLUDING WHATSOEVER THINGS YOU NEED HERE AND NOW ON EARTH. If you do not receive these things, it is your fault. It is because you have not grasped the LAW or perhaps have not had it pointed out to you.

Away back yonder, back of the nebulae, back of all the planets, back of every created thing, you will remember that this mighty LIFE SPIRIT made an INVISIBLE CREATION. No other kind. I shall show you from now on, exactly how this mighty God Spirit brought into physical mani-festation, the Creation that HE HAD ALREADY MADE. Then I shall show you how YOU, by pursuing the same methods this GOD-LAW pro-vides for, will bring into ACTUAL MANIFESTATION, the things YOU need. For certainly the LAW is here. Certainly it operates. If it could take a spiral nebula and from it make a marvelous creation such as we now enjoy, then do you not think it can create for you the few paltry things you need? Of course it can—for it is the GOP-LAW, the very same Principle that brought every manifested thing to earth. It is a LAW and don't you forget it.

You are doing the little exercises I have prescribed for you. I shall impress on you once more the absolute importance of setting before your "mind" as we say, the thing you want. I don't care what it is. The proba-bility though is, that it is either business success, health, or happiness, and let me assure you that this Great GOD-LAW can bring them all to you when you learn how to comply with the conditions governing it in your own life. But make sure of what it is you want, and then let your every thought, when not otherwise occupied, be of that thing. If it is success then be intent in your little affirmation, and say:

"I AM MORE AND MORE SUCCESSFUL—I AM MORE AND MORE SUCCESSFUL."

Let this sentence eat into you. Let it become a very part of you. After a while you will be doing it unconsciously, and when that time comes you will be well on the way to the actual manifestation of this very thing. Throughout the spinal column and brain, there runs a fluid called the "spinal fluid." This is composed of what are called neurons, and these neurons join hands with each other as it were. The end of one grasps the end of the other one. Every thought going through your cerebro-spinal system or the sympathetic nervous system, makes a definite movement among these neurons. It makes a path, which path however, closes up the minute the thought has passed. This is a physiological fact. NOW—you let the same thought be repeated over and over again, and THERE IS MADE A DEFINITE PATH OR CHANNEL IN THESE NEURONS, which belongs peculiarly to that one thought. With repeated affirmations or repetitions of that one thought or statement, they become automatic so to speak, and they become a very part of you.

I only mention this to show you that there is a scientific reason for everything I ask you to do, and greater than that, there stands behind it all—THE GOD LAW. And certainly THAT cannot be held incompetent to produce whatever is needed. So let this statement of your success ever be uppermost in your mind. Remember, you REALLY WANT success to come to you. You are not indifferent at all, but you actually WANT it, and in order that it may come, you are willing to WORK a little bit, mentally, for it. For this is what it amounts to. You do not know at this point the mighty GOD-LAW by which these needed things will come, but you are willing to work intelligently with me in order that the GOD-LAW, about which practically nothing is known, can manifest.

Perhaps your trouble is one of health. In this case you shall use the statement to the exclusion of all other statements and thoughts:

"THE LIVING GOD IS MAKING ME WHOLE"— "THE LIVING GOD IS MAKING ME WHOLE."

Do you not feel that there is anything even faintly connected with "superstitious religion" about this statement, for there is not. "PSY-CHIANA" is a new PSYCHOLOGICAL religion, and therefore it is a SCIENTIFIC RELIGION—not a superstitious one. And the founder of this system, and your present teacher knows whereof he speaks. He KNOWS the GOD-LAW exists. No matter what the illness or the sickness may be, use that statement, and USE it. DRIVE IT INTO YOUR VERY BEING. You will be putting the GOD-LAW into play if you will.

If it is happiness you need, then say: "I AM HAPPIER— HAP-PIER—HAPPIER" and KEEP AT IT. At night, you are still relaxing. You are lying very still. You finally forget that you have a body, and you feel sleep slowly creeping on you. THEN—you focus your thought and your desire INTO YOUR VERY EGO, for that is what the "white spot" is a manifestation of, and—you are asleep. When you awake, the very first thing you do go into your statement, no matter which of the three it may be. And you mean it. It is becoming a very active part of you. And you MEAN BUSINESS. You want to actually find the great GOD as the mighty POWER exists—and you will, if you will follow me.

In the next Lesson I shall go into this same subject a little further, and will deal with the ACTUAL EXISTENCE OF THIS GOD-LAW THROUGHOUT ALL SPACE. I will show you what it is, and then a little later, how it operates. Strange as it may seem, you and I live, and move, and have our being in the very midst of the most potent dynamic power we have ever seen or heard of, and yet we wander around looking for something or other to bring to us the good things of life. The next Lesson will show you the actual existence of the GOD-PRINCIPLE, and I do not think such a Lesson has ever been written before. I do not think any of the scientists have seen it. Perhaps they have, but if they have I have never heard of its being called to anyone's attention before.

Don't forget to write me if you experience any difficulty in grasping these Lessons, I want to help you find GOD—the REAL GOD—not a personality of any sort but the greatest Creating Power in existence.

POINTS TO REMEMBER IN LESSON SIX

1. What was accepted as the truth a few hundred years ago is not accepted as the truth today.

2. The immense truth of the unseen Spiritual Law, as you are learning it in these Lessons, has always existed but has not been recognized until quite recently.

5. The only limitations there need be on your life are the limitations you put there yourself, for truth is all powerful and when the truth of the Spiritual realm is applied in your life this truth will enable you to do almost anything you want to do.

4. The applications of the God-Law in your life will be followed by material manifestations also.

5. If you are not well physically repeat the affirmation given in this Lesson continually until it becomes a part of your very nature.

6. Grasp this Lesson fully before you receive the next one for in that Lesson you will be given another forward glance into the great Spiritual realm of truth. Be sure and write me if you do not understand anything in this Lesson and I will try to help you with it.

Sincerely your friend,
FRANK B. ROBINSON

LESSON 7

I promised you last week that in this Lesson Seven we should go into quite some depths, and we have. The Lesson gives you a picture of creation that you have never had before. It shows you the reason for the "thought exercises" I have been prescribing, and it also shows you the dynamic power behind these exercises.

You may have thought that you have been "talking to yourself" in doing these little exercises, but now you will know that if you have done them faithfully, you have put into operation a great Spiritual force and opened up the channel through which there can come to you just about whatever you need for complete success, health, and happiness.

Read and study this Lesson many times. It is really a marvelous Lesson and will probably start you thinking in earnest. So remember, help yourself to grasp the truths that I am helping you to grasp. What I am telling you now is TRUTH. And truth always liberates.

Sincerely your friend,
FRANK ROBINSON

In our efforts, to find and understand this dynamic GOD-LAW which I claim operates throughout the whole universe, you will remember that in your last Lesson, (number 6) I told you of the probable cause of this universe. I showed you the generally accepted modern scientific theory of the primary cause resulting in yon vast bodies floating in the ether millions and billions of miles away, and called NEBULAE. It is absolutely necessary that you understand the primary cause and the following stages of the creation, in order to get the picture as I see it exists.

And the creation is no less marvelous if we accept the nebula viewpoint than if we accepted the instantaneous six day creation. It is perhaps more marvelous as it is. It would, of course, be a wonderful thing if some power of other could call into being this universe in such a short time as six days, but it is infinitely more marvelous that this slow process of evolution has been going on through the millions and billions of years. Besides—I consider the exact manner of the creation to be not so important after all. The important fact is that we are here. The important fact is that every created thing was ever created at all.

The Law of which I speak and teach, exists, and no matter whether we are right of wrong in our understanding of the first creation, the main thing is the existence of the great GOD-LAW. For it would be absolutely impossible to conceive of such a creation as this is, without some guiding intelligence behind it all. The mistake too many people make is in thinking that some PERSONALITY is behind it all. They consider some PERSONAL GOD of other responsible for it all. This is the very worst kind of foolishness however, for no PERSONAL power of any soft could have had any thing to do with it. Those of us who are scientifically inclined, and those of us who have gone about as far as science can take us, KNOW, and we know full well, that no PERSONALITY ever had anything to do with this marvelous creation.

The story that some such personality of other did have, is but part of the superstitious religions I mentioned at some length in my last Lesson. But there are many people who, the minute you take PERSONALITY out of the picture, cry in anguish, "You have taken away my lord—you have taken away my lord." No such a thing. In all my teachings of different kinds, about all I take away from people is their erroneous religious and highly superstitious ideas regarding the "deity." That's all I take away. And by taking away such old dark-age superstitions, I am paving the way for a reasonable and intelligent understanding of the GOD-LAW which did. and still does, create every created thing, and which did, and still does, hold everything by that mighty LAW.

It is hard for some people to grasp the thought that it need NOT be a personality. They do not seem to absorb the fact that in the spiritual realm, it is quite possible for a spiritual LAW to be a self-existent, a self-thinking, and an intelligent LAW. They have the idea that if you take away personality from the spiritual realm, you have nothing left. But such is a thousand miles from the truth. For not only is it possible to have a spiritual LAW which Law is self-existent, self-sustaining, and intelligent, but SUCH IS THE FACT AS IT IS IN THE UNSEEN OF SPIRITUAL REALM. Just because the Power is a LAW, is no reason to suppose that it is an unintelligent LAW. Not at all. For there is no such thing as "unintelligence" in the spiritual unseen realm. All is intelligence—and marvelous intelligence at that.

To me, the beauties and the power are stripped from the spiritual of unseen realm in the very moment we begin to interpolate personality. For you may depend upon it, no personality is responsible off yon nebulae. No personality is responsible for yon starry vault. No personality ever was responsible for those heavenly satellites, meteorites, etc. No personality is responsible for the discovery of electricity of the radio. Not at all. The GOD-LAW, without personality is responsible for it all, and the men who bring these marvelous discoveries into being, are but men who are PRODUCTS 0F THIS MARVELOUS GOD-LAW, that's all.

How manifestly foolish and utterly unfair would it not be, to consider for an instant that an intelligent personality, even though he be called God, is responsible for the chaos, the crime, the misery on this earth today. Nation watching nation. One religion waiting to fly at the throat of another one. Racketeers—bootleggers—murderers—poverty—sin—crime—suffering—injustice, etc. And you ask me to believe that an intelligent PERSONALITY IS BACK 0F ALL THIS? You go and ask someone else to believe that—not me—for I KNOW BETTER. It would be an insult to whatever God there might be, to class Him as a personality, and then to say that He was responsible for things as they exists today.

But if you presume the existence of an intelligent, unseen, spiritual GOD LAW, and if you could but see that all existing evils are but due to ignorance of this mighty GOD LAW, do you not see how the picture changes? And do you not see how much more reasonable such an explanation is? of course you do. And the pity of it all is—and the crying shame of it all is, that men and women have for so long been kept in ignorance of the existence of this mighty GOD-LAW, and thereby have had its blessings and its help taken from them. For you cannot use a LAW YOU know nothing of. You cannot use a power that you do not understand. As far as you go, and as far as you are concerned, such a Power of GOD-LAW does not exist, if you have never known of its existence.

There must be however, such an intelligent LAW of this old world and yon starry heavens could not last one moment. And remember another thing here, my friend and student, if there is such a LAW, then it is one of the most stupendous things that ever could happen. For YOU CAN DEPEND ON A LAW. You cannot depend on any of the many "gods" the world has seen to date, off you can't get any intelligent information regarding them. One religionist says this—another says that. But where a spiritual LAW is concerned, YOU CAN ALWAYS DEPEND UPON SUCH BECAUSE IT IS A LAW. Be sure you see that. Now what soft of a Law do you think it is, to be responsible for the utterly marvelous demonstrations it has made to date on this earth? What soft of a Law can it be, that can take two little germ-cells, and, BY SPIRITUAL LAW, MAKE FROM THOSE TWO CELLS, A HUMAN BODY? For that is exactly what happens.

Would you have me believe that such a LAW as that was not able to create for you whatever few things you can possibly need to make you, happy, healthy, and successful? Would you have me believe that? Of course you wouldn't—and you do not believe it yourself. You will probably be amazed at the thought of such a mighty GOD LAW operating here and now on the earth, but may I assure you that such is the fact just the same. You may depend upon it too, that if there be no such a LAW, then there is certainly no use of your looking somewhere else to find it. You can cry to "god" in the sky to your hearts content for all the good it will do you—for any being up there, even if there were one, is positively useless to you of to me. I know, because I tried to find it for years. And it is not to be found. There is no personal "god" of any soft waiting to help you of me out of our troubles. And here let me add that if you are ever helped out of your troubles, it will be because of your understanding of the SUPREME CREATIVE GOD-LAW, which operates whether you recognize it of not, and certainly not through any help from "god in heaven" for such a "god" and such a place do not exist. They never have existed.

Omar Khayyam had it when he said something like this:

"And yon inverted bowl we call the sky,
Lift not your hands to it for help,
For it as impotently moves as you of I."

But Omar Khayyam didn't say all he might have said. What he might have added was the fact that if you and I could but get in touch with THE POWER THAT CREATED Y0N INVERTED BOWL, we might be getting somewhere with a vengeance. A preacher said to me on the street yesterday, "Well, Doctor Robinson—if you take all supernaturally revealed religion out of the world, what are you going to replace it with?" Do you know what my answer to that man was? Let me tell you. I answered that question by asking him another one, and this is what I asked him:

"When a surgeon cuts out a cancer of a tumor—do you ask the surgeon what he is going to replace it with? When you dig the weeds from your garden. do you ask yourself what you are going to replace them with?"

This silenced the brother as it was intended to. No, we have to come to the acknowledgment of such a spiritual Law as I teach. Otherwise the world is hopelessly lost. Supernatural religion will never do anything for it. We have had too many of those already, and instead of straightening this old world out, all they have ever done is to plunge it into deeper darkness and night. They have caused bloodshed to come instead of peace. They have caused sorrow instead of happiness. They have brought fear, instead of hope. They have blighted and disappointed human souls galore instead of helping them. And we want no more of them. They have been weighed in the balance and found wanting.

And now, for the first time, men and women are getting a faint glimpse of this mighty GOD-LAW responsible for it all. Through my teachings, men and women all over the civilized world are beginning to see somewhat of the marvelous spiritual power at their disposal. and, heaven be praised, they are using this mighty power, and "whatsoever things they desire" are coming to them. That is as it should be. And you personally my friend, and I know not whom you may be, will find your answer to the poverty question in this ever-present GOD-LAW. You will find your answer to the health problem in this GOD-LAW. You will find the answer to your happiness question in this ever-present GOD-LAW, which, in the beginning, caused yon nebulae to create suns. and yon suns to create worlds, and yon worlds to create people. Nowhere else will you find it.

There lies on my desk at my elbow now, a telegram the Western Union boy has brought to me. Here it is—it comes from Akron. Ohio. I shall give it to you as it reads:

"OUR BOY HAS STREPTOCOCCUS THROAT TERRIB-

LY SICK WILL YOU DO WHAT YOU CAN."

I have just dispatched a wire stating: "OF COURSE I WILL DO WHAT I CAN. AM HAPPY TO BE ABLE TO HELP YOUR BOY." And while I do not know this man at all, I know one thing—I KNOW THAT THE MIGHTY POWER OF THE GOD-LAW I HAVE ALREADY THROWN AGAINST THAT STREPTOCOCCUS THROAT, WILL MAKE THOSE STREPTOCOCCUS LOOK SICK IN MIGHTY SHORT ORDER.

You ask me why it is I am able to knock sickness out as we try to do, and I tell you that it is only by a faint understanding of the workings of this mighty GOD-LAW. For it is sure. It never fails. IT DOES THINGS HERE AND NOW. And it will do them for YOU in the very moment you know how to use it. So don't forget that brother or sister. Not me—but the mighty GOD-LAW. And if the good folks who continually wire me for help would but recognize that fact, what a joy it would be. The time is at hand however, when the world at large will know the revelation of the Living God as I am giving it, and sometimes I stand still and wonder what will happen when this marvelous spiritual revelation of truth is universally known.

No, it will not be done overnight, for there is a lot of "supernaturally revealed religion" in the world yet, and until that goes out, the progress of the GOD-LAW will naturally be retarded. For many are looking to the church with its "god in the sky" for the answer. And I find it a fact, that children give up their playthings very slowly, and until a few generations have died off, this teaching of the true GOD-LAW will not sit very well with the good church-folk. It upsets their structure. It is very apt to put their ministers out of jobs. So they don't like it. But that is their worry—not mine.

It will be a shock to them to discover that they have been giving the world a false god, but that will soon be forgotten in the joy which men and women will experience in finding the TRUE LIGHT—the GOD-LAW—THE CREATIVE LIFE PRINCIPLE WHICH IS THE ONLY TRUE GOD THERE EVER HAS BEEN. Has it ever occurred to you that sort of a life yours would be were you conscious of the existence in your life of the ONLY SPIRITUAL POWER THE WORLD HAS EVER KNOWN? Has the thought ever occurred to you just what you might do if you knew that such a power existed for you? Well, you are to learn, my friend, before you have finished your studies with me that there is, as I said in the national announcement which attracted you to this course, a power, so dynamic that all other powers and forces fade into insignificance beside it.

Did you know, there exists in the ether, a ray which permeates all space, and the existence of which is absolutely known. You did not know that did you? Way out yonder, for millions and billions of miles, this

Cosmic Ray, discovered by that marvel of science Dr. Millikan of the California Institute of Technology in Pasadena, is existent. There is no part of the universe where this ray is not. Recently a famous English scientist debated with Dr. Millikan as to whether of not this marvelous ray came from a universe that is building up, or from a disintegrating universe. The Englishman claimed that this ray comes from a universe on the rapid road to destruction. Millikan claims the very opposite. The Englishman says that life is an accident, and the universe is doomed to destruction. He is wrong, but that is the only view he can consistently hold, if he accepts the theory that this Cosmic Ray comes from a disintegrating universe.

Dr. Millikan, on the other hand, contends that the ray is an emanation from a universe that is building up. He is correct and I shall have lots more to say about this "ray" a little later. But I want you to try and conceive here if you can, of an electrical "ray" permeating the atmosphere throughout every tiny little bit of space. An electrical "ray" if you please. And the existence of this "ray" is absolutely known. Its penetrability into a body of water can be measured. Does this mean anything to you? It does to me I assure you. For more than one scientist has made the claim that THIS COSMIC RAY IS THE PRIMARY CAUSE OF EVERYTHING THAT HAS EVER BEEN CREATED ON THE EARTH; think that over for a moment. The scientists claim that they are on the verge of a mighty truth. In fact they have spoken the truth but have not realized what they were saying. I am going a little farther here than any other scientist has ever gone yet. I AM GOING ON RECORD AS STATING THAT THESE COSMIC RAYS HAVE INTELLIGENCE—AND CREATIVE INTELLIGENCE AT THAT. Now does that mean anything to you at all. It does to me, and in the further pursuit of our studies together, you will find that the remarkable fact of this Cosmic Ray is one of the most stupendous facts ever discovered by man. IT'S ON THE BORDER LINE OF THE SPIRITUAL, and in this discovery of Dr. Millikan's lies a world of truth and a world of power. We shall tap a little of that power ere long.

Now we have the cause of creation lying in the far off nebula. We have an electrical ray, (we shall call it electrical for the time being) in existence through out all nature. Coming to this earth from millions and billions of miles away, this electrical ray is ever-present, and just what significance this has can only be surmised by you at this point in your studies. I cannot take you too far all at once. And before I go more fully ˙ into this "ray" I shall have to leave the subject for a while, in order that I may link it up later with what I want to. You will understand the logic and the sequence of what I am saying to you in a future Lesson when I show you what this marvelous "Cosmic Ray" really is.

One thing you may know at this point though. and that is the fact that when I tell you to have in your thoughts the thing you need when you retire, and most of the day for that matter, I have a reason for that. Suppose for one instant that there might be some connection between that

Cosmic Ray and your own thoughts. Just suppose that there is. We have seen that some scientists have accepted it that THIS COSMIC RAY IS RESPONSIBLE FOR WHATEVER CREATED THINGS THERE ARE ON EARTH, and for the time being just let us consider that this is a fact. Do you see any connection now? Suppose that in some way or other, Dr. Millikan's "Cosmic Ray" is, in some unknown manner, a PART OF THE SPIRITUAL LAW AND THE SPIRITUAL REALM IN WHICH EVERYTHING CREATED MUST FIRST BE CREATED—THEN WHAT?

If that should prove to be a fact, then do you not see the significance of the little exercises I am giving you to do? I think you do. And I KNOW that by this time you are saying to yourself, "Well, just where is this man Robinson going to take me?" I know that you are realizing the mighty and the stupendous import of these Lessons. and all I shall say to you here is this—DO AS I TELL YOU TO DO. GET FIXED FIRMLY IN YOUR MIND WHAT IT IS THAT YOU NEED MOST ON EARTH FOR YOUR HAPPINESS, HEALTH, AND SUCCESS. And then, let the thought of its actual coming reign supreme in your thought-realm. You now know for the first time, that there may be a very staggering connection between your thought realm and the creative power of the universe. And, in the immense possibilities of this thought, you should certainly be extremely expectant. You should be very happy. Your whole life should brighten up, it will if you are following me closely—and I know you are. There are those of my students—not many of them—but there are those who are just merely curious. For instance, yesterday a retired banker enrolled for this work. On his enrollment blank he stated, "I am not interested in health—I am not interested in wealth—I am not interested in happiness—for I have them all. I am only interested in learning some more from the spiritual realm. That is well and good, for this gentleman will surely learn a little more if he follows me.

Most of my students however, are not in the fortunate condition in which this brother finds himself. I wish they all were. And it is to the intense—to the earnest that these Lessons will appeal. Even though these revelations are probably the most revolutionary and the most advanced to date, at the same time there are those who are not ambitious enough to really do the simple little exercises I am prescribing. I realize, of course, the immense value of these Lessons even from a scientific and literary standpoint. but more than all I am interested in the actual manifesting from the spiritual realm, the things my students most need. I tell you it is a joy far beyond any monetary consideration when I receive the wonderful letters I daily receive, and while of course we are living in a material world, yet somehow or other, as we find the GOD-LAW, some of the material seems to drop away, and we find ourselves more in tune with this great spiritual realm than we do the material realm.

For the spiritual realm is the realm of manifestation. It is the realm of realization. It is the realm where GOD is. Not of course the "god" of the superstitious religionists but the realm of the GREAT SPIRIT GOD, WHOSE POWER IS SUFFICIENT TO PROVIDE FOR US TODAY. HERE AND NOW, WITH WHATEVER WE NEED. That is the God I am talking about. That is the God I am daily showing many how to find.

Now. after having absorbed this unusual Lesson, you will have a new incentive to do the little evening exercises. You will have an intelligent understanding as to something of the reason for my prescribing your little thought exercises. And you will see that they are not quite as simple as you thought they were at first. You will see now that there is a dynamic and almost unbelievable power attached to them. When you repeat your affirmations from now on, especially when going to sleep, I want you to realize the existence of the "Cosmic Ray" and I want you also to realize the fact that a THOUGHT IS A THING. I WANT YOU TO REALIZE THAT WHEN YOU RELEASE A CONCENTRATED THOUGHT INTO THE ETHER, YOU ARE RELEASING IT INTO A MASS OF ELECTRICAL RAYS WHICH RAYS PERMEATE THE ATMOSPHERE FOR MILLIONS AND BILLIONS OF MILES. Never mind now just what these rays do, nor where they come from, nor where they go to. The thing I want you to do now, and the only thing I want you do, is to release your thoughts with the realization that you are TURNING THEM LOOSE INTO A VAST SEA OF ELECTRICAL WAVES, AND THAT THESE THOUGHTS ARE GOING VAST DISTANCES AWAY. That is what I want you to be conscious of now.

We shall have a lot more to say about this unseen "ray" in a future Lesson, but for the time being, get the point of this Lesson, namely, that your thoughts, concentrated, are by you being consciously released into a LIVE SPIRITUAL REALM—THE REALM OF THE COSMIC RAY.

If your little thought-affirmation is for success, as you state "I AM MORE AND MORE SUCCESSFUL," realize that you are sending that thought out into what we may say is a static atmosphere of electricity. It is far more than electricity, but we won't go into that now. Just realize that you are not talking to yourself, BUT ARE TALKING INTO THE GOD-REALM. And you cannot talk into that realm without getting the answer. Keep this up until you receive the next Lesson which will be in about two week.

POINTS TO REMEMBER

(1) There is in existence throughout the ether, a thinking substance which is spiritual in its essence.

(2) Your thoughts are the things that draw from this Spiritual Realm the things you need.

(3) Don't limit the power of the God-Law. Expect great things—then go after them.

Sincerely your friend,
FRANK ROBINSON

EXAMINATION QUESTIONS FOR LESSON NO. 7

These examination questions are for your benefit and you should know the answers to them all. If they are not clear to you, read your Lesson again and again until they are clear.

1. What is the modern scientific theory of the probable cause of this universe?

2. Because the Creative Power is a Law affords no reason for concluding that it is an unintelligent Law?

3. Who or what is responsible for existing evils?

4. For what reason may a Spiritual Law be preferable to a Personal God?

5. If you are ever helped out of your troubles, to what will it be due?

6. What answer may be made to the objection, "If you take all supernaturally revealed religion out of the world, with what will you replace it?"

7. What reason have you for asserting that supernatural religion will never do anything for the world?

8. Why may it be expected to take considerable time before these supernaturally revealed religions are removed from the world?

9. What is the Cosmic Ray? By whom was it discovered?

10. What was the subject of the debate recently held between Dr. Millikan and a famous English scientist in connection with the Cosmic Ray?

11. What is the reason why the little thought exercises are prescribed in these Lessons?

12. When you release a concentrated thought into the ether, what happens?

LESSON 8

In sending you the 8th Lesson it is very important that you study it with the fundamentals in mind as the allegorical illustrations are only for the purpose of bringing out the points involved. Literally the stories are merely allegories. but the principle behind them is scientifically true and it is for this reason that I have used them in this connection.

Read and study this lesson until you are sure that it is clear, as it is very important. Be faithful in your exercises and do not fail to memorize the little poem at the close of the Lesson.

Sincerely your friend,
FRANK B. ROBINSON

In your last Lesson I told you a few things which were quite new to you probably, and I think I opened up a realm of thought to you which is fraught with very vast possibilities to say the least. You will remember that the picture was as follows: We saw first the initial creation of the universe from the vast nebula. Probably through explosion, or from some other cause a sun was formed, as they still are being formed in the heavens. Then we saw the earth and its planets as a "throw-off" from the sun. All this, of course, was millions and billions of years ago as far as our own individual earth is concerned. but this same process is still being repeated now in the formation of other planets similar to our own.

You will, of course, realize that this is an immense scheme. and must be governed by some marvelous CREATIVE LAW. We saw that no personality as such ever had anything to do with it, nor indeed can ever have anything to do with it. We saw that no "god" as such could ever be responsible for it, if one looks upon such "god" as an anthropomorphous being of any sort. We saw further that it was a SPIRITUAL LAW which is in operation in this staggering system of creation, and we saw further that the unseen or the spiritual realm is the REAL and the PERMANENT realm. from which all material things must first come.

The Bible paragrapher was quite correct when he stated: "For the things which are seen are temporal. but the things which are not seen, (or unseen) are ETERNAL." And here in this course of study we are dealing with unseen things. Therefore they are ETERNAL things—they are spiritual things. Almost every scientist of note is quite fully agreed that behind the physical and material universe, there moves a great unseen force. More and more are men coming to realize that the material matters very little—but the spiritual matters very much. Certain it is that there can be no material thing at all, unless such material thing first had its inception and its conception in the unseen realm. It must have been created or its creation directed by the great unseen forces the scientists of today are talking about.

Then. you will remember, we saw ACTUAL EVIDENCE of such an

unseen force in the famous "cosmic ray" made famous by Dr. Millikan. This "ray" opens up a vast realm. and it is my opinion that in the realm of this "ray" lies the answer to the riddle of the universe. At any rate, if it does nothing else, this "ray" absolutely proves the existence of some unseen force or other. and it is quite reasonable to suppose that as we discover more of these famous rays, we shall also know much more about their nature. Today, however, we know that they exist. There is no chance for argument there. And we know that their discovery is quite recent. We know something else also. We know that a field of immense magnitude has been opened up through the discovery of this "ray."

In the last analysis my friend, and when the last thing about the spiritual realm is known, we shall discover that everything that today is deemed "super natural" will be found to be quite beautifully "natural." You know, the Bible has a story in it that there were large walls built around the city of Jericho. We are told that at a certain signal—a blast of a trumpet—these walls fell down killing the enemy. The reason the walls fell down at the blast of the trumpet is because "god" in some supernatural manner or other, caused them to fall. It was looked upon as a "divine intervention" and the walls, we are told, fell miraculously through the miraculous blast of a miraculous trumpet.

But recent investigations and excavations in the ruins of Jericho have told us an entirely different story. These excavations show us that these walls had been carefully undermined, and propped up with heavy stakes. and at the signal of the trumpet, HUMAN HANDS KNOCKED THE PROPS FROM UNDER THE WALLS AND THEY FELL. This is the reasonable and proper explanation of it. And behind every true "super natural" story, no matter how wonderful it may be, there lies a perfectly NATURAL answer. For there is NOTHING supernatural in the universe. Many things, of course, seem to appear "supernatural" to us, but that is only because we do not understand the LAW involved. And, to us I suppose, they are supernatural.

Those of us who are experimenting and delving into the unseen or spiritual realm though, know that there is nothing of the "supernatural" connected with it at all. It's all on account of our own lack of understanding of that realm. And when "earth's last picture is painted," and when the full knowledge of spiritual or natural Law breaks on the earth, the glory of it and the beauty of it will be indescribable. It staggers the imaginations of some of us now, but then you see, that is quite reasonable for we see the import and the amazing glories of the day in which spiritual Law, or natural Law, which is the same thing, will be fully understood. Truly, the Lion shall lie down with the lamb. Truly a child shall lead them. Truly the "glory of the knowledge of the Lord shall cover the earth as the waters cover the sea." Not, of course, the old murdering church god—"Yah-veh" who struck dead at one lick over 50,000 men women and children. No. Not that human made man-god at all.

But people will then realize how utterly foolish such conceptions of deity are and ever have been. And then, in that day, and in the place of the old pagan philosophies we have today, there will break on the world the knowledge of the existence of the CREATIVE LIFE SPIRIT as it actually exists. Then, will the LAW of GOD, or the Law of the Spirit realm. or in other words, the Law of the natural realm, be all-supreme. For—listen to me my friend—the solution to this whole problem, including life and death, LIES IN ABSOLUTELY NATURAL LAW, AND THERE ARE THOSE IN EXISTENCE WHO ARE DRAWING MIGHTY CLOSE TO THE SOLUTION. Some day soon—it will break, and the majesty and simplicity of it all will cause every knee to bow to the MASTER INTELLIGENCE—THE MASTER GOD-LAW responsible for it all. Then shall we know as we are known. Then will material things be the least of our troubles, for they will be quite secondary to the things of LIFE, and how our present pettifogging ideas will fade into nothingness when we realize the vast, the almost incredible majesty of the GOD-LAW. We have been told by those professing to be "agents of god" on the earth that "the finite cannot grasp the infinite." NO? Well the finite CAN grasp the Infinite. The finite IS grasping the Infinite. And it is grasping it simply because the finite IS A PART OF THE INFINITE. That's why. And no matter who you may be studying this Lesson, you may depend upon it that YOU have at your disposal NOW, every single bit of power that exists in the realm of the GOD-LAW, because YOU ARE A PART OF THAT LAW. You see that don't you?

Never let anyone tell you that you have to die and "go to heaven" before you can ever know God. If you ever die and don't know this God-Law here, then the chances are many to one that you will never know it. But the culmination of it all lies in the fact of ETERNAL LIFE HERE AND NOW. Not in the future. Is this too revolutionary? Well it's not quite revolutionary enough. At any rate it is the way all scientific and psychological and spiritual research is pointing, and whether you believe it or not, the GOD-LAW will manifest itself that way, and will be the highest manifestation of it the world has ever known. And I shall not go on record as saying that this will not be in your day and mine. I do not know with certainty, but I DO KNOW that it will be.

This is the logical sequence of life. This marvelous existence was never meant to be cut short, and this marvelous body was never meant to be reduced to ashes by death. It's too beautiful a construction for that. It is too high a manifestation of the GOD-LAW for that. It should not be. Someone here will say, "Oh—yes—that's a nice theory all right—but to date everyone has died." No question about that. But that is no reason for premising that all shall always die. Certainly not. Twenty years ago there was no diphtheria serum either, and diphtheria meant DEATH. But it does not mean death today—it means LIFE. Twenty years ago it was not possible for me to sit in my study and hear the fire-engines racing down

Broadway, New York, but I can do that today. Twenty years ago nothing was known much of the power of so-called "mind" over matter. but much of it is known today. Not many years since the "cosmic ray" was discovered—but it is known now.

So you will have to be a smarter man or woman than I think you are before you say definitely that it CANNOT BE. You have a perfect right to say that it has not been to date, and of course I shall agree with you. But you have NO RIGHT to say that it never can be, for if eternal life is not the one thing promised through every system of religion the world have ever seen, then I know nothing about these systems. It has always been promised. And beside—there is no other logical conclusion to which we can come other than that. There is no other answer to the problem of life. The religionists have told us of course, that the end of all things is to be eternal life, but they have added a proviso: they have told us that only those shall enjoy this eternal life who believe as THEY teach and obtain their "salvation" THEIR own peculiar way, and in accordance with their system of theology. But I differ from them. There is no evidence that this is a fact. It's pure guesswork. Never has there been the slightest scintilla of evidence on which to base such claims. And yet every system of "supernaturally revealed" religion the world has ever seen, and it has seen lots of them, has taught that theory. And they have taught it absolutely without authority of any kind or sort. Of course, they all have their "divine" books, and always these books contain a "divine" revelation from "god" to some prophet or other, but when you try to run down the evidence that the story might be true, you just simply cannot do it that's all. For there is no evidence outside of the internal evidence of these differing religious structures that their stories are true. And that sort of pseudo-evidence is not real evidence at all.

NO—"supernaturally-revealed religion" has had a long time in which to prove its theories, but they still remain unproven, and yet millions still follow them. Not so many millions in America for I doubt very much whether there can be found 500,000 intelligent believers in "supernatural religion," which believers have examined the foundation of their structure and are satisfied that the foundation is reasonably sound. I know it is NOT sound. I know that there never has existed any historical proof of the truth of any "supernaturally-revealed god" the world has ever seen. And it has seen lots of them. This applies to the Christian religion also. There are many people who think that the only man who ever appeared on earth who was called a combination "god" and man was Jesus Christ. This is not correct by any means. He was the LAST one. The church doesn't tell us about the rest of them. It would be just too bad if it did.

I think it might be interesting however, to tell you the names of a few of the "world's crucified Christs," and I know of no better book to quote than the wonderful volume written by Kersey Graves, copyrighted and published by the TRUTHSEEKER COMPANY, 49 Vesey St. New York City. I suggest that my students buy that book. It's one of the most learned things ever written. So I quote the names of these "crucified saviors" from this wonderful book:

> "Krishna" of India was supernaturally born and crucified in
>   1200 B.C.
> "Sakia" the Hindoo "god" was crucified in 600 B.C.
> "Thammuz" of Syria was crucified in 1160 B.C.
> "Wittoba" was crucified in 552 B.C.
> "Iao" was crucified in 622 B.C.
> "Hesus" of the Celtic Druids was crucified in 834 B.C.
> "Quexalcote" of Mexico was crucified in 587 B.C.
> "Quirinus" of Rome was crucified in 506 B.C.
> "Indra" of Thibet was crucified in 725 B.C.
> "Alcestos" was crucified in 600 B.C.
> "Atys" of Phrygia was crucified in 1170 B.C.
> "Crite" of the Chaldeans was crucified in 1200 B.C.
> "Bali" of Orissa was crucified in 725 B.C.
> "Mithra" of Persia was crucified in 600 B.C.

I do not mention these names to get into any religious controversy at all, I have lots of it now, but I do mention them in proof of my statement that Christ was not the only "world savior" to be crucified—he was the most recent.

All these other fellows were "supernaturally-born" combinations of "god" and a man, and they all, came to "save" the world. And they all got crucified too. These names and facts are very carefully concealed by those teaching "supernaturally-revealed" religion though, and I think it just as well that my students know the facts as they exist. It is interesting to note that history discloses the fact of the crucifixions of all of these supposed "world-saviors," BUT IT DOES NOT RECORD THE CRUCIFIXION OF CHRIST. That is mighty significant. Neither does it record his "supernatural birth," nor does it mention his life. It knows nothing of the crucifixion, nor the resurrection, nor the ascension, nor the falling stars, nor the dead people climbing out of their graves. History is silent on this whole Christ story, and it has never been explained to me by any theologian why that should be. To me it just simply means that these marvelous things DID NOT HAPPEN.

But let us get back again. I said to you that "supernatural" revelation had had lots of chance to prove its claims, and I say here that it has utterly failed to do so. The answer to the problem DOES NOT LIE IN THE SUPERNATURAL REALM AT ALL. It lies in the natural realm if ever it is to be found anywhere. And we are fast finding that out too. At this point I am going to go into one of the "supernaturally-revealed" stories, and show you how, although but allegory, the basic fundamental idea behind the story might very well be true, and may I ask you to please follow me very closely, for it ties in with the rest of these Lessons in a very remarkable manner. Also it corroborates very clearly the message of Life I am giving to you.

I am not quoting from this Bible story because I believe it to be true for I know that it is not true, as written. I know that the Master Intelligence which created this earth—yon nebulae—yon planets with their satellites, did NOT engage in a conversation with a talking snake. I KNOW that is not a fact. I know further that it is not a fact that this great LIFE SPIRIT made a mistake when he created man, first pronouncing the creation "GOOD" and then discovering his mistake, pronounced it very wicked, and drowning them all out in a terrible flood. I KNOW that did not happen. Spiritual or God-Law does not operate that way. However, the Bible says it does so either the Bible or I am wrong. I leave it to my students to be the judge.

We shall look into the story however, for it's worth while analyzing and it gives perhaps the spiritual cause for mans "fall" if he ever had a "fall." Personally I don't believe he did. I believe it has been one continuous and incessant climb from the lower to the higher. We know positively that man is a product of evolution, and we know that he has never retrogressed. This Bible story, however deals with the "changes in manifestation from the spiritual to the physical, so I want to look into it at some length. Later on in this series of Lessons, I shall give you the scientific understanding of it, and that will be far more interesting, and far more true. There is an element of truth in this Bible story however, and I particularly want my students to be familiar with this phase of it. It bears heavily on your intelligent understanding of the Spiritual GOD-LAW, and while it may seem a little out of place perhaps to study any part of the Bible here, yet later you will see the wisdom of my doing so. Here it is and remember we are now dealing with the creation and fall of man.

The creation of man is not so important, but the fall is very important. Once more we find opinions differing as to how man was actually created. The story as given us by Moses was that God made man from the dust of the ground.

That statement to the Scientist and trained Psychologist is probably literally correct. But not in the way it is interpreted by those who believe in the word for word interpretation of this story of the creation as Moses gave it to us. I shall not take time here to enter into a scientific discussion of this question, as it is far too deep for this sort of a work. Those who believe the Moses story verbatim will probably fail to see what I mean when I state that the story is scientifically correct.

But it is—so we shall let it go at that. We have seen so far that God is Spirit, and there is no record to date of anyone having seen God as such. Not even Jesus ever saw the Living God. Furthermore, the scriptures teach that "no man hath seen God at any time." Moses stated that God formed man out of the dust of the ground, but God being SPIRIT, we cannot believe that He, with physical hands, moulded and shaped the dust or earth into the shape of a physical man, and then, when the man was made in earth, breathed into his nose the "breath of life." From what we have learned so far of what God essentially is, that would have been a physical impossibility. And besides—we shall see a little later that God does not create things in that manner.

So it seems that we must look for another explanation of the creation of man, other than the one given us by Moses. As far as the creation of woman goes, I personally cannot accept that, either. Moses says that God caused a deep sleep to fall upon Adam, and, when fast asleep, took a rib from his side and made a woman. It would have been far more simple for God to have made both man and woman out of dust at the same time, than for Him to have performed such a delicate operation as removing a rib and then transforming the rib into a woman.

However, probably the whole story of creation as Moses wrote it was only according to the wisdom of his day, and we shall not spend any more time discussing it—especially when we have a subject of far greater importance to discuss in this Lesson.

We are told that after God had finished His creation of man and woman He planted a garden and placed both the man and the woman in it to care for it. Now please remember at this point that there was not another human soul on this earth but this couple. Then, we are told, God gave to this couple certain things to do, telling them just what they could do and just what they could NOT do. From here on I shall ask you to follow me very closely please. for to grasp the following truths fully gives one a grasp on this "so-called" fall of man that he has never had before.

Here they were, the man and the woman, fresh from the hand of the Living God, and both in each other's presence, NAKED AND NOT KNOWING IT. Now I ask you to try and conceive of what sort of a being a man and woman would be, to be both together and naked, AND NOT BE ABLE TO COMPREHEND THE FACT THAT THEY WERE NAKED. For it was not 'til later that they knew they were naked.

Spend a little time in thought here, and try to imagine a couple so constituted that the presence of each other in a naked condition had no effect upon them at all. In fact, THEY DID NOT KNOW THEMSELVES THAT THEY WERE NAKED. Now listen a moment, please, I want to ask you a question here. Suppose for a moment that you and I were of such mentality that we could be placed in the same position as this first created couple were, AND NO THOUGHT OF THE PHYSICAL EVER ENTER OUR MINDS.

We would be a pretty spiritually minded couple, would we not? The fact of the matter is, however, that the first created couple, as this mighty Life Spirit made them, HAD NO SENSE OF THE PHYSICAL AT ALL.

They could not even see the physical. For had they been able to see each other as fleshly bodies, they would have known that they were unclothed. BUT THEY KNEW IT NOT. I am of the opinion here that they were purely spiritual creations, having no such thing as a physical body at all—either that, or they possessed a physical body and were not conscious of it, which means the same thing. I am of the further opinion that this part of the creation of man is identical to the part of the creation of the universe UP TO THE TIME GOD CALLED IT INTO EXISTENCE BY WORD OF MOUTH. We have very plainly seen that the initial creation of the earth was a mental creation. I believe the story of the creation of man up to this point to be similar creation. It could not have been any other kind.

Now we shall see what happened to cause man to become a physical being, and what caused that event to take place. What a pity it is that the event ever took place—but it did—there is no denying that fact. The next step in the story of man's creation (for you must remember that he is not yet in the form in which we have him today) runs about as follows: This first created man and woman had been told by this mighty Life Spirit which had created them that there were certain things which they MUST NOT DO.

Whether it was a literal apple tree or a literal gooseberry bush does not enter into the discussion at all. It makes no difference whether it was such or whether it was not. The fact of prime importance here is the fact that GOD TOLD THIS MAN AND THIS WOMAN THAT IF THEY DID CERTAIN THINGS, INEVITABLE DEATH WOULD FOLLOW. That is the prime factor just here. (And in passing let me call the student's attention to the fact that instead of the opening of the eyes of the man and woman bringing LIFE to them—it brought DEATH. Now note carefully—THIS DEATH IS WHAT WE CALL LIFE TODAY.)

And then we are told God left them alone. We are to presume here that both the man and the woman BELIEVED GOD when He informed them that they would die if they did a certain thing—disobeyed Him.

At this point there comes into the picture a sinister figure—and a figure that is responsible for the entire suffering of the human race to date. Moses says a serpent entered the garden. It makes no difference whether it was a snake or a porcupine that actually entered this garden where those two created beings of God were. The whole picture is entirely illustrative.

This snake, or whatever it might have been, speaking physically, went to the man and the woman, and asked them if it were a fact that God had told them that they would die if they did a certain thing. It makes no difference if that thing were the eating of an apple or anything else—remember that. The actual act is beside the point.

On being told that it was a fact that God had so informed this man and woman, this snake, or something it represents, said unto the couple, in effect: "DID GOD SAY THAT YOU WOULD DIE? WELL, THAT ISN'T SO. DON'T WORRY ABOUT THAT. YOU WON'T DIE." Now, beloved student, hear me well. HAD THAT MAN AND THAT WOMAN THEN AND THERE HAVE SAID TO THE SNAKE "OH, YES, WE WILL DIE—GOD SAID SO," I should not be here writing this to you, and neither would you be in your room reading it.

NEITHER WOULD THERE BE A SINGLE SOLITARY THING IN THE ENTIRE UNIVERSE CONTRARY TO THE GREAT, IMMUTABLE GOD—NOT EXCEPTING THE EARTH ITSELF—for this entire world as we have it today is, in itself, contrary to and opposed to the great spiritual God. Had there been no disobedience on the part of that first couple, there would be nothing PHYSICAL IN THE ENTIRE CREATION. Remember that.

Had this man and woman taken THAT stand—how different it all would have been; but they didn't, and right here is the ACTUAL DEED THAT BROUGHT UPON THIS EARTH ALL THE MISERY, POVERTY, SICKNESS AND DEATH IT HAS EVER SEEN. AND THE FACT OR DEED WHICH CAUSED IT ALL WAS THE FACT THAT THE MAN AND WOMAN BELIEVED THE SNAKE IN PREFERENCE TO BELIEVING GOD. Do you see that?

Not only did they choose to believe the serpent, or what it represents, but they deliberately SHOWED THEIR DISBELIEF IN THE SPOKEN WORDS OF GOD BY ACTUALLY DOING THE VERY THING THAT GOD HAD COMMANDED THEM NOT TO DO. In other words. they showed this mighty Spirit that had created them that they would rather OBEY SOMEONE ELSE THAN HIM.

Now listen to what happened—and listen well. THE MOMENT THEY DELIBERATELY CHOSE TO OBEY THE SNAKE RATHER THAN GOD, AND THE MOMENT THEY ACTUALLY DISOBEYED GOD, THEIR EYES WERE OPENED AND THEY KNEW THEY WERE NAKED. If their eyes at this point were opened, then it must follow that they had been "closed" up to this point. Now just what effect did the opening of their eyes have on them? Only one effect, and that terrible in its consequences.

IT GAVE THEM THE CONSCIOUSNESS OF PHYSICAL EXISTENCE WHICH UP TO THAT POINT THEY HAD NEVER KNOWN. So you see, prior to the disobedience of God, there was NO SUCH A THING AS PHYSICAL CONSCIOUSNESS. THAT came when man's eyes were opened. And I shall state, in passing here, that when the same eyes are closed that were opened in the garden, then, and only then, can man be what he was before the "fall." This, Jesus came to do, as we shall see later.

What happened from that time on is more or less history, and we shall not concern ourselves with it here. The purpose of this Lesson is to show you the mighty significance of the fact of the "fall" of man, so that you may intelligently understand it, and understand the things which are to be told you further along in your studies.

What a simple thing it seems to listen to this story of the "fall" of man—and yet what vital truths are herein contained.

By this time you are beginning to grasp the truth as it has been presented to you, and as you slowly, but surely, grasp it, you will most assuredly see that this earth, and everything connected with it is the result of unbelief. You will also begin to grasp the truth that whatsoever we have on this earth is ONLY SECONDARY TO THINGS AS THEY REALLY ARE. The REAL things are the UNSEEN things. The things which are seen are temporal—but the things which are UNSEEN ——are eternal.

Another thing you can see is the fact that if the opening of the eyes of man to physical things closed his eyes to spiritual things, or. in other words, to THINGS AS THEY ARE, then, as long as we are physical, OUR EYES WILL STILL BE CLOSED TO THE REAL OR THE SPIRITUAL THINGS.

This, you will see, is the spiritual interpretation I put on the bible story of the creation and fall of man. It is a wonderful allegory. But truth is oft times veiled in myth and allegory, and you will do well to carry this picture in your mind, for it is in a way correct. It will help you later though, when I give you the true and the scientific explanation of the whole matter.

Now your exercises for the next two weeks are to be the very same as they have been. You are to keep constantly before you and in your thoughts, the thing you want to manifest in your life. As we progress, you will see the principle involved, and finally, the whole question will open up like a rose, and you will see the reason for what you are doing now. You are now releasing your DESIRES into the vast Cosmic—or God-Realm, and let me say to you that such desires, reaching the COSMIC-GOD, are ALWAYS REALIZED. Think over that for a moment. THEY ARE ALWAYS REALIZED. That is the Law or the Cosmic Realm. That is the Law or the great Life Spirit. That is the Law of God. THAT IS GOD.

The more earnestness you put into your thoughts and desires and affirmations, the faster will you progress towards your goal, and don't forget that while these exercises may seem simple, they are far from that, for they are spiritual or unseen exercises dealing with spiritual or unseen things, and remember. the spiritual realm is the realm from hence all physical manifestations come. I shall leave you here for two weeks. Be earnest. Be insistent. Be constant. DRIVE THE "THOUGHTS" INTO THE COSMIC OR GOD-RESERVOIR THAT WHAT YOU WANT TO BE IS ON ITS WAY TO YOU NOW. And it won't be long after the God-Law has begun to operate until you KNOW what is happening.

Cordially your friend.

SPECIAL FOR THIS LESSON

In addition to continuing the exercises as given in the previous lessons I want you to thoroughly memorize this little verse during the next two weeks.

INVICTUS

Out of the night that covers me,
Black as the pit from pole to pole,
I thank whatever gods may be
For my unconquerable soul.

In the fell clutch of circumstance
I have not winced nor cried aloud.
Under the bludgeonings of chance
My head is bloody, but unbowed.

It matters not how strait the gate
How charged with punishment the scroll,
I am the master of my Fate;
I am the Captain of my Soul.

W. E. Henley.

EXAMINATION QUESTIONS
FOR LESSON NO. 8

These examination questions are for your benefit and you should know the answers to them all. If they are not clear to you, read your Lesson again and again until they are clear.

1. Scientists are now nearly all agreed that behind the physical and material universe there moves a great unseen Force. Have we any ACTUAL EVIDENCE of such an unseen force?

2. Where must the inception of every physical or material thing be sought?

3. Compare the Bible story of the Fall of Jericho with the facts as disclosed by recent investigations and excavations.

4. That something has never occurred to date is no ground for asserting that it never can occur?

5. In what connection was the above statement made?

6. Does history record the crucifixion of any alleged "world-saviors"? How many?

7. Does history record the crucifixion of Christ?

8. Does history record any of the marvelous occurrences relating to Christ that are related in the Bible?

9. Between what years are the crucifixions of 14 alleged "world-saviors" recorded by history?

10. The Bible story of the "Fall of Man" is susceptible of a spiritual interpretation. Can you give it?

11. If the "opening of the eyes" of man to physical things "closed his eyes" to spiritual things, what conclusion must be drawn with reference to our present condition?

12. Can you repeat any of the stanzas of Henley's poem entitled "INVICTUS"?

LESSON 9

Dear friend and student:

I take pleasure in handing you lesson #9. You have probably been taught that you were a fallen creature who was born in sin and live in iniquity and other things along that order. This lesson will show you that you are no such a thing. It will show you that instead of having fallen, man has steadily climbed from the lower to the higher.

I want you to give a lot of time and thought to this lesson, and furthermore I want you to actually put the God-Law to the test in your own life. And let me repeat that there does exist a Spiritual power which you may contact and use in the attaining of every right desire of your heart.

Stay quiet and grasp to the full the immense Truths this lesson discloses for they ARE immense Truths.

Sincerely your friend and teacher,
FRANK B. ROBINSON

You will recall that in your last Lesson we took a glimpse at the subject of the creation and fall of man—among many other interesting things. We saw a little of the magnitude of the Power behind Creation. We saw that man has never FALLEN at all, but to the contrary, he has continually CLIMBED up through the ages, and from the "caveman" species up to his present stage of development. So please get away from the idea that you ever were a "fallen man" or a "lost sinner" in any sense of the word. What sort of a Creator would it be who would start a world rolling, and populated by a race of "guilty, lost, hell-deserving sinners"? What sort of an intelligence would that be? Do you think that story is true? Of course you don't—and neither do I.

Instead of the mighty Life Principle placing man on the earth to "fall into sin" and to retrograde, reserving a place of eternal punishment for him in the future, the mighty GOD-LAW, instead of holding a club over the heads of men and women, IS TRYING TO MAKE THEM SEE SOMETHING OF THE DYNAMIC UNSEEN SPIRITUAL POWER THAT IS AT THEIR DISPOSAL. That's what the God-Law is trying to do. And just as fast as man can assimilate the staggering fact of the existence and presence of this mighty God-Power, then just so fast will man continue to rise and climb to higher heights and nobler places than he has ever attained before. No matter what the VISION may be—no matter now high we place it—there is always power enough IN EXISTENCE HERE AND NOW, to make that vision attainable. You cannot WANT or DESIRE anything without first visualizing it, and you cannot visualize anything right and proper, WITHOUT ATTAINING IT, IF YOU USE THE MIGHTY DYNAMIC GOD-LAW FOR THAT PURPOSE.

All down through the ages, step by step, just as fast as man could visualize, the tremendous GOD-POWER has taken the human race by the hand, and, very slowly (For man is a stubborn animal) has led that man up to a little higher vision. You look into the Spiritual Realm a little bit—you believe what I am telling you about it—you venture just a tiny bit—and YOU FIND THE SPIRITUAL GOD-LAW WORKS. Then, you go just a little bit further, and there, as ever, you find this great unseen God-Law still awaiting you. Still it is beckoning you on to greater heights. And THE ONLY LIMITATIONS ON YOURSELF ARE THE LIMITATIONS PUT THERE BY YOU YOURSELF. For you certainly cannot limit God—can you? Do you think for a moment that this unseen dynamic Spiritual Law which brought life to the earth in the first place, cannot or will not rise to the occasion or to the emergency? And I place no limitations there either.

This great realm is above us and all around us—in fact all creation is pervaded by an unseen dynamic spiritual power—or LAW—whichever term you care to use, AND THIS UNSEEN DYNAMIC POWER OR LAW IS GOD. Now did you grasp that? It's revolutionary to be sure, but if you think this realm and this power do not exist—then try it out sometime and see.

One Bible paragrapher said: "IN HIM WE LIVE AND MOVE AND HAVE OUR BEING." And never was truer word than that ever spoken. My teaching takes that statement from the abstract realm, and places it right where it belongs—IN THE MATERIAL REALM HERE AND NOW. It may be all right for us to have a power in the sky that can do all sorts of things for us in the "future", that may all be true. But what good does that do you and me now. IT IS HERE AND NOW THAT WE WANT GOD TO OPERATE—not after we are dead. And besides, how much more valuable to us will a God be, who can, and will and DOES operate here and now, making it possible for us, THROUGH USING THE GOD-LAW, TO ACCOMPLISH WHATEVER WE WANT TO ACCOMPLISH. How much more reasonable is that than is the theory that after we die, then we shall have our desires in "the glory land" and other things on that and a similar order.

I would not have it inferred that I want to destroy anyone's hope of a future realm, but I DO want it understood, and understood plainly, that it is NOT TRUE THAT THE MIGHTY CREATOR ORDAINED THAT HIS POWER AND HIS BLESSINGS AND THE KNOWLEDGE 0F HIM ARE ALL RESERVED FOR "BEYOND THE TOMB". No one can prove that there is any life "beyond the tomb" in the first place, and if the "god" idea is logical at all, and if there be such a "god" which there is, then UNLESS THAT POWER CAN ACTUALLY AND LITERALLY OPERATE HERE AND NOW—IT IS OF NO USE TO US. Some good "Christians" here will now tell me that they would not sacrifice their childhood teachings under any consideration. All right—hang onto them—if they do you any good. Stick as close to them as you care to. But I shall warn you here that YOU MIGHT BE WRONG. It may be that scientific re search will show you that the theories you are depending on are not quite true after all. And suppose they are NOT true—what then?

You know—it is quite possible that a man may be mistaken. AND, IT IS QUITE POSSIBLE THAT AN ENTIRE ORGANIZATION MAY BE MISTAKEN TOO—ESPECIALLY IN THE REALM OF RELIGION—FOR A MORE SUPERSTITIOUS REALM NEVER EXISTED. Long before the "Christian" era, men and women could live as "pagans" in absolute security. But when the superstitious "Christian" religion came into vogue, then also came the peculiar "Christian" practice of burning men and women and little children alive at the stake. That cannot be denied. And such facts should be looked square in the face if the reasonable truth is to be discovered. At any rate, I am looking them square in the face. and it is such facts as that one that caused me to look elsewhere than the present day religious systems for the answer to the "god" proposition. And what a revelation I found.

I saw very plainly that those who were presuming to direct our spiritual destinies, were doing so on the authority of stories which were pagan and heathenish in the extreme. and stories utterly devoid of truth. Then, later, I saw the first faint inkling of the LIGHT 0F GOD. And what a light it is. Just think for a moment, my student, of the existence of a GOD-LAW, so dynamic that all other LAWS or FORCES fade into insignificance beside it.

Just think of the existence of a mighty spiritual power—a mighty "GOD" whose power in creating the world is HERE AT YOUR DISPOSAL HERE AND NOW. Think of that. Is that too startling? Well it isn't startling enough to express the profundity of the fact itself. For that Law exists. THAT LAW IS GOD——THE ONLY TRUE GOD THE WORLD HAS EVER KNOWN OR EVER WILL KNOW. And with the Law comes the method of putting the LAW into operation. And what a simple method it is. Had there never been any "supernaturally-revealed" religion on earth, then the fact of the existence of God would automatically have been discovered. But now that "supernaturally-revealed" religion has gotten hold of folks. it is going to take some little time to eradicate the radical tendencies inherent in man's mentality. For you cannot blot out the teachings of generations over night. You cannot change a line of thought at once. It will take time. But the time is now here and the old globe is awaiting a new revelation from God. Well—it will have one—although not in the way the churches expect it to come.

It will never come by the return of Jesus Christ from the skies or anything on that order. BUT IT WILL COME THROUGH MEN AND WOMEN ACTUALLY AND LITERALLY BELIEVING IN THE EXISTENCE 0F THE LIVING GOD AS AN UNSEEN SPIRITUAL POWER—HERE AND NOW. And that is the only way the revelation will come. We saw in a previous Lesson that the very ether is full of emanations called "cosmic rays". We saw the immense possibilities of this staggering fact. Recently I received a letter asking the very direct question as to whether or not I believed that these "cosmic rays" were God. I shall not say here what I believe about that particular point, for it might hinder the understanding of God that you are going to receive before you finish your studies with me. For I want every single student without exception to see the marvelously real fact of the present existence of this Master Intelligence—GOD, or as I call it, THE GOD-LAW.

I want every student to know, and to know beyond a shadow of a doubt, that this mighty Power exists. Whether the "cosmic rays" are God or not is aside from the point here. We do know that these "cosmic rays" exist. We do know that the fact of their existence proves the existence of at least electrical energy throughout the entire universe. We know also that there is such a thing as directing ones thoughts along this line into what has heretofore been known as "THE GREAT UNKNOWN" and with this realization in mind, we can very easily see the feasibility of directing our thoughts into this great realm on what might be called infinity. That is a fact. The "subconscious mind" theory is NOT the answer. That is a man-made theory arrived at by some quite popular and brilliant scientific men, but advanced science has disproven that theory. As science advances, it first accepts a theory, and then when another PROVEN theory is found, it embraces it and discards the other one. But it ever changes, dealing always and ever with the FACTS AS THEY ARE KNOWN TO EXIST. The one who will NEVER change his or her ideas to meet the advances of scientific and psychical research, will stagnate and die. Yet we find them though, still willing to hang to theories so old that they create an obnoxious odor whenever and wherever they are aired. No—religion can well discard a lot of things handed down to it from the dark ages, and in the discarding of these things, it may find God. They will never find Him in them, because what they teach does not exist and never did exist. There lies on my desk as I write this, a letter from a Baptist preacher, and here is what he says, in part: "Your teachings are certainly DYNAMITE to orthodox religion—BUT I FIND MYSELF ACCEPTING THEM AND DISCARDING THE RELIGION I HAVE BEEN TAUGHT FROM BOYHOOD."

That's fine—and I can tell him where there are thousands more who are discarding it too. They are throwing away the "future" for the "now". They are refusing to no longer take a chance on sacrificing their happiness, success, and health here and now, on the theory that will get all these things in "heaven." Many of them have suspected that "heaven" does not answer the story, and so they are looking for God here and now, and bless your soul they are finding Him. They are becoming acquainted with the greatest spiritual unseen dynamic LAW the world has ever known. And, finding this GOD-LAW, they KNOW now what is the truth of God. They find that the LAW satisfies. They find that it can and does, do the work when the CONDITIONS GOVERNING THE OPERATION OF THE

LAW ARE MET.

At this point in our studies, the question of suffering, and that mythical monster SIN enters the argument, and I deem it quite necessary at this point of our journey, to get hold of Mr. "Sin", and take a look at him and find out if we can, just what he is and just what he is not. This is necessary to an intelligent study of the Lessons to come. And bear in mind, those of you who may be tempted to get in a little hurry, that you must learn the truths I am giving you slowly. Yesterday a man wrote me asking me to send the Lessons all at once. He stated that he was of sufficient mentality to grasp these supreme facts of life INSTANTLY. Well—perhaps he is—but if he has that sort of a mentality the world surely would have heard of him—but it hasn't to date.

And if you think for a moment that a cursory reading of these Lessons, interesting though they are, will teach you these mighty truths of God, then let me assure you that you are much mistaken. You will have to ACTUALLY PUT THIS GOD-LAW TO THE TEST YOURSELF IN YOUR OWN LIFE, before you will know whether it works or not. It won't do you any good to have me tell you that it exists, and have you mentally agree with me—that will get you nowhere. BUT THE ACTUAL CONTACTING OF THE GOD-LAW, AS THE ACTUAL TEST OF THESE TRUTHS WILL CONVINCE YOU, AND VERY QUICKLY TOO. THAT THIS GOD-LAW EXISTS AND EXISTS HERE AND NOW FOR YOU. What is it you want? Well believe me you can have it, if it is a right and proper thing, through the GOD-LAW. Through the Living God-Spirit. But not by reading about it. You will have to actually DO THE THINGS I TELL YOU TO DO, AND THEN, you will KNOW whether I know what I am talking about or not. But we shall have to progress for I want to look into the story of Mr. "SIN" and see what we can discover about him. Here once more we shall deal with the subject as present day religion handles it, and for the time being I shall quote their story. For, as ever, underneath the fable—underneath the myth—underneath the allegory, there lies the germ of a great spiritual truth. The religious heads haven't seen it yet. They will though, and when that time comes I think perhaps some of them will be honest enough to come out into the limelight and tell us that they were mistaken in their theories.

According to their story, the two first created people on this earth were responsible for this "sin" proposition. They were put into a garden and told not to do a certain thing. They were not to eat any fruit. It makes no difference what sort of a tree or a bush it was, whether an apple tree or a gooseberry bush—the fact remains that this first created man and woman were put in this garden by "God" and told not to eat fruit. Fruit is good for us today but evidently in that day it was not suited to the peculiar manufacture of their bodies, else God would not have forbidden them to eat it. At any rate, into the garden came a snake. A talking snake. And this snake entered into a conversation with Adam and Eve, and he evidently had ideas of his own about the effects of fruit. For he denied the story that God had told Adam and Eve, and did it in such an effective manner, that he made his point, and God had to take second place with this talking snake in the matter of salesmanship. For the only two people on earth. fresh from the hand of God, paid more attention to this loquacious serpent than they did to the God who had just created them. They ate the fruit.

So, according to the Bible story, we plainly see that it was our own ancestors away back yonder, who, when they were enjoying the bliss of perfect communion with God, deliberately chose to throw it away, and all the joys attendant with it. They deliberately threw away the liberty which comes from perfect communion with a perfect God, and by so doing, they lost this communion and brought death, disease, sickness and poverty not only to themselves, but to the entire human race,—YOU AND ME INCLUDED. What a pity. But the result is here though, and just because those two, fresh from the hand of God ate fruit when God told them not to, you and I are under a terrible curse, which curse cannot be removed unless we go through a certain experience prescribed by certain religious organizations teaching this story. As a matter of fact, however, neither you nor me nor any other sane person ever really believes such a story as this one is. Reason reigns supreme where this sort of a yarn is concerned, and even the "super-orthodox" sometimes give way a little bit and question the truth of it.

The big idea under it all though, is the fact or rather the theory that this first created couple WOULD NOT BELIEVE GOD. They showed their utter disregard for what God had told them, and incidentally insulted him by taking the word of a talking snake in the place of the word of the Living God, the Creator of the universe.

Now watch closely here, for this whole story of the "fall of man" even though it be pagan myth and allegory which it undoubtedly is, IS DESIGNED TO TEACH THAT RANK UNBELIEF OF GOD WAS THE FIRST CAUSE OF MAN'S HELPLESS AND FALLEN CONDITION. And at this point, if the religionists will discard the "garden of Eden" and the "talking snake" story, I heartily agree with them. They will not be able to see it, but I do though. And more than that, unbelief in the Power of the mighty LIFE-SPIRIT TODAY, IS THE VERY THING THAT IS KEEPING MEN AND WOMEN WITH THEIR NOSES TO THE GRINDSTONE TODAY. And furthermore, THIS UNBELIEF OR DOUBT OF GOD IS THE ONLY SIN THERE IS IN THE UNIVERSE. For every sin in existence can be directly traceable to that great monster of "SIN" or doubt of the Power of the Living God, to do for us what it is we want done today, AND NOT IN THE "FUTURE" AT ALL.

People doubt the existence of God, and I don't blame them either for doubting the existence of such a God as the present day religionists teach—not at all do I blame them, and for that matter, the whole story is myth for such a God as that one never did exist. The mighty Master Intelligence behind this universe DID NOT NEED TO RESORT TO CONVERSATIONS WITH TALKING SNAKES, and any story that he did is a LIE. And a one hundred percent LIE at that. But the fact that doubt of the Life Spirit itself being the cause of all sin, cannot be questioned. Here today, we have in existence a Power, so dynamic and so potent, that it is able to take two little germs, and in nine months make a complete and superbly marvelous human being out of them and IS CAPABLE OF DOING THAT ANY DAY IN THE WEEK AND HERE AND NOW. And yet, men and women WILL NOT BELIEVE IN THE EXISTENCE OF THIS POWER EVEN THOUGH THEY ARE SURROUNDED BY IT AND EVEN THOUGH IT BROUGHT THEM PERSONALLY INTO BEING. THEY STILL DOUBT IT.

People write to me by the thousands telling me that they are sick and tired of poverty, illness, etc., and they try this—and then they try that. The most of them have discarded the church teachings long ago, and many of them take up with Christian Science. The "supernaturally-revealed" religion story did not have anything to offer them or stories on a par with the "talking-snake" story, and being honest, these good folks, of course, are looking elsewhere for the truth. A good many of them are finding it too. But here they are—on every hand—crying against this and crying that. This circumstance doesn't suit them, and neither does that circumstance. Their hearts are crying for the truth—bleeding for it some of them. and, just because they have been taught that they could never know God until "after they die", they are of all people the most miserable. They cannot and do not believe that this same God who held the conversation with the talking snake sent a one-third of himself down to earth to be brutally murdered in order that those few who accept that story might be "saved".

Like any other reasoning mind, they do NOT BELIEVE THAT STORY. And neither do I. So they wander round and honestly and intelligently try to find the answer. And most of them find that the further they get away from "supernaturalism" the more apt they are to find God, for if ever God were anything at all, HE IS A PERFECTLY NATURAL GOD AND ONE THAT CAN VERY EASILY BE COMPREHENDED BY THE REASON OF A CHILD. And never you forget that. For, as a famous "doubter" once said: "Anything in religion that does not appeal to the mind of a child—is not true." Nor is it. This world is made up of human beings. Some are black, some are yellow, and some are white, while others are brown and various other colors. Now it must be a fact, that a universal GOD must be a GOD who appeals to ALL NATIONS AND RACES, and one who CAN BE UNDERSTOOD BY THEM ALL. This teaching that only ONE system of religion has the truth and all the rest are damned, is an utterly false teaching, and the very brand of falsity is stamped on it by such a teaching.

GOD—AS HE EXISTS—IF THERE BE A GOD—MUST NEED BE SUCH A GOD THAT EVERY MAN OF EVERY NATION CAN GRASP HIM. And that is exactly the facts of the mighty LIFE SPIRIT as it exists. Rather a marvelous thought is it not? Well, it's the truth. And when the conditions—the very simple conditions—governing the mighty unseen GOD-LAW are complied with, it makes no difference whether it is a China man who complied with them, or a South Sea Islander or a good old-fashioned Yankee. You cannot put into play the conditions governing this mighty GOD-LAW, without RECEIVING FROM THAT MIGHTY LAW, WHATSOEVER THINGS YOU DESIRE, and please remember that. A universal God is the only sort of a God that will fit a universal race. And a universal God-Law is the only sort of a spiritual power the race will accept.

It will take so much paganism. It will take just so much "supernaturally revealed" religion, but it won't take too much, and it is taking very little of that any more. And then the time will come when men and women will discard the whole thing if they can't get any satisfaction from it. And millions today have lost their faith in any God, because of what has been taught them by professing "religionists" who, by the way, teach a system of "supernaturally revealed" religion. So, finding that this brand fails and does nothing tangible for them now, they miss the point by stating that there is no God at all. And the professing religionists are alone responsible for this condition. No one else. But this is evidenced by the upward trend of evolution.

John Calvin, being the founder of Presbyterianism, persecuted Michael Servitus and was the cause of his being burned alive at the stake, and not 400 years ago either. But John Calvin founded one of the strongest Protestant systems of religion in existence just the same. Would you want to follow today any system of religion founded by a man of that type? I don't think so, and while, of course, these differing structures have changed somewhat, yet ESSENTIALLY THEY ARE THE SAME AT HEART FOR THEY ARE FOUNDED 0N THE SUPERSTITIONS SUCH MEN AS CALVIN BELIEVED. These are facts. They may hurt the feelings of the good Presbyterians but they still remain facts. And that is all I am interested in—THE FACTS. Naturally I have a lot of enemies amongst "orthodox religionists" but that is but natural. The time is here when we MUST know the truth of GOD or go down to absolute oblivion, missing the greatest Power the world has ever known.

For over and above all present day "supernaturally-revealed" teaching, there exists, and there has ever existed, AN UNSEEN DYNAMIC SPIRITUAL POWER SO STAGGERING IN ITS IMMENSITY THAT IT IS ALMOST UNBELIEVABLE. And this Power has been in existence all the while those professing "religion" have been vainly endeavoring to make people accept their foolish story. Outside of all that—there has always been this Power. There has always been this

GOD-LAW, but unrecognized by the professors of religion because they believed that they had the only God there is, when as a matter of fact all they have is "Yah-veh" or Jehovah. who never was more than a Jewish tribal God, and who never had any existence at all for that matter. But this is the God the "supernaturalists" worship today.

Just this morning came in a letter from a minister saying: "Can it be possible that there is a God-Power in existence that the church has never known? Can it be possible that we do not know God at all?" And my reply to that brother was that not only was it possible, BUT IT IS THE VERY CONDITION THAT NOW EXISTS. And that is the reason people on the street smile when religion and the church is mentioned. That is the reason the pews are empty and spasmodic "revival" tactics adopted in a useless effort to "stimulate trade". The reason goes deep. It has been hidden for a long time—but it's coming to light today though, because MEN AND WOMEN HAVE MADE UP THEIR MINDS TO FIND GOD. And when that happens you may depend upon it some man will arise to point the way. That is my mission in life. To point men and women to the existence of the most dynamic power this world has ever seen—THE POWER OF THE GOD-LAW.

And are they accepting it? I think so. And if you could see my files you would think so also I assure you. And this is the Power I am slowly but surely leading you to find. Don't be in a hurry, for I must logically make every point along the journey plain to you. This teaching is quite revolutionary, and so I must explain why this God-Law has not been recognized before. And to those who believe "orthodox theology" may I say that the new vision of the God Law coming to the earth will very effectively show up the hollow sham that has masqueraded for so long in the name of GOD. This is not a pity at all, it's the most blessed thing the world has ever seen. For you let the knowledge and the power of the Life Spirit once become universally known, and all this so-called "sin" proposition will very soon vanish away. This poverty business will go also. And as my students are rapidly finding out, they will KNOW THAT THIS GOD-LAW EXISTS, AND EXISTS HERE AND NOW, AND IS ABUNDANTLY ABLE TO DO FOR THEM WHATSOEVER THEY CANNOT DO FOR THEMSELVES.

The fly, crawling around on the ceiling, is perfectly oblivious to the fact that it is a ceiling he is crawling on. He does not know that that ceiling is part of what is called a room. Nor does he or she know, as they crawl around there that the room they are in is but one room in a house. Nor is the fly cognizant of the fact that the house is part of a block of houses. Nor does he know that the block is part of a street. And it does not know that the street is part of a city. It thinks that ALL IT SEES IS THE WHOLE OF THE WORLD. AND IT IS AS FAR AS THAT FLY GOES. FOR ITS VISION IS LIMITED BY ITS MATERIAL SENSES. It does not know that the city is but one of thousands of cities making up a nation. It does not know that nations are many on this earth, nor does it know that nation flies at the throat of nation, and that every so often bloodshed tints the earth a deep crimson red—bloodshed that never would be had there never been any "supernaturally-revealed" religion in the world. The fly does not know that. Nor does it know that there is a sun, or a moon, or stars, and certainly it does not know that there are planets and nebulae millions and billions of miles away from the earth.

All that fly knows is what it can see. It can see its immediate surroundings—and that is all. The human race is somewhat like that fly. And especially is this so of the religious phase of human life. And, because there are things in existence which the religious eye could not see, it has immediately gone on the assumption that such things are reserved for "after death" and has put a "supernatural" construction on everything it could not understand, and then buried and cast off the whole under the cloak of "GOD IN HEAVEN". As a matter of fact, nothing is farther from the truth. But—like the little fly—he is not conscious of the immensity of the universe, neither are many people conscious of the majestic and invulnerable SPIRITUAL GOD-LAW OPERATING HERE AND NOW FOR THEM. For YOU if you please.

Try and grasp the picture this Lesson has taught you. In your evening efforts, continue the same practices I have been giving you, and LET THE THOUGHT OF WHAT YOU DESIRE GO OUT INTO THAT GREAT COSMIC REALM. FOR SOONER OR LATER IT WILL FIND THE GREAT SOURCE OF THE LAW, AND THEN WILL BEGIN TO MANIFEST IN THE UNSEEN REALM, THE VERY THINGS YOU WANT TO MANIFEST HERE. THEY WILL BEGIN TO MANIFEST IN THE "HEART" OF GOD SO TO SPEAK. Don't bother your head here about HOW these things will come. Just KEEP THE THOUGHTS AND THE DESIRES GOING OUT INTO THE SPIRITUAL REALM IN A CONTINUAL STREAM—and you will know some day whether or not there is a GOD-LAW in existence which unseen Spiritual Law is so dynamic that all other laws and forces fade into insignificance beside it.

One word of caution here—keep continually on the EXPECTANT side of Life. LOOK FOR THE THINGS YOU ARE NEEDING TO HAPPEN. I will not go into the "manifestation" of these things here, because another Lesson deals with that subject. BUT KEEP THOSE THOUGHTS UPPERMOST IN YOUR THOUGHT REALM, AND REALIZE THAT YOUR DESIRE, AND THE ACTUAL THING ITSELF, ARE BUT DIFFERENT ENDS OF THE SAME THING. Did you understand that last statement? Read it again, and grasp the fact that YOUR DESIRE and the ACTUAL MANIFESTATION OF THE THING DESIRED, are in the spiritual realm, BOTH THE SAME THING.

You are at the receiving end of it, while the GOD-LAW is at the other end. This is as far as we shall go in this Lesson, but don't forget to write me if everything is not clear. Don't anticipate, however, as many questions on your lips now will be answered in forthcoming Lessons. I shall be glad to hear of the changes that are coming to you, and also of the actual manifestations as you make them. Be as happy and as enthusiastic as you care to be over the changes which come to you, and don't try to control whatever joy comes to you. When that comes, that is the time to shout if you want to. For this feeling of supreme happiness is but an evidence of the actual presence of this mighty GOD-LAW.

Many of you will feel certain "vibrations" perhaps, but many more will not. They are marvelous to those who do experience them, but are not at all necessary, and if you do not receive evidence of the existence of the GOD-LAW through these "vibrations" you will receive it some other way.

And now, without the slightest semblance of religious superstition may I leave with you my very kindest and heartfelt wishes, and until the next Lesson may I say to you—BE STRONG IN THE POWER 0F THE MIGHTY LIFE SPIRIT.

Cordially your friend,

P.S. I am not emphasizing any special point to remember in this lesson as the important point runs through all the material. To obtain a clear idea of the thought contained in this lesson it should be read over a number of times.—F.B.R.

EXAMINATION QUESTIONS
FOR LESSON No. 9

These examination questions are for your benefit and you should know the answers to them all. If they are not clear to you, read your Lesson again and again until they are clear.

1. Does history support or contradict the story of the "Fall of Man"?

2. How far can one go in his use of the God-Law?

3. What will be the character of the New Revelation?

4. To know whether or not the God-Law works, something more is necessary than to merely accept these Lessons as true?

5. What is the great spiritual truth that lies underneath the story of the "Fall of man"?

6. What are the conditions of a Universal God? Are these conditions fulfilled by the God-Law?

7. For what purpose does this Lesson use the illustration of a fly crawling on the ceiling?

8. Where will the thought of what you desire be manifested first?

9. What is meant by saying that your desire and the thing itself are both the same thing?

10. Who was John Calvin? By what act of cruelty was his life as a religious teacher discredited?

11. Is it necessary for one to receive "vibrations" as evidence of the existence of the God-Law?

12. Upon what side of life does this Lesson instruct to "keep continually"?

LESSON 10

Dear friend and student:

I take pleasure in handing to you now Lesson No. 10. This Lesson is one of the most profound Lessons of the entire course of instruction, and you will do well to follow it very closely. Also—please remember—the more time you spend alone with these Lessons, and the more time you give to your exercises, the better it will be for you. Remember also that if there is any limit to the Power of the Great God-Law, then I have not been able to find it.

Keep quiet at all times. If you keep quiet enough, the God-Law will have an opportunity to work through you and to manifest to you something of its Presence and Power. Be sure and comprehend the part of this Lesson dealing with your "thoughts" for it is quite possible that you will have a different idea of "thoughts" before you finish these studies. Remember this—THE LAW WORKS WHENEVER AND WHEREVER THE CONDITIONS ARE COMPLIED WITH. This LAW is GOD, and it HAS to work because GOD is TRUE.

Sincerely your friend and teacher,
FRANK B. ROBINSON

In this Lesson I am going to go over the ground covered by us to date in our studies together, and then I shall show you the principle involved, and show you something of the way the GOD-LAW works in the human life. I want you to pay very special attention, to this Lesson, for you MUST grasp it. You MUST know how to put this infinite GOD-LAW to work in your own individual Life. That is what you want, and that is what I want for you. Generalities are fine. Interesting reading matter is fine. Theories are fine. Many of them are true—but unless you understand the theory, and put it to work in your own life, THEREBY MAKING A FACT OUT OF A THEORY, then your studies will not be as valuable to you as they otherwise would be. The LAW exists, and by this time you know it. You must know it.

Now, what we want to do is to put it to work in your own life. And I am speaking here to every individual student I have all over the world. It makes not so much difference where you are, nor does it make so much difference just what you do. For the universal GOD-LAW is more than sufficient for every and all circumstances, and it operates with unerring precision, whether in Shanghai or in Timbuktu. It also operates equally as efficient in a black man as it does in a white, or a yellow man. Just as long as a person is a sane and normal human being—then the GOD-LAW will work, and it will NEVER FAIL. So you will be very foolish if you do not perfectly understand its operations, and not only that, if you do not avail yourself of these marvelous operations.

This mighty Law operates in a spiritual realm. It is a Spiritual Law.

Therefore you must not expect to SEE the Law work. You will see the results of its workings, but you will NEVER see it work. Nor can you explain by means of the five senses, just how it worked. Nor can you understand perhaps, the principle involved in its working. But these things you do not need to understand. All you need to know is that the LAW actually does work, and works here and now. That will be sufficient for you to know. For I doubt very much whether or not you care very much HOW this mighty GOD-LAW works, just as long as you know that it DOES WORK. You do not understand how or why electricity gives light. You cannot see electricity. You have never seen electricity. You never will see it. You see its effects. Nor do you, when you need the electric light, stand at the switch and start to try and figure out just how and why the electricity, contained in a bulb and through a wire, can, and does give light.

You are not interested in the "whys" and the "hows" at all. You are only interested in GETTING THE LIGHT. So it is in this invisible spiritual realm. You need the spiritual light, and. if you are wise, you will throw the spiritual switch, and the light will come, in much the same way that it does when you throw the electric switch in your home. If you throw the switch and the electric light in your homes does not light—then immediately you say, "WHY—THE POWER IS OFF." And you probably would be correct.

But in the dynamic unseen realm of the GOD-LAW, THERE IS NO SUCH THING AS THE "POWER BEING OFF." The switch may get out of order, or you may fail to throw it fully in, but ONCE THE SWITCH IS FULLY THROWN—THE POWER NEVER IS OFF. It is ALWAYS on. You will see here that the wise man will throw the switch into the spiritual realm—AND WILL LEAVE IT THROWN. HE WILL NEVER NEED TO PULL IT BECAUSE THIS SPIRITUAL POWER COSTS NOTHING. No Power Company sends a bill around at the end of the month, and insists that you pay it—not at all. For the Great Master Life Spirit IS, and IS as free as the very air you breathe. So throw the switch—leave it in—and then, through the power of the spiritual realm and the GOD-LAW, go out and do what you want to do in and through this mighty GOD-LAW. For it is a mighty LAW. Shall we look at that LAW for a moment and see just now mighty it is?

In passing, however, let me remind you that you must not try to understand this LAW now. For later you will see that it is none of the five senses that can recognize this GOD-LAW at all. It may be recognized, if necessary, through what may correctly be called a sixth sense. But I am not so much concerned here with the recognition of the operations of this LAW, as I am with the facts of the material results FOLLOWING its operation. For instance, I place a few grains of barley in a barrel filled with earth. I also place the same number of grains in a barrel filled with iron filings. In the course of time—the little grains I buried in the barrel containing the earth, will begin to sprout, and the first thing you know, sticking their tiny heads through the soil, will be seen little barley shoots. Quite natural—you say. YES—but try and explain it—if you can. You cannot, as a matter of fact, and it is useless for you to try to. BUT THE GOD-LAW WAS OPERATING IN THAT BARREL AND THROUGH THOSE BARLEY GRAINS JUST THE SAME. And all the scientists on earth can put their heads together, and scheme and plot and plan, and try, and they can never either explain those processes, nor can they duplicate them.

For this is outside of their realm. And the man has not been born yet who can define spiritual LAW or its operations. We KNOW the GOD-LAW exists. We KNOW its results are sure. But we cannot define its actions, nor can we understand what makes the LAW work as it does. So let us forget once and for all trying to comprehend the spiritual manner in which the GOD-LAW brings into manifestation the things from the spiritual realm. We know it does just that. And to date I have given you a little inkling of how it may be done. but I shall never attempt to tell you that I understand the marvelous spiritual processes by which it is done—for I would be lying to you if I did. And I try not to lie ever. Many people are amazed at the results I obtain in the field of spiritual healing. They absolutely cannot understand it. They see these things done, and they know that according to accepted "rules" they should not be done. BUT THEY ARE DONE. For in many and many cases in which the physician is stopped—I receive a wire and throw the mighty Power of the GOD-LAW into play—and the results ofttimes make people sit up and think.

Time and time and again I am asked by both physicians and ministers "HOW DO YOU DO IT?" "JUST WHAT IS THE POWER YOU USE?" "HAVE YOU ANY SPECIAL GIFT THAT ENABLES YOU TO DO THESE UNUSUAL THINGS?" And to all those questionings I reply that I do not know just how these things are done. An article recently appeared in a national magazine written by me, and dealing with this very thing. In that article I told my readers that I could not explain the processes by which these remarkable "cures" etc., were accomplished. And I repeat that statement here. I KNOW that when this mighty LAW is used, it is absolutely all-powerful, but I can not tell you just exactly how a germ such as the streptococcus is made to leave the throat of an afflicted child. Nor am I interested too much in that angle of it.

When people wire me in an emergency, all I am interested in is the recovery of that ill one. I don't sit down and try to figure out "how" the God-Law can do it, but I DO throw into play whatever little knowledge of God that I have, and the result is usually all that is to be desired. I don't lose very many cases. And here it may be well also to tell you that the GOD-LAW works far more effectively when you do not try to understand how it works. That's rather strange to some—but not to me, for I always remember that this is a Spiritual Law we are dealing with, and therefore, operating in a spiritual realm, we might better employ our time otherwise than in trying to find out "how" and "why" it works.

So in the case of the grains of barley. Surely neither the iron filings nor the earth in these two barrels are at all conscious that grains of barley have been placed in them. No one would say that. Neither can one say that the grains of barley themselves know that they are placed in barrels, the one to sprout and the other not to sprout. The grains are all about the same, and it would be the rankest kind of folly to say for one moment that either these little barley grains, or the earth, or the iron filings EVEN KNOW anything at all. Yet one grows and the other does not grow. But the answer cannot lie in the intelligence of either the grains of barley, the earth, nor yet the iron filings. I think you will see that. But these grains DO GROW. And they reproduce their kind also. Those in the filings will not do this.

The answer to this problem lies in the fact that the great spiritual GOD-LAW I am teaching you about, is operating in the case of the barley grains in the barrel of earth. IT CANNOT OPERATE IN THE BARREL CONTAINING THE BARLEY GRAINS MIXED WITH THE IRONS FILINGS. You ask me why it cannot operate in that particular barrel—you will receive your answer in a future Lesson and I shall not anticipate here. The grains of barley in the barrel containing the iron filings do not grow, BECAUSE THE SPIRITUAL GOD-LAW IS NOT BEING COMPLIED WITH. This answer will do for the present time. We know that when the grains are transferred to another barrel containing good earth, they WILL grow. They are now in a position in which the GOD-LAW can operate, BECAUSE THE CONDITIONS GOVERNING THAT LAW HAVE BEEN COMPLIED WITH.

So it is in your own life. Whenever the conditions in governing the GOD-LAW are complied with, THE RESULTS ARE VERY SURE. When they are NOT complied with, nothing but failure and disaster can ever manifest. Either that, or a very mediocre existence is lived, in which joy and happiness and health do not manifest themselves in a very marked manner. THE LAW IS NOT BEING COMPLIED WITH—AND FAILURE AND DISEASE AND UNHAPPINESS RESULT. So if there are those among my students who have been bothering their heads trying to understand just "why God permits this and why God permits that" then to such let me say that God has absolutely nothing whatsoever to do with these things. The GOD-LAW is NOT being complied with, and these unwanted things happen. But don't blame the GOD-LAW for that. DON'T BLAME IT FOR SOMETHING THAT HAPPENS THROUGH NONCOMPLIANCE WITH THAT MIGHTY LAW, for the Law is not concerned with anything in opposition to it. It is very vitally concerned with everything concerned, when these things are being done through the GOD-LAW itself. BUT IT IS NOT CONCERNED ABOUT WHAT HAPPENS IN VIOLATION OF

THE GOD-LAW. Remember that. And put it down right here and now that if there is manifesting in your life, things that are not so good, and things that you don't like any too well, put it down that your life is not being lived under conditions which the GOD-LAW can operate.

Where the GOD-LAW operates, there can be none of those unwanted things. You, however, are studying with me to try and find out how to put the GOD-LAW into operation in your own individual life. You want to know HOW TO INDIVIDUALIZE THE GOD LAW so that YOU can obtain the many benefits it can and does bring to every human soul complying with LAW, and that is the object of this Lesson—to show you just that. Always remembering, of course, that we shall not try to understand the methods the GOD-LAW uses to manifest these things. You may string piano wires zigzag across a dark room if you want to. Then place in that room a bat—a blind bat—and that bat will fly around in that room, AND NEVER HIT A PIANO WIRE. HOW? Well you don't know and neither do I. But here we see again the subtle unseen GOD-LAW, and we see it IN ACTUAL OPERATION. For it GUIDES THAT BAT BETWEEN THOSE PIANO WIRES, AND IT DOES IT WITH UNERRING ACCURACY.

You may place a female moth in an empty capsule. Seal that capsule inside another capsule. Then seal that capsule inside of still another capsule, and do that six times, making sure that no smell of any sort can escape from the innermost of those six capsules. Now—you may introduce a male moth into that room, and the first thing the male moth will do is to try and get inside those capsules. WHY? Well you don't know and neither do I. But I DO KNOW that here again we see the GOD-LAW IN ACTUAL OPERATION. You see what I mean? In my home I have in the parlor a beautiful glass goldfish bowl, and in that bowl are three wonderful goldfish. At the same time every night I feed those goldfish and at the same hour I change the water and wash the bowl out. When I enter that room every night to feed those fish, there is quite a commotion in that bowl and these three fish swim towards me and express their knowledge that I am there to feed them. WHY? You do not know and neither do I. But I DO KNOW that the mighty GOD-LAW TELLS THOSE FISH THAT IT IS FEEDING TIME. You would not attempt to tell me that just from force of habit those fish know that it is feeding time. If you do then I shall ask you HOW DO THEY KNOW IT? Here again we have but another manifestation of the subtle manner in which, whenever and wherever there is LIFE, the SPIRIT OF LIFE IS THERE IN SUFFICIENT POWER TO PROVIDE FOR THAT LIFE WHATEVER IS NECESSARY FOR THAT LIFE. Think that over a little bit. Whenever and wherever there is a human life, there is also the GOD-LAW. For this GOD-LAW created this human life in the first place, and it cannot be that after that creation (and I mean that individual creation) the GOD-LAW disappeared, to be seen and heard from no more. Not at all.

Now we have seen that your thoughts directed into what we may call "the ether," are met by, and perhaps go out upon or into these millions and billions of "cosmic rays." We know that a thought is the most powerful weapon which can be used to bring the GOD-LAW into play. We have seen that a thought is a very vital PART OF this mighty GOD-LAW. We have seen that the thoughts, to put this GOD-LAW into operation, must be directed into and charged with the one supreme thing in life most needed. EVERY NEGATIVE THOUGHT MUST BE PUT A THOUSAND MILES INTO THE NOWHERE. UNDER NO CIRCUMSTANCES MUST A FAILURE THOUGHT OR A NEGATIVE THOUGHT OF ANY KIND EVER BE ALLOWED TO ENTER YOUR HEAD. If they are allowed to enter, then your work is undone, for it takes twice as many positive thoughts to put out these "fear" thoughts. So don't entertain them. I might just as well say to you here that if you do entertain them, you will lose.

Some one about here is going to write to me and tell me that they "CAN'T HELP" these fear thoughts or these negative and destructive thoughts from coming into their heads. Well—if there be such a person in existence, then I feel very sorry for him or her. For when a person gets to the place where he tells me that he "CAN'T HELP" these thoughts from coming, then I say to such a one—"what a pity—where did you lose your manhood or your womanhood?" Yes, it's thrice a pity, for even a baby knows its own mind. And yet full grown men and women come to me and write to me and try to tell me that they can't control their own thoughts. What a pity I say again. For when one gets to the place in which he is not absolute master of his own thoughts, then I honestly feel sorry for him. For a thought is certainly the one thing above all others that CAN be mastered. It CAN be directed. It CAN be made to bring results from the spiritual realm—and it WILL bring them, when you are IN EARNEST ENOUGH TO SEE THAT YOUR THOUGHTS ARE WHAT THEY SHOULD BE.

There is no room in this world for the man or woman who cannot absolutely control his or her own thoughts. For that simply means that such a person cannot control him or herself. For the man or the woman is but the thought crystallized—and if one cannot direct his own thoughts, or choose which thoughts he wants to entertain, then I am doubly sorry for such a person. Life's choicest blessings are for the man or the woman who is absolute master of his or her own thoughts, and who, IN THE THOUGHT REALM, DECIDES TO BE WHATEVER HE OR SHE WANTS TO BE. For such a one by this attitude, IS THROWING INTO PLAY THE SPIRITUAL GOD-LAW, and SOONER WILL THE HEAVENS FALL THAN SUCH A ONE BE DISAPPOINTED. For the Power behind it all—the GOD-LAW behind it all—HAS ORDAINED THAT THE LAW GOVERNING ITS OWN OPERATION IS A LAW OF ABSOLUTE CONFIDENCE.

FIRST: Confidence in the Law itself.

SECOND: Confidence in one's self to use the LAW.

THIRD: Confidence in one's fellow men and women.

That will bring the Law into Play. That will make you an over-whelming victor in life—and don't you forget it brother or sister. For I know of no more dynamic way to GET THE RESULTS THAN TO SHOW THE MIGHTY INTELLIGENT GOD-LAW THAT YOU HAVE UTTER CONFIDENCE IN ITS EXISTENCE, AND ALSO IN ITS POWER T0 DO FOR YOU, HERE AND NOW.

Jesus said, "If ye had faith as a grain of mustard seed—etc.," and how well he knew what he was talking about. FAITH? There isn't very much of it on this earth, my friend. There is very little in one's fellow men, let alone in God. And yet—FAITH—and lots of it—is one of the necessary conditions necessary to the operation of the GOD-LAW. In fact it IS the LAW itself. Let me try to make that statement a little plainer if I may. The Law is that FAITH IN THE LAW BRINGS THE RESULT OR THE ANSWER TO ONES DESIRES. Now let me illustrate—and this informa-tion is first hand for it happened to me, and therefore I can speak with absolute certainty. Some time ago, and when this business of mine was in its infancy, there came a time when I did not know just what the future would be. I had had no publishing experience whatsoever and never before had I written anything for publication.

Here I was—practically a "greenhorn" one might say, and with an entirely new business on my hands, and running in opposition to long established and wealthy concerns. I had practically nothing. I had one thing though—I had an unshakable faith in the GOD-LAW and that means in reality I had everything. Now—there came this time I speak of. Magazines were wiring me—calling me from New York and Chicago on the telephone, and begging me to give them a page ad for their next issue. For the success of "PSYCHIANA" went through news agencies and advertising agencies at a very rapid rate, and I was besieged with requests for these full page ads I run. Now bear in mind please that full page ads in national magazines cost money—and some of them cost lots of it. I had practically nothing at that time—and further more—had I had no confi-dence in the GOD-LAW you would not be reading this Lesson now, for I should have been swallowed up in a very short order, as many have since that time who sought to imitate my methods and this teaching. They found that it could not be done—so they ran a couple of ads and then shut up shop.

Here I was though—not knowing for certainty whether I should "make the grade" or not. A few fellows had trusted me with a few hun-dred dollars each, and these boys could ill afford to lose it—and I didn't want them to lose it either. But I knew that if I had discovered some little of the ACTUAL TRUTHS of the REAL GOD—this teaching would go like wildfire. (Today—two years later I am sending my literature into 73 different countries). But as far as actual knowledge was concerned, outside of my faith in the GOD-LAW, I had no assurance that even my full page announcements would bring one single reply. But I knew that the world needed my teachings. I knew they were true, and, I ALSO KNEW THAT IF MY THEORY OF THE PHILOSOPHY OF LIFE AND GOD WAS CORRECT, THE GOD-LAW WOULD BE BEHIND ME ONE THOUSAND PER CENT. So, with a quiet smiling trust, I went ahead. One corporation wired me and I inserted ads to the tune of about two thousand dollars. Then the next day another one wired me, this one costing $1450.00 I ordered that ad in also. Then on top of all that I ran the circulation up to many millions, without even having the slightest idea where the money was coming from to pay for these ads, and the funniest part of it all was that I HAD NOT THE SLIGHTEST DOUBT OF THE GOD-LAW THAT THE MONEY WOULD COME FROM SOMEWHERE.

NOT FOR ONE INSTANT DID DOUBT OF GOD EVER ENTER MY MIND. So I did the thing that was needed to be done—and ordered the ads. Not many men would have done that—but I KNEW THAT I HAD CONFIDENCE IN THE GOD-LAW, AND I KNEW FURTHER THAT THIS CONFIDENCE WAS THE VERY THING WHICH MADE THE LAW OPERATE. I KNEW THAT. And so—never giving the bills a second thought, and with a sweet smiling confidence in the mighty ever-present unseen spiritual dynamic God-Law, I went about my daily business—and when the time came to pay the bills—they were paid. If I were to tell you the way in which the GOD-LAW worked in this case, you would have some time crediting your ears. For it was little short of uncanny—and I don't mean perhaps either. But the money came—the bills were discounted—and this thing is daily growing by leaps and bounds, as, all over the world men and women are finding that GOD LIVES AS THE MOST SUBTLE INVISIBLE FORCE IN EXISTENCE TODAY. And don't you forget it brother or sister.

NOW LISTEN TO ME SOME MORE—IT IS UTTERLY IMPOSSIBLE FOR YOU TO RELY ABSOLUTELY ON THE GOD-LAW FOR ANYTHING WITHOUT RECEIVING IT. You can try a thousand different ways to get what you want without the operation of the God-Law—but you CANNOT PUT IT INTO OPERATION WITHOUT YOUR DESIRES OR PRAYERS BEING ANSWERED. What do you think of that? And now let me tell you something else—WHEN ONCE YOU DEMONSTRATE EVEN THE TINIEST LITTLE BIT, THIS MIGHTY SPIRITUAL POWER—IT WILL BECOME SECOND NATURE TO YOU TO USE IT. You will never for one instant act outside of its realm. For you will know that to live apart from the God-Law would be very foolish. And let me say to you this also—there comes a sense of POWER to the man who relies upon the existence of the GOD-LAW in his life. That man gets somewhere and all the world knows that he is going somewhere too. For He is LINKED UP TO THE GREATEST POWER THIS WORLD HAS EVER KNOWN. It is the very same power that took the two little germ-cells I spoke about, and made YOU out of them. It is the very same invisible subtle POWER that gives the bat the guidance to miss the piano wires. And it is also the very same intelligence that tells the male moth that a female moth is hidden inside six sealed capsules. That is the sort of a POWER it is.

And it would be vain to try and tell me that such an intelligence could not and cannot guide EVERY MOMENT OF YOUR LIFE, AND EVERY ACTION OF THAT LIFE OF YOURS, SO THAT THE VERY THINGS YOU DESIRE CAN COME TO YOU. IT CAN. IT WILL. IT DOES. And the funny part of it all is that you will not be conscious of the fact that the GOD-LAW is at work for your benefit until the thing you want begins to shape itself up. Remember this please. Remember that this mighty GOD-LAW is invisible. Remember also that it only operates in an invisible spiritual realm—therefore YOU CANNOT SEE ITS OPERATIONS.

BUT YOU MAY KNOW WITH ABSOLUTE CONFIDENCE THAT IT IS WORKING IN YOUR BEHALF JUST AS LONG AS YOU ARE IMPRESSING ON THAT GOD-LAW THROUGH YOUR THOUGHT REALM, THE THINGS YOU DESIRE. Therefore—how manifestly foolish it would be for one to say that just because he did not understand the GOD-LAW—and just because he did not SEE it in operation—it was not working. That would be sheer nonsense. And the man or woman adopting that attitude NEVER WILL RECEIVE ANYTHING FROM THIS INVISIBLE LAW—THIS INVISIBLE GOD. He cannot. The LAW is not being complied with. This LAW is here for the very purpose and for no other purpose than to PROVIDE EVERY RIGHT THING THE HUMAN HEART CAN NEED. IT IS A LAW OF GOD THAT ALL SUCH THINGS SHALL BE. AND HE HAS PROVIDED IF YOU PLEASE, A NEVER FAILING LAW WHICH OPERATES TO THAT END. And the LAW has never failed yet.

The conditions fulfilling the Law or rather governing the Law are very simple. But until they are grasped those soaked in orthodox theology cannot see it. But that does not alter the fact of the existence of this mighty dynamic GOD-LAW. Denying the Law of Gravitation does not nullify that Law. It still works. Denying the Law of Electricity does not nullify that Law. It still works. Denying the existence of this God-Law does not nullify that Law. It still works. Those who deny its existence only STOP THE POWER FROM COMING INTO THEIR OWN LIVES. And again—where denying the existence of this God-Law stops automatically the Power from operating in the life of the one denying the Law—ACKNOWLEDGMENT OF THE LAW IS THE VERY FIRST STEP TOWARDS PUTTING THESE STAGGERING GOD-POWERS INTO PLAY IN YOUR OWN LIFE. FIRST—recognize the existence of the

LAW. Then—believe it. Then—test it out for yourself and see whether or not it works.

You turn on the electric light—never questioning. What is the result? Why the room is flooded with light. You trust in the God-Law and what is the result? Why the LIFE is flooded with this unseen spiritual God-Power. You automatically depend upon it—and IT NEVER FAILS. I wonder if you can do that. Do you think you can? Let me illustrate. Not so long ago a banker in the East wrote to me telling me that two of his banks were in distress. This good friend didn't know which way to turn. He knew of the existence of the GOD-LAW for he has followed me in everything I have written to date. But in the crisis of having two banks on the verge of failure—he weakened a little bit. Not much—but he did weaken a little. In the very moment he should have been strongest—he slipped a little. He was not sure of the proper move to make, and, as was quite natural—HE MADE THE WRONG MOVE. It did no harm in this case, for I should have said that he contemplated the wrong move. He got in touch with me though, and got straightened out, AND NEITHER BANK CLOSED ITS DOORS. From a totally unexpected angle came the relief. HE COMPLIED WITH THE GOD-LAW AND THE ANSWER WAS SURE. The bank was saved. BUT THE RESULT WAS THROUGH AN OPERATION OF THE GOD-LAW AND THROUGH THE CONSTANT REALIZATION ON THE PART OF THIS BANKER THAT SUCH A LAW EXISTED AND WAS SURE. In rather a miraculous manner, a certain way opened up—and lo and behold, instead of bemoaning the threatened failure of this man's two banks, he saw the foolishness of such worrying—and LET THE INTELLIGENCE OF GOD GUIDE. And it did. And as always—the man is more successful today than he ever was. And, as usual, there is no doubt NOW in that man's mind as to whether or not it is better to trust in the GOD-LAW, even through darkness, than it is to go ahead under one's own steam.

A letter came today noon from a man who owns a hotel worth $40,000. They took the hotel away from him last week on a mortgage of about $6,000—and this man writes me: "WHAT CAN I DO?" I haven't answered the letter yet—but do you know what I'm going to tell that man? I'm going to tell that man to DIRECT HIS THOUGHTS AND DESIRES CONTINUALLY INTO THE GOD-REALM—AND LEAVE THEM THERE. I shall tell that man to be wide awake for the leadings which will INEVITABLY COME TO HIM FROM THE SPIRITUAL REALM—THROUGH HIS OWN THOUGHT REALM—and if he will do that—and I know he will, before the year's grace is up he will have his hotel back and the mortgage will be paid. For he has one year in which to redeem it. And by the very simple plan of PUTTING THE GOD-LAW INTO OPERATION BY TRUSTING IT AND TELLING IT THAT IS DESIRED—THE RESULTS WILL BE SURE. There is no mistake about this. For just that is the whole purpose of the GOD-LAW. That is the reason it is here. That is the reason it was placed here millions of ages ago. DO YOU SEE THAT? For this GOD-LAW is RESPONSIBLE FOR EVERYTHING IN EXISTENCE—even you and me.

There never was a created thing that did not FIRST originate in the realm of this spiritual GOD-LAW. And there never can arise a circumstance which this God Law cannot change if a change is necessary. For this LAW is TRUTH. It is JUSTICE. It is LOVE. It is RIGHT. And greater than all—IT IS AN EVER PRESENT PROVIDING GOD. And don't you forget it. If you do not use this mighty Life Spirit—that is your fault—not mine. I am telling you of its existence, and I am showing you as intelligently and as earnestly as I possibly can, just how to use it. FIRST—recognize its presence. You know YOU are alive, so the God-Law must be there too. SECOND—recognize its POWER. THIRD—put the power into play NOW—and HERE—and for WHATEVER YOU NEED IN LIFE, and, to repeat, SOONER WILL THE HEAVENS FALL THAN YOU BE DISAPPOINTED. The only thing that can possibly hinder is a wavering faith. So don't waver.

Here is a student of mine working shall we say in a garage. He is a mechanic. He has nothing except his wages. He wants a nice home—he wants a good car—he wants to be happy. Now according to all the rules of the game, about the usual thing this student would say, before beginning his studies with me of course, would be something about like this: "Oh heck—I can't ever get any place. I can't ever save enough to buy a garage. It takes too much money to live these days." And the chances are that he never would get the garage he wanted. But you take that person, and let him make up his mind that HE WANTS THAT GARAGE. Let him make up his mind that he REALLY WANTS THAT HOME. And, being in earnest—he follows my studies implicitly. We find his predominating thought continually on that garage. We find him doing the exercises I have prescribed. We find that man SENDING HIS DESIRES OR THOUGHTS INTO THE GOD-REALM EVERY DAY AND EVERY NIGHT. We find that man having faith in the God-Law—and what happens. In the first place that man, perhaps unknown to himself, IS BRINGING INTO PLAY THE MOST DYNAMIC SPIRITUAL LAW THIS WORLD HAS EVER SEEN. HE IS BRINGING INTO PLAY THE VERY FORCE OR SPIRITUAL POWER THAT CAUSED THIS CREATED SCHEME TO BE. And, according to the God-Law, which by the way can NEVER FAIL, the things this young man wants ARE ALREADY BEGINNING TO MANIFEST SOMEWHERE. Somewhere—circumstances, and all unknown to this fellow—are shaping themselves so that this man can have his garage. What does it? Why the all consuming and universal GOD-LAW does it. For never was a man born yet—outside of that LAW. Never a circumstance yet—outside of that Law. Never a desire expressed yet—really expressed and the answer expected—outside of that Law—and these desire ALWAYS WIN. THEY

NEVER FAIL.

For don't you see—this great GOD-LAW is all in all. It is the Life Spirit that exists everywhere. It is the intelligence that guides the geese over the snow capped hills of Canada to sunny southern California. It is the MOTIVE POWER BEHIND EVERY MAN WHO WANTS TO ACHIEVE OR DO SOMETHING FOR HIMSELF. Get that, friend. The motive power—is the GOD-LAW. And this garage man, by directing his thoughts and desires to God, HAS ALREADY PUT INTO OPERATION THE LAW THAT CAN NEVER FAIL. And the only thing that can possibly stop the material manifestation of that garage, is for the young fellow to LOSE his FAITH—and quit. Even then sometimes these desired things manifest. The GOD-LAW, ONCE STARTED INTO ACTION FOR YOU AND ME, ALWAYS DOES WHAT WAS IMPRESSED UPON IT. This is what the Galilean Carpenter meant when he said: "ALL THINGS WHATSOEVER YE DESIRE, WHEN YE PRAY (DESIRE) BELIEVE THAT YE RECEIVE THEM, AND YE SHALL HAVE THEM." THIS IS THE LAW OF GOD. This is where the spiritual power lies.

And from time immemorial this same power has been going to waste because men and women did not know of the LAW involved. They couldn't see it—so they never suspected that such a LAW existed. They can't see radio waves either—and until a demonstration was made men didn't believe they existed either. But just as surely as the radio waves exist—.so does the God-Law exist. They listened to what the churches and superstitious religionists had to say about God, and they made up minds that the church God (in the sky) never could help them here and now. And they were correct. But the existence of this now known GOD-LAW never has been suspected, even by those who think they know the most about God today. What a pity.

But as I say, as this teaching becomes known, and as men and women begin to talk about it and spread abroad the results our students are obtaining, it will not be very long until this Power is universally known for what it is. Demonstration after demonstration will be made. Healing after healing will occur. Poverty will begin to wane. For men and women, for the first time in history, through my teachings I humbly must state, ARE GETTING A TINY GLIMPSE OF THE MARVELOUS GOD-LAW AT THEIR DISPOSAL. And no wonder they step out on this mighty Power and do things.

Here I am going to leave you once more until next week. Then I shall perhaps tell you the story of how, in less than two years, through the operations of the God-Law—I CHANGED ABSOLUTELY FAILURE AND POVERTY INTO GLORIOUS SUCCESS AND PLENTY. For you will remember—it is not two years yet since I lived in a rented apartment—had no money—no car—no life insurance—just a "job"—and a wife and baby. The GOD-LAW, however, in less than two short years changed all that. Now, through using the God-Law, I own a beautiful home, one of the best in Moscow, I own a wonderful Sedan—an extra lot next door to my home—I have had installed a beautiful pipe-organ in that home—I have many thousands of dollars worth of life insurance, and million upon millions of people have seen my picture and hundreds of thousands have heard my voice over the radio.

And the next Lesson will tell you something about how I did that. And you will certainly be interested in hearing about it, for I don't think it has ever been duplicated by anyone. Changes have been made all right—but I don't think as radical a change in as short a time. And on top of all that, I have thousands of students all over the world who are using the same methods for the same results, and my files tell mighty interesting stories of their successes.

Keep the thought of what you want directed into the spiritual God-Realm, and KEEP at it. REALIZE THAT THE CHANCES ARE THE THING YOU WANT IS ALREADY ON THE WAY TO YOU. DON'T FORGET THAT—AND LIVE IN THE CONSTANT EXPECTATION OF ITS MANIFESTATION. For it is yours in the moment you can rely on this mighty God Power to bring it. And remember—when the God-conditions are complied with, the God-Law never fails.

Cordially your friend and teacher,
FRANK B. ROBINSON

EXAMINATION QUESTIONS
FOR LESSON NO. 10

These examination questions are for your benefit and you should know the answers to them all. If they are not clear to you, read your Lesson again and again until they are clear.

1. What is the subject of Lesson 10?

2. You must not expect to see the God-Law work; Why not? What will you see?

3. Wherein does the God-Law resemble the electric light? Wherein does it differ?

4. What is the illustration of the barrel and the grains of barley? The lesson conveyed thereby?

5. How may this lesson be applied to your own life?

6. What is the most powerful instrument by which to bring the God-Law into play?

7. . "The God-Law ordained that the law governing its own operation is a law of absolute confidence." Confidence in what?

8. Faith in the God-Law brings the results desired. Doctor Robinson gives a striking example of this in the early history of PSYCHIANA?

9. When may you know, with absolute confidence, that the God Law is working in your behalf?

10. What is the first step towards putting the God-Law into play in your own life?

11. Three steps are required in all?

12. Jesus correctly expressed the God-Law in giving his directions for prayer. Can you quote the passage?

LESSON 11

Dear friend and student:

Here is Lesson number eleven. It is very important and also highly interesting and instructive. It will show you what one man was enabled to do and what he did do when he realized first of all his own impotence WITHOUT the Great God-Law, and his own IMPORTANCE WITH this Great God-Law. It is an admitted fact I think that the great unseen Spiritual God-Realm is by far the most important realm in existence. An electric light bulb is positively useless without electricity running through it. So are you without the God-Law running through you.

Study this important Lesson closely. Do faithfully the simple little exercises prescribed. PUT THE GOD-LAW TO WORK IN YOUR OWN LIFE. Then—when you really do that—just see what happens. For God is true. This mighty invisible Creative-Intelligence and Law really exists. Let it work for you.

Your friend and teacher,
FRANK B. ROBINSON

This is the Lesson in which I promised to tell you exactly the remarkable change from poverty to success which happened in my own life. For it was a remarkable change. I don't like to tell the story personally though, and wish someone else would tell it to you for me. There is quite a temptation where one is telling the story of his own success to over-estimate himself a little, but I know of that tendency so shall guard against it. I would not tell the story at all were it not for the fact that it will help you to realize something of the existence of the God Law, and in passing let me say that everything I have been enabled to do in the past two years is directly due to the presence and existence of the mighty spiritual power. So the GOD-LAW must have the credit for it all. True, it is that a knowledge or a faith in the existence of such a Spiritual Law or Power had to be there, but in reality the actual demonstration of the things done by this Power through me, is the very strongest sort of evidence that the Power exists.

I am no different now from what I have ever been. I am the same Frank B. Robinson. No change in my nature has occurred. I have not experienced any "supernatural" or "divine" change called "conversion"—not at all. The only change that has come to me is the fact that now, I believe in the existence and Power of the mighty LIFE SPIRIT, and I believe in it HERE and NOW. I used to believe that "GOD" is in "heaven" and would reward the "pilgrims" after death. Now I don't believe such chatter at all, for I KNOW that GOD is a LIVING and DYNAMIC POWER, EVERYWHERE, ALL OMNIPOTENT, AND BETTER THAN ALL, OPERATING OR RATHER IN EXISTENCE IN

ORDER THAT EVERY HUMAN BEING INCLUDING YOU AND ME CAN, HERE AND NOW, TAKE FROM THIS MIGHTY GOD THE THINGS WE NEED. This is exactly what the Galilean Carpenter preached, but it also is exactly what those pretending to be following Him DO NOT PREACH TODAY.

Until I had advanced this philosophy of life and God however, I had been a most miserable failure. Just the same sort of a failure that thousands write me today and tell me that they are. But in the very moment that I put the mighty GOD-LAW to work in my life of failure, then this life of mine was changed into a life of success and influence—AND IT WAS DONE IN MIGHTY SHORT ORDER TOO. For as this is written it is not yet 22 months since I was selling paints and powders and lipsticks and perfume behind a drugstore counter right here in Moscow for $175.00 a month. And I can say to you very frankly and very honestly here that had I not stepped out on the promises of God, I should still be there in that drugstore, and the chances are many to one that I would never have been heard of. It goes to show you how the mighty GOD-LAW really works.

I want you to follow this Lesson very carefully, for I shall cover the path trod by me step by step, and shall endeavor very earnestly to show you the things I did in order to put myself where this mighty God-Law could operate. In passing let me say that all failure that ever manifested in my life was not due to "the other powers of evil" as so many write me about, but was due in its entirety to my ignorance of the existence of the GOD-LAW here and now operating for my success. There are NOT two powers in the world—the one good and the other evil. There is but one Power—and that is all GOOD. People often write to me asking where the "devil" originated, etc. Only yesterday a preacher wrote to me asking where sickness, poverty, illness disease and "sin" came from if there were no "evil spirit" in existence as the Bible teaches. Well, I'll tell you. All of these unwanted things are NOT due to the "power of evil" at all. THEY ARE THE NATURAL RESULTS WHICH MUST FOLLOW A LIFE LIVED IN IGNORANCE OF THE GOD-LAW.

Darkness is NOT a thing. When you turn out the light at night in a room—you have darkness. But no such thing called "darkness" enters when the lights are turned off. Certainly not. For there is NO SUCH THING AS DARKNESS. If you think there is then take a shovel and try to shovel it out of the room. No, my friend, DARKNESS IS ONLY THE ABSENCE OF LIGHT. It is the normal natural condition that MUST exist where there is no light. And so failure, sickness, so-called "sin," and poverty, and disease, and unhappiness—ARE ALL THE NATURAL AND NORMAL RESULTS OF THE ABSENCE OF THE GOD-LAW IN THE HUMAN LIFE. Where the God-Law is NOT used—there can manifest nothing but failure and all the rest of these other things that are not so nice. THEY ARE NOT DUE TO A POWER OF "EVIL" AT ALL.

REMEMBER THIS PLEASE.

The same thing applies to what we call "success" and "failure." There is NO SUCH THING IN REALITY AS FAILURE—IT IS BUT THE ABSENCE OF SUCCESS. Do you see that? I think you will. The presence of "unhappiness" is not real—it is but the ABSENCE of the Law governing happiness. The same thing applies also to health. I do not say, of course, that there is no such thing as illness or disease, for anyone with ordinary brains knows that there is a lot of just those things in the world today. But I DO say that these things are all very unnatural, and EXIST ONLY BECAUSE THE GOD-LAW GOVERNING THEIR VERY OPPOSITES IS NOT BEING USED. You see—where the LAW exists, it exists only for the very things we desire. It exists only to manifest the very finer things of life. NO GOD-LAW COULD POSSIBLY MANIFEST UNHAPPINESS, SICKNESS, OR POVERTY. Such things are foreign to the GOD-LAW. Neither could this mighty invisible POWER manifest unhappiness or illness or disease.

And you may depend upon it that if you are poor, if you are unhappy, if you are ill, it is purely and simply because the GOD-LAW is NOT being used by you in your daily life. I don't care how far you want to carry this—by no possible means can the spiritual LAW of GOD manifest any of these very undesirable things. It is only the ABSENCE of the Law that makes these things real, or in fact that makes them exist at all. Many of us however, have believed for so long that poverty, failure, and unhappiness are a very fundamental part of the human race, that it seems mighty hard to grasp the fact that these things need not be. And they won't be either when the Power of the Living God is used against them. For is not God—LIFE? Can he be death in any sense of the word? Can this mighty God Law be illness or unhappiness in any sense of the word? I don't think so. One of my most frequent clashes with religionists is on account of their attitude and teaching that you and I are but "guilty, lost, hell-deserving sinners" or "pilgrims along life's highway," destined and expected to go through life with nothing more solid than hope of a "home in heaven" to comfort us. I don't believe that. I believe in the existence of the Spiritual GOD-LAW here and now. More than that, I KNOW that this spiritual LAW exists.

For many years I lived in complete ignorance of this mighty Law—but no more. For there is not a moment of the day in which I do not use it. I live in it—and so do you. So why not use it? If you don't use it, then it is simply because of your ignorance of its existence, or your apathy of life. However—I think the vast majority of my students really do want to be happy, successful, and healthy in life, and so I shall address myself to such students. Never does a day go by that I do not receive letters from happy and very satisfied students regarding the finding of the GOD-LAW and this fact alone, if no other, more than demonstrates the fact that such a Law—such a Power really exists. This being a fact, then the thing for you to do is to apply this mighty Law in your own life.

I shall never forget the fear and trembling with which I first stepped out—just a little step—on the mighty God-Law I believed to exist. Never shall I forget it. Here I was—a failure, and in me were all the racial tendencies of millions of years probably. All down through the ages these tendencies have been to "worship" some unseen power or other. But none of these quasi-religious teachings have ever taught anything other than the presumed fact that the unseen power they teach is a "divine" and therefore an unnatural power. There has had to be a "god" of some sort or other. Almost invariably this "god" lives "in the sky" somewhere. Men and women have been taught down through the ages to live in FEAR. FEAR of God. Fear of some of God's agents. Fear of one's self. Fear of hell fire. Fear of purgatory. Fear of being a "lost soul", etc.

And it is my contention that no really true religion can have its basis in fear of anyone or anything. Yet they all have. And this is the reason for their impotence—for it is useless to deny that the present day systems of religion are utterly impotent and useless as far as this human life goes. They are not destined to be of any use here. They deal with the future. They deal with an unknown "god". Therefore, it was but natural that there was a certain amount of hesitancy about my putting the GOD-LAW to the test. This was not at all a lack of faith on my part —but it was the natural sequence as I state, of hereditary tendencies and beliefs of thousands and perhaps millions of years, and I could not be blamed too much for it. I had it—I confess. You have it too the chances are, and it is but natural that the question as to the existence of a real Living God-Law which can operate here and now should be at times quite pertinent. Children give up their playthings reluctantly, and so these old idolatrous superstitions go slowly. They are going though—and they never went as fast as they are going today. We see it all over the world—and it's good to see too. And the reason they are going is simply because the human race as a whole is recognizing the fact that there is nothing of further interest in any of these systems of "supernaturally-revealed" religion.

We've had them on earth for centuries. And nothing enlightening has ever come from them. No help on earth has ever been received yet by anyone. True—it might be a fine thing for "after death" but you see there is no proof of that, and so, as the matter stands now, these systems are universally recognized to be quite useless. So we are discarding them. Their strain will remain though for many years to come, and it will probably be quite a few decades before the human race entirely discards ALL "supernaturally-revealed religion" and finds and uses only NATURALLY-REVEALED RELIGION. For that is the need of the world today. Men and women are caring less and less for the future and are more interested in the "here" and the "now." As I write this story of how the mighty God-Law changed my life, I find myself looking back over the years. I see the little country church at which my Dad preached. I remember the little house we lived in. I remember the stone wall with the wallflowers growing on top of it, and which separated our little home from that of the gentleman next door I remember distinctly sitting before the fire of the living room with a book in my hands containing pictures of Indians. I remember the old well in the yard with the water bucket attached, and I remember how I was warned never to go near that well under any circumstances.

I can remember back pretty well to the time I was less than one year old, but the one outstanding memory which will be forever planted in my mind is the memory of the day—a beautiful summer's day—on which I laid on my back on the grass in the little yard we had connected with the house. The sky was of an azure blue that day, and both sun and moon were visible. I just laid there—it was my third birthday I remember, and looked up into yon heavens. And I was somewhat awestruck with the magnificence of it all. My thoughts ran along the line of religion as taught in the old Baptist church by my Dad. Suddenly it seemed that I was lifted from that lawn, although of course I knew I was not, and there seemed to come to me a sense of the very nearness of God—the mighty Life Spirit I now am teaching. I was told it seemed, in an unmistakable manner that I should be used to bring to the world a new revelation of God. I seemed carried into a realm completely beyond this earthly sphere, and the impression then and there indelibly written on my young mind, WAS THE FACT OF THE EXISTENCE OF GOD RIGHT HERE ON THIS EARTH. I seemed to be told that what was masquerading as "religion" was utterly false, and I saw myself that day, leading a new and true system of thought with men and women by the thousands accepting it. (That dream of 43 years ago is coming true now—today). The vision or what-ever it was, was forgotten for many years though, and, like the rest of my brothers, I was brought up in the good old-fashioned "orthodox" way. A lost sinner, etc. No hope beyond the tomb. Divine revelation, etc. Repen-tance and conversion. And all the rest of it. But somehow or other it wouldn't take—and I surely am glad now that it didn't take. I have always thanked the powers that be for giving me an open honest nature, and a nature that will not accept anything as truth unless the presumption is strong that it is the truth. I will analyze what people say. I will put what they say up against what they do. I will very carefully examine a story—and if there be no evidence of the truth of the story, then, in the absence of other circumstances, I shall discard the story.

I shall not weary you with the complete story of my struggles through the years. It probably wouldn't interest you anyhow, and that is all being now written in another book, and perhaps you will read it in detail some day soon. Suffice it to say that all through the years, deeply religious as I was, there was ever and always an undying hunger for God. I wanted to know who and what He was. I wanted to know about Him. I suspected faintly that there might perhaps be some way that I did not know of, of coming to that mighty God and obtaining from Him whatever happiness my soul craved. But I didn't find it. I knew—and from close connection that my parents knew nothing about God even though Dad preached ABOUT this "god" of his, every day and twice on Sunday. But you see—I lived in that home—and I KNEW THAT NO POWER OF GOD WAS EVER MANIFESTED IN DAD'S LIFE AT ALL.

I knew that he didn't even believe the story he preached. With the mother however—it was a different story—for what an "angel" she was if ever there was one. She didn't live long after my birth however, perhaps ten years, so I never had the chance to know her real well. But say, that memory ever lingers with me. When she died, and the specialist was called, I was taken into the bedroom for a last look at her. I gazed on that dying form knowing full well that she was going. But I didn't realize what it meant. I didn't realize what death was. And a couple of days later when the casket lay on the bier in front of the old Baptist church, I sat with Dad in the front row. And still I didn't seem to realize what it all meant. The old reed-organ played "The sands of time are sinking,—the dawn of heaven breaks," and as the choir sang that wonderful old hymn with several others amongst which was "A few more years shall roll," I looked up at Dad. I saw there the tears streaming down his strong face, as his friend, the Rev. Henry Davis preached the funeral message and tried to comfort him. Looking up into that grief-scarred face I said—"Daddy, what are you crying for, you still have me." I only mention this experience here in order that you may intelligently picture the various steps through which I came in my search for God, which search ended in finding his mighty Power. Then the service was over. They carried her to the little cemetery and there, to this day, what remains of that tranquil soul rests.

On the way back in the hack, seeing Daddy heartbroken, I crept up to him and, putting my arms around his neck I said: "Don't cry Daddy—you'll see her in the morning." But the morning came and he didn't see her. And many mornings have come and gone since then, and still he hasn't seen her. And he never will. I think perhaps that death made a marked impression on me, for I continued my search for God according to the methods prescribed by the "orthodox religionists" and others who believe in the "unnatural story" of Jesus Christ coming down to earth to save the entire human race from its sins. But as I have stated—these methods did not work. They may work for others—but they DID NOT work for me. I think I have been to the "penitent form" over 100 times, and I know I was baptized seven times—and still it wouldn't work. However, one day after many years' searching—I just discarded the whole thing, and then things happened—I found God. Isn't it passing strange that I should find the God I was looking for when I denied that the story as told by those who said they represented God was true. That is the fact of it though.

But the years rolled by, and soon we found ourselves with absolutely no future at all. I had a job in a drug store here in Moscow. I was over 40 years of age and no life insurance, no money, no car, nothing at all. I was a registered pharmacist in several States, but as far as accomplishing anything worth while—well I had never done it. I was a rank and an out-and-out failure in life. We lived in a little rented apartment, and as fast as the skimpy salary came—it went again. The future was black. It held nothing for me. Upon discarding the theories taught to me in my youth, which theories of course were expected to make a "Christian" out of me, the light of the truth of God broke in my life. I have told you of that however, in the large lecture I sent to you so will not repeat it here. Just in passing may I say that after an entire lifetime spent in a fruitless attempt to find God by the methods given to me by the church and also my parents, the day came in which I was convinced that such methods DID NOT WORK. Therefore, I concluded that they must be untrue.

I also had very grave doubts shortly afterwards in regard to the entire Bible story and the plan of "salvation" as taught me in my childhood and youth. In my free lecture I told you of the day on which I finally, in desperation and disgust, threw all "supernaturally-revealed religion" to the four winds. I denied that the story of a "combination of man and God" coming to the earth to "save" people by the "repentance" and "salvation" method, was true. I knew that not a living soul had ever tried to find God any harder than I had, and I also knew that if he were not to be found after such efforts as I had put forth, the chances were that there never was such a being at all, who had created a "salvation" as hard to find as this one was. I have never denied the existence of a Master Intelligence, and even though I threw overboard the whole "Christian church" formula, that does not by any means infer that I threw overboard my beliefs in God. It just simply means that, that I threw overboard all faith in the "god" my parents and the numerous churches I had attended taught. As I looked into the story a little further, the more I learned of it and its origin, the less faith I had in any of it. I KNOW now that it is not true, although of course I could not know that then. Trustingly I had believed everything that my parents and the different preachers had told me, and swallowed the story hook, line, and sinker—as thousands are still doing.

Never for one instant did it ever occur to me that the story might be false, as I later proved it to be. I have thanked my parents many a time for raising a man who was so filled with the indomitable desire to find out the truth of God, that he was willing to challenge the entire structure if necessary in his search for the truth. And as the years rolled by, and as I attended theological school and continued my studies into "holy writ," I found out that the chances are that it is "wholly wrong" and nothing more or less than a remnant of idolatrous and pagan superstition. I claim the story told by the "orthodox church" today to be nothing more or less than that. Thousands of years before Christ was ever heard of, millions of people knew the story of the "supernatural" birth, in the "resurrection," the "ascension" etc., and I found that there was not a single thing that could be said in favor of Christ being the "savior" of the world, that could not also be said in favor of a dozen other crucified "saviors."

I learned that the authorship of the four gospels is absolutely unknown. I learned that no proof of the story was to be had. It was all based on "believe." And it is my contention that any system of thought or philosophy of life upon which we are asked to trust our soul's future welfare, should at least be capable of proof. And no system of religion should be allowed to operate in this country that cannot prove its claims. The church comes to us with a story that a certain man lived who was God. It tells us that we are lost sinners. It tells us that we're born in sin and shaped in iniquity, and it further tells us that unless we repent and be baptized and saved that we shall in no wise inherit the kingdom of heaven. It tells us that we are lost souls unless we accept the story it brings to us. It is my contention that the church should be made to PROVE the truth of that story—and if it cannot prove it, it should certainly not be allowed privileges no one else is allowed. However—this Lesson is not to show the falsity of the existing religious system at all, I merely mention these facts in passing to show that the definition and story of God that the church gives to the world is not true. At any rate—it cannot be proven, and in the absence of proof of its verity, I shall, in the light of my experiences with it, pronounce the teaching false.

So I say—I discarded the entire thing, and, strange to relate, the discarding of religious church tradition was the very thing that brought to me the first faint smattering of the truth of the LIFE SPIRIT—GOD—as He really exists. And the more convinced I became of the falsity of the church story, the more convinced and assured did I become of the existence of the real God—the Power the church knows nothing about. I KNEW ABSOLUTELY THAT THERE EXISTED HERE AND NOW, A DIVINELY NATURAL SPIRIT OR FORCE OR POWER THAT COULD BRING INTO EXISTENCE EVERYTHING THE HUMAN SOUL CAN POSSIBLY NEED, WHETHER IT BE HEALTH, SUCCESS, OR HAPPINESS. I say I knew that. I was as sure of it as I was that I was alive. I had not demonstrated any of its power in a material way yet, but I had been filled with a sweet peace of mind that I had never had before. I KNEW IN WHOM I WAS BELIEVING, and the ever present Power of the Living God was a revelation to me every day of my life.

But the gnawing at my soul for the good things of life was insistent and I wanted to do the things necessary to be done in order to actually manifest the good things of life I needed. Here I was, happy in the presence of the mighty Life Spirit, but still in the drugstore and still lacking the things I wanted to have, which things were necessary to my happiness to complete it. While pondering on the stupendous question of the literal existence of God amongst his created beings here on earth, one day I seemed to be given a revelation of the entire picture. I saw the Life

Spirit—GOD—as this spiritual being exists. I saw the significance of the story of the fall of man. In fact, it seemed that there was given to me that Sunday afternoon in that drugstore the full and complete picture of this world—its Creator—and His creation.

I saw with remarkable clarity things as they are—and the vision has never left me. I saw then, and still see, how very false is the teaching that the mighty Intelligence behind all created things, sent himself down to earth in the form of ONE individual man, to "save" the entire creation which otherwise would be eternally lost. I knew then and there that such a story was but superstition and tradition—and very poor tradition at that. But I also saw the true relationship man bears to the great Creative Life Spirit—and as I write this to you this Thursday afternoon—I am staggered still at the stupendous import of it all. Many times I am not understood. Many times there is heaped upon my head epithets which are very cruel and wrong, and which I do not deserve. But I cannot give to men and women the full significance of that picture except as led to do so. I am doing it as carefully and as intelligently as is humanly possible, and I suppose I must go through a period of misunderstanding on the part of the religiously inclined, before they will see the divinely natural truths I am giving to the world. That must be as it may however, for I cannot do any worrying about what others think of me. I KNOW—and I KNOW FULL WELL IN WHOM I BELIEVE. I KNOW WHOSE POWER SUSTAINS ME. I KNOW SOMETHING OF THE DIVINELY NA-TURAL SPIRITUAL POWER OF GOD—AND—KNOWING THAT POWER—I SMILE AT TRIALS AND TRIBULATIONS AS FEARLESS-LY AND VERY SUCCESSFULLY GO FORWARD, knowing that shortly the existence of this mighty Power—Law—God—will be universally known and believed.

It was Sunday afternoon when this picture came to me, and I was in a feverish haste to transfer it to writing. I had no typewriter however, so the next morning I borrowed one from a dentist friend of mine, in the mean-time making notes in my pocket book. On Monday I took the little vest-pocket typewriter to the apartment, and advised my family that I desired to be left strictly alone. As fast as my fingers would travel I wrote that story down on paper. Inside of one week it was finished, and not a word of it has been changed from that day to this. That was that. Here I was with the typewritten story and the copyright on it—and no money.

I want you my student to note carefully what happened from now on. I did not sit on my haunches waiting for some rich uncle to die and leave me enough money to publish this works. Nor did I get down on my knees and pray for the money to come. I knew better than that. I KNEW IN WHAT POWER I WAS BELIEVING and I stepped out on that very Power. Remember please, that it was all new to me, and was contrary to all that I had been taught about the operations of God. But then you will remember I had discarded the old traditional "Yah-veh" and had exchanged him for the TRUE LIGHT, and from now on I was living in that LIGHT. For months and months, prior to this revelation or whatever you care to call it, I was trying to learn how to have faith in the Living God-Law. I wanted success. I wanted a good home. I wanted a car. I wanted a pipe-organ, and I wanted to be in a position where the wolf could not get at my back door.

So I did the only thing I could have done. I KNEW that the Life Spirit existed for the express purpose of being my all-in-all and for the purpose of giving to me whatsoever things I desired. I say I KNEW that. But how was I to get these things. I did the only thing I could do, and the thing that thousands write and ask me about in their own lives. I DIDN'T BOTHER MY HEAD ABOUT THE MEANS TO BE EMPLOYED IN BRINGING THESE THINGS I WANTED TO ME. I JUST SIMPLY PLACED MYSELF IN A RECEIVING ATTITUDE, KNOWING FULL WELL THAT GOD WOULD NEVER DISAPPOINT ME. HUN-DREDS OF THOUSANDS OF TIMES I REPEATED THE SEN-TENCE—"YOU HAVE BROUGHT ME SUCCESS—YOU HAVE MADE ME WEALTHY." I kept everlastingly at this. In every spare moment I had. In the basement of the drugstore while unpacking boxes and crates. Every waking moment was filled with that thought—for I knew it was a fact, and I WANTED THE GOD-LAW TO KNOW THAT I KNEW IT WAS A FACT. For I knew that by so doing, I WAS PUTTING INTO ACTUAL OPERATION THE VERY LAW THAT WOULD BRING THESE THINGS TO ME.

That is the Law of the Spiritual Realm. It is the Law of God. It is God. And—though but a man—never let anyone tell you that Jesus Christ did not understand Spiritual Law. For He understood it to the very full. But you will remember —the church members crucified Him as they would do again today if He returned with the same revolutionary message that He brought in that day and age. He preached a PRESENT religion. He preached a PRESENT and perfectly NATURAL Power—but it was not wanted. People did not want a reasonable religion at all. They did not want a God who could do things for them then. They, in keeping with all other systems of supernaturally-revealed religion, wanted the same old trinity and crucifixion, and resurrection story, so they took that story, dressed it up in a garb of their own, and foisted it off on the unsuspecting world as the real religion—just as all the others with the same story claimed. And today it is being found out for what it is—and that is UNTRUE.

These repeated affirmations of truth were not influencing God at all, but they were ESTABLISHING THE CONNECTION THROUGH WHICH THE DIVINELY NATURAL GOD-LAW COULD WORK. FOR THIS LAW CANNOT AND WILL NOT WORK WHERE ONE IS UNWILLING TO TAKE FROM THE LAW THE THINGS ONE MOST NEEDS. How could it work any other way? This God-Law is what might be termed an automatic Law. In the very moment one actually believes in its existence, and TAKES IT AS AN ESTABLISHED FACT THAT THE GOD-LAW CAN AND WILL GIVE THEM WHAT THEY NEED—WHEN THAT IS DONE LET ME REPEAT—THE RESULTS ARE VERY SURE. Don't forget this. Then—the answer came. I received the picture of this spiritual truth, and THE MEANS WAS PUT INTO MY HANDS BY WHICH THESE THINGS I WANTED COULD COME TO ME.

The following night after obtaining the copyright, I put the Lessons I have received in my pocket, and, in a blinding snowstorm started downtown. Mrs. R. asked me where I was going. I told her that I should need about $2500.00 to get my teaching printed and further informed her that I should return that night with $500.00. I had not the slightest suspicion where I was going or whom I was going to see, for I had not a friend in this city. I had only been here a short time, and no one, of course, knew me. So who I was going to see that night I knew not. However—the first man I met was a young fellow who happens to be now the Vice President of this corporation. I asked him if he had any money. He told me that he had $500.00 and I explained to him what I wanted to do. I got the $500.00 and inside of two days had another similar amount from his brother-in-law.

I won't go into detail here any more than to say that inside of a week, I had enough money to get a thousand completed copies of the revelation printed, and also ten thousand of several different sorts of letters printed. After placing my first advertisement in a magazine, we had $16.47 to our name. But the public recognized the truth of the advertisement, and it wasn't very long until things were entirely changed around. At first I worked all day in the drugstore, and looked after the mailing at night. Then I rented a cheap little office and hired a girl to work half days. Then I was forced to give half of my time to the rapidly growing business, so I went on half time at the drugstore. This was not to be though, for the inquiries continued to rush in and shortly I was giving all of my time to the work and—(see how God works) I was drawing a salary of $500.00 a month. From that day to this (21 months later) the story is well known. Every conceivable thing I could desire has come to me through the power of the self-existent Life Spirit—GOD.

Inside of one year some part or other of my teachings was going into 67 different countries, and we had two books in existence. The second year we had our own magazine, and Brotherhood. Now, it takes an office staff of ten people to handle the mail, etc., and this is but 21 months later. I live in my own home now—which I wanted—I own a very fine car—which I also wanted—I have thousands of dollars of life insurance—which I also wanted—I have a very beautiful pipe organ—which I certainly did want—and all of these things have been obtained in 21 months, THROUGH APPLYING THE DIVINELY NATURAL LAW OF GOD IN MY LIFE. I did not ask "How is it going to be done." Nor did I argue with God in an effort to try and help him out a little. Not that. I just simply adopted the attitude that Life Spirit could and WOULD supply all my needs according to its infallible power and might, and when I REALLY BELIEVED THAT, it didn't take very long for the needed things to come. And when you actually and literally believe God, it won't take very long for them to come to you either, my friend.

Millions of people see my picture every month, and hundreds of thousands have heard my voice over the radio. "PSYCHIANA" is going all over the world—and best of all—thousands of others are daily finding that the message I give them comes pretty nearly being the truth. Some folks might have thought that I was a little off if they knew that hundreds of thousand of times I FORCED myself to mentally say "YOU HAVE BROUGHT ME SUCCESS—YOU HAVE MADE ME WEALTHY," but I meant business. I BELIEVED GOD. And the results speak for themselves I think. Had there never been any superstitious religious teachings, it would not be necessary for one to have to force themselves to believe in his Creator. But it is necessary now. And it will probably be for many years yet, until people as a whole see how utterly wrong it is to believe such foolish traditions.

God is LAW. A mighty operating Spiritual Law. This Law is here for your benefit and for mine. This Law made you. It made me. It made every created thing that ever was made. And it did not spit on the ground to do it. This is a self-existent God-Law. It is eternal. It ruled and existed since the beginning of time, for in reality—there is no time. It is but an effect and Einstein is right. It is a SPIRITUAL LAW and it IS the entire spiritual realm. It is all of the spiritual realm. There is no such a thing as A spiritual realm without God—the Great LAW. There are no "angels" hovering around, or was there ever a "fallen Angel" called Lucifer. That is allegory and superstition and you should know it by this time if you don't.

This great Spiritual Law—or God—controls and governs the whole universe BY THE POWER OF HIS OWN LAW—OR, IN OTHER WORDS, BY HIMSELF. There never was a created thing that did not originally have its inception in this realm of God—the Great Spiritual Law. No matter what the processes of creation may be, behind them all stands this God-Law—and is ever yet creating, creating, creating. And it will ever be creating. In the upward trend of man and his evolution, there looms in the immediate future, a spiritual understanding of this spiritual realm. This realm of God. Without attempting here to analyze the various processes by which the material is manifest from the spiritual, we know enough of God to know the one GREAT FUNDAMENTAL GOVERNING ALL PHYSICAL MANIFESTATIONS. It is not necessary that we know the "why" or the "how." All that is necessary is that we recognize the stupendous fact that GOD IS, and that he is ever creating as his creatures need. We know, I say, what the one great predominating and overshadowing fact ruling this marvelous Law is. We know for a positive fact just how to draw this mighty Spiritual Power into our own lives with its omnipotent wisdom and its unerring and unfailing power. We know that. Jesus Christ knew it. The great souls of the ages have all known it. True, many of them were not conscious of the LAW, but they used it just the same, even though unconscious of what it actually was they were using. You will see here why many benefits have been credited to Jehovah or "Yah-veh" when as a matter of fact he had nothing whatsoever to do with them.

There are many good honest-intentioned souls in existence who will swear to you that they pray to Jesus Christ and in return for such prayers they receive this and they receive that. But we know that Jesus Christ died two thousand years ago. And we know that the story that he came back from the dead is but legend, and is nothing more than the old "resurrection" story of other religions told over again. We know positively that Jesus Christ is NOT in heaven seated at the right hand of God and making "intercession for us with groanings which cannot be uttered." We know—for our reason tells us—that such is not the case. Yet many, many good souls will tell us with much conviction that they receive their answers to their prayers direct from this source. This is not a fact, for once more this story of the world's "savior" sitting at the right hand of his "father" in heaven is, like the crucifixion and resurrection stories, pagan myth retold.

What actually happens is this—in these cases of presumed answer to prayer by "Yah-veh" or Jehovah, the earnest "believer" pins his faith in Jehovah, or Christ, or Krishna, or Buddha, or Confucius, or any one of the many other "divinely born" saviors, and, THEY PUT INTO USE THE LAW GOVERNING THE TRUE GOD EVEN THOUGH THEY THINK THEY ARE PRAYING TO AN ENTIRELY DIFFERENT BEING. So sure is the Law of God that when faith is used, it makes no difference what that faith may be pinned to—IT WILL WORK. This, of course, proves positively that the GOD-LAW exists and actually works, EVEN THOUGH THE PETITIONER KNOWS NOT FROM WHENCE THE ANSWER COMES. And to this extent there is some good in the Christian religion. Not in its beliefs however, for every thinking mind knows full well that these are neither reasonable or scientific. BUT THE PRACTICE OF PRAYER BRINGS THE RESULT EVEN THOUGH THE BEING PRAYED TO NEVER EXISTED. Do you see that? I am sure you do.

There are people who worship the sun. These good folk can show us many "answers to prayer" coming from the sun. But you and I both know that the sun had nothing to do with the answering of their prayers. Yet evidently they receive their answers. No matter what philosophy of life one may choose to adopt, if one believes in it hard enough and lives it—IT WILL WORK OUT. How much more intelligent is it therefore to really draw from the CREATIVE GOD POWER ITSELF THE THINGS WE

NEED, THAN TO HAVE AS A GOD A BEING WHOSE EVERY MOVEMENT FROM HIS BIRTH UP HAS BEEN SHROUDED IN UNBELIEVABLE MIRACLES AND MYSTERY. I cannot believe the Bible story at all. There is too much to be taken for granted in it. Or can I believe that angels came down from heaven and said to Krishna: "Rise—holy Love—rise"—at which the shroud unwound itself from the dead body of this "savior" and he came back from the dead and ascended to his father in heaven. I say I cannot believe that story. Neither can you if you study its origin and its history. BUT I CAN BELIEVE IN THE EXIST-ENCE OF THE CREATIVE LIFE-SPIRIT OF THIS UNIVERSE. For my reason tells me that such a power or spirit MUST exist. Chance can have nothing to do with it. Or can personality have anything to do with it either. If it could, then you and I would be able to understand the Creative Personality and that can never be. Personality of any sort has nothing to do with it. The GOD-LAW however, BECOMES personal—ONLY AS YOU AND I APPLY IT AND USE IT IN OUR OWN INDIVIDUAL CASE. This is plain to see.

But every system of religion in existence tells us that they alone pos-sess the TRUE light when as a matter of fact they never were farther from the true light than they are when they attempt to attribute to God, super-natural powers. There is nothing supernatural about God. If there were anything on the supernatural order about that Power, it never would have made a natural universe. The power is NOT supernatural—but is DIVINELY NATURAL—if I may use that expression. Religions have, how ever, placed their own interpretations on stories of Gods galore, and have missed the truth through trying to confine the "god" in the middle of their own structure. You may depend upon one thing though. You may be sure of the fact that the Creative Intelligence behind this created scheme of things is not contained in the creeds or the beliefs of any one society or denomination or organization. IT EXISTS OUTSIDE OF THEM ALL, AND IF ANY OF THE FOLLOWERS OF THESE DIFFERING SYSTEMS OF RELIGION KNOW ANYTHING ABOUT SPIRITUAL POWER, THEY KNOW IT THROUGH THE GREAT GOD-LAW WHICH IS OPERATING THROUGHOUT THE UNIVERSE, AND NOT IN THEIR OWN STRUCTURE TO THE EXCLUSION OF EVERYONE ELSE. The story that "unless ye repent and be baptized you shall be damned" is not true. And you know it's not true. So does the church know it's not true.

They did not know it 50 years ago—but they know it now. All of them are leaning more and more to the truths I am teaching you in this course of instruction, and the time is coming when the mighty God-Law will be known by them all. But that time is not here yet. Hence I say that the man on the street is far more liable to know something of the truths of God than are those who think that God is to be found in their own little denomination. As a matter of fact they know that this is not so. They know they have never found God through any of the practices they indulge in. Yet they hang on and make a profession. This is not honest.

I think my students see at this point that there is in existence a mighty operating force which is ever-present and omnipotent, and which can do anything needed to be done for the human race and for every individual soul, and do it though entirely apart from what we have been used to as "agents of God." This Power does not operate through any organization or does it operate through any one man or any of his agents. Or is the power supernatural at all.

Nor is prayer necessary to contact this marvelously potent Power. Nor is repentance. Nor is salvation. It is as free as the very air we breathe. Remember here though that this mighty Power or Law is, like gravitation, an invisible Law. But remember also that it is just as sure. Now—at this point, I want you to continue your affirmations with renewed vigor. I want you to make them become a very part of your being. I have told you how I did it, and I want you to do it also. Remember—a wishy-washy system of affirming will get you nothing—just that. But the grim jaw—the clenched fist—the stiff spine—the solid backbone—the determined will—in other words THE FAITH—will bring the answer every time, and it will bring it in the moment when you least expect it.

As you continue your affirmations, sooner or later there will come a time when you will instinctively KNOW that the connection with the Law has been made. You will then TAKE IT FOR GRANTED THAT YOU WILL RECEIVE THAT FOR WHICH YOUR HEART LONGS— and your attitude will be one of WATCHFUL EXPECTANCY. Then— there will come to you perhaps an idea. It may be a leading. But YOU WILL KNOW BY THE VERY QUIETNESS OF THE IDEA OR THE LEADING THAT IT COMES FROM THE SPIRITUAL REALM. Then, when that lead comes—OBEY IT FULLY AND INSTANTLY. UNDER NO CIRCUMSTANCES PROCRASTINATE. There will never be any question in your mind as to whether the "lead" or the idea is from the God-Law or not—FOR IT WILL APPEAR TO YOU TO BE THE PERFECTLY NATURAL THING TO DO OR THE THING YOU WANT TO BE MADE MANIFEST IN YOUR LIFE. It will be a direct step along the road and in the right direction. Now please realize here that this Lesson is being read by thousands and tens of thousands of students coming to me from every walk of life.

I cannot know the individual problems of them all. One is a light-housekeeper. Another is a garage mechanic. Another is a minister. Another is a Government official. Many, many different sorts of people study this course of instruction—and I cannot possibly know them all. Nor can I know their individual problems. But I CAN give general instructions for contacting the GOD-LAW which will work, no matter who the student may be, and no matter what the problem may be that is worrying the student. I can give you the fundamental Law of the Living

Creative Life Spirit, and I can say to you with absolute assurance that IT IS IMMUTABLE. YOU CANNOT USE IT AND FAIL. YOU CANNOT BELIEVE IN THE EXISTENCE OF GOD WITHOUT RECEIVING WHAT YOU DESIRE. For this is the Law of God. This IS GOD.

Now—in previous Lessons I have given you varying affirmations to use. You have already decided what it is you need in life the most. I have shown you the Law. I have shown you how, by applying the Law and continually affirming to be a fact the things I wanted made them actual literal facts. Now I want you to affirm with twice the interest from now on. Be in earnest. Remember that through years of racial tendencies you have been taught to believe in an entirely different God from the one I am teaching you now. This is the reason affirmations of faith are necessary at all. Let the desire for the thing you want be from now on an all consuming desire. If you mean business show the God-Law that you believe first of all in its existence—and also in its power and willingness to provide the means to bring to you whatever right thing you desire.

There is another affirmation I used many, many times when I was struggling to have a little faith in God, and that is the following affirmation. I would clench my fist, and, with a firmness and a desire that never would admit defeat, I would say "By God I Will." That is not profanity at all. It is a scientific fact—a theological fact—and a Spiritual truth. For if you ever attain the things you need it will be—not by God's help—but BY GOD. In those days my friend, I can tell you I meant business. There was no halfway measure there. I KNEW THE GOD-LAW EXISTED AND I KNEW THAT IT EXISTED FOR ME, AND MY MIND WAS MADE UP TO FIND AND USE THAT POWER. AND WHEN THE NECESSARY FAITH OR BELIEF IN THE GOD-LAW WAS ONCE MANIFESTED—MY SEARCHING WAS AT AN END. I have never since doubted this mighty God-Law. AND I RECEIVE EVERYTHING I WANT TOO. I wanted a beautiful home—and I received it. I wanted a car—and I got it. I wanted money in the bank—and I have it—I wanted a pipe-organ—and I have a beautiful instrument now. I wanted life insurance—and I have it. I wanted friends—and I have them—lots of them. I wanted to tell men and women about God—and I am doing it. AND ALL IN 21 MONTHS FROM THE TIME I REALLY TRUSTED THE LIVING GOD-LAW. Think of it. From poverty to success in twenty-one short months—and after over forty years of failure. You tell me the Law doesn't work? Not me. You must tell someone else that. For since that time I have seen many hundreds who have found this same Law I am teaching. I have seen sickness banished by its power.

I have seen death thwarted in its attempts to end the life of some sufferer. I have seen the Power of God applied against illness and have seen very unusual things happen. I have seen lives transformed by this mighty Power. I have seen wealth supplant poverty. I have seen happiness supplant misery, and I have seen thousands discard an idolatrous superstition and a pagan "god" for the LIFE SPIRIT. My files contain hundreds and hundreds of letters from students who have found the God-Law. Inside of one year my teaching was all over the world one might say. As I write this we are planning to move for the fourth time into larger quarters—WHY?—because all over the world, wherever our teaching goes, men and women are actually FINDING THE TRUTH OF OUR TEACHINGS.

So you—no matter who you may be I say: "USE THIS UNSEEN DYNAMIC GOD-LAW. NEVER LET UP UNTIL YOU GET WHAT YOU WANT." Be something like Jacob of old—HANG ON BY FAITH IN THIS MIGHTY LAW, AND YOU WILL NEVER BE DISAPPOINTED—NO MATTER WHAT YOUR NEEDS MAY BE. In the next Lesson we shall go quite a little farther into this subject of the existence of this mighty Power—GOD. Study carefully. Be slow about it. Let these truths sink in. Above all—BELIEVE IN THE GOD I AM SHOWING YOU.

Sincerely your friend and teacher,
FRANK B. ROBINSON

EXAMINATION QUESTIONS
FOR LESSON NO. 11

These examinations questions are for your benefit and you should know the answers to them all. If they are not clear to you, read your Lesson again and again until they are clear.

1. Contrast Doctor Robinson's present with his former belief.

2. If there be no "power of evil" or "devil" in the world, whence come sickness, poverty, disease, etc?

3. If you are poor, unhappy or ill, what is the cause?

4. Why is mankind now discarding supernaturally revealed religions?

5. How did Dr. Robinson answer the question, "How am I to get the things I need?

6. Did his repeated affirmations influence God at all? What did they do?

7. In what sense may the God-Law be called an "automatic" law?

8. What is it that actually happens in the case of presumed answer to prayer by Jehovah or Christ?

9. Why is the practice of prayer useful, even though made to a being that never existed?

10. To what extent does the God-Law become personal?

11. Is prayer necessary in order to contact the God-Law? What, then, is necessary?

12. How does Dr. Robinson justify the use by him of an apparently profane affirmation when he was struggling to have a little faith in God?

LESSON 12

Dear friend and student:

Of all of the Lessons, Lesson 12 is probably one of the most important of all of them. It deals with life, and, as you know life is the only real thing on this earth.

Some day we shall know in full what we begin to suspect now. So study this Lesson very carefully and see if you can't grasp the thought I am trying to give to you. Read between the lines for these Lessons contain a deep Spiritual Truth which I want you to grasp.

Your friend and teacher,
FRANK B. ROBINSON

In this Lesson I deem it advisable to go a little farther with you into the realm in which we are pursuing our studies, for too much cannot be learned about the existence of the mighty operating Spiritual Law we are here discussing. Before I go any farther into it however, I want to call your attention to an Associated Press dispatch which appeared nationally in the columns of the press through out this country on February the 22nd this year. The clipping is mighty interesting, and is in absolute line with what I am teaching you here in this course of studies. Long before any scientist had advanced this theory, I was publishing it to the world. Had the statement come from a man of less standing than its author, I should not have paid much attention to it. As a matter of fact, however, scientists the wide world over are recognizing the staggering fact that THERE IS IN EXISTENCE AN UNSEEN POWER SO DYNAMIC IN ITS ESSENCE, THAT ALL OTHER POWERS AND FORCES FADE INTO INSIGNIFICANCE BESIDE IT. I put that statement into print over two years ago, and the fact that the scientific thinking minds of the world are now scientifically recognizing the truth of that statement, is evidence beyond any reasonable shadow of doubt that I know whereof I speak.

Not only the gentleman in question here makes the statement, but others of equal standing are recognizing the fact that, as I am teaching you here, the UNSEEN REALM IS THE REAL CREATIVE REALM WHEREAS THE CREATION ITSELF IS OF SECONDARY IMPORTANCE. The cosmic ray of Dr. Milliken is an established fact. The scientists are mostly agreed also regarding this ray that it is an emanation of, or perhaps the cause of A UNIVERSE THAT IS BUILDING UP. I have already referred to one man who thinks that this ray is an emanation from a disintegrating universe, but I think that gentleman is very wrong. He is entitled to his opinion however, and I am glad that we are not all agreed on the subject. It is always the doubter and the thinker that finds the truth, and not the one who blindly accepts. So I am happy that the English scientist I mentioned in a foregoing Lesson holds the view that he does hold. That gives those of us who hold the opposite view a chance to investigate further and find out if possible which is correct.

Certain it is that the mighty truths of creation are at our hands. They do NOT lie in some future life. We cannot perhaps grasp them fully now—but you may depend upon it that it is HERE ON THIS EARTH WHERE THESE MIGHTY TRUTHS WILL BE GRASPED—not in "heaven." And, as I consistently claim, there will be found under, and over, and all around this marvelous creation, A VAST SPIRITUAL LAW. Not a personality of any sort or kind—but a Law. A SPIRITUAL LAW though. But a LAW just the same. It must be a LAW. It can be nothing else. It may upset the hopes of those who are looking to "heaven" after death for their hopes, but just the same, and, without being at all dogmatic, all the evidence to hand clearly discloses that LAW—and not an anthropomorphic "god" is responsible for it all.

Now shall we look at this clipping for it is marvelous in its significance. And, by the way, this is not the only news item that has been sent out recently along this line of thought. Many of the scientists and thinkers who in the past have been considered somewhat "atheistic" are changing their viewpoint, and the differing religious organizations are finding considerable solace and consolation out of this seeming fact. They have yet to discover though that not a scientist in existence believes the Christian story of creation as told in the Bible. There is not a scientist or thinker in existence who believes for one moment that the secret of the ages lies anywhere else than in LAWS WE ARE ALREADY USING. "The life beyond" does not answer the question. "Heaven" does not answer the question. "Repentance" does not answer the question. "Salvation" does not answer the question. LAW—THE GOD-LAW DOES ANSWER THE QUESTION. Many of the old prophets knew this, and so they recognized and depended upon this mighty LAW for their daily help. And just before I quote this article, let me say to you whoever you may be, that in the day when you learn to absolutely trust and depend on the existence of this spiritual God-Law, then in that moment will your life be one of overcoming victory. All the finer things of life will come to you. Its holiest and most sacred sentiments are contained in this remarkable God-Law, and never fear that if you accept the existence of this mighty Law you will have to become cold-blooded and sacrifice the very finest and most hallowed things of life. For this is NOT a fact. There never was a holy instinct yet that did not have its origin in the God-Law. There never was a heart that throbbed or thrilled with pity that this emotion did not have its origin in the mighty God-Law. There never was a holy instinct of love yet, that was not part of the mighty God-Law I am teaching you about. Not one. And it is very foolish for theological professors to tell me that there can be no such thing as a "law" which in itself contains the very finest and most sacred powers and emotions of life. This is what some of them sometimes attempt to tell me. And in reply to such statements I usually reply: "Who said so?"

Who was it that ever said that such a spiritual "law" could not exist? Why those who have manufactured a "god" of their own—that is all. Naturally you could not expect a Roman Catholic to believe in the existence of the mighty God Law I am teaching. Or could you expect a good Presbyterian brother to believe it either. Consequently—to them—I am all wrong. I know nothing whatsoever of spiritual law. I am an "outcast" from all that is good and noble. I do not believe in Jehovah or "Yah-veh" and so am teaching a gospel that is not true. This is what a lot of them tell me and write me. Now as a matter of fact, the fact that these good brethren deny the power I teach is not at all evidence that such a Power does not exist. They deny every other teaching than their own. But you see—there is another side to it, and a side which I know and which they can not possibly know. Certainly if there exists the Law or Power I teach, these good brethren cannot know of it, because my teachings seem to be so fundamentally different from theirs.

But just the same—I can produce an overwhelming mass of evidence which will prove that I am not entirely wrong. I can prove to the satisfaction of any reasonable man or woman that I am using and teaching my students to use A Law or Power or Force of which these religionists know nothing at all. I say I can PROVE that. I don't just make an empty statement that all these other fellows are wrong, although if I did they could never PROVE their story. But I DO make the statement that this spiritual power exists, and furthermore, I can PROVE it. And will prove it to your satisfaction before I get through with you. Religion is all—IF IT CAN BE PROVEN. BUT IT ISN'T WORTH TWO WHOOPS OF A CAT'S TAIL IF IT CAN'T BE PROVEN. You may take all the varying and multitudinous systems of religion and put them all in a sack, and, if they cannot be proven—I wouldn't give you ten cents for all of them. I would rather stake my hope of the joys of this life and whatever future life there may be on the existence of one KNOWN TRUTH, than I would on miles and miles of religious theories that cannot be proven. For truth is truth. It never changes. It never varies. It is ABSOLUTE.

And these mighty searchers into the spiritual realm—these thinkers and scientists are fast finding out the fact that for over two years now I have been steadfastly advocating. And that is the existence of this mighty divinely natural spiritual God-Law I am here teaching you. Here is the clipping. Read it carefully. I don't say that I agree with it all—I don't know. But in essence I DO AGREE WITH IT. In fact it is exactly what I am trying to put across to you:

DISTANT SPACE MAY
HOLD LIFE MYSTERY

SCIENTIST CONCEIVES CIVILIZATIONS DWARFING OURS, ON OLDER WORLDS

CHICAGO—Inhabitants on distant worlds as far superior to man kind as men are to single life cells are visioned by Dr. William MacMillan, professor of mathematical astronomy at the University of Chicago.

"He outlined his theory in amplifying a brief article of his published January 16 in which he voiced for the first time the skepticism of many American scientists toward the 'explosion of the universe' idea advanced by the Cambridge Astronomers, Eddington and Jeans.

"They hold that the universe is gradually wearing down to a state where all matter will become a vast inert mass, formless, lifeless, and cold."

UNIVERSE INFINITE

Dr. MacMillan conceives a universe infinite in time and space, and pervaded by a fine structure of unknown composition which diffuses energy amidst all forms of matter, so that the supply of energy remains the same.

"Out in the heavens, perhaps," he said, "are civilizations as far above ours as we are above the single cell, since they are so much older than ours."

Magnificent forms of life have grown up over magnificent stretches of time only to perish in some cataclysm. Magnificent forms of life will always grow up if this theory be true that the universe is continually being rebuilt at some unknown sub-electronic level.

If there is one thing more than any other thing that brings to me the spiritual strength I need so much daily, it is the thoughts of this immense spiritual realm with its accompanying power. Just to realize for one moment the vastness of the Creative Life Spirit fills me with a buoyancy that nothing else can duplicate. I do not say this to boast at all, but I probably produce more real work every month than any other one man writing and teaching. I am told by college professors and ministers that

1   Taken from Associated Press report.

they do not understand how it can possibly be done by one man. Well, it would not be done did I not know the source of my strength and power. Of myself I could do absolutely nothing along this line. The articles I write which grip people so—the books—the Lessons—the letters—the source of them all lies in the recognition I have of the CONTINUAL PRESENCE OF THIS MIGHTY INVISIBLE GOD LAW. If I cared to not recognize this LAW, I could just simply throw all restraint to the winds and could be one of the most dissolute and useless characters in existence. For I know how to make far more money than I am making now. My services are at a premium in the advertising field if I want to employ them there.

I could just say "Let us eat, drink, and be merry—for tomorrow we die." But I don't do that. For I have just as much joy in life as any living mortal has. And, instead of going along caring nothing for the rest of my fellow men and women, I do whatever I may be able to do to lift their eyes from idolatrous superstition unto the Great Power—God—whence cometh all their help in the very moment they recognize that invisible Presence. I do not profess to know all about spiritual Law. I wish I did. But I know something of the existence of the GOD LAW—and I know how to apply it just a tiny little bit. And, so powerful and so immutable is this Law, that there is no wonder that no matter what I do it is over-whelmingly successful. The secret—you ask—well, brother or sister—listen to me—I just simply KNOW of the existence of the Life Spirit, and when I want a little guidance along any line, I just keep still, and, with a smile on the face, I RECOGNIZE AND DEPEND UPON THE GOD-LAW TO POINT OUT THE WAY—AND I HAVE NEVER BEEN DISAPPOINTED YET. And I never shall be.

No prayer of any kind ever enters into my life—there is no need of it. My knees are never bent at the bedside. That would be idolatry and pagan superstition. For I know that the God-Law knows better than I know the thing for which I am best suited. And I know also that there is absolutely no need for me to beg and implore God to do this for me or that for me. I KNOW A FAR BETTER WAY. I KNOW THAT GOD IS. I KNOW THAT IT IS THE LAW—LAW—LAW OF THE SPIRITUAL REALM THAT GOD HAS ALREADY PREPARED FOR YOU AND ME WHATEVER WE CAN TAKE. And, knowing this, then either praying or petitioning would be quite futile and absolutely unnecessary. For what sort of a God-Law would it be that could be cajoled into giving you some-thing that otherwise would be withheld because you did not ask prop-erly—or perchance forgot to ask for at all? What sort of a power would that be? No—brethren—IT HAS TO BE A LAW, AND FURTHERMORE, IT HAS TO BE A LAW WHICH IS NEVER FAILING. IT HAS TO BE IMMUTABLE. IT HAS TO BE OMNISCIENT. IT HAS TO BE ABSOLUTE. And, knowing that this is the case—then I just simply DEPEND UPON THIS GOD-LAW—and the results are sure.

But you may say—"well, Dr. Robinson—are there not limitations to what you can get from God?"—and my answer to you is "NONE AT ALL." At least if there be such limitations then I have never yet been able to find them. They may exist—but I doubt it. Remember please at this point that the human race has not yet emerged from the state of religious superstition and tradition. And, until it fully emerges there can be no universal recognition of the existence of such an almost unbelievable Power as there is. As I write this, the eyes of the world are on the far eastern situation—and, well, they might be. For if I sense the situation aright this old world is due to be bathed in the most terrible slaughter it has ever seen. It may not be—but I am fearful for it. If such does happen, and I trust I am wrong, it will be the greatest conflict the world will ever see, for out of the WRECKAGE WILL ARISE SOME ONE WHO WILL DEMONSTRATE TO THE VERY FULL THE SPIRITUAL POWER OF GOD, and when that power is once known, wars will be no more. Men and nations will see how absolutely criminal it is to even build a battleship to either attack or defend. But that time is coming. Humanity has reached the point at which it is beginning to realize the fact that even though one has all the material possession he may desire, it means nothing if the blood of others is on their hands. NO—THE ROOT OF "SIN" AS THE CHURCH FOLKS CALL IT HAS TO BE DESTROYED. And you will remember that there is but one sin in the entire creation. And that sin is doubt of the existence of God. Doubt of the existence of the Spiritual God-Law. Doubt of an overshadowing intelligence behind it all. Doubt of everything and everyone. And this "doubt" or "fear" will have to be absolutely annihilated before men and women can possibly know God.

And, I am going to say right here, even though my religious friends don't like it, that "supernaturally-revealed religion" is DIRECTLY RESPONSIBLE FOR THIS CALAMITY OF FEAR THAT RULES THE WORLD TODAY. For centuries the Japs have been teaching their youth that the finest thing in the world is to DIE IN BATTLE. They are taught that if they die fighting for their country, they are sure of "heaven." And they have been saps enough to believe it. And, as a result, no one knows where the end of this far eastern situation will lie. It is bad any way you look at it, and I am somewhat apprehensive that blood is to run very freely before God steps in and takes a hand. By this I do not mean the church "god" by any manner of means—but you will find out that if this calamity comes—THE GOD-LAW WILL, THROUGH ITS OPERATION, PUT A STOP TO IT BEFORE IT IS COMPLETED. Mark this down and remember what I am saying to you about this calamity—for calamity it is.

But, the human race had to go through it, it seems. It seemed to be in the cards, and the quicker we get it over with the quicker will men and women see the ghastly farce of it all. Will the lion ever lie down with the lamb? I think so—but neither the return of Christ or anything the "church" can do will have much to do with it. Christ will never return—perchance some man will become so imbued with the spirit of Christ—the greatest of all prophets, that he again will put into actual practice something of the marvelous power of God—and the human race will see it next time. This Lesson is not intended to be a discourse on religion, but it is very pertinent to our studies that you be fully conversant with every phase of the operations of the mighty God-Law here and now. And, above all, I do so want you to KNOW in whom you are believing. I want you to actually KNOW and perhaps understand something of the mighty power of the God-Law, which Law, properly applied, can and will bring to you through its operations, everything that you can possibly and reasonably expect to receive throughout life. It may be discovered that it can bring you more than that. But I think you will be satisfied if it brings you the desires of your heart—will you not?

This article I have reproduced here will, I think, give you a stronger picture than ever before of the real size of the universe, and should open your eyes a little to the spiritual power behind it all. It will give you perhaps a faint glimpse of the power I am trying to show you how to contact, in order that both health, success, and happiness may manifest themselves in your own individual life. We have seen that the chances are many to one that there does exist through the ether, and in fact throughout the entire creation, AN INVISIBLE COSMIC FORCE OR LAW OR SPIRIT, WHICH AS SUCH IS RESPONSIBLE FOR THE ENTIRE CREATION. Now get that fact firmly planted in your mind here and now. We have seen further that the unseen or spiritual part of you is the real part. We have seen that your own invisible thoughts are the THINGS WHICH ARE A PART OF THIS GREAT INVISIBLE CREATIVE SPIRIT OR FORCE OR POWER. We know that now to be a fact. I have shown you that when you concentrate your thoughts into this great vast unseen spiritual realm THIS GOD-LAW IMMEDIATELY HAS BEGUN TO BRING TO YOU IN ACTUAL MANIFESTATION THE THINGS YOU DESIRE. Not because this great God-Law can be changed to suit your individual needs, BUT BECAUSE THIS GREAT GOD-LAW IS RESPONSIBLE FOR YOUR EXISTENCE IN THE FIRST PLACE. AND IF IT KNEW ENOUGH TO PRODUCE YOU AS YOU ARE, THEN CERTAINLY IT KNOWS ENOUGH TO GIVE TO YOU THAT WHICH IS NECESSARY TO COMPLETE THE JOB OF YOUR OWN PERFECT HEALTH, HAPPINESS, AND SUCCESS. NOW LISTEN TO ME A MOMENT PLEASE—the only thing that stops you from having the things you desire is YOUR UNBELIEF IN THE GOD-LAW. But, you will remember, you are doing exercises designed to put into operation in your case this invisible God-Law, and the thing for you to do now is to KEEP ETERNALLY BEFORE YOU THE THING YOU WANT. Keep eternally at this sending of your thoughts into the God-Realm, and then—wait with an expectant attitude—always ALERT TO

THE PROMPTINGS OF THIS MIGHTY LAW.

For the spiritual LAW works through what we look upon as natural channels. Gold does not drop from the sky in your lap. Health will not immediately manifest if you are not in a state of mind to receive it. The conditions necessary for the blessing and gifts from the spiritual realm to manifest are: First—an absolute faith in the existence of the all-creative intelligence which created you in the first place. Second—the desire for what you need impressed into the spiritual realm with never-wavering precision. Third—the ability to follow the leadings of the spiritual realm, from whence these things MUST come. If you are a weakling—then get strong. The God-Law likes nothing better than to have you put it to the test. It's like you going into a bank and asking the banker for a loan. You go in there, state your needs, and the banker says "O.K.—I'll let you have the money, just sign this note."

You go to the tellers window and the banker hands him the note telling him to honor it and put so much money to your credit. But how utterly foolish you would be if, when the money is handed to you, you were to back away, saying: "No, it's too good to be true—I don't believe that banker wants me to have the money." Well, it's the same identical thing in the God-Realm. You perhaps think that this Power cannot give you these things. Well—if you do—then take it from me no one will lose but you. It won't affect me any. I know I can get whatever I need from God. You can too. I believe in this God-Law—you don't. That is the difference. I don't think though that many of my students doubt the existence of the God-Law now, for too many letters continually come to me telling in no uncertain terms of the benefits to be had by my students from the God-Realm.

Cannot you see that this material world will pass away? Do you not know that it is fast cooling off? Do you not know that the moon you see so often is but a cooling sun? Surely you must know that the REAL power behind creation is an UNSEEN AND ETERNAL POWER. Of course you do. Then why not definitely say to your self right now—"I AM RECEIVING THAT WHICH I NEED FROM THE GOD-LAW." If it will make you feel any better, you may say "I AM RECEIVING THAT WHICH I NEED FROM GOD." The answer will be just as sure no matter what you call the Power or the Law. For it is not your idea of God that brings the answer—it's the LAW—or GOD—itself. I don't care what you think God to be. There are as many differing ideas of God as there are stars almost—but the fact is that outside of them all, there operates the Law of God—and none of these many religions have any more truth in them than the other one has. For the God-Law cannot be contained in any manmade system of theology, and GOD HIMSELF DID NOT MAKE A SYSTEM OF THEOLOGY. IT WOULD BE ENTIRELY UN-NECESSARY WHEN THE TRUE FACT OF THE EXISTENCE OF GOD IS KNOWN. Theology is not needed then.

For the God-Law is self-existent—self-supporting—and fully satisfying and fully able to give you whatsoever things are right and true. If your main desire is for health—the Power of the Life Spirit can give it to you. If your desire is for success—the Power of the Life Spirit can bring it to you. If your desire is for happiness—the Power of the Life Spirit can bring it to you. NOW—THE QUESTION IS—CAN YOU TAKE IT? If you need it bad enough you will. For the truths told in this course of instruction are coming as life-buoys to hundreds who have been downed in the battle of life, and who are floating on the sea of time like so many pieces of flotsam and jetsam. They hear my message. They see the honesty and earnestness of my attempts to help them. AND THEY DON'T STUDY WITH ME VERY LONG BEFORE THEY BELIEVE. Then its all over. The moment the belief is manifest—all that is necessary is for a continuation of that belief until the actual manifestation. Remember though—you must mean business. You must actually NEED these good things. You must actually WANT them. And more than all, YOU MUST RECOGNIZE THE SOURCE FROM WHENCE THEY COME.

In the next Lesson I am going to deal with the most remarkable character ever born. That Man Jesus. There is a lot of tradition surrounding His name and history and many things are told to us that are not so. But personally I find Him of sufficient interest that I pattern my life after His. I apply the same God-Law that He applied—and so I shall give a Lesson—maybe two to Him after this one. Now—a new affirmation of truth for you—and a very Powerful one also. I have seen more results achieved from this one affirmation than from any other. It's very dynamic, I assure you. I want you from now on to adopt an attitude of restful waiting as it were. Don't say any more positive affirmations until I tell you to. From now on let your affirmation be this: "I THANK THEE FATHER THAT THOU HAST HEARD ME." Don't let up on that statement, for don't you see, YOU ARE PUTTING THE GOD-LAW TO THE TEST. There is no better way that I know to obtain things from the Spiritual God-Law than to acknowledge the fact that your needs have been made known, and WILL BE ANSWERED AND PROVIDED.

So don't forget from now on its: "I THANK THEE FATHER THAT THOU HAST HEARD ME." Keep quiet. Keep smiling—for soon the assurance of the answer will probably come to you in the moment when you least expect it. This is far as I shall take you this time.

"I THANK THEE FATHER THAT THOU HAST HEARD ME"

EXAMINATION QUESTIONS
FOR LESSON NO. 12

These examination questions are For your benefit and you should know the answers to them all. If they are not clear to you, read your Lesson again and again until they are clear.

1. From what moment does Dr. Robinson say that your life will be one of overcoming victory?

2. What is Dr. MacMillan's conception of the universe? It is opposed to the conception of certain British astronomers?

3. To what does Dr. Robinson attribute his ability to perform so much work?

4. What does he do when he desires guidance? Does he pray?

5. Why would prayer be futile and unnecessary?

6. What does Dr. Robinson designate as the one "sin" in the entire creation?

7. What part of you is the real part?

8. What part of you forms part of the great invisible creative Spirit or Force or Power?

9. What is the only thing that stops you from having the things you desire?

10. Name the conditions necessary for the blessings and gifts from the Spiritual Realm to manifest?

11. What is the affirmation given in this Lesson?

12. Why is this affirmation recommended?

LESSON 13

I promised you that in this Lesson we should deal with the Carpenter Man of Galilee. Not from any religious angle in the accepted sense of the word, however, nor shall we deal with him as any "god" man at all. All our dealings with this wonderful character will be from the standpoint that He never was more than a human being—even as you and I. There are many though who believe Him to be a "one-third part of the trinity" although why they believe it they cannot tell. They have never spent the time or given the effort to find out just what is known about that phase of His existence and what is not known. If they did that they would instantly realize that if they choose to call Him a "god" and look upon Him as such, it will have to be through a strained sense of "faith" for certainly there is no evidence in existence which would tend to justify the statement that He ever was other than a man.

Personally, I am willing to believe anything that can be proven. But I am NOT willing to believe anything that cannot be proven—especially along religious lines. For I know the history of most of the systems of religion, and I know that there is no more proof of the "divinity" of their "gods" than there is that the moon is made of green cheese. Also—you will find if you care to investigate, that these differing systems of religion sprang into existence long after their respective "gods" were dead and buried—if indeed they ever lived at all. For instance—there was no such a religion as Christianity when Christ was on the earth. It was unknown. It sprang into existence far later, and still we have it with us. It's not very potent today, however, for men and women in the first place are not believing the story; and in the second place, when they force themselves to believe it (if possible) they find that its claims cannot be borne out and its precepts do not work. So they are discarding it.

I think perhaps it may be wise here to just submit a few facts regarding the infancy and birth of this Galilean Carpenter to make my point. For ever so often some "dignitary of the church" attempts to take me to task for my stand on religion, as Billy Sunday did recently. They don't get very far with me however, but they might with someone less familiar with church history than I am. I shall just call passing attention to a few pertinent facts which will stop any argument not based on "faith" and then we shall get down to the real significance of this man—for there is a marvelous significance to Him to be sure. The message He came to preach went a thousand miles over the heads of the religionists of His day, and for that matter is still a thousand miles over the heads of the orthodox religionists of today. We shall look into that later in the Lesson though.

The first thing I want to call your attention to is the fact that the time and the place of His birth were never historically known. The time is placed any where inside of 15 years, and is credited to almost every day of that 15 years. If it be a fact that He was a one-third of the Master-Intelligence overruling this great creation, then it certainly would be known just where, and when, and in what year, and in what month, and in what week, and on what day He was born. But history knows nothing about that. Either church or profane history. Then again, another mighty significant fact is that practically all of the rest of the world's "crucified saviors" were born on December the 25th. Moreover, most of them were saved from destruction in infancy. Their births were all miraculously foretold, and in many cases the "sun became dark," etc.

Astronomy gives us no record of these happenings in the stellar regions but religious tradition has lots to say about it, and every "supernaturally-born" "god" the world has ever had was born under circumstances similar to those under which Christ was born. Therefore, if Christ were a "god," so were the rest of the old Grecian "gods" all could do what is claimed for Christ, even to raising the dead and walking on the water. Their mothers were usually "holy virgins" and Plato's mother was conceived by God. Pythagorus was a spirit in heaven before he was born on earth, and his birth was miraculously foretold. He, like the Christ, restored sight to the blind. He cast out devils. He walked on the sea. He healed all manner of diseases and handled poisonous snakes with impunity. He read the thoughts of others and discerned them. He could foretell the future and do thousands of other wonderful things. To be precise here, let me say to you that there is nothing that can be said in favor of Christ's miraculous birth and resurrection that cannot also be said in favor of a dozen other world's saviors also.

Not alone is there no record whatsoever in history of such a character, but neither has there ever been of many of the other "gods" this world has been blessed (or cursed) with. As a matter of fact there is far more evidence that Plato lived than there is that Christ lived. However—I am not questioning His birth at all, for history gives us enough indirect evidence that a person called Jesus Christ probably lived on earth. Where I differ with "supernaturally-revealed" religion is on the point of His "immaculate birth," His "resurrection" and other impossible things attributed to Him. Those who gave us these pagan yarns little knew the harm they were doing to humanity when they gave them. For if the Bible story of this man Jesus is true—then it very effectively removes Him from us. If He had a miraculous birth, and if He were the supreme "god" in human form, then you and I, being but mortals, cannot ever hope to duplicate the life He lived.

For He was "god" and you and I are human beings, born in exactly the same manner as the rest of the human race. But—if Jesus Christ were only a man, THEN IT PLACES HIM IMMEDIATELY WITHIN OUR REACH AND YOU AND I CAN ALSO DO THE THINGS THROUGH THE SAME POWER HE USED, WHICH THINGS HE DID. There can be no question about that. I shall not touch here the things He did and the things attributed to Him that He did not do. The point I want to make is that if He were God, then by no means can you or I ever attain the heights to which he is supposed to have attained—unless, of course, we are all Gods. And there is a lot of truth in that statement, for I believe we are the same identical physical and mental structure that Jesus was. If He were a "god"—so are you. But we shall not halt long here for I want to draw in this Lesson the picture of this Galilean Carpenter as I believe it to exist. And by the way, thinkers the world over are very rapidly coming to this viewpoint of this "man" Jesus Christ.

The personality of Jesus Christ is a very interesting one, and also one which is very revolutionary too. To me, this man Jesus is about the sweetest character that has ever lived. The pages of history have been graced by many unusual and sweet characters, and it is really a pity that history's pages are absolutely silent on this man Jesus. In church histories, of course, there is to be found much reference to Him. In fact they are builded around Him. But I am here talking about authentic recognized histories of that land and age—and this message of history is complete and absolute silence regarding this man who was "god"—as the church would have us believe. Personally I believe He lived, and from that premise I shall write from now on. Many years did I spend studying that character, and many, many hours have I spent just quietly reading of Him. I have realized, of course, that the writings concerning Him, viz. the four gospels are absolutely anonymous writings. No one knows who wrote them, or has there ever been known to exist a single original manuscript covering this story of this Carpenter of Galilee.

So in my studies of Him and in this present writing about Him, I shall ask you to remember that I am writing about Him as I have pictured Him, and even though there is nothing much authentic about Him to be discovered. I might do the same thing about Confucius or Krishna, and incidentally, one might do far worse than make the philosophy of Confucius his philosophy of life. For there are to be found some of the most profound spiritual truths in the teachings of Confucius, as in fact there are also to be found many spiritual truths in every system of so called "supernatural" religion. This but proves the truth of my contention that the God-Law operates outside of all varying creeds and denominations, and probably in spite of a good many or them.

However, believe it or not, I have learned to love this Galilean character, and if I am wrong, and if the future should prove that He was God, then no harm will have been done for, I repeat, I have learned to love that man. Not on account of His presumed godship, but on account of His natural understanding of the spiritual God-Law. With all His strength of character there is intermingled a sweetness almost inexplicable. And you must believe me when I say to you now that my intensely human and faltering heart thrills a little bit at the prospect of writing a Lesson on this Master of Spiritual things. For He was a Master—make no mistake about that. What a pity it is that well-meaning but uneducated religionists and religious promoters attempted to spoil this wonderful character by trying to make Him "divine." For in so doing they robbed mankind of a possibility that it has never had offered to it since.

For when one begins to know this man, there invariably starts a friendship that lasts through time—and perhaps eternity. And so I may confess to you that this much misunderstood Carpenter man and myself have become pals as it were. I learned a lot of spiritual truth from that man. Sometimes in the stress of a busy life, I weaken just a little—or rather, I feel that perhaps I might weaken. in such moments as those, however, I remember His superb strength in the face of all obstacles, and, revivified with the power this man of Galilee knew so well, the weakness is always turned into overwhelming strength, and once more am I vindicated in my claim that the greatest Power in this world today is the power of the Living God-Law. And if it should be that this life does not end it all, and if it should further be proven that we live again "on the other side," then that fact will be to me the very sweetest fact I know. For the friendship I have formed with my Carpenter pal will then be carried over yonder, and the day will come in which I shall see that face of ineffable sweetness.

Beloved—there is one enemy to yet be destroyed and that enemy is death. This last lone enemy WILL BE DESTROYED just as soon as the truth of the Living God Spirit is made known. It will not be through any "judgment bar" or anything on that order, but it will be through a full knowledge here and now of the mighty power my friend the Galilean Carpenter knew and used. And the friendship I have formed here for this man will be a different sort of friendship when this last enemy of man is destroyed—I can say that to you with assurance. THAT friendship will continue throughout the myriads of ages when there shall be no more time, and when you and I are once more restored through understanding of the present God-Law to that state of existence we had away back yonder prior to the time the first "DOUBT" of God entered the picture. What a pity that it ever did enter—but it did—and you and I have discovered to our sorrow that it did not pay to doubt the spoken word of that mighty Life Spirit or God, and had that two back yonder known what the awful consequences would have been, as you and I know what they are, they would have thought a second time before believing any outside "suggester," as they did. It is just as disastrous to doubt that same Life Spirit now as it was then, and I trust that before this course is finished, my students will have learned the utter foolishness of ever again doubting this great Presence, whose power is so unmistakable, right here and now.

But the lesson had to be learned, and so it is that you and I were plunged, through the act of another, into a world as different as night from day, from the first creation of it.

However, in passing, may I say to my students that they may depend upon it that at the right time, and in the right manner, that state of existence will be restored once more. And it may be that a far more radiant state of existence than that was will be manifested. "Eye hath not seen, ear hath not heard, neither HATH IT ENTERED INTO THE HEART OF MAN, THE THINGS THAT THIS MIGHTY LIFE SPIRIT HATH PREPARED FOR THOSE THAT LOVE—OR KNOW HIM—FOR TO KNOW HIM IS TO LOVE HIM."

People sometimes ask me if I believe that we shall know each other in "heaven." You will never be in "heaven" as it is generally understood today, my friend. The heaven that God created is the entire space outside of this earth. The stars are in heaven, the planets are in heaven, and in the sense that God is everywhere, then He is in heaven—but in no other sense. He is not in some place where there is any physical existence of any sort. Neither is He preparing a place for us if, by that, we mean any residence for us as we are manifesting here—in the flesh.

What the future may bring forth we do not know. But you may be sure that when the fullness of the spiritual power of the mighty Life Spirit is fully known, there will be naught of so-called "sin" in the world—naught of poverty—naught of suffering—naught of disease—but there will be a perfection that the world today knows nothing of. The ideals of Confucius will never bring this to pass. Nor will the ideals of Krishna, Vishnu, or Christ or any other PERSONALITY. For there are as many different interpretations put on His teachings as there are ministers almost. What will bring this about will be the actual knowledge and presence of the POWER OF THE LIVING SPIRIT HERE AND NOW. Ideals cannot do it. If they could this old world would have been straightened out a long time ago. But it's far from being straightened out at the present time I can tell you.

True it is that I believe the whole universe is on the verge of the greatest spiritual upheaval and demonstration it has ever witnessed, but today it is in its dark period just before the dawn. I should not be in the slightest degree surprised to see mankind bathed in blood such as never before had it been. I hope not. I trust I am wrong. But there is abroad in the world a spirit or rather a disregard for the Spirit of the Living Creative God-Law, and this is becoming quite pronounced. Men and women are not quite ready yet to accept the Spirit of Truth. They will be some day—and soon I hope—but they are NOT there yet.

Those of us, however, who are trying to know something of this mighty spiritual God-Law, KNOW, and we KNOW FULL WELL that the Life Spirit of God exists here and now, and is gloriously more than sufficient for our every need no matter what that need may be. It remains still for the world at large to know the existence of this power, and I am today the happiest man alive on account of the part I am playing in sending all around the civilized world, the mighty truths of God. I can tell you that it's a responsibility. But it is a joy. I receive criticism and lots of it. But that is only natural and is always the case when one begins to upset ancient traditions and religious doctrines. And it makes no difference whether the new truth overshadows them with power or not, the hard-shelled religionists don't want it.

A few years ago I heard of a preacher in Portland, Oregon, who made the statement from the pulpit that there was no question at all that the scientists and psychologists knew far more of God than the church knows, but, said he, "We have built this church organization ourselves. It is exactly as we want it. AND WE WILL NOT CHANGE IT EVEN THOUGH THE OTHER FELLOW HAS MORE OF THE TRUTHS OF GOD THAN WE HAVE." It is mighty easy to find the reason this brother is preaching, isn't it? But to come back to the Carpenter of Galilee—my friend. My true friend. The friend who would love me were He on the earth, and the friend I love even though I have never seen Him. For had it not been for the spiritual insight into the God Realm which He had, things might have been different in my life.

Was it not He who first preached the message of the ACTUAL LIVING PRESENCE OF THIS MIGHTY GOD POWER? Was it not He who first brought the story to this earth? And was it not that same story, and that story alone, which made it possible for me to know the actual presence, the living, marvelous presence, of this mighty GOD-LAW we are here learning about? None other was qualified to make such a revelation as He was—and had not that revelation been made, I should never have been able to learn the way, and neither would you for that matter—or anyone else.

And as I look back this evening over the years, to the time when that boyhood heart of mine was touched by the story of His rejection, I wonder, had I known then the roughness of the trail ahead of me, whether I should have attempted to tread it or not. Had I known the sharp, jagged edges against which I would tear myself—had I known the loneliness of the nights spent in wrestling with God—had I known the almost impenetrable blackness which was to confront me for years—had I known all this—I very much question whether or not I should have gone on or thrown up the sponge, and denied the very existence of God at all.

You may depend upon one fact, however, and that is this: the man through whom God chooses to make a revelation to this earth, will be a man who is WILLING TO BELIEVE AND TRUST EVEN THOUGH HE GO TO HIS DEATH DOING SO. Through no other sort of a man CAN any revelation from God ever come. History has proven that, time and time again. And had it not been for that Carpenter Pal of mine—I should never have been able to have come through at all.

But He charmed me—He drew me—His story rang true—and it made no difference to me if the church crucified Him, I believed both in Him and in the remarkable story He came to tell—and—as is always in the realm of God—THE BELIEF ITSELF WAS THE ANSWER. I wish I could put that more plainly—but I cannot. It is an immutable Law of the

Living God Himself; in fact it is the God-Law that, ACCORDING TO YOUR FAITH BE IT UNTO YOU, and, being absolutely, unalterably immutable in essence, THE BELIEVING PRAYER, OR DESIRE (for prayer is only another name for desire) you may believe me when I say to you, that IT IS UTTERLY IMPOSSIBLE FOR YOU TO DESIRE OR PRAY FOR ANYTHING WITHOUT RECEIVING IT FROM THE LIVING GOD-LAW—IF YOU BELIEVE IN ITS PRESENCE.

I very much question if there are 15 ministers in the entire world who actually believe the truths as Jesus taught them and spake them. By truths I mean the words He said, as He said them, and without any other inter-pretation on them, other than what He put on them. I doubt very much if there is a single, solitary minister in the entire universe who is willing to take the words of Christ literally—exactly as He spake them—and risk either his neck or his job upon these words.

And so it is that I have come to love this man of Galilee—far better than I love my life. And the very exercises I am prescribing for you, and asking you to follow, are the self-same exercises that have brought to me what little faith in God that I may have. And in the final summing up, had I been able to literally believe the words of this Carpenter friend of mine long ago, I would have done so. In a sort of mental, hazy way I believed that He was the "son of God," but as far as actually receiving anything from Him goes—well—I just couldn't do it. It wasn't in me. I believed that it WAS possible to rely absolutely on this God, but how to do it I knew not. Little did I suspect that this dynamic power was all around me, a mighty, immutable, unchangeable Law, operating for my benefit, and charged and supercharged with power that could be contacted by me. I know it now, however—and am passing the knowledge I have obtained on to you .

I shall not hold out to you any false hopes that overnight you will be able to come into a full realization of the actual presence of the Living God, although that is perfectly possible, and, had you the faith necessary, you could do that very thing. But the chances are that you will have to grow slowly—as I did. Have you ever seen a beautiful lily blooming on the hillside? Sure you have. Well, one of the Bible writers called attention to that lily, and asked us to consider how it grew.

Shall I tell you how it grows?—Well, it grows by JUST STAYING THERE AND MAKING NO EFFORT—at least, no physical effort to grow—THAT'S ALL. It is quietly absorbing moisture and food from the earth, and, as it absorbs, THE GROWTH TAKES CARE OF ITSELF. IF IT MADE ANY ATTEMPT TO GROW IT WOULD SPOIL ITSELF. So it will be with you. The truth about the Living God will GRADUALLY unfold itself to you, and when once it unfolds, you will never lose it. And remember this—the more anxious you are to know the power of this mighty Life Spirit, the faster will it unfold itself to you. Soon you will come to the place where you will not need me or anyone else to show you the way. IT WILL UNFOLD ITSELF AUTOMATICALLY FROM THE LIVING GOD HIMSELF. Then it will be when you shall be perfect master over all your material surroundings, and you will know how to supply your every need, and your progress from then on will be in your own hands. All I can do is to show you the way to begin, and to show you how to actually get in touch with this great Living God of ours. How far you go with Him is in your own hands.

The exercises given to you are to train you to do that very thing. We have been steeped in unbelief and superstition so long that our very nature has become impregnated with it, and in this day and age we cannot mention God without putting on a long face, or shrinking into the background. God's name ought to be the most talked of thing in the world, but it isn't. The mighty Living Life Spirit ought to be on every tongue—but it isn't. Only on Wednesday night and on Sunday is it proper to talk about Him, and then we let one man do all the talking, and pay him for doing it, and all he gives us is pagan superstition and dark age beliefs.

Now mark me well, please—the only way to get that rotten unbelief and superstition out, is to PRACTICE ACTUAL EXERCISES IN FAITH AND BELIEF. For instance, if I can make you believe that your affirmation concerning the power of the Living God is true, then, step by step, can I make you believe in the ACTUAL PRESENCE 0F THE LIVING GOD HIMSELF?

You may see now why I am so insistent that you constantly repeat the statements and affirmations. If I can make you believe in the "power" of this great living spirit, then I can make you believe IN THE GREAT SPIRIT ITSELF—don't you see? I am doing, in these exercises and in this course of study, by scientific means what the religious leaders of the country have vainly attempted to do by just simply telling you, or asking you, to "believe." That method is wrong. We have had it preached to us so long now, that a great majority of those preaching it do not believe it themselves.

Now, if I can, step by step, intelligently show you who and what this wonderful Living God actually is, and if I can step by step give you exercises that I myself have actually proven will manifest the actual presence and power of this Great Living God in your everyday life—then I have accomplished what the "church" has utterly failed to accomplish. I have brought into being by intelligent interpretation and understanding of facts as revealed not only to me but to the entire race if they chose to believe them. FAITH IN THE LIVING GOD.

And the end more than justifies the means. I have made the statement once to you that blind belief is unscientific and to ask a man to believe something that his intelligence cannot grasp is to ask that man to do the impossible. I speak now as a Psychologist.

The trouble with religion today is that it has taken the plain. unvarnished facts of God as Jesus spake them and as they exist, and as they have ever existed, and has clothed them in superstition to such an extent that Christ Himself or God Himself could never recognize them.

Thank God though a remnant have remained which remnant were unwilling to continue the sham of "churchism" and this remnant have made up their minds to KNOW the truth of the God of the universe—or else explode the whole theory. And what did we find? Well we found that there is in existence a Living Life Spirit, which can and will in the moment we can trust it to the full, supply our every need here and now on this earth. It makes no difference what we may need. It makes no difference what the trouble may be, whether lack of health, lack of happiness or lack of success—THE LIVING GOD-LAW CAN SUPPLY IT AND CAN SUPPLY IT HERE AND NOW. This man Jesus knew the secret of it all. Before this spiritual God Law as He knew and used it, seeming miracles were done. But they were not miracles at all. They were the perfectly natural things for Him to do. What was thought to be "supernatural" LAW is but divinely "natural" law. And that is the Lesson the world has yet to learn.

It made no difference to this Carpenter man what was needed—the spiritual God-Law supplied the need. Shall I tell you the secret of the Power of the lonely Nazarene? Listen for a moment, and digest it well—it will open up to you like a rose when you see it. This Nazarene KNEW THE EXISTENCE OF THE MIGHTY LIFE SPIRIT I AM TALKING TO YOU ABOUT—AND HE KNEW HOW TO KEEP HIMSELF IN TUNE WITH THIS MIGHTY LAW. And so may you. For I shall tell you a little secret now: IT IS PERFECT HARMONY WITH THE GOD-LAW THAT BRINGS COMPLETE VICTORY OVER EVERY MATERIAL CIRCUMSTANCE. The existence of the great cosmic world filled with its cosmic energy or ray, is an established fact. It is also an established fact that your thoughts are THINGS. It is also well known to you now that your THOUGHTS are a PART OF THE GREAT SPIRITUAL COSMIC REALM. I have been very careful to explain to you how this thought realm of yours was part of the great cosmic consciousness or energy. I have told you to continually and without lapse direct your desires right straight into this realm of cosmic or God-energy.

You have done carefully the things I have asked you to do, and judging by the letters I daily receive, the great proportion of my students have found that this great cosmic or God-consciousness really exists and really does the things needed to be done. And may I say to you that the more of the cosmic consciousness you absorb—the more spiritual and happier will you become. Your work from now on is but to keep yourself in HARMONY WITH THE GREAT COSMIC GOD-LAW OR REALM AS IT EXISTS. THIS IS TO BE DONE BY UTTER RELAXATION AT NIGHT, AND BY A CONSTANT RECOGNITION OF THE POWER OF THIS COSMIC GOD REALM BY YOU. I think you will be able to see now the reasonableness of my hypothesis, and now I want you to go quite a little farther in your simple little, but dynamic exercises. I want you to practice being very quiet. and TUNING YOURSELF TO THE GREAT COSMIC CONSCIOUSNESS. You can do this through the channel of your thoughts.

At night, just say from a thankful heart, the affirmation I gave you in the last Lesson: "I THANK THEE FATHER THAT THOU HAST HEARD ME" and then stay quiet for a long time, or until you go to sleep, KEEPING YOUR THOUGHTS FAR OUT YONDER INTO THE REALM OF THE GOD-CONSCIOUSNESS. LET THE INVISIBLE EMANATIONS FROM THIS REALM FLOW THROUGH AND THROUGH YOU, AND REALIZE AT ALL TIMES THAT YOU ARE NOW USING THE VERY CREATIVE POWER OF THE EARTH AND THE HEAVENS IN YOUR OWN LIFE. If you place a piece of steel against a magnet, and rub the two together, after a few rubs the piece of unmagnetized steel will become magnetized. And when you place yourself up against the God-Consciousness, then you will absorb the power of the great God-Law and your life will be transformed from then on. The religious people would have us get down on our knees and "pray" to some mystical creature in heaven called "god," and then, only "if it be His sweet will" in His own good time they will receive the petitions. But they never do. How much better is it to know that God is a real living spiritual power, CAPABLE OF CHARGING OTHERS WITH THAT POWER. How much better is it than "praying" to actually place yourself in vital living contact with the all-creative Living Life-Spirit here and now.

It is an old saying and incidentally a well-known fact that as one's thoughts are, so is one. This is especially true in the God-Realm. When once you begin to realize the fact that God is a living reality to you, and a living Law, CAPABLE OF FULFILLING YOUR EVERY NEED, then what a power there is for you to use is there not? Why my friend—all the God-Power of the whole creation lies in your hands. and the closer you get to it and keep to it, the more powerful will you be. You can see that. You know this power exists. You know it exists for you. All right—then just from now on. ABSORB OR TAKE FROM THE GOD-REALM THE POWER IT SO FREELY OFFERS YOU. IN YOUR BUSINESS OR IN YOUR HOME, IT MAKES NO DIFFERENCE WHICH, YOU USE THE MIGHTY POWER OF THIS MIGHTY GOD-LAW MOMENT BY MOMENT. I want you to so saturate yourself with it that it will bubble out of you and everything you touch will be a success. Is there disharmony in your home? There will not be if you are filled with the spirit of the God-Law. Is there failure in business? There will not be when you become so filled with the wisdom and business acumen of the God-Law that failure cannot manifest at all.

Send your thoughts into the great cosmic realm, draw from that realm the things of God that you need, or the material things for that matter, and. when you have isolated yourself and your thought to God or to this great cosmic God-Consciousness, THE THINGS YOU NEED TO MANIFEST WILL MANIFEST. Perhaps not tomorrow, BUT THEY WILL MANIFEST, AND THE THINGS NEEDED TO BE DONE TO BRING THAT MANIFESTATION WILL COME TO YOU. I think you can see this, so until you receive your next Lesson do as I ask you to. Get so close to this God-Realm and keep so close to it that you become full of its power. This is the way in which Jesus obtained his power. You will remember that He loved to be alone either on the mountainside or by the sea. And I can tell you what His thoughts were on these occasions. They were thoughts of the power of what He called "his father." This was only another way of saying the power of God. And this is but another way of saying the great cosmic creative intelligence behind the universe.

POINTS TO REMEMBER IN THIS LESSON.

(1) Jesus obtained His power from close communion with the great Life Spirit of the universe.

(2) He learned the secret of being alone with God. or with the great God-Consciousness of the universe.

(3) You may have the very same power that Jesus had when you will become so close to this cosmic power that you become like it.

(4) Let your evening exercises and your waking exercises be designed to rest quietly. and let the God-Consciousness thrill you and flow through you to the very full. If you should experience strange vibrations—write and let me know immediately. Many students will experience them, and many will not. If you do however I want to know of it at once. Also if you see different colors before your vision when you are contacting the spiritual realm, I want to know that also.

EXAMINATION QUESTIONS
FOR LESSON NO. 13

These examination questions are for your benefit and you should know the answers to them all. If they are not clear to you, read your Lesson again and again until they are clear.

(1) From what standpoint is the character of Jesus considered in this Lesson?

(2) How can this standpoint be justified?

(3) Mention some of the facts that throw doubt upon the Bible story of the miraculous birth of Jesus?

(4) If the Bible story were true, humanity would be the sufferer. Why?

(5) What answer is given to the inquiry, "Shall we know each other in Heaven?"

(6) If just one condition be fulfilled, it will be utterly impossible for you to desire anything without receiving it from the Living God-Law?

(7) How will you be enabled to come into a full realization of the actual presence of the Living God?

(8) In what way can you get rid of unbelief and superstition?

(9) What is it that brings complete victory over every material circumstance?

(10) By what means are you enabled to keep yourself in harmony with the great Cosmic God-Realm?

(11) What instructions are given you for night-time?

(12) How did Jesus obtain his wonderful power?

LESSON 14

Dear friend and student:

This Lesson is the focal point of everything that has gone before. It is the point at which I show you how to actually and literally find and use the Power of the Mighty Life Spirit of the universe.

In the other Lessons I have led you slowly step by step up the ladder until you have now arrived at a point where you may see the view stretched before you. This Lesson will show you how to do that, for it is the most dynamic thing I have ever put into print. What you do with it lies in your own hands. If you use this cosmic Power for your own good and the good of others it will repay you many times.

Let me warn you not to use it for the harm of others for if you do it will turn like a serpent and sting you.

Sincerely your friend,
FRANK B. ROBINSON

In our last study together we dealt with the character—Jesus of Galilee. In this Lesson we shall look a little farther into that man's life, and try and discover the secret of His impelling charm and power. For it would be useless to try to tell me that there is not a magnetic attraction and charm attached to this man. I know better. And while, of course, He could not have been other than a human being, still—the attraction and charm is there just the same. This comes from the Spiritual Realm where the God-Law operates, and in passing may I say to you that it is not possible for a man or woman to know very much about the Spiritual Realm of God, or the God-Law, and not be full of charm, and power. There is a very subtle something to the man or woman who has learned the secret of "abiding in God" or the great God-Law that I am teaching you about.

It is often hard to explain, but there can be no question of the presence of this subtle something in the human life that knows the spiritual power of the God-Law. Men may try to explain the impelling and compelling power in such a life, but it cannot be done—for the power is spiritual and therefore cannot be explained by natural means. As a matter of fact however, we have seen that the spiritual realm, which has so often been alluded to as the realm of mystery, is, after all, nothing but the divinely natural realm. And the same spiritual power that exudes from this Christ man, should exude from you. More than that—it WILL exude from you in the moment you KNOW and USE spiritual God-Law as this Carpenter man knew and used it. And this is the normal natural condition of every man and woman. If you are living apart from the so-called "divine" power as manifested by this Christ man, then you are not enjoying life to the full, and neither are you YOURSELF.

For the natural and normal condition of every man should be that he lead a life of overwhelming victory over the world around him, and over everything that crops up in his life which is not wanted. There should exude from the NORMAL man a power that can create whatever it is he needs, and more than that, SUCH A POWER IS NOW AT THE DISPOSAL OF EVERY MAN IF HE WILL TAKE IT. It is NOT necessary to wait till after death before the power of the unseen or spiritual realm may be known. Can you imagine what sort of a life yours would be, if you had and could use the same power that this Christ man used? Would not your life be a much more blessed thing than it is now? I think so. Well, the power is here. It is the God-Power. It is NOT the power of any so-called "subconscious mind" for such a mind does not exist at all, and never has existed. It is just simply the overwhelming power of the mighty Life Spirit, anxious and waiting for you to USE IT IN YOUR DAILY LIFE AND AFFAIRS.

Everything I have said to you to date in these Lessons has been designed to bring you to the point where you will be able to absorb and understand the truth this 14th Lesson teaches. And it is a mighty spiritual truth too. Slowly I unfolded to you the facts of nature and of nature's God as I believe them to exist. I showed you that your thoughts are the real spiritual part of you. I tried to show you something of the magnitude and reality of LIFE itself. Then I brought to your attention the fact of the existence of the "cosmic rays" and you will have observed that through these Lessons to date, I have been slowly and carefully taking you by the hand and leading you along the spiritual Life-Path, until such time as I considered that you were capable of absorbing a little bit of REAL spiritual truth, and more than that, OF LITERALLY APPLYING IT IN YOUR OWN LIFE.

Had I given to you the truths this Lesson contains right on the start, the chances are many to one that you would have said "Oh, well, that fellow's crazy—I'm not going ahead with this course of instruction."

BUT—leading you slowly and gently over a period of months as I have led you, if you are a normal and intelligently thinking person, you should be ready by this time to start to really APPLY THE GOD-LAW IN YOUR OWN LIFE AFTER YOU HAVE FOUND IT. The first thing to do is to find it. I don't think there are many of my students that have come along this far with me, without finding a little bit about the existence of this mighty GOD-LAW. They will not have known it to the very full of course, for I have not yet explained fully just what this Law is and just how it operates. I am giving you a glimpse of what to expect in this Lesson now. And under this Lesson lies a lot of spiritual truth. I trust you will grasp it all, for if you do, then the world may be yours and everything it contains. At any rate, enough of this world's pleasures may be yours to satisfy you. The religiously inclined of course, will quote to me here the old Bible saw: "lay not up for yourselves treasures on earth, where moss and rust doth corrupt, and where thieves do not break through and steal."

All I have to say to that doctrine is that it is but one more old church teaching, of certainly unknown origin, and therefore not credible at all. Never let anyone tell you that any pleasure you may have here on earth is not pleasure obtained from the Life Spirit. Don't let anyone tell you that you should not try to obtain the blessings of life while you are here, for such is NOT a fact. The spirit that gave you LIFE in the first place, is interested in seeing you ENJOY life. More than that, such a Spirit is interested in your enjoying life—not in the "future," but HERE AND NOW IF YOU PLEASE. What sort of a being would the Creative Life Intelligence be if he would create or implant in you the desire for the very best things of life, and then tell you that you never could have them here and now, but will get them "after you die—beyond Jordan." That is church myth once more and it is NOT the truth.

As far as the "moss" and the "rust" and the thieves go, we have some very good safety deposit boxes in our banks, and there is not much likelihood of very much moss growing on our money, nor do I think with the up-to-date banking contrivances we have, there is much chance for it to get very rusty. I can assure you mine doesn't—it doesn't stay in one place long enough for that. And those thieves—well, there are burglar-proof vaults in most any bank, quite sufficient to keep out the average burglar. In any event, if while in the charge of a bank, your money gets "rusty" or covered with "moss," or if it is stolen by thieves, the bank will be held responsible, and will either clean up and restore your money to you, or will replace it with new money. So you see the Bible argument here is not so good—it will not hold water. At any rate, I shouldn't stop trying to accumulate money if I were you on account of this ancient Bible paragrapher's story about the rust, and the moss, and the thieves.

My advice to you is to use the power of the Living Spirit for the accumulation of whatever good things you need in this life. This is what the Spirit of God exists for. It would be useless to us otherwise. If the Great Creative Life Principle cannot do for you here and now the things you desire, then the chances are that neither can it do these things "beyond the tomb." And this "tomb" proposition is all so very vague and indefinite anyhow. There is not enough evidence of any life after death to justify your living in poverty here and now, denying yourself the things you could enjoy on the strength of the hope that you will get them after you are dead. This "life after death" theory is a very beautiful one to be sure. But it was born in the minds of men who DID NOT KNOW SPIRITUAL LAW. They knew nothing at all of the power of God or they would not have originated such a theory as that. The theory is as old as the hills anyhow, and was in existence thousands of years before the Christian era commenced. It is far older than Christ, and was known to millions of Egyptians thousands of years before Christ was ever heard of.

And in the meantime, thousands of good "followers of the Lord" have been living in abject poverty because they believed such a story as this one purports to be. THEY ARE RESTING THEIR OARS ON PAST-

AGE DOGMA AND TRADITION, ALL THE WHILE PASSING UP THE REAL TRUTHS OF GOD, AND HAVE ALSO PASSED UP ALL INVESTIGATIONS INTO THE SPIRITUAL REALM, WHICH IN-VESTIGATIONS MIGHT FINALLY DISCLOSE THE TRUTH THAT DEATH IS NOT A PART OF THE SCHEME OF LIFE IN ANY SENSE OF THE WORD. IN OTHER WORDS, SUPERSTITIOUS RELIGION-ISTS HAVE LEFT WITH US THE IDEA THAT NO MAN CAN OB-TAIN HAPPINESS UNTIL AFTER HE IS DEAD. Such an impossible teaching. Such an awful dogma as that is. And it has been given to us in the name of God, by men and women who claim they know God. As a matter of fact I am pretty well convinced in my own mind that they know nothing about Him at all. And I am convinced of something else too—I am convinced that as long as the asinine theories of "supernatural birth"—"Immaculate conception"—"resurrection," etc., are indulged in and taught, nothing tangible about God can be learned by those teaching and believing such incredible yarns about the mighty Creator.

Life is LIFE—and IS NOT DEATH IN ANY FORM. REMEMBER THAT. I shall not go into what life means in this course of instruction. I deal with that somewhere else and in a more advanced teaching which students of this course are not quite ready for yet. But the question con-tinually comes into every normal man's mind at some time or other in his lifetime. He wants to know where LIFE originated. He wants to know what it is. He wants to know why it ends so suddenly. The religionists have told us that such things were only hidden in the "heart of God" and were not to be known by mortal man. And in reply to such statements I say: "WHO SAID SO?" That these truths are hidden in the "heart of God" is quite correct. But not in the heart of any old pagan "Yah-veh" such as the old Jews owned for a God.

Shall I tell you just where these secrets are hidden, my friend? THEY ARE HIDDEN IN THE HEART OF GOD ALL RIGHT—BUT GOD IS THE CREATIVE SPIRIT AND INTELLIGENCE THROUGH WHOSE POWER AND IN WHOM WE LIVE AND MOVE AND HAVE OUR BEING, That is where they are hidden if you can properly use the word "hidden." And I am not so sure that they are hidden at that. Those of us who have paid the price and who know something of the Law governing the Spiritual Realm, know full well that these things may all be known here and now. We know that it won't be very long until we SHALL know them here and now. The "future" story does not appeal to us for we know its origin. But you may be sure of one thing my friend. You may be sure of the fact THAT THERE IS LAW—SPIRITUAL LAW—AND ORDER UNDERLYING THE ENTIRE REALM OF GOD—THE SPIRITUAL REALM. The future will disclose the fact that the truths of God are NATURAL TRUTHS WITHIN OUR GRASP HERE AND NOW. True it is that we have not yet seen them fully—but that means nothing.

There was a time when the radio Law was unknown too. There was a time, and not so long ago, when electricity as a lighting agent was absolutely unknown. It is not very long since a certain city petitioned the city council to "pass an ordinance denying people the right to install electric light—because it is an invention of the devil." And that was right here in the good old United States at that. So there is no argument at all in the statement that because these things have never been fully known they never can be fully known. And I don't want a single one of my students to ever believe that heathenish story. Who knows—probably one to whom I am writing now will be the one who will venture into the spiritual realm, and will disclose to the world some of its hitherto unknown secrets. Who can say? For it may be that YOU—yes YOU—will progress so far into this marvelous realm of God, THAT YOU WILL BE CAPABLE OF UNDERSTANDING THE REVELATION THAT THIS REALM CAN GIVE TO YOU, AND WILL TRANSFER TO US HUNGRY MORTALS, SOMETHING MORE THAN WE KNOW NOW OF THE TRUTH OF GOD.

For the last thing has not yet been learned about this realm. This realm will not be plumbed to the full until the secret of DEATH is known. We are not there yet—BUT WE ARE GETTING THERE, AND MAYBE BEFORE THIS COMES FROM OUR PRINTING PRESSES SOME NEW AND MARVELOUS REVELATION WILL HAVE BEEN GIVEN TO MAN FROM GOD. Let me put that another way. Let me say that some MAN or WOMAN will have been WILLING TO TRUST THE GOD-LAW TO THE LIMIT, AND SO WILL DISCOVER WHATEVER HE CAN HOLD OF GOD.

The Spiritual Law cannot operate to the full as long as death reigns supreme on the earth. It was NOT meant that it should so reign, and beloved student, hear me well when I say to you that THE FULL UNDERSTANDING OF THE SPIRITUAL LAW OF GOD WILL ABSOLUTELY BANISH DEATH. Carry that thought with you, and live in the spirit that death is not necessary. We know that disease is not necessary, and we know that poverty is not necessary either. And you may rest assured that neither is death necessary. It takes one of two kinds of men to make the above statement. Either a man must be a fool or he must have progressed to quite some depth in the realm of God. I wish to assure my students that I am not looked up on nationally as any sort of a fool, and in making the above statement to you, I know whereof I speak.

In a much further advanced course I go into the realm of the creative power of the Life Spirit; but, as I stated, I shall not pursue that study here in this course, for if you master this course you will have enough to keep you busy the rest of your life, learning day by day a little more of the marvelously beautiful power of the Living Life Spirit—GOD. Never get away from the fact though, that there is a definite PURPOSE running through all creation, AND DEATH HAS NO PLACE IN THAT DIVINE

PURPOSE. Day by day brings us closer to our goal. Day by day sees some student of mine doing what might be considered very unusual to say the least. I have in mind how one lady student, who, before she was half way through this course of instruction, SAW THE LIGHT, and her manifestation of the Living God shows to others through the gift of healing. She is able to take cases that no physician can possibly help, and through her knowledge of the Spirit of Life, she is enabled to do for them what is often considered a miracle.

But there are no miracles where God is concerned. Nor were there ever any miracles in spiritual Law. What seems miraculous to human and material eyes assumes a perfect naturalness when the light of the Creative Life Spirit is thrown upon it. It is literally amazing the things the natural human life can accomplish, WHEN THEIR UNION AND HARMONY WITH THE GOD-LAW IS FULLY OR EVEN PARTIALLY RECOGNIZED. I am often asked, "Well, Doctor Robinson—do you mean to tell me that your teaching can do this, or can cure that, or can rectify the other thing?" And my reply invariably is that if there is any limit to the power of the LIVING SPIRIT—GOD—then I have never yet been able to find it. I am not looking for it either because I know that such limit does NOT exist. The limitation is not on the part of the God-Law, but IS on your part and my part. For would we throw all doubt and fear to the four winds, absolutely and completely, THERE IS NOTHING THE HUMAN MIND CAN CONCEIVE THAT THE GOD OF THIS UNIVERSE WOULD NOT DO. Every inch of ground that the sole of your foot shall tread upon shall be yours. Every bit of confidence you can put in the God-Law will bring forth much fruit. And if it is material blessings you are looking for—IT WILL BRING THEM TOO. Don't forget that.

I shall not deal with the subject here as to whether or not the Galilean Carpenter ever worked miracles. I deal with that elsewhere and shall not touch upon the subject here any more than to say that if He did, He did it through a complete knowledge of the spiritual God-Law at His command. Take the allegory of the Lazarus story. You will remember that when word was brought to the Master that LAZARUS was dead, the first thing He did was to get away for a while. One would have thought that He would have gone immediately—but He did not. And I think perhaps I know the reason why He did not go. Anyway—He abode where He was. Finally He went, however, and the statement He made in the form of a "preacher" is very, very significant. Lifting His eyes to heaven He said, in effect: "Father, I don't need to pray for myself because I KNOW that you can raise this dead man, so don't take this prayer as an evidence of my own doubt—BUT I AM MERELY PRAYING THIS PRAYER IN ORDER THAT THE THRONGS THAT ARE WITH ME MIGHT NOT MAKE THE MISTAKE OF ATTRIBUTING ANY MIRACULOUS POWER TO ME—BUT THAT THEY MIGHT KNOW THAT

YOU—GREAT LIFE SPIRIT—ARE THE ONE WHO WILL DO THIS HEALING.

And then, as the story runs, He called with a loud voice and the dead came to life again. In the first place, Jesus Christ realized first and last and all the time, THAT THE POWER HE USED WAS NOT WITHIN HIMSELF. He realized further that every living soul can use this same power. He said to the crowds who looked on in amazement, "THE THINGS THAT I DO SHALL YE DO ALSO"—and I am convinced that He knew full well what He was talking about. He must have—otherwise His name would not be as universally known as it is today. For—I repeat—there is an attraction to that name to be sure. And in whatever moments of weakness I may at times have, (and I should not be human if I didn't have them) it is to this great Prophet of God that I turn. He needed no miraculous conception in order to manifest the power of the Life Spirit. You have no immaculate conception to your credit, have you? Well, it is spiritual Law that you and I can duplicate every AUTHENTIC work this humble Nazarene ever did is it not? Nor were you conceived without a human father were you? I think not. That He was "CONCEIVED BY THE HOLY SPIRIT OF GOD" I am perfectly willing to admit, FOR YOU AND I AND EVERY OTHER LIVING SOUL WERE ALSO CONCEIVED BY THAT SAME GREAT LIFE SPIRIT—BUT THROUGH PERFECTLY NATURAL MEANS.

The other "supernatural" story robs this man of His power and his greatness, for it attributes to Him an unusual power He never did possess. It takes Him away from us. It puts Him on a pinnacle where He does not belong—and it is very wrong and very blind of the churches to do this. Some day soon they won't do it at all. NO—friend—this man of Galilee KNEW THE VERY SAME GOD-LAW I AM TRYING SO HARD TO TEACH YOU ABOUT. Where did He learn it, you ask. I do not know. There are many places where one may learn the spiritual truths of God. Probably this man fulfilled a maternal ideal, and therefore was the culmination of lifetimes hopes on the part of his mother, and fulfilled them through her own wishes and desires. That is aside from the point though. In my little Alfred I see myself. My traits are his traits. In little Florence the same thing applies. If you breed a Clydesdale to a Percheron—you get a mixture. It is a well established fact that prenatal care and prenatal ideas certainly have their part in shaping the foetus and the born baby. The great thing here though is that this man Jesus KNEW AND RECOGNIZED THE POWER THERE WAS AT HIS DISPOSAL. HE KNEW THE POWER OF GOD, even though He were but a man. He lived in that power. He loved it. Did it ever occur to you that a great constituent part of the life of this Nazarene was loneliness? He was ever to be found either on some lone mountainside, or perchance, beside the sea. His was a lonely life—and I can tell you why it was a lonely life. IT WAS A LONELY LIFE BECAUSE HE RECOGNIZED THE FACT THAT THE

GREAT TRUTHS OF GOD ARE ALWAYS REVEALED IN THE QUIETNESS OR THE LONELINESS OF THE HUMAN SOUL. That is why. Why do you think I have been giving you these exercises in relaxation, concentration, restful trust, etc.? Did you think for a moment that I did not have a very definite plan behind all these simple appearing little exercises? Perhaps you thought that I was but trying to have you relax the body in order that the relaxation would do you good. It may be that you wondered why I prescribed these exercises, and it may be that perhaps they seemed somewhat useless and perhaps a little foolish to you. Well, let me say to you that nothing is farther from the truth than that. I GAVE YOU THESE EXERCISES TO PREPARE YOU TO GET INTO LIVING VITAL CONTACT WITH THE ACTUAL LITERAL POWER OF THE MIGHTY CREATIVE INTELLIGENCE OF THE UNIVERSE. Well, but you say to me, "Dr. Robinson—do you mean to tell me that you are going to show me how to literally get in touch with the realm of God?" And my reply is that I mean just that. I am going to show you how to make the ACTUAL LITERAL CONNECTION WITH GOD THAT YOU HAVE WANTED TO MAKE ALL YOUR LIFE.

And when this Connection is made, I assure you your future is in your own hands, and I can then very safely hand you back to yourself, to live, and learn under the guidance of the Master Hand—the mighty Life Spirit. And most of your Lessons under this teacher will be learned, not by begging from Him for this or for that, BUT BY KEEPING SO STILL THAT YOU CAN HEAR WHAT HE HAS TO SAY TO YOU. For the spiritual realm always responds to the soul that is in tune with this wonder-working realm. The Life Spirit always responds to that life. It is the GOD-LAW that such be the case. And when this flash from the God-Realm comes to you—you will know it and will never forget it. You will remember here that your thoughts are things. You will remember further that God works in the "quietness." It is the still (quiet) small voice that brings the victory and sense of the overwhelming presence of the Living God to you.

Now, in these relaxing exercises I have had you fix your mind continually on the light area. I have had you concentrate on the thing you want. I have told you to definitely set your mind on the one thing above all others that you really need in life. I have, furthermore had you repeat the affirmation, "I THANK THEE FATHER THAT THOU HAST HEARD ME." Now—from now on, I am going to ask you to do something else. It is definitely established in your mind what you want. You are, night by night, throwing your thoughts (things of the spirit) into the great cosmic consciousness which is God. You have been doing these exercises now for several months, and are now where I consider you should be. You are now at the place where you should be able to make the definite spiritual contact with the power of the mighty Life Spirit—and make it to your everlasting joy.

Now let me warn you in advance that I cannot tell you just exactly WHEN you will experience the sensation of the presence of God. I do not know you personally. I know nothing about your temperament nor do I know anything about your daily mode of life. But I don't need to. The Law of GOD works for all. The difference in the time taken for the actual manifestation differs in accordance with the speed with which YOU can REST IN PERFECT HARMONY WITH THE LIFE SPIRIT. For what I am going to show you now is how to actually get into harmony with God. When you do that—you will know that the trolley of your life has touched the electric wire of God fullness, and you will then go wherever you want to as long as that connection is still there. In putting yourself in harmony with this great Cosmic Consciousness, it is necessary that you choose some part of the day or evening for this one exercise. Forget the other exercises for the time being, and set aside some regular time of the day for your LESSONS IN ACTUALLY CONTACTING GOD.

Perhaps the morning will suit you best. Perhaps the afternoon is more convenient. Perhaps just before going to bed would fit your needs better. These things I do not know and you will have to pick out the time best suited to your circumstances and surroundings. The main thing is that you have a definite time set for your daily exercise in GOD'S ACTUAL PRESENCE—FOR THAT IS LITERALLY WHAT YOU ARE DOING.

You will get after a while so that you would not miss this half hour for worlds; for the strength coming to You from the Cosmic Life Spirit will stagger You. I want you, in your time for finding God, to lie down. Be absolutely at rest. Just as you have been doing, only more so if possible. Not a move. Very quiet and slow breathing. You lie like a log of wood or a piece of lead. NOT ONE SINGLE MOVE. KEEP ABSOLUTELY STILL. Not a strained stillness at all, but an absolute and utter relaxation of every nerve and every muscle. The best illustration I can give you, although not at all appropriate, is that of a drunken man. He is in a state of utter relaxation. Not the stiffness of a corpse at all, but just simply the leaving go of every attempt to do anything at all—except breathe to the full—slowly fill the lungs—slowly exhale—and DO IT NOISELESSLY TOO.

Then—FORGET EVERYTHING IN YOU—CAST IT OUT—AND LISTEN. Did you hear what I said? L I S T E N. Don't move at all—just listen. Forget who you are if you can. Forget everything—just LOSE YOURSELF IN THE GREAT COSMIC CONSCIOUSNESS OF THE UNIVERSE. Keep widely awake—intently listening. DO NOT GO TO SLEEP IF YOU CAN KEEP AWAKE. If you cannot keep awake then do the exercise sitting in a chair.

Wide awake remember. Intensely alert—listening—listening—listening. An absolute quiet should be there. Not a move made. No one to disturb you. Then LISTEN. At some time or other, and before you have been doing this "waiting on God" exercise very long, THERE WILL

COME A MOMENT IN YOUR LIFE WHILE YOU ARE DOING THIS EXERCISE PROBABLY, WHEN IT WILL SEEM THAT THE WHOLE REALM OF HEAVEN HAS BEEN OPENED UP TO YOU. You may want to sing—and if you do, why sing. You may want to shout, and if you do, why shout. No matter what form of manifestation this flash from the spiritual realm takes—IT WILL SOMETIME OR OTHER COME TO YOU. And it will fill you with a spiritual peace that you never knew before. It will transform you. It will make you extremely happy.

Now I must also warn you a little here also. UNDER NO CIRCUMSTANCES TRY TO PROLONG THIS MOMENT, BUT JUST LET IT TAKE ITS NATURAL COURSE. BE SURE THAT YOU DO NOT TRY TO FORCE ITS RETURN FOR YOU WILL NOT BE ABLE TO DO THAT. IF IT DOES RETURN TO YOU, IT WILL BE WITHOUT YOUR HELP AND IT WILL BE IN A MOMENT WHEN YOU LEAST EXPECT IT. Some day or other, there will come surging into your consciousness waves upon waves of joy. Tears will flow perhaps—but you will KNOW THAT YOU ARE IN HARMONY WITH THE GOD OF THIS UNIVERSE. You will have had a "flash" from the skies one might say. And you will be supremely happy I assure you.

I cannot say to you definitely just when this experience will come, nor can I tell you where it will come. It may come after you have been doing this exercise for only a few days and it may not come to you for months or years, but sooner or later it will come. It is a Law of the spiritual realm that it must come. Your natural environment and your natural life should be in harmony with the cosmic principle of the universe, or in other words with God. Intenseness of desire will be a great help, for it is the desire for this harmony with the cosmic consciousness that brings it into being.

Once this flash is recognized you need never fear further about your relationships with the Master-Intelligence behind the universe. Of course, it is possible even after that for you to do things which might break this connection, but the law is that after this consciousness is established you never will do many things you are not supposed to do. You will not commit very many of what the Christians like to call "Sins."

In passing let me call your attention to the fact that a good many things which the church would have you believe are sins, are nothing of the kind. To the contrary many of the things they look upon as being opposed to God are,. as a matter of fact, nothing more or less than a normal material manifestation of the Spiritual Law working through you.

The principle behind this manifestation from the spiritual realm is this—there has come to you a little bit of the joy and happiness which is contained to the full in the realm of God. The God-Law has been brought to play in your life momentarily. Now the question may arise why cannot this supreme happiness be made permanent, and let me say to you in answer to that question that if it were made permanent while you are manifesting as a physical being you would be utterly no use to yourself or to any one else. Some of the most spiritual people I know are some of the loneliest people, and their connection with the Spiritual Law invariably results in a breakdown in which the tears flow copiously. This spiritual realm manifests to different individuals in a different way; most of them, however, are made quite happy while others are reduced to tears. Still others can go out and command sickness to leave inflicted bodies, in presumed violation of all natural laws.

As I stated I do not know whether this experience will come to you but you must keep up this exercise earnestly, intelligently until it does. Let there be absolutely nothing fanatical about this, for I assure you, you are dealing with a psychological and spiritual law which is as sure as the law of gravitation. It would be a sorry scheme of things if it were not possible for a human being to get into vital living contact with its own creator.

You will remember that the Bible allegory tells us that after God had spit in the ground and made man out of a hunk of mud, or clay, he breathed into his nostrils the breath of life. The story, of course, is absolutely fiction and an old myth, but at the same time there lies under that story a very deep and a very true spiritual truth. Leaving out of the question entirely the method by which man was made, we know that he was made physically at some time or other, we also know that the Great Master-Intelligence of the universe was directly responsible for that making, so we shall accept that fact and let it go for the time being.

The point I want you to understand here is that this same life principle I am teaching you about, at some time or other, breathed into this material thing called MAN the breath of life; in other words, he permeated his creation with himself and he is life. Therefore, every living thing is a living actual manifestation of the first creative life principle of the universe. There can be no such a thing as a man living without the God Principle causing him to live.

Whatever it was that happened so long ago, which caused man to lose sight of the life principle, I shall not go into here for it is beside the point. The thing I want to do here is to restore that communion between God and my students.

I have stated many times and I repeat it here that there is a vast harmony running through the entire created scheme of things as they exist today. Certain it is that if you are out of harmony with that great Intelligence, by no possible means can you fulfill your place in the universe; furthermore, if you are out of tune with this God-Law you cannot obtain from it anything you might need for the simple reason that the channel between you and the rest of the universe is not open.

When the weather gets very cold in my home and the temperature drops, all the violin pipes on my organ go flat and have to be retuned to fit the cold weather. If on playing the organ in cold weather I use the violin pipes, disharmony results so I never play the violin pipes in the winter time. When it warms up, of course, they naturally go back into tune again, but when those pipes are out of harmony with the rest of the organ they are useless to me and consequently I never use them. Neither will the great Life Spirit use you in the eternal scheme of things as long as you are out of harmony with it. Now to get back into harmony with it I have given you, covering a period of months, certain fundamental truths and certain dynamic spiritual exercises to do. In this way I have directed you back again into the great spiritual realm of life and I am only asking you to desire earnestly enough and keep quiet enough for the original connection which has been broken, to be re-established between you and the creative life spirit which gave you life in the first place. That is all that I am trying to do but it is enough.

Many points may arise at this stage of our journey, but don't write me letters about them unless you feel that you really must. I am flooded with mail now, and I know the questions that you are going to ask me and the balance of this course will be given over to dealing with those questions that have come into your minds since you studied this Lesson number 14.

From time to time as you keep in harmony with the cosmic Law this experience will probably be repeated, and here let me warn you very carefully against the great mistake that most people make. They think that if the consciousness of this cosmic presence is not there at all times that they are out of tune with the Infinite. No such a thing. The proof of the Spiritual Law lies in its efficacy to control a human life even though that life be not conscious of it. You would not want to be supremely happy every moment; I mean the happiness which manifests itself in either singing or shouting or crying, for there is something in life which is far greater than that sort of happiness. There is what we choose to call peace, and that is a quietness of life which I cannot explain to you. I experience it to be sure but as far as putting it to print or defining the cosmic peace, I cannot do it. You, however, will experience it after you have received that manifestation from the spiritual realm.

At this point I am going to leave you until the next Lesson, and do this exercise very faithfully remembering that your whole future is now dependent upon your making this connection with the spiritual realm. Don't be in too big a hurry about it for the chances are that it will come when you are not looking for it.

POINTS TO REMEMBER IN LESSON 14.

(1) The spirit of the God-Law is contacted and comes into consciousness in the quietness of the human life.

(2) Intense desire is very effective in bringing the manifestation from the Cosmic realm into your own life.

(3) If, when the manifestation of cosmic power is made, you feel like singing or shouting or jumping, do so.

(4) Do not try to force these moments to come into your life at will, for you will never be able to do it.

(5) It is a law of the spiritual realm that you cannot desire anything from this realm without your desire being granted. So if you do not make this contact immediately it is because you are not keeping quiet enough, but do not worry for you will make it.

(6) Don't forget in this period of relaxation not to use any affirmation of any kind. Just listen and out of that stillness will come to you the flash of the consciousness of God.

EXAMINATION QUESTIONS
FOR LESSON NO. 14

These examination questions are for your benefit and you should know the answers to them all. If they are not clear to you, read your Lesson again and again until they are clear.

(1) The power used by Jesus is available here and now, but it is not the power of the subconscious mind. What is it?

(2) What is the real spiritual part of you?

(3) What comments are made in this Lesson upon the Biblical injunction, "Lay not up for yourselves treasures on earth"?

(4) Did the "life after death" theory originate with Jesus?

(5) There is one secret that, until it is learned, the God Realm will not have been plumbed to the full?

(6) Why did Jesus pray to his Father before raising Lazarus?

(7) In what sense was Jesus conceived by the Holy Spirit of God?

(8) Why was the life of Jesus a lonely life?

(9) What were the exercises given in preceding Lessons intended to prepare you for?

(10) How do you prepare yourself for the exercise in actually contacting God?

(11) Describe that exercise in detail, and its objective?

(12) Most of the lessons to be learned from the mighty Life Spirit will not be obtained by begging or prayer. How then?

LESSON 15

Dear friend and student:

Here is your 15th Lesson. It takes you into a new experience of the God-Law and shows you something of your harmony and unity with it. This is not a Lesson to be hurriedly read and then cast aside. It is a Lesson which will disclose new spiritual truths every time you read it. So take your time with it. Read it every day. Spend your evening hour in quietness and then, when fully relaxed and very quiet, make your desires known—and LISTEN TO WHAT GOD, THROUGH THE SPIRITUAL REALM, HAS TO SAY TO YOU.

Don't look for "feelings" of any sort—just rest safe and secure in the knowledge that YOU are part of the LIVING GOD-LAW.

Sincerely your friend and teacher,
FRANK B. ROBINSON

P. S. There are no "SPECIAL INSTRUCTIONS" to this Lesson. It needs studying every day. It will win its way into your heart—so spend much time with it, and follow me closely in it.

F. B. R.

In this Lesson I shall give you the picture as it really exists of your relationship to the Great Cosmic Creator of the universe. You will, of course, understand that whenever I refer to the Creator, I do it in the sense of this power not being a "he" or a "she," and I only use the terms containing gender to make the application clearer. God can have no gender. It is not necessary as far as that goes to ever refer to the Creative Intelligence as "God" at all. The Life Spirit—Intelligence—or whatever you choose to call it, just simply IS. It is not male nor is it female. It belongs to the "spiritual" realm and there is no such a thing as either male or female in this wonderful realm.

The last Lesson showed you how to come to the conscious realization of the presence of the Creator in your life. This Lesson will show you the staggering fact that YOU ARE A VITAL PART OF THIS GREAT CREATIVE INTELLIGENCE ITSELF. In other words—you—the real YOU—is spirit and nothing but spirit. True—you have a physical body, but as far as the REAL YOU goes, YOU ARE SPIRIT. And as part of this great scheme of the universe YOU NEVER HAD A BEGINNING. As a physical body—yes—you had a birth or a creation. But as a vital part of the Life Spirit—you never had a creation. The physical matters nothing where the spiritual is concerned, and never forget the point I shall make here, which point is that you are essentially SPIRIT.

The Life Spirit which I showed you how to literally and actually contact in our last Lesson, NEVER HAD A BEGINNING. There was no beginning to the spirit realm. It is self-existent because it is intelligence. It is God if you care to use the term. And there should be no difficulty on your part in understanding this fact. Many people write me and ask "Who created God?" I never reply to such a question for in the first place it is absolute foolishness to ask the question, and in the second place it would do no good to try to explain the fact of the self-existence of God to such a mind. You do NOT understand what electricity is—but you would not deny its existence. Neither do you know what law it is that causes an article to drop when unsupported. We call it the Law of Gravitation. But that is only a name. You DO NOT understand why this is.

So why then should you doubt the self-existence of the spiritual-power of the universe. Why is it so hard for you to conceive of a SPIRITUAL POWER being self existent and from time immemorial? As You know something of the spiritual realm you will begin to see that there never was a beginning or can there ever be an end to anything spiritual. Having no beginning, and being self-existent, there never can be an end to the spiritual realm. It exists for ever and ever. It has always existed, and will exist till the end of time. And even time has no end. There really is no such a thing as time—it is merely a conception. Einstein saw the truth of this, and in a very brilliant way he tried to prove it. There is a lot more of spiritual truth tied up in the Einstein theory of relativity than the average mind can grasp. It is a truth of God though, and I honor such a mind as this man possesses. He is a thinker—and what the world needs today is not more battleships or more submarines—BUT MORE THINKERS. FOR, AS EVER, THE SOLUTION TO THE WORLD'S PROBLEMS LIES IN THE REALM OF THOUGHT WHICH IS THE SPIRITUAL REALM.

You wing your thought away out yonder into the ether when you retire for the night. The thing you want to come is uppermost in your thought-realm. There is a need for this thing to manifest in your own life, and, in accordance with my instructions, you have faithfully done as I have asked you to do. You have arrived at the place where you KNOW the Presence of the Cosmic God-Law has been manifested to you. And sooner or later will you receive that for which your soul hungers. For it is NOT possible for the heart's desire to be registered in the God-Realm, with faith, without the answer coming. Sooner will the heavens fall than that happen. For yon heavens are but SPACE—and there is no end to space. For space is but the abode of the spiritual God-Law, and as such it is limitless. No time—no space—no beginning—no end. Do you now begin to see the magnitude of the great Spiritual Realm I am teaching you about? And remember, throughout this entire universe and from time immemorial as we speak of time, and throughout all space, as we speak of space, THERE LIVES OR EXISTS OR OPERATES THE SPIRIT OF THE LIVING GOD-LAW, WHICH LAW CAN BRING INTO EXISTENCE WHATEVER IT IS THAT YOU NEED FOR YOUR OWN

WELFARE IN THIS LIFE. GOD IS EVERYWHERE. HE LIVES EVERYWHERE. HE CREATED EVERYTHING THAT EVER WAS CREATED. Then can you doubt that as you wing your desires into this great father-heart, that they will be heard and answered? It is not a matter of asking something in the sky to hear and answer your "prayers," that is not it at all. It is just simply a case of YOU, YOURSELF, APPLYING THE SPIRITUAL GOD-LAW FOR THE ACTUAL MANIFESTATION OF THE THINGS YOU NEED—AND IT IS THE LAW OF THE SPIRITUAL REALM THAT YOU SHALL RECEIVE THEM, WHEN YOU UNDERSTAND THE LAW OF THIS MARVELOUS REALM, AND KNOW HOW TO TAKE THESE THINGS FROM THE HAND OF THE GREAT MASTER INTELLIGENCE.

It is not sentiment. It is not any personal "god." It is not religious superstition. It is not tradition. It is not dogma. It is not any "church" or other. None of that. IT IS GOD. IT IS THE LAW OF THE GOD REALM. So why shall you not receive the things you need? You will receive them when you realize the FACT THAT YOU, YOURSELF, ARE A PART OF THIS GREAT COSMIC GOD REALM IN ESSENCE. Had not the Power of the Life Spirit operated IN YOUR INDIVIDUAL CASE—YOU COULD BY NO MEANS HAVE BEEN HERE AND ALIVE ON THIS EARTH. So you must not tell me that there is no hope for you, for I know better. The only thing that can possibly prevent your having the things you need in this life, WILL BE YOUR INABILITY TO BELIEVE GOD. Perhaps I should say your UNWILLINGNESS TO BELIEVE GOD, for that is what it really is in the complete analysis of the question. And you are not to blame. You have been taught certain things about "god" which things are NOT SO. You have been given to under-stand that you are a "pilgrim" on the face of the earth. You have teen told that the aim of life is to "prepares to meet your God." Well, let me say to you that nothing is farther from the truth.

Why prepare to meet "god" in the sky after you die, when IN HIM YOU LIVE AND MOVE AND HAVE YOUR BEING? What would be the sense of that? No my friend, never mind about finding "god" in the sky—after you die—forget all that sort of stuff, AND TRY AND FIND HIM HERE AND NOW. TRY AND DISCOVER SOMETHING ABOUT THE ABSOLUTELY SURE LAW OF GOD THAT OPERATES HERE AND NOW AND THAT LIVES AND EXISTS THROUGHOUT ALL THE COSMIC SPACES OF THE ENTIRE UNIVERSE. And remember also that space is unlimited. You cannot find the end of space for it has no end. And also remember here, the staggering fact once more that YOU ARE A VITAL PART OF THE SPIRITUAL CREATION. Where does that put you? Listen to me here a moment, "IT PUTS YOU IN THE POSITION OF BEING PART OF THE CREATIVE INTELLIGENCE THAT WILL BRING WHATEVER YOU NEED IN LIFE INTO BEING." It makes you the RULER of your OWN LIFE. In a former Lesson I quoted "INVICTUS" to you and asked you to learn it by heart. You probably did this. Now you know why I wanted you to learn that justly famous poem. Now you can see just why it is a fact that you ARE the master of your own fate and the captain of your own soul. IT IS BECAUSE THE SPIRIT OF GOD IS A PART OF YOU, AND YOU ARE A PART OF THE SPIRIT OF GOD. You see that, of course.

Now, are you ready to acknowledge your sonship with the great God-Spirit or the Spirit of God? Are you now willing to do that? Are you ready to accept this fact of your unity with the great Creative Life Spirit, and, resting securely in this bountiful knowledge, DEMAND FROM THE UNIVERSE WHAT IT IS YOU NEED, AND NOT ONLY DEMAND IT, BUT PUT TO WORK THE ACTUAL LAWS AND FORCES THAT WILL MAKE THE MANIFESTATION A LITERAL FACT? Are you willing to do this? That is what I am asking you here and now. There is no questioning the fact that, you are a very vital part of the spiritual God-Law. Neither is there any questioning the fact that the spiritual realm is ruled by a SPIRITUAL LAW, WHICH LAW IS NOT DEPENDENT UPON ANY GOOD DEEDS THAT YOU DO HERE ON THE EARTH. THIS LAW WORKS. IT LITERALLY WORKS. AND IT WORKS IN WHATSOEVER LIFE IT IS GIVEN A CHANCE TO WORK. AND BEING A LAW—IT WILL ALWAYS WORK. Let me go a step farther with you my friend, please, at this point and please mark me well, and get this statement if it is the last thing you ever do—IF YOU DO NOT RECEIVE THE SPIRITUAL AND MATERIAL BLESSINGS YOU NEED IN THIS LIFE, IT JUST SIMPLY IS BECAUSE YOU WILL NOT ACCEPT THEM FROM THIS MIGHTY GOD-LAW. YOU WILL NOT TAKE THEM. YOU WILL NOT ACCEPT THE EXISTENCE OF GOD. And there are tens of thousands like this. They don't want any GOD that could possibly do something for them now. THEY WOULD RATHER HANG ONTO THEIR OLD HELL-FIRE AND BRIMSTONE CREATION THAN TO HAVE ANYTHING TO DO WITH A PULSATING, VIRULENT, STABLE, OMNISCIENT GOD-LAW HERE AND NOW. And those kind, of course, have their reward. The trouble with them is though that most of them die before they can appreciate anything that their "god" can do for them. Nothing at all in this life—nothing for a poor lowly pilgrim, humbly following in the steps of the "master." This is what they have been taught, and I say again there are tens of thousands who would rather go on in misery and unhappiness and poverty, than to discard their old idolatrous and pagan ideas of the old traditional "god," and KNOW THE JOY OF A LIFE FILLED WITH THE ACTUAL SPIRIT AND POWER OF THE LIVING GOD—THE EVER-PRESENT LIFE SPIRIT IN WHOM WE LIVE AND MOVE AND HAVE OUR BEING.

Often ministers come in my study to talk with me. I always talk with them. They know my stand very well, but still they try to connect the

Living God with the old Bible traditions. And it just simply cannot be done. They try to tell me that the God I am teaching is the very same God they try to teach. But this is not a fact. Even though they attribute to their deity the same attributes I give to the mighty Creator of the universe, IT IS NOT POSSIBLE TO LINK THE CREATIVE GOD-LAW WITH SUCH HAPPENINGS AS WE ARE ASKED TO BELIEVE OF THE DEITY PREACHED BY THE PREACHERS WHO CALL UPON ME EVERY SO OFTEN. Can you imagine the God-Law playing favorites? Can you imagine the God-Law working for one and not for another? Can you imagine anyone who really finds and grasps the fact of their unity with the God-Law ever being disappointed? Of course not. I don't care for theory. I don't care for dogma. I don't care what this church teaches nor what that church teaches. The only thing I care about is telling men and women how they may FIND THE ACTUAL and LITERAL PRESENCE of the mighty LIFE-SPIRIT, here and now. I want every one of my students to KNOW that a connection eternally exists between them and the one responsible for their being alive. When that fact is fully grasped, then things begin to happen. Men and women go out and with a soul full of the knowledge of the actual GOD-POWER of the Great Creative Life Spirit—these men and women WORK FOR THEIR ENDS WITH THIS KNOWLEDGE OVERSHADOWING ALL OTHER KNOWLEDGE, AND THEY INVARIABLY WIN.

It is NOT POSSIBLE for a man or woman to actually accept the fact of the literal presence of God, and make a failure out of his or her life. It cannot be. For if they accept this mighty God-Presence, then they KNOW that there is no other power in existence than this same God-Power, hence they conquer in that POWER. Whenever and wherever defeat manifests, you may be sure of the fact that the one in whose affairs such defeat manifests, KNOWS NOTHING ABOUT THE PRESENT EXISTENCE OF THE LIVING GOD-LAW. How foolish it would be for a man to stand outside a restaurant hungry, and wishing for something to eat, and all the time have $20.00 in his pocket. It could not be done. Either the man would not be hungry or HE COULD NOT BE COGNIZANT WITH THE FACT THAT HE HAD AMPLE FUNDS IN HIS POSSESSION. And this is. exactly the case with many folks in their relation to the spiritual realm. THEY DO NOT KNOW OF THE POWER AT THEIR DISPOSAL AND IN THEIR HANDS, AND SO THEY STARVE TO DEATH SPIRITUALLY WITH THE GREATEST SPIRITUAL POWER IN THE UNIVERSE IN THEIR HANDS. What a calamity. So I want you to realize every moment of the day from henceforth, the existing POWER of the GOD-LAW in your own life. remember too, that this great spiritual LAW is abundantly able to CREATE or build whatever it may be that you need. Don't fool with the God-Law. PUT IT TO THE TEST; FIND IT; USE IT; LIVE IN IT; DEMAND THAT IT SUPPLY YOUR NEEDS; DEMAND THAT IT SHOW YOU THE WAY TO FUL-

FILLMENT; TRUST IT; for this God-Law is an understanding Law. It's a Law of Love. A LAW—SURE IT IS—BUT A LAW OF INFINITE INTELLIGENCE—INFINITE COMPASSION—INFINITE LOVE. For the Law was conceived in Love. It lives as Love; it is a loving Law; stern—unbreakable—irresistible—but still LOVING.

This God-Law will take you by the hand if you will let it, and it will slowly but surely lead you into the right paths. It will lead you into green pastures. It will take you beside the still waters. It operates in stillness, for in SPIRITUAL STILLNESS THERE IS POWER. In other words, there is even now as you read this, a surging sea of invisible spiritual creative POWER at your disposal. This spiritual POWER will leap into play when the LAW governing it is used. WHAT IS THAT LAW? Well, it's simple. The Law governing the spiritual realm is simply THAT YOU TAKE WHATEVER IT IS YOU NEED FROM THAT REALM. Some may say, "Well, Dr. Robinson, can I take what I haven't got and don't see?" Of course you can. That is the only sort of thing you CAN take—the thing you do not have. You certainly cannot take what you already have, can you? Of course not. Then the only things you can actually take from the spiritual realm, ARE THE THINGS YOU NEED BUT D0 NOT HAVE.

You are going to ask me here how you can take them. And my reply—my sure reply to that is that YOU YOURSELF WILL APPLY THE MIGHTY SPIRITUAL LAW GOVERNING ALL THE AFFAIRS OF THE UNIVERSE, TO BRING WHATEVER IT IS YOU NEED INTO ACTUAL MANIFESTATION. Don't think that I am playing with you here my friend for I assure you that I have neither the time or the inclination to play with the sacred things of your life. Nor am I advancing a theory of any sort, nor yet am I wandering into the hazy realm of metaphysics. I am telling you here of SPIRITUAL LAW AS IT OPERATES IN THE SPIRITUAL WORLD—OR THE NATURAL WORLD, FOR THEY ARE BOTH ONE AND THE SAME THING. Try and assimilate that statement. I am telling you here of the process by which every created thing was created. I am telling you here, and trying to show you here, of the staggering import of the fact that the SPIRITUAL REALM IS THE CONTROLLING REALM OF YOUR LIFE. Never a thought or a desire can ever be sent into that great realm without the answer already being on its way to you. It may take some time for the physical material manifestation to come—but—with unwavering quiet simple childlike faith in the LAW of GOD—THE ANSWER IS SURE.

It took me less than six months to manifest the things I needed in my life. It really took longer than that; it took two years. BUT THE ANSWER WAS ON ITS WAY TO ME THE VERY MOMENT THE REQUEST OR THE DESIRE REGISTERED IN THE SPIRITUAL REALM. That very moment, all the creative powers of the God-Law were immediately and automatically brought into play in my behalf. IMMEDIATELY—there was put into motion, whatever power was necessary to bring from the spiritual realm to me the material things I so much desired. One might say that the desire was really the things itself in actuality. You know, and I know, that the creative Intelligence behind this universe is both big enough, and powerful enough, and resourceful enough to bring to you the things you need. If it can instill into a wild goose the "instinct" that guides it over the trackless waste from hunger to plenty, and does it with unerring accuracy, do you not think it can bring into your little life the things you need. If this all-creative God-Law can clothe the beautiful lily as it grows, so quietly, so slowly, on the lone mountainside, do you not think it can also give to you the very best wearing apparel? If God Himself, through His self existent power can implant into your life and into my life the material things we need to make us both happy, successful, and healthy, then do you not think He is able to supply all your needs according to the great spiritual riches that lie in this unseen spiritual realm? I think He can. I think this God-Law is perfectly able to supply all your needs by its own power, AND WILL DO SO IN THE MOMENT YOU LINK YOURSELF UP WITH THIS GOD POWER. As a matter of fact, it is not a case of whether or not the God-Law can give you everything you need, it's a case of whether or not YOU WILL TAKE ENOUGH FROM THE GOD-LAW. Any old fool can get on his knees and ask anyone for anything—BUT IT TAKES A MAN OR A WOMAN IN TUNE WITH THE SPIRITUAL GOD-LAW TO GET THEM. I have shown you the operations of the spiritual LAW. I have given you exercises designed to show you how to obtain this superb and matchless spiritual power. NOW IT'S UP TO YOU. This Law is here. It actually works. It has ever worked. It always will work. Through this Law the universe swings in the heavens in its respective orbits. Through this God-Law it is sustained. Then will you get into complete harmony with this mighty spiritual LAW? I think you will.

Hundreds of my students are already in harmony with it. Just as long as they are they will be manifestly successful in everything they undertake. Will you be? If you are inherently religious, then you may look upon this power as your God. You may call it the power of the CHRIST if you want to. I don't care what you call it as long as you recognize its presence WITH YOU EVERY MOMENT OF THE DAY. I WANT YOU NEVER TO QUESTION THIS DIVINELY NATURAL PRESENCE, BUT TAKE IT AS A MATTER OF FACT THAT IT IS THERE WITH YOU. FOR IT IS. It make no difference what the occasion may be. You can never go into error with the presence of the greatest spiritual power the world has ever known in your life—can you? You can never make a wrong move just as long as the CREATIVE GOD-INTELLIGENCE IS GUIDING YOU— can you? Of course not. All right—call this power what you will. Look upon it however you care to. I care not about that. BUT I DO CARE THAT MY STUDENTS LIVE IN THE CONSCIOUSNESS OF SUCH A GOD. Therein lies victory over everything. Herein lies complete mastery of all circumstances. Just as long as you are a canting hypocrite, trying to hypnotize yourself into believing something impossible that your reason will not allow you to believe, then by no possible means can you ever taste and see what a spiritual power there is for you through a personal knowledge of the existence of the GREAT GOD-LAW.

And besides, you will be only fooling yourself. You cannot fool others. They know that you have no more faith in your "traditional god" than has a jackrabbit. But you let yourself once use and apply the GOD-LAW in your life, and believe me people will stop and take notice of you. People will know that you know both what you are doing and where you are going. But call the power what you like. The term "GOD" is probably as good as any other term, for the God idea seems to be stamped into many of the human race. But depend upon this unseen invisible God Power please, and learn the secret of communion with it. Learn well the Lesson that your every need shall be supplied through the operations of the GOD-LAW, and this in the very moment in which you RECOGNIZE AND ACKNOWLEDGE THIS UNITY OF STRENGTH AND PURPOSE. Do you question whether or not your "prayer" or desire car come to you if this desire is for physical things. Why? "If God so clothed the grass of the field that today is, and tomorrow is cast into the oven, HOW MUCH MORE SHALL HE CLOTHE YOU—OH YE OF LITTLE FAITH."

I saw a wonderful verse somewhere yesterday. It was in some newspaper or other, and I don't know where I saw it. But I learned it—and I shall give it to you here for it is a beautiful thing and just fits in with my thought here very wonderfully. Here it is:

"If radio's slim fingers can pluck a melody from out the night and toss it over a continent or sea; if petalled white notes of a violin are blown across a mountain or a city's din; If songs like crimson roses are pulled from thin, blue air, Why should mortals wonder if God hears prayer."

Those of us who have found something of the dynamic Spirit of God don't wonder—WE KNOW. The trouble is that religionists have foisted onto the human race a God who "SAVES SOULS IN THE FUTURE." I am giving to the world, a God who "SAVES BOTH SOULS AND BODIES HERE AND NOW." This God-Law of mine may also save souls in the future. I know nothing about that. Nor does the cleverest preacher that ever lived. All along that line are theory and self-made hopes. But we of "PSYCHIANA" KNOW that our Master-Law does these things here and now.

Now I ask you which is the better of the two "gods;" the one who MAY save your souls in the future, or the one who DOES OPERATE FOR YOUR ETERNAL BENEFIT HERE AND NOW. The church people don't like me because I remove thinking people from their traditional "god." But I am not moving people from their "god" at all. I am moving the "god." And in its place I am putting another, and far more reasonable GOD-LAW the effects and results of which can be known to the very full here and now. That is all I am doing. But it's enough. For through trial, and toil, and tribulation, the old church, and the entire human race, has groped its way out of God's NATURALLY-REVEALED RELIGION. And, as ever, such groping and such changes are slow. Those advocating them are always looked upon as a "leper" or something equally as bad, when, as a matter of fact, it is the pioneers into the spiritual realm that revolutionize religious truth. And there never was a truth of God discovered yet that did not upset tradition and dogma. I wish I had my way—I would smash every dogma and every tradition to the wall—and what a smash it would be.

But my students may depend upon it that just behind the tradition, and just behind the dogma, and just behind church creeds—lies the TRUE GOD. And this TRUE GOD is SPIRIT. And SPIRIT is LIFE. And SPIRIT is PLENTY. And SPIRIT IS HEALTH. And SPIRIT is HAPPINESS. And SPIRIT is YOU. And YOU are a vital part of GOD. You see this? Of course you do. Then all right—tomorrow morning go out to your daily task with the knowledge of the actual presence of the GOD-LAW with you. Never mind feelings at all. They are the most unreliable things I know. Even a picture show can change feelings—and CHANGEABLENESS IS NOT AN ATTRIBUTE OF THE GOD-LAW nor of the spiritual realm. Feelings belong to the superficial things in a man's makeup—and there are many superficial things there too. But you must get behind all feelings. Get down to the realm where God is. Recognize the actual literal presence of the God-Law in your own life—always—ever—and for your everlasting benefit. Never mind what happens beyond the tome. You know nothing of that. Neither does anyone else—spiritualists to the contrary. But you may depend up on one thing—if the mighty Spiritual Creator of the Universe is your companion and your strength here, you need have no fears for the hereafter. Only a coward worries about the future. If your life is spiritual—and if it is straight here and now—never mind the future. For the same spiritual God-Law operating with you and for you NOW, will very effectively take care of "the future." This has been a favorite old "dead-dog" of the churches. And it's a fine thing to keep people "meek and lowly in heart." But such a doctrine never produced a spiritual advancement yet.

The men who move other men, are men who KNOW THE POWER OF THE GOD-LAW AS IT OPERATES HERE, AND ARE THEMSELVES MOTIVATED BY THAT LAW. AND YOU MAY DEPEND UPON IT, MY FRIEND, THAT WHEREVER YOU SEE A MAN WHO IS MOLDING THE RELIGIOUS AND SPIRITUAL LIVES OF OTHERS, THERE YOU HAVE A MAN MOLDED HIMSELF BY THE POWER OF THE DYNAMIC GOD-LAW OF THE UNIVERSE.

DON'T FORGET THAT. It makes no difference whether or not shallow-brained ministers or priests call him a "heretic." That means nothing at all. For the "heretic" of today is the prophet of tomorrow.

This Lesson may appear to be a little on the religious order to you—I hope not, for I don't ever want to write anything that might be classed as "orthodox religion." "PSYCHIANA" is a New Psychological Religion. It's certainly new—and most certainly comes at the psychological moment in the world's affairs when men and women are running around like sheep with their heads cut off, looking for something tangible on which to pin their faith and hopes. And in the dispensation of the truth as released through "PSYCHIANA" I must be very true, first of all to the God-Law, then to my students, and then to myself. I haven't any friends, I don't want them. The only friend I have is the Spirit of God—the Life Spirit—and that is the only friend I want. Oh yes, I have a swarm of personal friends amongst my thousands of students—but I haven't seen many of them—so they must remain friends at a distance. But as far as real friends go—well, I just simply haven't many I assure you. But—in this lonesomeness of life and heart—I am driven to the God-Law, and in that Spirit of Life—I find whatever it is that I need. And I mean this materially and spiritually.

Any religion, whether it be "orthodox" or whether it be "psychological," must be a religion pure in intent. It must teach a PURE God, or a PURE God-Law. Hence, I should be untrue to both you and myself if I did not call your attention also to the finer things of life as well as the material things. For, to the one knowing the Life Spirit they go hand in hand. Or they should. So don't think it strange if I tell you that while this unseen God-Power can and will bring you the necessary material joys of life, it also can bring the many spiritual joys. It can, and does bring to the one knowing it, the finest, and highest, and noblest impulses possible. It lifts one out of all moral wrong. It cleans up a dirty life. It makes the one intent and desire of the life for a fuller and more complete knowledge of the Great God-Law itself. It has no time for rottenness. In fact, the one knowing the God-Law to the full will not commit very much rottenness. It's only the hypocritical "religionists" who believe in something their reason can not accept who will do these tricks. A man motivated by the Spirit of the Living God never will do them. He is too big a man in the first place, and he knows it's a violation of the Spiritual Law in the second place.

Now as to your relationship with the Cosmic Law of God; I think you have the picture clearly in your mind now. You have had the "flash" from the spiritual realm, or you will receive it sooner or later. Now, act as if all the power of the spiritual realm were working through you. For it is—just to the extent to which you let it. Carry always before you the thing you need most. Never forget it. And then it is securely anchored in the realm of the Spirit—LEAVE IT THERE. It's something like the grain of wheat.

It is sown a single grain; it is harvested as many grains. So let your whole life, day by day, be lived in the consciousness of the God-Law. There are many more things I could say to you at this point, but I shall leave them for future Lessons. GET THE CONSCIOUSNESS OF YOUR HARMONY WITH THE SPIRITUAL LAW AND YOUR UNITY WITH IT INTO YOUR THOUGHT-REALM—AND KEEP IT THERE. STUDY THIS LESSON EVERY DAY UNTIL YOU RECEIVE THE NEXT ONE. You will find something new in it every time you read it.

Sincerely your friend and teacher,
FRANK B. ROBINSON

EXAMINATION QUESTIONS
FOR LESSON NO. 15

These examination questions are for your benefit and you should know the answers to them all. If they are not clear to you, read your Lesson again and again until they are clear.

(1) Of what relationship is there a picture given in Lesson 15?

(2) In what sense may it be truly said that you never had a beginning?

(3) To obtain what you need is not a matter of asking some being in the sky to hear and answer your prayer. What is it then?

(4) When you realize the "staggering fact" that you are a vital part of the spiritual creation, where does that put you?

(5) Why is it a fact that you are the "master of your fate and the captain of your soul"?

(6) Is it correct for orthodox preachers to assert that the God taught in these Lessons is the same God that they try to teach?

(7) You may be sure of something regarding any one in whose affairs defeat manifests?

(8) What is the illustration given in this Lesson of the man standing outside a restaurant? How is it applicable?

(9) What is the Law governing the Spiritual Realm?

(10) What answer is made to the charge of church people that these Lessons are removing people from their traditional God?

(11) Why need you have no fears of "the hereafter"?

(12) In addition to material blessings, the God-Law can also bring spiritual joys?

LESSON 16

Dear friend and student:

This Lesson number 16 gives you, if you can grasp it, a faint glimpse of one of the most remarkable scientific truths ever discovered. We do not know the last thing about creation yet, nor has the last discovery been made. You may depend upon one thing, though, and that is that when the full knowledge of Spiritual Law and the scheme of creation is known, it will be found to be enveloped in laws which, although not recognized now, are in existence now and are perfectly natural laws.

It will be good for you to study this Lesson many times and I am asking you to do just this.

Sincerely your friend and teacher,
FRANK B. ROBINSON

It is a well known scientific fact that in the last analysis, everything material in existence is nothing more or less than particles of electrical energy called electrons and protons. These little energy balls, if I may use that word, comprise every created thing, and it is scientifically correct to state that so far as is now known, the most minute particles into which matter can be divided is into these electrical protons and electrons. You may take the very hardest piece of steel, and in that piece of steel the electrons are chasing themselves around at the speed of an express train. This does not appear, of course, to the physical eye, but it is a known fact just the same. This was perhaps the most important scientific discovery ever made, and certainly it bears me out in my understanding and teaching of the God-Law. Without the least thought of pride on my part, let me state here that I have had in print practically the same theories that the scientific world is making now, and have had them in print long before the scientists even thought of them. I gave an instance of this in a former Lesson in this course. Now I shall give you another instance.

My clipping bureau sends me this morning a newspaper clipping dated February 27th., 1932. It is headed in large type:

"FIND EMBRYONIC FORM OF MATTER."

Then under this large heading is a subheading which states:

"DISCOVERY OF 'NEUTRON' HAILED AS POSSIBLY GREATEST SINCE THE X-RAY."

Then there is another large heading under that which states:

"NEW EVOLUTION CLEW"

"ULTIMATE PARTICLE IN NATURE IS SAID TO HAVE UNKNOWN POWERS OF PENETRATION."

Then follows the article which I reproduce here in full and verbatim, giving credit, of course, to the Associated Press which organization released this report. Here it is—read it carefully and think about what I have been teaching you in the light of this latest scientific finding. It will show you whether or not I know what I am talking about in this great spiritual realm of the GOD-LAW.

> BALTIMORE, Feb. 27. (*Taken from Associated Press report)— The discovery in Cavendish laboratory, Cambridge university, London, by James Chadwick of the "neutron," a particle so minute it carries no electrical charge, and hailed as the greatest find in the scientific world since the electron, the proton and the X-ray, was announced today by the Baltimore Sun in a dispatch from the Manchester Guardian.

HAVE NO WAVE LENGTH.

The "neutron" was described as one of the ultimate particles in nature, so tiny it would take 200,000,000,000,000,000,000,000 to make a mass weighing an ounce. Neutrons are not waves, the dispatch said, but particles, but they have as particles hitherto unknown powers of penetration.

In the realm of astronomy and the evolution of the universe, neutrons are of fundamental importance, representing the first step in the evolution of matter out of primeval electrons and protons, the paper said.

EMBRYO OF MATTER.

The ultimate substance of the world is electricity and the simplest element built of electricity is helium. The neutron is half way between electricity and helium; it is the embryonic form of ordinary matter growing but not born.

Neutrons are so penetrative and elusive because they have no electric charge. The neutron is composed of a proton and an electron bound closely together. It is speculated the neutron may be the unit of magnetism, for it presumably is a doublet, as magnets are, with both a north and south pole, the dispatch continued.

"FIND" OF FIRST IMPORTANCE.

Physicists at the Johns Hopkins university, when told of the discovery, hailed the achievement as one of first importance.

Dr. Joseph S. Ames, president of the university said:

"The discovery, if substantiated. is worth all the importance attributed to it. Chadwick is a physicist of high repute and Rutherford (Chadwick's superior) would let nothing go out of his laboratory without its having been carefully checked and tested."

Dr. Ames was a physicist before assuming the presidency of Johns Hopkins.

While this is, of course, going into the realm of physics at some depth. I think that all of my students will see the principle behind it all, and will know by this time that the important and controlling forces of this universe are spiritual or unseen forces. This is exactly what I have claimed and what I still claim. As the months and the years go by, science is continually bringing forth facts that PROVE that there is a LAW behind every created thing. They are showing in a very unmistakable way that nothing ever happens by chance. There is no chance in the universe; all is governed by immutable LAW. And naturally this LAW which was and still is the original creative force of the universe, must be alluded to as "god" if one cares to have the God-idea at all.

I am not so sure that the "god-idea" is any too logical, but we have it here, and perhaps for the time being it will be as well to argue from the premise that the idea is logical. To me—however—I care nothing for any idea of "god" that removes him from me here and now. I want to know nothing of any theories and creeds and dogmas, for there isn't a word of truth in any of them. They are all manmade and they all will die the death that anything manmade dies. I am only interested in the great spiritual cosmic unseen force or spirit or power behind this marvelous scheme of things. For it is indeed a very marvelous scheme of things. Furthermore, there is an astounding spiritual God-Law behind it all, and these scientists and physicists are fast finding that out.

It is now the acknowledged and stated opinion of the realm of scientists that the UNSEEN forces of nature are the forces of causation. Were there no unseen spiritual forces existent, then nothing material could or would exist at all. And now science comes along and tells us that it has discovered a thing called a "neutron" which thing is so small that it would take about 200,000,000,000,000,000,000,000 of them to make an ounce in weight. Up to the time of the above announcement, the electron and the proton were the smallest known ingredient of matter. And these two were electrical waves of energy. Now, we have the neutron which is NOT electrical, and which "POSSESSES ALMOST UNKNOWN POWERS OF PENETRATION." Think that over for a little while. For if this isn't getting down to basic facts then I don't know what it is. I have consistently claimed that one scientific fact is worth a ton of old religious tradition, and I make that claim more forcibly now than I have ever made it before. And you may depend upon it, my friend, that if the men delving and pioneering into the realms of both science and psychology do not give us the answer to the entire problem—the preachers never will. For all they have to go on is blind belief. And, again I state that blind belief is unscientific. For to ask a man to believe something that his reason cannot understand is asking that man to perform a physical and mental impossibility.

Thousands of people say they really believe that the great "god" of this universe sent a one-third part of Himself down from "heaven" to earth to die a horrible death in order that those who believe this story might "inherit eternal life." But as a matter of fact not one of them really believes that. For it is an impossibility for a normal thinking mind to believe anything as irrational as that story is. If the man really does believe it, then I should class such a one as being not at all normal. Furthermore, such a one would be capable of inflicting similar cruelties on others. We have an example of that going on in the world today. Here in the East is a military mad nation. Their religion teaches them that if they die in battle they are assured of heaven. Imbued with the spirit of this lie, they fight like madmen in order to "make sure of heaven." You see, any "supernaturally-revealed" religion cannot be very good for anyone, for most anything might happen in the realm of the "supernatural."

However, thinking people possessing reasonable minds have just about discarded all that sort of twaddle, and they are looking to nature, and to nature's God for the answer. And they are slowly but surely finding it. For it is only reasonable to suppose that in life itself is to be found the answer to the riddle of life. It is very cowardly and is in itself an evidence of shiftlessness to state that we cannot know here but must wait till we die before anything concerning the realm of God can be discovered. The soul that has found something of the existence of the mighty Life Spirit, KNOWS and KNOWS FULL WELL that there is plenty of power, plenty of wisdom, plenty of intelligence right here on this earth and wrapped up in a human soul if you please, to answer whatever questions may arise regarding this life we are living. Whenever and wherever a man or woman is in harmony with the God-Law, then there always follows a completeness of every good thing. If the body is sound, and the thought-realm in tune with the great cosmic intelligence, then that man or woman accomplishes wonders. Too many of us, however, look upon the good things of life as the exceptions whereas they should be the natural thing. It is natural—divinely natural for you to have a strong physical body. It is also divinely natural for you to be successful in everything you undertake. It is divinely natural for you to be supremely happy, and you may depend upon it that you will be whenever you come into conscious relation to the unseen but very potent and vital power of the God-Law.

The Power exists; it exists NOW; it exists for YOU. The only thing for you to make up your mind about is whether or not you will throw yourself unreservedly into the ocean of love and power provided for you through the existence of the Spirit of God—the GOD-LAW of the universe. If you will do that—nothing good will be impossible to you. There can be nothing you need that the God-Law can not provide. For the LAW actually WORKS. It is here for that purpose. It is a spiritual LAW and therefore an unseen LAW and is far higher than any earthly LAW you have ever had anything to do with. Think of it—in the ether all around you there is a "THINKING SUBSTANCE"—which we know is COSMIC or SPIRITUAL IN ITS ORIGIN. From this unseen cosmic realm came everything physical or material in the universe. YOU came from the first great cosmic cause. YOU are a living demonstration that this mighty POWER exists. YOU are a part of this cosmic God-Law; so why should you be afraid? Why should you say that the good things of life are for others and not for you? You delude yourself, my friend.

True, you have been taught that "it is appointed unto man once to die, and after that the judgment"—but don't you believe it. There will never be any "bar" of "god" before which you will be required to stand and give an account of the deeds done in the body. That is pagan superstition. The answer to the human desire for life is L I F E. And I do not believe that LIFE can ever come through DEATH. Life is here now—you have it. It comes to you from the Spirit of Life which spirit is not "in the heavens" but is all around you. When the time comes in which men and women understand just a little bit of the beauties and the power of the spiritual realm of God, then will the answer to this question of life and death be known. I BELIEVE THE WORLD TO BE ON THE VERGE OF THIS ANSWER. Let no one misunderstand me please—I am no hare-brained fanatic of any sort, meandering around in the hazy realm of metaphysics. I keep both feet solid on the floor at all times. But I KNOW SOMETHING 0F THE SPIRITUAL REALM, AND I KNOW SOMETHING OF THE POWER OF THE LIVING CREATIVE LIFE SPIRIT. And what little I do know about that power suffices for me to make the statement I have just made. For spiritual Law is so far above material Law, although the same in essence, that there can be not so much comparison. The LAW is the same. Man is different from what he was originally intended to be.

But—as time rolls on, and as men's hearts get away from baser material things of life, automatically they will look to the spiritual realm for the answer, and when enough of them do that—they will find the answer. In this matter of success and happiness and health, there is one angle of the Law that I want you to be quite clear about. That is this; there is enough of the power of the spiritual God-Law to provide you with every good thing you need. That Law exists. We know that. YOU, however, MAY NOT BE USING THE LAW, and if such be the case, then your condition can never be other than it is now. You see that? In other words. the spiritual realm cannot benefit you until you USE THE POWER OF THIS SPIRITUAL

REALM. The power is there—but it's useless to you unless you use it. The thing to do now then is to use this spiritual power for the manifestation of whatever things you need in life. You want to get to the other side of a river. Here is a boat starting out for the other side in a few moments now. You will never get to the other side of that river standing there arguing about the boat. You will never cross that river just by standing there and looking at the boat and wondering whether or not it will ever get to the other side. YOU MUST GET ON BOARD OF THE BOAT. When that is done, you will safely reach the other side.

The same principle applies in the spiritual God-Realm. You may take these Lessons of mine, which are Lessons of many-times-proven power, and you may argue whether or not I know of what I am speaking. You will never get anywhere by doing this though. You may take these Lessons, you may read them, and then you may compare them with someone else's Lessons and see wherein they are different—and still you will never contact the unseen spiritual power of God that way. That boat had been going over the river many a time—and yet you doubted as you stood on the shore whether or not it was good for one more trip. These Lessons have benefitted the lives of thousands—and they are certainly good for one more life. BUT YOU WILL HAVE TO GET ON BOARD THE BOAT. YOU WILL HAVE TO ACTUALLY DO AS YOU HAVE BEEN TOLD TO DO, AND WHEN YOU DO THAT—YOU WILL FIND THE POWER OF THE MIGHTY LIFE SPIRIT TRUE. You will find that I know so well of what I speak, in the very moment you are willing to get in spiritual touch with the power of the mighty Life Spirit.

But you can't just hope for it—you must GRIT YOUR TEETH, SOME OF YOU, AND WITH A BULLDOG DETERMINATION THAT WILL NOT BE DENIED, YOU MUST WRESTLE WITH YOURSELF UNTIL YOU WIN THE VICTORY. You will find that there will come a time in your life in which you will come face to face with your doubting self. There will be a battle. If the doubting self wins that battle, you might JUST as well throw these Lessons away for they will do you no good whatsoever. BUT—IF THE BELIEVING SIDE WINS—then jump for joy, for your faith in the Living God-Law will bring you triumphant over every wrong, and will set your feet on a path of spiritual travel which cannot but bring to you the things from the spiritual realm you need. Every so often someone writes me stating that he would like to receive the Lessons more frequently than once every two weeks. "There is nothing new to me in the Lessons so far"—writes one man. Another writes: "I am quite an advanced student of scientific psychology, and therefore you must understand that your Lessons are quite elementary to me." I meet quite a few of such mortals, and I am interested in watching their reaction when I advise them that the more they THINK they know of the spiritual realm, the less they ACTUALLY DO KNOW.

For one cannot approach this great unseen realm of the God-Law except as a child. I care not what this man has studied nor do I care what that man has studied. Nor do I care what academic degrees a man may have. All that means nothing. Academic degrees mean nothing. I can use several of them if I care to. THE ATTITUDE THAT WINS IN THE REALM OF THE SPIRIT IS THE ATTITUDE OF CHILDLIKE FAITH IN THE POWER OF THE MIGHTY LIFE SPIRIT. That is the winning attitude. I love to read the beautiful parables of Luke, for although I know they are but perfectly anonymous writings, and purely imaginary, still, the spiritual thread running through them is, to me, very beautiful. You may see nothing in them at all, and if this is your reaction then I advise you not to ever read them. But to me, many of them are very beautiful. The other gospels contain many good thoughts, but the parables of Luke are pregnant with a spiritual power that is easily recognizable by one spiritually attuned.

Whenever I feel my need of special recognition of the power of the God-Realm in my own life (which is very often) I like to refer to the passage found in the gospels where the Galilean Carpenter forbade those who would drive the children away, saying: "Suffer (or let) the little children come near me, for the Kingdom of Heaven is made up of such." And realizing to some extent the immense spiritual magnitude of the God-Law I so often use, and realizing how very small I am compared to its fullness, I very often adopt the attitude of a little child—for I really am nothing more than that. For everyone loves a child. They are so helpless and so sweet that we all love them. We want to help them. On the other hand we are not at all in sympathy with those who "know-all" and we feel less inclined to offer assistance spiritually to those who would have us believe that they are just a little bit advanced in knowledge to the rest of their fellow men—in the spiritual realm.

Whenever I meet such a person, or receive a letter from one of them, telling me how far advanced they are in this spiritual life, I immediately put it down that such a one really knows practically nothing of the Realm of God. For those who have experienced even a very little of the joys of the spiritual realm, know that it is far too big a realm for them to understand to the full. You could not know all there is to know of the spiritual realm of God and live. I won't go into this here though—I might be misunderstood, but you may depend upon it that the more you begin to learn of the realm of the God-Law, the more humble will you become before it. You will be staggered by its immensity. And when you actually begin to KNOW that this realm of God CAN, and WILL, and DOES care for your every need here and now, and when you begin to only faintly recognize the fact that "more things are wrought by prayer than this world dreams of," you will be only too willing to keep quiet, and listen for the "still small voice" of God—coming to you from the God-Realm, FOR THIS VOICE NEVER LEADS ASTRAY. IT NEVER DISAPPOINTS. IT ALWAYS BRINGS THE CORRECT SOLUTION TO EVERY PROBLEM. IT

ALWAYS GUIDES ARIGHT. And you my friend—no matter who or what you may be, can never make a mistake in throwing yourself wholly and unreservedly into this vast ocean of the Spiritual Power of the God-Law.

Prayer—you ask me what prayer is, and I shall tell you. Prayer is NOT asking God for anything. PRAYER IS SIMPLY EXPRESSING THE DESIRE OF YOUR HEART INTO THE GREAT SPIRITUAL REALM OF THE GOD-LAW, AND THEN, HAVING FAITH ENOUGH TO START THE SPIRITUAL REALM TO WORK ACTUALLY BRINGING TO YOU THE THINGS YOU NEED. That is prayer. That is the prayer that wins—and there is no other sort of prayer. Often there comes to me a letter in which the writer tells me that he or she has been praying to God for a certain thing for years and years and years. The old story is that they never receive the thing they are praying for. Certainly not.

God is an operating LAW. It is a condition of that LAW'S operation that to ask is to receive—why?—because the petition and thing itself are one and the same thing in the realm of God. And in the infinite wisdom of the Creative Intelligence, it has been so ordained that THE ANSWER TO PRAYER ALWAYS COMES IMMUTABLE, AND WITH NO EFFORT ON ANYONE'S PART THAN YOUR OWN. The Law is there. It works. It is God. And any failure to obtain the things you need from the Great Master Life Spirit—IS NOT FAILURE ON THE PART OF THE GOD-LAW, BUT FAILURE ON YOUR PART. And there can be only ONE CAUSE OF SUCH FAILURE. That cause is DOUBT. It is the snake that the old allegory symbolizes in the allegory of creation as the Bible gives it. It is yet, and it has ever been the only thing standing in the way of the operations of the immutable unchangeable Law of God. YOU CANNOT FAIL AND USE THE GOD-LAW AT THE SAME TIME. It would be an utter impossibility. It would be quite paradoxical. You cannot use POWER and still have nothing. You cannot live in harmony with the God-Law and be a failure. The cards do not lie that way. You cannot fall into the Pacific Ocean without getting wet. Neither can you fall into the ocean of the love and power of God without getting this love and power all over you. It beats down every enemy. It defeats every disaster. It covers you with a Spiritual power and intelligence that you probably cannot understand. It watches over every step you take. It guides those steps. Always aright. It exercises over you a magnetic charm and spiritual attraction which very effectively keeps you from harm. It fills your whole life with happiness, with health, and with success. And the reason it does these things is because THIS SPIRITUAL POWER IS GOD And in due time, and through a bitter period of evolution, the world will know that it is God. There will have to be several serious cataclysms before that day of the fullness of the knowledge of God dawns universally on the earth, but there are those who have had a foretaste of the beauties of that power now. There is always a remnant remaining, which remnant have an undying faith in the spiritual Law of God. There will ever be found those who are gifted sufficiently to peer ahead through the clouds of the future and get a tiny little glimpse of what is to be. And this world will universally know God, and before too long. I am afraid that blood must run red throughout the universe first. I hope not. I trust that this appreciation of the literal presence of God can be made known universally without that—but I am afraid not.

Personally, I look for the future to bring forth a calamity the like of which this already blood-bathed world has never before seen. I hope I am all wrong. But as I receive light and inspiration from the realm of God—I think I see that a little way ahead of us. For every race of men in existence is looking to the sky for their God. They all have a "supernatural god," and "supernaturally revealed" religion. And there never was either a supernatural "god" or a supernatural system of religion yet that was true. Never were they true. And this is where men and countries and nations are missing the goal. Peace conferences are futile. And while I am heartily behind any and all movements for peace, I am afraid that national and universal peace will not be secured as long as there are so many different nations preparing for war, and all of them looking to "their god" for assistance. The nations haven't yet learned the foolishness and the farce of it all though. But they will learn. I only hope it's a bloodless learning. But if it is not—then let's have the learning period over, and let's come quickly to the day when the Lion shall lie down with the lamb, and a little child shall lead them.

That day will come. It is around the corner. The nations may err and stumble many times going around that corner—let us hope not. But they may. I am wandering perhaps a little bit here, but these things are all so pertinent to our studies that I must mention them in passing. I must call the attention of my students to the fact that the only thing in the world that matters now is the actual presence on this earth of the greatest spiritual power the old world has ever known. What a pity that their eyes are so blinded that they cannot see it. But the spiritual always triumphs over the material, and in the last analysis when earth's last picture is painted, it will perhaps be discovered that the spiritual will be all in all. It may be discovered that the eye which can behold the physical will close. Then will be the time when this great spiritual God-Law, ALONG WITH EVERY CREATED BEING WILL BE ONE VAST WHOLE—COMPLETE—PERFECT—ETERNALLY HAPPY AND ENJOYING ETERNAL LIFE TOGETHER—CREATOR—AND CREATED.

In the meantime, what shall be the attitude of my students towards these times in which we live? They shall keep very close to the Life Spirit, I have in these Lessons taught them to contact. Their whole life shall be a spiritual life, or a life in which the spiritual or unseen power of the spiritual realm absolutely rules. This will necessitate a quietness of heart which will be quite refreshing for I know of no peace like that coming to the soul that AUTOMATICALLY LIVES IN THE POWER OF THE SPIRITUAL REALM. This is not abnormal at all—neither is it the results of "salvation" or anything on that order. It is the normal condition in which ever man and woman should live. This is the power-life. This is the life in which the unseen spiritual Law assumes complete control. And when that happens then there need be no worry over the material things of life for they will all be provided. I care not what the circumstances may be, I know that in my own case they were changed in pretty short order when I STEPPED OUT ON THE SURE PROMISES COMING TO ME FROM THE REALM OF THE LIVING GOD-LAW. And they will be changed for you too when that time comes. I suspect that in your own individual case this time has already arrived, and you are finding something of the power of the overwhelming spiritual God-Law in your life and circumstances. Happy man or happy woman. It but remains now for you to LIVE CONTINUALLY IN THIS POWER. If you have not been so sure that you have contacted it—then go through the exercises again which were designed to show you how to find this mighty eternal spiritual realm. There will be some to whom the realization of this realm takes some time to manifest. Some are handicapped by circumstances—others by doubt—most of them by a little bit of doubt. But the overwhelming majority of my students will have grasped the vital and staggering truths this course of instruction has revealed to them. And from now on their lives and their futures will be in their own hands.

The more time given to the application of the God-Law in the human life, the greater will the results be. I realize, of course, that my students are in as many different circumstances as there are students. But remember that the spiritual God-Law works wherever there are circumstances. It is LAW and it is SPIRITUAL LAW. Therefore it is just. It is right. It never fails. No matter who you may be, and no matter what your circumstances may be, the spiritual God-Law will MAKE YOU WHAT YOU SHOULD BE IN THOSE CIRCUMSTANCES OR WILL CHANGE THE CIRCUMSTANCES. You have a definite place in the spiritual scheme of things. It would not be complete without YOU. Therefore, allow the spiritual God-Law to show you where your place is, and this it will unerringly do whenever you keep in harmony with it. For all is one vast harmony. Seems as if there is a lot of discord in the world for sure—but in the fullness of time it will be demonstrated that harmony shall come out of discord. Trust shall come out of doubt. Peace shall come out of turmoil, and plenty will take the place of want. Health will take the place of disease, and happiness—overwhelming happiness will take the place of suffering and sorrow. This will be universal. My students may know this mighty God-Law and these good things NOW.

I shall ask you all to pay strict attention to this Lesson until you receive the next one, for in that I am going to deal with a subject of vital importance to you all. Let the next two weeks be very quiet ones spiritually; rest in the Life Spirit. Trust sweetly in the divinely natural God-Law, and above all, MOMENT BY MOMENT RECOGNIZE YOUR ONENESS WITH THE GREAT GOD. Realize the fact that you are a growth from God if you understand what I mean. "I am the vine—ye are the branches," that is true. The Living God-Law is the vine—and you are definitely a PART OF THIS LIVING GOD. Remember this. Almost every evening at 9 o'clock Pacific Standard time, I sit for an hour or so at the console of my beautiful pipe-organ. After a busy day's toil I find much relaxation through so doing. It will help me quite a little if you care to, if you will direct your thoughts to me at that time. I love this vast family of students of mine all over the world. I love them all. I shall never see most of them—but there is a very strong bond of friendship there I assure you. And it might be that by turning your thoughts to me at that time, there may steal into your life a little of the peace of God. For remember, God works always through perfectly natural and human channels, and it is more than likely that if you will think of me at this hour every evening, you may be benefitted. I know I shall be.

When thousands and tens of thousands of people all over the civilized world are directing their thoughts to me at the same hour every night, I shall receive added spiritual strength and power for this great work. For—you will remember—a thought is a thing. It is a part of the God-Realm, and it is a LIVING SPIRITUAL REALITY. In the realm of God, a thought may be likened to an actual messenger. So if you will not think I am imposing on you, may I ask you, for my good as well as your own, to try directing your thoughts every evening for the next two weeks (or longer if you want to) to me. I in return am thinking of you, and this spiritual exercise has been the means of blessing many of my students.

Don't forget—a quiet restful trust from now on until you receive your next Lesson.

Sincerely your friend and teacher,
FRANK B. ROBINSON

EXAMINATION QUESTIONS
FOR LESSON NO. 16

These examination questions are for your benefit and you should know the answers to them all. If they are not clear to you, read your Lesson again and again until they are clear.

(1) What is the ultimate substance of the world? Its simplest element?
(2) What are the most minute particles into which matter can be divided?
(3) What are neutrons? Of what are they composed?

(4) To find the power of the mighty Life Spirit true, more is required than to merely read the Lessons and argue about them?

(5) What is the attitude that wins in the Realm of the Spirit?

(6) The student can never make a mistake by throwing himself into the vast ocean of the Spiritual Power of the God-Law?

(7) What is prayer? What is it that prevents prayers from being answered?

(8) Why is it that men, countries and nations are missing the goal of universal peace?

(9) What is the only thing in the world that matters now?

(10) If the student is not quite sure that he has already contacted the God-Law, what course is recommended?

(11) What should be the student's attitude towards these times in which we live?

(12) How is the Scriptural text, "I am the vine, ye are the branches" applied in this Lesson?

LESSON 17

Dear friend and student:

This 17th Lesson deals with the most stupendous problem we have to face. That problem is life itself. In life itself will be found the answer to the problem of life. This Lesson is designed to show you how there may be a fullness of perfect supply, for it is a fact that the greater the need, the more sure is the supply.

This Lesson has quite a distinct bearing on the next one you will receive, so study it carefully for it may contain the answer to your personal problems.

Sincerely your friend and teacher,
FRANK B. ROBINSON

Now in this Lesson I want to deal with the subject of LIFE a little further. You have seen that there is nothing in existence except LIFE. Every other thing is but a result of the operations of this mighty Life Spirit of which I am teaching you in this course of instruction. Remember that please. If you were to take LIFE out of the world, there would be nothing left. Nothing. What is now here would decay and a grim silence—the grim silence of death would ensue. Suppose you imagine for a few moments here, what this old world would be like if there were no life in it. Imagine your awakening in the morning and finding that every single living thing but yourself had ceased to be. Not a living thing in existence only you. SILENCE—nothing but SILENCE—and DEATH all around you. The stores would stand as they now stand, but customers and clerks would be missing. Not an animal on the street. The trees all die, and on every hand nothing but disintegration and death.

It should not be so hard to imagine such a condition as that, so try it. Take the city in which you now live and try and imagine this city as being a city of no life except yourself. Then you will be able to see what an immense thing a living person is. Take electricity, and the great factories, and workshops; take the thousands of automobiles that flash past us on the streets; take all the bustle and noise; take our large scientific laboratories; they all exist only because LIFE exists. And it is perfectly allowable and also perfectly true to say that nothing exists except LIFE. This being a fact, then YOU, as you read this, are yourself, the greatest thing in the created universe—YOU ARE LIFE. I so hope that I successfully drive this fact home to you, because if I do, it will give you a picture of yourself that you have never had before—I promise you that.

We are so used to seeing life, and things, all about us, that we overlook the magnitude of the scheme as it exists. The farmer on the farm becomes so used to sowing the grain and reaping the harvest, that he seldom ever thinks of the miracle of the transformation of one grain of wheat into several hundreds. LIFE was created where before it did not exist. It was transferred to where it was not before. But the farmer never does sit down and try to analyze just how or why this marvelous transformation occurs. Nor does he seem interested in it. He has become so used to the miracle that it is a matter of everyday fact with him, and so he pays no attention at all to it. So you and I have become so used to life that we take it as a matter of course, and unless deadly in earnest, we do not take much interest in it. For all we know, the secret of the whole scheme might very easily be within our grasp but we never give a second thought to that possibility.

We see LIFE around us on every hand. Black life—yellow life—brown life—every conceivable form of LIFE—and yet we pay no attention to it just taking it as a matter of course. Therefore—the greatest thing in the world has become so common to us that we do not pay attention to it at all. Those who want to be successful in life will go chasing this rainbow and that rainbow. They will search here and they will search there. They will buy this theory and they will buy that theory. They will follow every psychological faker that comes along. They have gone to the church and the preachers to try and find out more—but silence has rewarded their efforts. Some charlatan or other comes along, and these good earnest souls are to be found following in the band wagon. First here, then there. First they look to religion—then they look to the skies and elsewhere.

I wish I had the money right now that has been spent by honest intelligent souls in trying to find something of the secret underlying the universe. They want to be successful. They want to be happy. They want to be healthy, and so millions of dollars have been paid by them in what to date seems to have been a somewhat fruitless search for TRUTH. And they never find it. I am not interested in money very much, as such. I am only interested in it as a means to an end in the age in which we are living, which age happens to be a monetary age. But had I the cash that has been thrown away on this eternal search for the TRUTH, I should be able to put my teaching all over the world in mighty rapid order—and not charge for it either. It has gone practically all over the world as it is, and this not withstanding the fact that I do make a charge for it. But let me repeat that had I the money that good souls have spent trying to find "god" or some little truth of life, I should certainly have a lot of it.

And it is quite reasonable for these good honest souls to try to find out the very finest things of life. It is perfectly all right for them to try and discover the secret of life if they can. These souls are the ones who will pioneer the way into the spiritual realm, and they will, many of them, never let up until they do find the truth as it does exist. But they look everywhere except in the right place. They follow this cult, and after having proven that it does not give them much lasting satisfaction, they switch to that cult. After having tried them out also, they finally drift into the study of so-called "psychology." Well and good—they will learn something in that realm all right. They will learn nothing of the truth of the spiritual realm through any system of "supernaturally-revealed" religion, but they will find it in the realm of the New Psychology. It was in this realm that I found the first faint glimmer of light that led me to discover the truth of God as I believe it to exist. It exists for me, and I know full well it exists for many hundreds of my students.

This Lesson is being written at 3:45 in the morning, and after a busy Monday at the study. Hundreds of letters came to me from students, and while it is perhaps not pertinent to this Lesson, I am going to mention a fact which fact cannot be duplicated by any teacher in existence. I don't believe. I probably answered today over two hundred personal letters from students in all parts of the country. I receive many, many letters from students in all parts of the country. I receive many, many letters of praise. I receive hundreds of letters in which my students thank me from the bottom of their hearts for showing them the spiritual truths this course of instruction discloses. And these letters make me very happy, and I get quite used to them. I should think something radically wrong if ever one mail went by without bringing me many letters from students thanking me for these truths. But in dictating the last group of letters today, (yesterday really) twenty-nine of them, one after another, all contained the word "wonderful." Think of that. Twenty nine letters, one after another and taken as they came, all spoke in no uncertain terms of the actual literal value of my teaching, and all used the word "WONDERFUL."

Most of the writers of those letters—in fact all of them—were people of intelligence and ability, and some of them were quite prominent people. But they have learned to look for the answer to life's problems in the proper place. Many of them used to attend this church and that church. They bought this "course of psychology" and they bought that course. And they did NOT find spiritual truth in any of them.

But when their thoughts were intelligently directed into the realm from which all LIFE and all TRUTH come—naturally they are made happy, and they write to me out of the fullness of their hearts. LIFE—that is the place in which to learn the secrets of the spiritual realm—for there is no other realm. Take LIFE out of the world, and DEATH results. There is nothing in existence more than LIFE. And you my friend, are LIFE. Think it over. YOU ARE LIFE. And LIFE is EVERYTHING THERE IS IN EXISTENCE. At least it is the primary cause of everything in existence. And I am not so much interested in anything that is not connected with LIFE—which is God—or which is TRUTH. GOD IS LIFE—INVISIBLE LIFE. He never was anything else. And the LIFE you possess is a part of the GREAT LIFE WHICH GREAT LIFE IS EVERYTHING IN EXISTENCE. You would not attempt to tell me that there exists any power other than the power of the mighty LIFE SPIRIT would you? It would do you no good for I know better. There has never been known to exist any other power or any greater power than the power of LIFE—the mighty invisible LIFE SPIRIT. And YOU are a part of that Spirit of Life. Then it MUST follow that wrapped up you are ALL THE POWERS OF CREATION. It could not be any other way.

And you may depend upon it my friend that this is a fact. If you want things in life that you do not possess—then the power to obtain these things lies in the Great Life Spirit which spirit operates now as an invisible God-Law for your use. AND YOU CAN USE THIS MIGHTY LAW WHENEVER YOU WANT TO USE IT FOR THE MANIFESTATION OF WHATEVER IT IS YOU NEED. You are alive are you not? Then you are GOD. YOU ARE THE MIGHTY LIFE SPIRIT IN ESSENCE. You MUST be. You HAVE to be. If you were not you couldn't exist one split second. So don't go howling around the country telling people that you never had a chance. You had all the chance in the universe and there was all the power in the universe to back you up also—BUT YOU DIDN'T KNOW IT. You are finding that out now though, and if you are one of the many, you have already used and are still using this mighty God-Law for the manifestation of the things you desire.

I have not the slightest use for any doctrine which tries to tell you and me that we are supposed to be "content with our lot" here, spending whatever spare time we may possess in an attempt to win a "home in heaven." I do not want to hurt anyone's feelings, nor would I wish to discredit any doctrine they may believe, for everyone has the right to believe that the moon is made of green cheese if they care to. That does not make cheese out of the moon though. Neither does the fact that hundreds of thousands believe the "home in heaven" dogma have the slightest effect upon the truth or the falsity of that dogma. Personally I don't believe it. Nor can any proof in substantiation of its unusual claims ever be adduced. It has no evidence to offer proving its claims. It never has had any evidence. and further more. it never will have. But I have no quarrel with those believing such an impossible theory. For it's a senseless theory. It does not appeal to one's reason. And there is nothing unreasonable in the whole spiritual realm. Remember that.

Yet these good people and these good denominations spend a lot of time and much money in trying to "convert the world" which by the way, they have been trying to do for quite some time now. And the world is much farther from acceptance of their impossible story than it ever was before. But these good folks continue to propagate their story and they give it to the public as truth. This they have a right to do. I, in turn, have the same right to tell people that the story is NOT true if I wish to, and if I can prove my statement. This I can do. There is no reasoning mind that can accept this story with reason. It is based entirely on "faith" and the funny part of it is that no one knows on what the faith is pinned.

No—my friend—you can very safely discard all such hopes and all such stories, and you will have to discard them before you ever find anything at all about the Spiritual God-Law as it really exists. Never mind the "home in heaven." Try and get a home down here. Never mind the "wings" and the "angels" and the "great white thrones," try and get you a throne of your own down here. Let the "angels" be your own thoughts of the mighty Life Spirit, and manifest the presence of God through deeds here and now. The future will take care of itself if you find God here.

I am not at all a materialist for I know too much about the mighty Spiritual God-Law as it really exists to be such. But I am in favor of an understanding of the spiritual realm of God—here and NOW. LIFE is here. We have it. DEATH to date has always appeared also. But I am not one of those who accept the fact of death without at least making an intelligent analysis and investigation of the whole subject to find out whether with spiritual TRUTH fully known, death is at all necessary. Certainly the solution to the scheme lies in LIFE itself. It cannot lie "beyond the tomb" for there can be no land of that sort. The chances are, my friend, many to one—that when they lay you down under six feet of earth, that is the end of you. I shall not dogmatize here, however, for, of course, I may be wrong. I don't think so, however. And, as far as "eternal life" goes, I am not so sure that the day will not come when it will be the natural thing right here on this earth.

It is a very cowardly thing to do, to tell you and me that we are "not supposed" to know anything at all about life and death until we die. Well, heaven knows, it will probably be too late then to find out anything about it. And if our good church friends should be wrong (and they can't prove they are not wrong) then what a responsibility lies upon their head. "Never mind this world's goods" they tell us. "The Lord will take care of you in heaven." Well, I don't believe that either. There may be a life after death. And again there may not be. But whether there is or not, WE KNOW THE MIGHTY GOD-LAW EXISTS HERE AND NOW, AND WE KNOW THAT THIS GOD-LAW IS LIFE—AND WE ALSO KNOW THAT IT CAN BE USED FOR THE MANIFESTATION OF EVERYTHING WE NEED HERE AND NOW. So why worry about "heaven?"

You are NOW, a very vital part of the Creative Life Spirit which brought every created thing into being. Without you, there could be no life at all. Take every individual out of existence and try and imagine what a world it would be. It would stagnate—and die—and I want you to think of this a little. ALL WE KNOW OF GOD IS TIED UP AND MANIFESTED HERE IN THE HUMAN RACE. NOT IN ANY ONE SECT OR RACE—BUT IN THEM ALL. There may be other planets on which similar life manifests, but this we do not know. AS FAR AS THE MIGHTY LIFE SPIRIT GOES, ON THIS EARTH AT LEAST, IT IS CONTAINED IN ITS ENTIRETY IN THE HUMAN FAMILY. And any revelation from the spiritual realm of God must come from some member of the human family. There will never be any angels come down from the sky to tell us something about God. Not at all. There never have been such happenings and there never will be.

For you and I have seen that GOD IS A SELF-EXISTING UNSEEN SPIRITUAL LAW WHICH OPERATES HERE AND NOW IN BEHALF OF EVERY MAN AND WOMAN. I might say that the GOD-LAW operates automatically for that is just what it does. Whenever and wherever the conditions are complied with—THE LAW WORKS. And if there be limitations to it, I have not yet been able to find them.

And this God-Law is awaiting your call now. The power of the mighty Life Spirit is at your disposal. YOU MAY NOT KNOW IT, HOWEVER, and if you do NOT know it—then what a pity it is. For the power of the Life Spirit will only work when PUT INTO ACTION. It is something like a radio battery. You cannot see the electrical energy stored in it, but it is there, and you will know it is there when you touch the battery. So with the mighty power of the invisible God-Law. Here it is all around you. You can't see it. You want to use it. You believe it to be there—in fact you KNOW it is there. Now—how to put it into action is the thing to lock into now. The first thing for you to realize is that YOU ARE LIFE. In other words "YOU ARE YOURSELF A MANIFESTA-TION OF THE SAME SPIRITUAL GOD-LAW THAT BROUGHT INTO BEING EVERY CREATED THING. YOU MUST REALIZE THAT TO THE VERY FULL.

Try and think of one single thing that can compare to a man. You cannot do it. Look around the world—take its seven wonders and com-pare them with man—and YOU cannot make a comparison at all. For man is so far superior to anything else that he. cannot be compared. Now listen—THERE LIES, TIED UP IN EVERY HUMAN LIFE, ALL 0F GOD THERE IS. REMEMBER THE ILLUSTRATION I USED SOME TIME BACK ABOUT THE PACIFIC OCEAN AND THE BUCKET OF WATER? That is what I mean here. AND YOU MUST STAY WITH THIS THOUGHT UNTIL YOU ABSOLUTELY FEEL ITS KNOWLEDGE, (WHICH IS ITS POWER) GOING THROUGH AND THROUGH YOU. There never was a created thing manifesting as much of God as you manifest. You can talk—you can think—and you have already seen that there is a permanent and always-open connection between you and the entire spiritual realm, and you must LIVE IN THE CONSCIOUS REALIZATION OF THIS MOMENTOUS SPIRITUAL FACT.

When you awaken in the morning, you should be so still that you can realize anew, the marvels of conscious relation to the Life Spirit. If you were NOT a manifestation of the mighty Spirit—YOU WOULD NEVER LEAVE YOUR BED. But you ARE a manifestation of this mighty Spirit, and the permanent connection with it is in your hands as long as you are alive. And the conscious realization of this Power is all that is needed to bring the material manifestation of whatever it may be you need. This life of conscious union with God is not a blustery life. Usually it is a very quiet life. But from its hidden depths spring wells of quiet in visible POWER. This SPIRITUAL POWER, (which may not be recognized as spiritual power) always overcomes whatever things there may be that are not so good for you. IT INVARIABLY POINTS THE WAY TO THE VERY HIGHEST AND NOBLEST THINGS LIFE HOLDS. IT LEADS TO THE SOURCE OF ALL SUPPLY, FOR IT IS THE GOD-LAW AND NEVER CAN IT FAIL. And you must here realize this fact.

There can arise in life no circumstance which cannot be overcome by applying the great, invisible God-Law which is so close at hand. Let us take, for instance, a specific case which is very characteristic of possibly hundreds of thousands of other cases. Here is a family living in a little home. Business depression has cost the husband his job. The little kiddies are not dressed as well as they should be and there is not an over-abundance of supply of food in the house. Wages being small at best, there is, of course, no money in the bank; perhaps what little might have been there we diminished through sickness of some sort. But, at any rate, here is this family with a future that is none too rosy.

Now, according to the average way of thinking, there is no possible way out for this man or his family. He will probably begin to worry and fret and stew and the more he does that, the deeper does he get into the mire and the less competent is he to help himself. Finally. if things get bad enough, starvation faces the family and they are thrown upon the resources of their county or state or some other charitable institution. (In passing I might state that it would be a good thing if every charitable institution in existence were abolished). And so matters go on in this little family from bad to worse. This man knows nothing at all about the power of the great, unseen God-Law. He has been told, of course, that he was born in sin, shaped in iniquity and is supposed to be constant with his lot and leave everything in the hands of the Lord. This would probably be good advice if he were told the truth about this "Lord" proposition, but the only Lord he knows anything about is a judge who, after death, will stand him before a bar of judgment and punish him for his sins or reward him for his good deeds. This man has been told nothing about an existing Intelligence or Spiritual Power which can and does operate for the supplying of his material needs here and now; consequently, the man cannot be blamed for worrying and becoming desperate and in many cases cursing the system of which he is a part. Such teachings concerning God invariably lead to Communism and other things worse among certain classes of people.

Now, what is the actual fact concerning this little family and its circumstances. If this man knew of the existence of the great, mighty, invisible God Law, and if he knew for a positive fact that this Creative Intelligence is responsible for every created thing upon the earth, and if he knew this great Spirit was Life, itself, and if he knew that all supply of everything came from this Master Intelligence, don't you see how little worry there would be in this man's life, provided he knew how to throw into Action the power of this great, providing, eternal, unchangeable God-Law? This man then would know that every need would be supplied and if he had been taught simple faith in this marvelous existing spiritual Power, don't you see that it would not be long until the conditions surrounding that little family would be changed? Then, instead of thinking and struggling against so-called "circumstances," this man would rise above them and by and through the Power that gave him life, the greatest thing in the world, by the way, he would rise superior to and master circumstances, and would, if you please, put into operation a Spiritual Law which would respond according to the needs and desires of his individual case.

It may be that the student reading this Lesson is in similar circumstances to the ones I have just related and it may be that such student is not quite clear as to how to apply this unfailing Spiritual Law for the changing of adverse conditions. If such be the case, I want to give this student just one fundamental rule to follow, and if he follows this rule to the letter, I can assure him that those circumstances will be changed in short order. The first thing for such a one to do is to realize that he, himself, is the greatest manifestation of the God-Law in existence. If he puts out of his mind all thoughts of being a "lost soul and pilgrim" and all the rest of that stuff and realizes that wrapped up in him is more of the Life Spirit than there is in any other Created thing, then do you not see the hope and the positive assurance and confidence which will come into that life? The moment this truth of existence is recognized, in the place of despair comes confidence, and confidence in the Law of God is the key which unlocks the door to the Spiritual Realm of supply and it is the switch which, when thrown, sends the God-current coursing through all this man's life and circumstances.

Now the second play for this person to make after he has recognized that he himself, is a very fundamental part of the great God-Law, is for him to let his desires be made known to this great intelligent, thinking, God-Law, itself. Now, how will he do that? Here is how he will do it. Filled with the confidence of the omnipotent, immutable, omniscient, all-pervading. self-existing and all-providing God-Law and knowing that this Law is Life, itself, he will speak into existence the material needs he desires. Let me try to make it a little more concrete by placing myself in those circumstances. If this morning I were in circumstances as above described, there would no worry, no fretting, no fear in my life at all; in fact, I could not give a second thought to it, for I have learned and proved the power and existence of the great Spiritual Law I am teaching. So, under those circumstances, I would keep exceptionally quiet and would audibly command material needs to be supplied by using the following sentence; "LET THERE BE A FULLNESS OF SUPPLY." I would transmit that desire with childlike confidence into the great Spiritual Realm of God and leave it there. Then, if I were out of work, I would make every effort to procure it and with all the power and wisdom of the great Creative God-Law behind me. I would instinctively be led by this great Life Spirit to where work was to be had. My own inclinations might lead me some where else, but if the switch were thrown and I were resting in that complete confidence which the knowledge of this great God-Law brings, then just as surely as the day follows the night would this supreme, living intelligence lead me aright.

It would be foolish and presumptuous for me to try to explain the processes by which I would be led into channels whereby these circumstances would be changed, for no man can do this. and neither would I be concerned about the spiritual operations which directed my footsteps and my actions in the proper channel. The results would be sure; therefore, I would be very foolish to question how or why. Furthermore, if I should raise these questions, the Law governing them would be hindered, for as I have tried to impress upon you all through this teaching, the key that unlocks the door of God's great storehouse is belief in the God-Law, itself. If a perfect confidence in this great Law be manifested under those conditions and the smile of confidence worn on the face, no matter how black the future may look and no matter how undesirable physical and material conditions may be, one could shout for joy if he only knew it because with one's connection with the God Law once established, relief is sure.

I think those of my students in circumstances not to their liking will grasp what I have so earnestly tried to teach in this Lesson and I mean it literally, too. I am not theorizing, nor am I taking any airplane trip in the hazy realm of metaphysics. I am talking about a reality. I am talking about the great God-Law which manifested life in the first place. I am talking about the great God-Law in whom dwells intelligence and wisdom enough to direct every man and woman so that all things whatsoever that they need for their own good can be supplied. One does not need to argue about the existence of the God-Law, for arguing about it will not change it or prove its existence. All one has to do is to just simply put it to the test with childlike faith and find out whether or not it works. If our statesmen and law-makers realized this stupendous fact now and if the nations of the world realized it, the saddened condition of affairs would be changed very shortly.

Now, until you get your next Lesson, if there are circumstances surrounding you which you want to change and if this change is in tune with the mighty God-Law, let me suggest that you first be sure of your spiritual connection with this God Law and then SPEAK INTO EXISTENCE THE CONDITIONS YOU DESIRE. Do not misunderstand me here. It may take weeks or months or perhaps years for the things you need to really manifest themselves. They do not usually spring into existence by any miraculous means, but I will say this to you: "THE GREATER THE NEED, THE GREATER AND THE QUICKER THE SUPPLY." As a matter of fact, the realization of one's own oneness with the great Life Spirit is in itself the beginning of the actual thing desired.

Thousands of people write me regarding conditions of poverty and illness, also. In cases of illness, let me suggest. the same method be followed. Place the right hand on the forehead of the afflicted and with perfect confidence and power say quite audibly and with lots of force, "LET THERE BE PERFECT HEALTH." If you have faith in the God-Law even as a grain of mustard seed, what will happen will stagger you. If you do not have very much faith, then repeat this operation every day all the while increasing in intensity and confidence. and let me say to you once more that according to your faith in the great God-Law will it be done unto you.

We shall not go any farther now. You have two weeks in which to actually apply the great God-Law literally in your life, or in the lives of others around you, and in conclusion let me state to you that you will never exhibit even the suspicion of a grain of real confidence in this great God-Spirit without the results being sure.

Sincerely your friend and teacher,
FRANK B. ROBINSON

EXAMINATION QUESTIONS
FOR LESSON NO. 17

These examination questions are for your benefit and you should know the answers to them all. If they are not clear to you, read your Lesson again and again until they are clear.

(1) Why would it be true to say that nothing exists except LIFE?

(2. We can become so used to a miracle that we cease to pay any attention to it. Illustrate this?

(3. What is the answer to a man who complains that he never has had a chance?

(4. In what respect does the power of the Life Spirit resemble a radio battery?

(5) Contrast the behavior of the husband of a little family overtaken by misfortune when

    (a) He knows nothing of the God-Law?

    (b) He regulates his conduct by the God-Law?

(6) There has never been known to exist any greater power than the power of LIFE. So, if you are a part of that Spirit of Life, what follows?

(7) As a human being, you manifest more of God than does any other

created thing? How so?

(8) What is the key which unlocks the door to the Spiritual Realm of supply?

(9) If there be circumstances surrounding you that you want to change, what is the first step to be taken?

(10) What is the next step? Anything further?

(11) What is the beginning of the actual thing desired?

(12) In treating cases of illness, describe the procedure?

LESSON 18

Dear friend and student:

You will find this 18th Lesson entirely different from those that have gone before and in a way this is rather a distasteful Lesson in parts; but in handling the truth as it exists, I must stay close by that truth and not allow sentiment to swing me at all.

You will find also some very beautiful instructions and a beautiful spiritual sentiment running through this Lesson and I want you to apply this principle every day in your own life, for to find the power of the great God-Law means supreme happiness, supreme peace, and supreme supply.

Sincerely your friend and teacher,
FRANK B. ROBINSON

The Lessons in this Course which you have received to date have been specifically designed and very earnestly designed to show you something of the existence of this great, unseen Power , we sometimes chose to call "God." I have shown you scientifically that there does exist an unseen, dynamic Spiritual Power, and I have further shown you that this Power does not and indeed could not operate through any one man or any one organization to the exclusion of the rest of the human race. I have so earnestly tried to show you the universality and the omnipotence and the omniscience and the everywhereness of this great, invisible, but dynamic Power. I have shown you furthermore that this Power is a Law, a Spiritual Law, which must respond and which does respond universally and in every individual case in which the conditions of this Law are complied with.

I realize that the common opinion of perhaps ninety-nine per cent of the human race is that financial and material success are the only things necessary to complete happiness in life. I realize that this is perhaps the universally held opinion of practically everybody, so in this course of instruction so far I have carefully and purposely designed these Lessons to show you how this great God Law can be used for the manifestation of these material things. I have shown you, however, that, the source or every material manifestation must lie and does lie in the great, unseen Spiritual Cosmic GOD-REALM. In that Realm lies the starting point and the very beginning of every physical and material thing on this earth. We covered that rather carefully in the Lesson dealing with that subject, and I think you will realize that without the unseen, creative Realm of the God-Law, there never could have been any material or physical manifestation of any kind, nor could there ever have been any physical manifestation of life as we know it now in all its varied forms. I took great pains to impress this fact upon you and right here I want to drive it home again. I want you to permanently understand that the origin of every created thing lies in the unseen, creative Spiritual Realm of this dynamic spiritual Power we call "GOD." I want you to further understand that whatever material things manifest in your own individual life in the future will first have a manifestation unseen by you in your thought realm, which, as you now know, is a definite part of the great universal Spiritual Realm of the great LIFE SPIRIT.

Most of my students are absolutely in earnest in desiring the better things of life, and by far the great majority of them are following me very closely, and are, day by day, and week by week, and month by month, laying the foundation in the Spiritual Realm, or rather let me say they are making the manifestation in the Spiritual Realm of those things which are to manifest materially or physically in due time. Many of these good friends and students of mine—in fact, quite a large percentage of them—have already written to me thanking me for leading them to the place in which they could actually manifest the blessings and the power of this great God-Realm. These thousands of letters to me. and to anyone else are conclusive evidence of the truth and reality of the power of the great God-Law which actually brings into realization by means of the unseen Spiritual Realm, the things needed and desired physically and materially here and now.

But there is another side to this question of manifestation, and while it is a fact that the vast majority of people imagine that happiness, success, and satisfaction lie in the material realm and in material possessions, let me say to my students that money, or material possessions never yet were the means to the very best things the Spiritual Realm holds for you and for me. There is no question whatsoever that money and a nice home and a good car are very much to be desired blessings in many cases; but the point I want to make is that the obtaining of these things is by no means an assurance of real happiness, real satisfaction, or real success in life, for real success in life lies not so much in getting as in giving. Real satisfaction in life lies not so much in material accumulation as it lies in the accumulation of the finer spiritual things of life; and real happiness in life lies not so much in the amassing of a fortune as it does lie in the fact of the conscious realization of one's inseparableness from this vast spiritual God-Realm.

So, in this Lesson we are going to get away from the material realm for a while and I am going to show you some of the finer and much more to be desired gifts that this invisible Spiritual Realm bestows upon those in that Realm, and which gifts are a part of this great God-Law itself. I have purposely given the impression in this course of instruction so far, that the spiritual God-Law is a cold-blooded, never-varying Law, working with absolute precision and with the certainty of a chemical formula whenever the conditions governing this Law are complied .with. I have deliberately done this, for that is actually the impression I wanted you to form. I wanted you to have a conception of Spiritual Law which would convince you beyond the shadow of a doubt that there is no possibility of Spiritual Law failing when the conditions governing it are complied with; so in order to more effectively do this, I have impressed upon your minds the fact, and it is a fact, that there is no more possible way to miss the results from this great realm of Spiritual Law than there is to stop a pencil from dropping to the floor by the law of gravitation. I have used my best brain power and my most earnest efforts in my attempt to give you this picture of this great God-Realm, and right here I wish to make it even stronger if I possibly can.

When dealing with the God-Realm, there can be no such a thing as petitioning this great Realm for something, and then hopefully and watchfully waiting in the expectation of the power behind the Spiritual Realm looking with favor upon your request, and some time or other in the far distant future perhaps granting it. This is the common idea given out by the religious systems of the day. If adversity comes along, you are told that it is all in the will of God, and you must not murmur or complain but just simply say in a very meek and obedient voice:

> *"Though dark my path and sad my lot,*
> *Let me be still and murmur not;*
> *But breathe the prayer divinely taught—*
> *'Thy will be done'.*

> *"What though in lonely grief I sigh*
> *For friends beloved no longer nigh,*
> *Submissive still would I reply,*
> *'Thy will be done.'"*

This sentiment is a million miles from the truth of God as it actually exists. The sentiment behind this teaching, however, is easily understood when it is traced back to its source. In those days the church was what it would like to be now but cannot—a great political power. Every means were used to cow people into submission and threats of "Hell" and "damnation" and everything else were held over their heads in an effort, and a very vain effort, by the way, to force this foolish and pagan teaching into the minds of ignorant and superstitious people incapable of thinking for themselves. In those days the world was a very fertile field for all sorts of religious superstition, and many and terrible were the atrocities committed in the name of "God."

A few weeks ago I was in New York City and made a special trip to see one of the most gruesome exhibitions I have ever seen in my life. It was interesting, but I never want to see it again. Mr. Joseph Lewis has brought to this country direct from Germany several dozens of instruments of torture which were used by the so-called "Christian" church only a few hundred years ago, in its effort to force down the throats of the "heretics," or in other words, those who believed differently, the teachings of that religious organization. The first thing I saw in this exhibition room were several pairs of horrible pincers two or three feet long with which the tongues of these "heretics" were literally torn out by the roots. Following after this, I saw another gruesome display of gouges by which the eyes of the "non-Christians" were literally gouged out in the name of "God" by a supposedly Christian organization. Over in one corner of the exhibition room was a rack which was a horrible piece of machinery. The victim was fastened down on this rack and both arms extended over his head and chained to a post on the two upper corners of this diabolical instrument of torture. The legs were also extended and similarly fastened. Then two men or more would get on a wheel and turn it until the victim's arms and legs were torn from their sockets. The next gem in this "Christian" persuasive category was a bathtub sitting on rockers. It was about six feet long and made of wood with sloping sides and ends. With points only one-half an inch apart horrible steel spikes about one and one-half inches long were driven into the bathtub and these points sharpened to points of terrible cruelty. The victim, stark naked, was put into this bathtub and rocked from side to side, and you can imagine the condition of this "unbeliever" when these cruel and ignorant and benighted "agents of God" were through with him or her. On a table in the center of the exhibition hall were several branding irons for the purpose of branding "unbelievers" on the forehead and other parts of the body as a punishment for their not believing in the God taught by this "Holy" religious organization. On still another table was a gruesome assortment of thumb screws which were fastened around the wrists of the victim and his thumb screwed around and around until it was literally wrenched from his body. Another horrible thing I saw there was the wheel and the rack. This consisted of a ladder about seven feet long and two feet wide constructed of very heavy wood with the rungs about six inches apart and having sharp edges on them. The victim was tied to this rack and the "Holy men of God" attempting to convert him seized a very heavy wheel. On this wheel a knife blade about six inches deep and one foot long had been fastened and while this helpless victim lay tied to the rack, these "saints" would bring down the wheel, with the knife blade attached, onto his body until he was literally hacked to pieces.

There was also a terrible chair there the seat of which was covered with one and one-half inch spikes, as also were the back and arms. The "unsaved" one was compelled to sit in this chair stark naked on these spikes, and then was chained in that. condition. One of the most fiendish things, though, was a brass helmet which was fitted over the head of the "unbeliever" and on each side of this helmet was a funnel-shaped affair hollow on the inside. Molten lead was then poured through these funnel-shaped affairs after this horrible thing WAS attached over the "sinner's" head and this molten lead ran into the ears and down the sides of the face of the victim. I saw in that horrible place mouth gags which were pear shaped and which were forced into the mouth and then screwed wide open. Lying in another corner of the room were several torture belts which were applied to the naked bodies of women. As long as the victim stood absolutely motionless, she suffered no pain; but the very moment she made one move, then spikes from this torture belt penetrated her flesh. Several whips were there with many lashes onto which pieces of lead with jagged points had been fastened every six or eight inches and the victim was horribly lashed to death or to insensibility. But the crowning masterpiece of all was a contraption called "The Iron Maiden." This is a hollow brass figure of a woman hinged on one side and weighing several tons. The "unbeliever" was placed, upright, in this contraption and the door was forced shut. On the inside of the door were spikes six inches long and fixed in such a manner that, .when the door was closed, the victim was impaled by these spikes and suffered an excruciating and agonizing death. With devilish ingenuity two of these spikes were placed so that they went through the eyes; another penetrated the nose; while another went through the mouth; three went through the breast; two through the stomach; and four through each leg. I will not prolong this picture, for I realize as well as you do that it is a horrible thing to talk and to write about.

My only object in mentioning these terrible things I saw in New York is to make a definite connection between them and the teaching I have just alluded to which tries to tell thinking, intelligent men and women today that they must keep submissive to the will of God. This "submission" teaching originated in the countries and by the organizations which used the cruel methods I have described to force men and women to accept their religious teaching, and this teaching of submission to both God and His "agents" was the fundamental feature and dogma of that horrible thing which masqueraded as a divinely appointed organization to which the truths of the great God had been exclusively revealed. Now that connection is established and now that it has been clearly shown that this petitioning of God is a false and pagan teaching, let us forget this picture and view another which is a much more sensible and reasonable one of the operations of the great spiritual God-Realm in a human life.

While I was very insistent upon painting this picture of the Spiritual Realm as being an immutable realm of LAW, I purposely left until this part of the course another side of this realm which operates with the same unerring accuracy and precision in the unseen Spiritual Realm as it does in the physical and material realm. For instance, I would not for one moment have my students think that all the Realm of God is, is an invisible storehouse from which, by complying with an immutable Law, they might obtain whatever material things they might need for their happiness. These material things positively are to be obtained from this great God-Realm; but, also, there is to be obtained from this same realm many unseen, and therefore spiritual, gifts, and it is of these gifts that I want to write for a little while now. Here is a student. He grasps the Law governing this great Spiritual Realm. He applies that Law and is eminently satisfied in a material way; but, he may stop there and if he does, disappointment and unhappiness and failure are almost sure to follow, because he has not gone the limit in appropriating to himself all that the spiritual God-Realm has to give, for there is in that Realm much more than physical and material wealth. And let me repeat, I question very much whether the accumulation of material things can ever bring permanent, lasting joy and happiness, because such happiness and joy may not be found merely in the possession of material things.

When my students have learned something of the existent power of the God Realm and something of the existent presence of this great creative God-Law, the first thing they are able to experience is a strange spiritual quietness which goes far beyond the so-called "joy" and "happiness" which may or may not come from the possession of material things. Some poet said, "Joy is like restless day; but peace, divine, like quiet night;" and by far the greatest gift attached to the Realm of God, or perhaps I should say the greatest attribute of the Law of God, is the attribute of peace. Just as surely as this great God-Law brings this health and happiness and success materially, it also brings this spiritual peace. Let me take one specific example which is perhaps characteristic of thousands I know. Here is a student. He has been suffering perhaps from some minor ailment or affliction. He comes into contact with the great God-Law and by complying with the conditions underlying or governing this God-Law, he secures freedom from this condition. Then he masters his material surroundings and perhaps obtains a good paying position, or as one student wrote me this morning, "I have made the first payment on a new home." He accumulates a little money in the bank and is well on the road to material success through the application of this invisible God-Law, and here is where I want to warn you to be very, very careful, for if you stop at this point, you will miss the goal and you will find that you have before you a life of continual struggle and continual restlessness and continual anxiety, for you will be limited in your use of the Spiritual Realm to material things and therefore will miss the true source of the power which naturally emanates from this great creative God-Realm.

You will find as you progress in this Realm of God that the master key which unlocks all the other locks in this great mansion may be called the KEY OF PEACE. Perhaps TRUST would be a better name for it. You see if I trust a person, then I am absolutely at ease in his presence. I can talk freely before him and I can also act freely. No question ever arises as to my being refused any request I might make of him, and therefore any worry or fretfulness cannot possibly enter into a situation where two people trust each other. I want you to enter into this arrangement, if you please, with the great God-Law. I want you to recognize that you, yourself, through your oneness with this great Spiritual Power, have in you all the power that is tied up in this great Spiritual Realm and that is certainly sufficient power to make you an overcomer in every phase of life. I want you to realize that as this great God-Law is a creative Law, so are you, as part of this great God-Law, also a creative being. You cannot stay in communion with the Spiritual Realm and not yourself be a creator, for this great Spirit of God will drive you to the creation of something or other. In my own particular case it drove me to the creation of this marvelous work of mine. In your case it may drive you to creation of something along an entirely different line. This great God-Law drove Thomas A. Edison into his marvelous inventions. The same great God-Law drove Henry Ford along lines of mechanical genius. The same great Spiritual Law is driving everyone in its power toward a creative end of some sort or other. Some people do not allow their reason to reign supreme and therefore they allow this great Law to drive them in the wrong direction in which case they inevitably meet with disaster and failure; for the same great Law which will drive me to create a movement which will change the lives of thousands will also operate with the same unerring accuracy and precision to the destruction of a man if he does not stay close to the Law and follow the greatest gift of the Law—that gift being the purest gem in the human mind, the gem of REASON.

Not. long ago I personally listened to a famous preacher. There is no question in my mind that the man is being driven by the great God Spirit, but this particular man is allowing himself to be driven according to old pagan dogmas and doctrines which on the very face of them are so asinine and so foolish that a child with its pureness of heart could not possibly believe them. Yet this man wonders why eighty per cent of the churches in his denomination are not self supporting. He wonders why he labors his heart out and yet is a failure as far as actually doing anything for the human race is concerned. He cannot for the life of him see why nothing but failure, and worse than failure seems to be ahead of his efforts which he recognizes are controlled by the great God-Law. If this good brother would sit down and think for about a week and decide to discard every thing unreasonable in his teachings, he would be one of the most stupendous leaders the world has ever seen, but he will not do this. Instead he chooses to limit himself by applying the driving force of the great God Spirit along a channel which is based purely on manmade, and therefore perfectly human, dogmas and traditions. This man will tell you that he actually believes that the great Creative Intelligence of this universe came down to the earth in mortal flesh and was born in that form through the medium of the wife of a Syrian Jew. He will tell you that he actually believes that through the crucifixion of this child of the Syrian Jewess, which child was at the same time God and man—he will tell you that he actually believes that by this barbarous act, those who believe the story shall be eternally saved from eternal damnation.

Now, I ask you if you think this is a reasonable belief. I ask you if you think it is a true belief, and your answer must be "No" to both questions. This being a fact, then, the entire story must be and is entirely outside of the realm of the great God Spirit. There is no question at all in my mind that the story does belong in the Christian religion, for the simple reason that the only God the Christian religion has ever known is old "Yahweh" or "Jehovah," which God never was anything more than the old tribal God of the Jews and which God never had any existence outside the imaginations of those old Jewish religious leaders. This is the God that smote dead over fifty thousand men and women for attempting to look into a little wooden box called the "ark" in which this old God, "Yahweh" or "Jehovah," lived.

So, I must in honesty to myself and to you say to you that any teaching by any religious organization, no matter who they be, must be false and untrue if it teaches anything contrary to illumined human reasoning. I have stated in many of my writings and been grossly misunderstood for stating it that the Christian religion as it exists today is founded wholly upon an unprovable fabrication originating in a perfectly human, but perfectly blind and ignorant superstitious structure, which structure in its attempt to manufacture a guide of its own, stole a crucifixion and resurrection story from another system, which story was known to millions of people thousands of years before the so-called "Savior" of this religion was ever heard of. You will never "save" this world, and you will never give to a human being one single enlightened and helpful thought from a system of religion which is based on fear and ignorance and superstition. What an atrocity it is to attempt to be a power for enlightenment in the world and come to the world with a story so foolish that even a child cannot believe it.

The religious organizations of today are dabbling with prohibition. They are fighting among themselves. We have over three hundred of them in this country and outside of their social organization, they do not have among them one reasonable, sensible, constructive truth to give anybody. They had better leave prohibition and politics and everything else alone and examine their own structure first and then, when convinced of its dishonesty, which they inevitably will be on only a superficial examination, they had better come to men and women with a true story of a true God, which is not and cannot be "Jehovah" or old "Yahweh," the tribal God of the Jews. What a difference in the life of a student of mine who knows some thing of the freedom and something of the quietness and something of the power of the great creative God-Law behind this universe. There is no fear in the life of such a one either of the past or of the future, for there is no fear in the Realm of God, I promise you that. Instead of fear there comes an absolute TRUST; instead of doubt, there comes an absolute FAITH; and instead of strife and turmoil, there comes CALM, for the realm of the Spirit of God is a realm of calm. It is a realm of peace; it is a realm of quietness; it is a realm of static power, and you can make it dynamic by applying it in your own life.

NOW for the next two weeks I want you to discontinue the use of all affirmations of every kind and I want you to enter into a period of absolute quietness. I want this period to be with the full consciousness that this quietness comes to you from the Spiritual Realm, or rather is part of the Spiritual Realm. You see, you cannot hear the still small Voice of the great LIFE SPIRIT unless you keep quiet. You could not hear a whisper at a ball game; and if your life is busy, if it is noisy, if it is hurried, and if it is fretful, you will not be able to hear this still small Voice of God. When you arise in the morning, sit still for a few moments and be quiet. Recognize your union with the great quiet Life Spirit. Take your bath quietly. Dress quietly. Eat your meals quietly. Go to work quietly. Do your daily duties quietly. And for the next two weeks let there be a silence over your entire life. This is what will happen. Out of that quietness will come to you a knowledge of your union with the great God Spirit. You will know as never before something of the power that lies in the peace and quietness of God. If you have a problem which needs solving, you will be much more able to get the solution of the problem in the quietness than you will be able to get it in the bluster and humdrum of life. If you are out of a job and if there are pressing bills to be met, and if you do not know where the rent is coming from, or if you do not know where the next meal is coming from, or if you have domestic troubles, you will find the answer much more quickly through a simple quiet resting in this great quiet Realm of God than you will in any other way. In fact, it is an immutable Law of God that the answer to every human problem, and this includes yours, may be found in the great quiet Spiritual Realm from whence comes all wisdom. You will be kind in this quiet realm; you will be loving in this quiet realm; you will say no unkind things or hurtful things to anyone because you cannot if you keep quiet. Relax your efforts to direct your little barque on the Sea of Life. You have left the coast clear for the Master Pilot to step a board your little vessel and THROUGH you guide it aright. You will not be like the preacher I mentioned, driven in the wrong direction; but by living this quiet life, with nothing imposed by you between yourself and the great God Spirit, you will invariably and most assuredly be driven where you should go, for this Master Intelligence—this unseen God Spirit—is the cause of life. It caused your life to be; consequently, it knows far better than you know in what channel lies complete happiness and success. You might by being noisy and unsettled, do the very thing which will hinder your hearing the direct leadings from the great God Spirit. When this life is lived, you will find that there will be created in you a desire to pass on your knowledge of the great Life Spirit to others. This Presence will become very close to you and very near to you, and in working with this Spirit you will find that it will show you the way to triumph over every undesirable condition. If you will live continually in this attitude toward the great God Spirit, you need have no more thoughts about your future for you will want to follow where this great Spirit leads and that is always aright.

So for the next two weeks, and indeed forever, let this be your condition of life. There is a little poem which comes to my mind now written by that saintly old man, Dr. Washington Gladden, who, by the way, was ostracized by his own church organization and practically called a heretic and an infidel for stating that the Bible was not infallible. This precious old Bible scholar of the Congregational Church said: "In the Bible, human ignorance and error have been suffered to mingle with the stream of living water throughout all its course. If our assurance of salvation was made to depend upon our knowledge that every word in the Bible was of divine origin, our hope of eternal life would be altogether insecure. It is not infallible scientifically; it is not infallible historically; and it is not infallible morally; and the attempt of any intelligent man to maintain the theories and to maintain the infallibility of this book is a criminal blunder." For making that statement this man was ostracized and, of course, the Congregational Church, to which he belonged, stated that he knew nothing about God at all. They bitterly condemned him and said all sorts of nasty things about him; but listen to what he wrote as I am about to quote it and then ask yourself who knew the most about God, the great Life Spirit—Dr. Washington Gladden, or the church, founded upon pagan superstition and idolatry, which condemned him. I want you to read these verses slowly and carefully and when the word "Master" appears in these beautiful verses, you look upon that word as being the great invisible God Spirit. Do not consider for one moment that it means Jesus Christ, or any other of the world's sixteen crucified God-men. For the time being at least just pass that out of the picture and in repeating these marvelous verses do so with the idea in mind that the word "Master" means the great Life Spirit you are learning to know and to love.

> "O Master, let me walk with Thee
> In lowly paths of service free;
> Tell me Thy secret; help me bear
> The strain of toil, the fret of care.
>
> Help me the slow of heart to move
> By some clear, winning word of love;
> Teach me the wayward feet to stay,
> And guide them in the homeward way.
>
> Teach me Thy patience; still with Thee
> In closer, dearer company,
> In work that keeps faith sweet and strong,
> In trust that triumphs over wrong.
>
> In hope that sends a shining ray

Far down the future's broadening way,
In peace that only Thou canst give,
With Thee, O Master, let me live."

I am going to leave you now with this thought and I wish you the happiness that it brings me to know that thousands of students the world over will be reading these beautiful lines, and will be quietly resting from now on in the peace and the power coming from the great Spirit of the .REAL GOD.

Sincerely your friend and teacher,
FRANK B. ROBINSON

EXAMINATION QUESTIONS
FOR LESSON NO. 18

These examination questions are for your benefit and you should know the answers to them all. If they are not clear to you, read your Lesson again and again until they are clear.

(1) Whatever material things manifest in your own individual life in the future will have had a prior manifestation?

(2) What constitutes (a) real happiness (b) real satisfaction © real success in life?

(3) Distinguish between the common idea regarding prayer given out by existing religious systems and the attitude of one who uses the God-Law

(4) The fundamental policy of the Church was expressed in the well-known hymn, "Thy Will Be Done"?

(5) What was the reason for describing the various horrible instruments of torture exhibited in New York?

(6) A student, by applying the God-Law may be eminently satisfied in a material way, but he must not stop there?

(7) What is described in this Lesson as "the greatest attribute of the Law of God"?

(8) What is described as "the master key which unlocks all the other locks in the Realm of God"?

(9) Why is it that you are a creative being?

(10) There exists a danger that. as a creative being, you may be driven in the wrong direction. How can this danger be avoided?

(11) Why is it beneficial to enter into a period of absolute quietness?

(12) Why need you have no more thoughts about your future?

LESSON 19

Dear friend and student:

This Lesson 19 is probably the one you have been looking for, for it opens up the entire Spiritual Realm and brings it down to where your reasoning mind can grasp it. No such Lesson as this has ever been written before by anyone, nor has this vast vista of Spiritual Truth been given to anyone before that I know of. You may be able to comprehend this Lesson in two weeks, and you may not. However, you think this Lesson out, for it puts into your hands a weapon which you can use, if you properly understand it, to overcome every undesirable condition in your life.

The great God-Realm is waiting for you to plunge into it; so whatever you do, grasp this Lesson and govern your life throughout the future in accordance with the Spiritual facts I have given you here.

Your friend and teacher,
FRANK B. ROBINSON

At this point in our journey into the spiritual realm of TRUTH I shall show you a little bit about just where the Power comes from and just how it acts in the human life. For there is no mistake about it—there is a magnetic or rather a Spiritual charm and force to the man or woman who is in tune with the mighty God Law. It cannot be otherwise for it is impossible for YOU to know and experience anything at all about the realm of God without being a dynamic and very positive character. By this I don't mean a blustery character, for you will notice that the men and women in the world who amount to the most, are very quiet characters—that is—internally. Some of them can get out and fight like a lion if they have to, but what I mean is that they have at their disposal a sure knowledge of an infinite Spiritual God-Law, and, safe and secure in this knowledge, they know their strength.

When troubles come along which would worry the ordinary man or woman to death, these God-men care nothing about them for they KNOW that the Spiritual Law of the universe is more than everything that can ever be formed against them. And so, safe in the knowledge and assurance of this mighty God-Law, they pay no attention at all to negative things, but they hold before their mind's eye all the time, the one thing they desire to do or to possess, and—as ever in the spiritual realm of God—obstacles are swept away and they invariably attain their goal. The world looks at them and wonders. Nothing seems to worry them. Whatever they do is successful. They do not know the meaning of the word "failure" for the simple reason that such a word is not in their vocabulary. They are charged and supercharged with the dynamic spiritual power of God—the Creative Intelligence and the Creative Spirit behind all created things—and they KNOW it. You do not need to tell such a one that the power of God exists—for he KNOWS it. He or she may not allude to "god" as a mythical being in the sky who came down to die for the sins of the world—they may know nothing about that particular dogma, for that is all it is—BUT THESE GOD-MEN AND WOMEN KNOW THE SOURCE OF THEIR OWN STRENGTH. THEY KNOW THE POWER THEY BELIEVE IN. AND THEY KNOW SUCH POWER IS IMMUTABLE. THEY KNOW IT CAN NEVER BE DEFEATED. THEY KNOW THAT THERE IS NO HIGHER OR GREATER POWER. THEY KNOW THE POWER IS GOD—the creative Life Spirit and Intelligence behind the universe and behind every created soul in it, INCLUDING YOU AS YOU READ THIS LESSON NOW.

I shall ask you here not to confuse this Spiritual God-Power with any so-called "power of will" or anything on that order. Nor must you confuse this Spiritual Power with any other known power, for there is no power in existence which comes anywhere near approaching the power of the God-Law. The question is ofttimes asked me whether or not I think the "Cosmic Ray" is God. Of course I don't—for GOD IS SPIRIT. The Cosmic Ray, however, brings God down to the level of a man, and one understanding the existence of this "Cosmic Ray" can also easily understand the existence of the mighty Life Spirit I am teaching. It has no personality because it is SPIRIT. And SPIRIT cannot have personality. Nor is this power material at all in any sense of the word. It is SPIRIT. It is GOD. It is LIFE. And from out the man or woman knowing and urging this power, I say there flows a magnetism, if you please, that BINDS THAT MAN OR WOMAN TO THE FORCES OF THE LIVING INTELLIGENCE—THE GREATEST UNSEEN POWER THIS WORLD WILL EVER KNOW.

Would it make any difference to you if you realized that working through you was a Spiritual Power so dynamic that all other powers and forces fade into insignificance beside it? Do you think that thought would help you much? Of course it would. For let me repeat—there is no stopping the man or the woman who so imbues him or herself with this Spiritual Power. And it makes no difference what the goal may be. It makes no difference whether it be wealth, health or happiness that is desired—the ever present power of this mighty Life Spirit is at the disposal of every man and woman who wants this power and is willing to find it in the way I advise.

Not so many days ago, a certain religious leader of quite some standing came into my office as he often does to while away a half hour or so. The gentleman in question is connected with a certain educational institution specializing in religious instruction, and the man has quite a big reputation. I shall not mention his name here. However, he is fairly broad in his religious beliefs but still not broad enough to get away from the insane "belief" or "faith" in a story that is so palpably foolish that by no possible means could it ever be true. This brother tells me that he does NOT believe in the "immaculate conception" of Jesus Christ. He states further that he does NOT believe in the doctrine of the Trinity. He also told me that he did not believe that "he that doubteth is damned." And there are a good many other old fundamentals that this brother tells me he does NOT believe. And yet—he will still teach "orthodox theology" in an institute of religious education, and will still take part in "orthodox" religious exercises whenever and wherever he gets the opportunity to do so.

Of course—I realize the fact that were he to come right straight out as I do, and deny the asinine theory of the "trinity" and the equally asinine theory of the "blood atonement" and all the rest of the old pagan myths, he would LOSE HIS JOB. I know that. But just the same, I should have much more confidence in the man if he would do just that. He knows that these old Bible myths were in existence long before Christ WAS ever heard of. He knows that the story of the "fall of man" and the story of the "flood" were recently found in literature used by the old Red Indians long before Christ was ever known. Yet, like hundreds of others, he still "hangs on," and when doom cracks this good brother will still be found "hanging on" to doctrines which, while in themselves will do no harm, yet they do effectively take ones eyes from the REAL Spiritual POWER of the universe operating HERE and NOW, and they put that vision "somewhere in the future," and make it entirely dependent upon a false belief in a false "god."

However, this brother said to me in this study the other morning, "Well, Dr. Robinson, will you please tell me what is the secret of the magnetic attraction whatever you write seems to have on those who study it?" He said to me: "You work seeming miracles of success and healing—folks wire you from all over the world—and evidently you get the results although I am frank to admit that I do not understand how you do it." This brother has made several calls on me to try and analyze the cause of our outstanding success. He knows that wherever this simple teaching of mine has gone remarkable results have often followed. He knows that there is a "something" that cannot be expressed or explained, which "something" seems to grip and revitalize the spiritual lives and also the physical lives of men and women. And he wants to know the reason for it. Many have asked me these same questions. And without taking any credit to myself let me say to you, and to one and all who may see this Lesson you are reading, that the answer is very simple.

The answer lies in the fact that the founder of this movement KNOWS GOD. He knows something of the dynamic invisible Spiritual Power that comes only out of the spiritual God-Realm. He KNOWS that Power. He USES that Power. He lives so close to it that he is ever conscious of its nearness and its magnetic charm and vitalizing effect in the human life. The founder of this movement is not looked upon as a "Christian" even by the "church," which looks upon him as an "infidel" and a "heretic." And I suppose they are correct as far as their "god" goes.

For I know nothing about such a creature nor do I want to know anything about him. Nor is there—nor has there ever been—any magnetic attraction or charm to that sort of a doctrine. Men and women on the street would laugh at you if you even suggested that there even might be any such thing as Spiritual Power in the "church." For they know better. They live amongst and know full well its "members" and you cannot fool the general public with any false ideas that the "church members" know anything about the "god" they profess. In the first place they cannot tell you who or what he is. Nor can they tell you where he is. Nor can they tell you how he operates. Yet they are very anxious to criticize one who does know something of the Power of the Living Life Spirit—which Power by the way the church knows nothing about for the simple reason that it has a "god" all its own, which God never was other than the old tribal Jewish "Yahveh" or Jehovah. And, of course, there can never be any attraction for anyone in such a being as that. I will admit to you that there is a decided charm to the man of Galilee, but that is NOT ON ACCOUNT OF ANY DIVINITY OF BIRTH AT ALL, BUT IS SIMPLY ON ACCOUNT OF THE FACT THAT THIS CARPENTER MAN KNEW SOMETHING OF THE GOD-LAW I AM HERE TEACHING YOU ABOUT. And naturally—the much discussed message has LIVED THROUGH THAT CARPENTER MAN.

So there is to some people, myself included, a very marked attraction to that old character who died by the way 2000 years ago and has never been heard from since. And this charm is simply because the message He taught was a message of truth. It was a message concerning the mighty God-Law behind the universe. And of course—His name has lived. (No longer than many others though). Whenever and wherever you find any part of SPIRITUAL TRUTH, you may depend upon it such Spiritual Truth will win its way around the world if it can find a man or woman with faith enough and courage enough to carry the message in spite of "religious" opposition. And that is the reason that there is such a magnetic charm and a compelling and impelling "something" to either the man or the movement that is grounded in the spiritual TRUTHS of the great Life Spirit. It cannot be otherwise. For God is God, and in your own life, when you get to the place where you can LIVE IN THIS SPIRITUAL REALM, you will be a dynamic power too. You will get somewhere. The compelling and impelling Power of God will make you succeed and will make you happy and will keep you healthy, and will draw you to this SPIRITUAL REALM until you wonder what the end of such drawing and such power will be.

You—individually—who are reading this Lesson now—and there are thousands of "you" all over the civilized world, ask yourself the question NOW, why is it that you to date, and before you studied this course of instruction, NEVER KNEW THE FIRST THING ABOUT SPIRITUAL GOD-POWER. And the reason will be quite plain to you. It is because you did not KNOW that such a God-Power existed—now did you? No one had ever told you about the existence of a Living Vital, Dynamic Force—Law—Spirit—God—which YOU could use—now had they? Of course they had not. Now, in these Lessons, you have received training in actually contacting this vital spiritual God-Law, and you are beginning to get a faint glimpse of the wonderful possibilities of the spiritual realm in your OWN life. You begin to see the immensity of it all. You begin to grasp just faintly perhaps, but you DO begin to grasp the existence of the Intellect of God. You are grasping something of the actually MATERIAL EXISTENCE of God—if you will understand that phrase.

More than that—you KNOW how to keep so quiet that the spiritual God-Law will SPEAK to you, and at the same time you KNOW that you are in touch with the Spiritual God-Realm. You KNOW these things now. You did NOT know them when you began your studies with me. And you should be a very happy man or woman I assure you. And you will be as the magnetism of God exudes from you, and as you begin to really FIND THE ACTUAL POWER OF GOD WORKING IN YOUR OWN LIFE AND BRINGING TO YOU THE THINGS YOU DESIRE. Your friends will see the change in you. For spiritual contact brings a change. Perhaps many of them will not be able to understand you—but what do you care? YOU and GOD—there is the answer to every problem that can arise in your life. Just YOU and the GOD-LAW. And in that Law, all Power is given unto you in heaven and earth, and no weapon formed against you can possibly prosper. As a matter of fact there is not, nor has there ever been any weapon ever formed against you. The disturbances you have experienced are due but to the absence of the God Law in your own life. The poverty which perhaps has dogged your footsteps is not due to the power of "Satan" or anything on that order. It is due but to the ABSENCE of the God-Law in your own life. Many people write and tell me about the "power" of "sin," and the "power" of "Satan" and the "power" of this and the "power" of that. THERE IS NO POWER IN THE UNIVERSE OTHER THAN THE POWER OF THE LIVING GOD-LAW. And that LAW is NOT contacted by church creeds and dogmas. There is not a single power in existence that could ever lift its head against the power that you are now using. There is nothing formed against you at all. But YOU—without the Power of God—are utterly useless and helpless. You may use the Power of God unknowingly—but how much better is it to use it intelligently, and to recognize the source from whence such Power comes?

You KNOW that your thoughts are SPIRITUAL THINGS. You KNOW that. You also must know that an Intelligence or a Creative Power great enough and mighty enough to call this created scheme of things into being, must of necessity be a great enough Power to more than satisfy the little cravings and longings of your individual life. Even though you crave millions—I care not. For millions in wealth to this great Spiritual Power

MEAN JUST NOTHING AT ALL. If you could pile all the wealth of the world in one spot—it would mean nothing at all when compared with the Power of this mighty unseen Spiritual God-Law. And you would not ask me to believe that such a Power as it was that formed the marvelous universe with all created life, could not provide you with the necessary brains or intelligence or IDEAS sufficient to satisfy your soul's longings—would you? You know better than that. You know that the God-Law is more than sufficient to give you whatever things you need, or to provide you with the necessary wisdom or intelligence to create those things yourself.

In the last analysis EVERYTHING comes from the God-Law. It alone is responsible for every created thing. Without it, you would not be here. Neither would I. Neither would there be a breath of life on any planet or would there be any planets. It would be a black, aching, empty nothingness if you can imagine that. But since this Life Principle was manifested on the earth, it gave LIFE to every created living thing. It causes the tree to grow unhelped by the hand of man. It causes the little squirrel to have intelligence enough to garner enough food through the summer to keep it through the winter when the snows cover the earth like a blanket. It gives me intelligence enough to sit at this typewriter and give to you a few of the truths of the Spiritual Realm as I believe them to exist. You have heard time and time again of some famous man who started life without a nickel. No education; no training at all and no friends. Take most of our great men and they all began that way.

Yet many of them climbed to the very peak of power. They made fortunes. They made up their minds to achieve and they achieved. They wrested success from life and they did it in spite of every handicap. Their names are written indelibly on history's scroll, and time will not efface some of them. Such men as Thomas Edison—J. P. Morgan, and hundreds of others I could mention. Yet—had not the Life Spirit been manifest on the earth, these men would not have ever lived. And you may depend upon it, whatever these mighty warriors of life did, was done through the Power of the Mighty Life Spirit alone. Their intellect could have come from no other source than the God-Law. Their lives came from that source and so did their brains. So did their ambitions. So did everything they ever possessed. And it is an incontrovertible FACT that whatever they achieved was achieved through no other power than the Power of the mighty LIFE SPIRIT—THE UNSEEN GOD-LAW—which Law I am teaching you how to use in these Lessons.

Mr. Carnegie made the statement when but a lad that he would be the wealthiest man in the world before he died. He was. Now, had you asked Mr. Carnegie if he was using a Spiritual God-Law in his life he probably would have told you "no." But he was just the same. He perhaps was not conscious of the Power he was using, but had he not used the Power of the God-Law he could not have TAKEN EVEN ONE SINGLE BREATH. Do you see what I mean? Everything that Carnegie did was done through the power of the mighty God-Law—AND NO OTHER WAY. And anything YOU ever do, and anything YOU ever accomplish will be done and accomplished through THE VERY SAME IDENTICAL GOD-LAW. Never forget that. Now then—the point I am making is this: THIS GREAT GOD-LAW THAT OPERATES THROUGHOUT THE ENTIRE UNIVERSE IS GREAT ENOUGH, AND BIG ENOUGH, AND WISE ENOUGH, AND INTELLIGENT ENOUGH, AND LOVING ENOUGH TO PROVIDE FOR YOU WHATSOEVER THINGS IT MAY BE THAT YOU DESIRE—and mark me well here please—AND IT WILL DO JUST THAT IN THE MOMENT YOU ACTUALLY PUT THIS GOD-POWER CONSCIOUSLY TO WORK IN YOUR LIFE. Oh yes—you can sit on your haunches from now till the crack of doom if you want to, and you can "pray" till you are black in the face—and that will never get you anywhere at all. You may go on in the manner in which you are going now if you want to, LETTING THE POWER OF THE GOD-LAW PASS YOU BY. The God-Law cares nothing about whether you do or not. IT IS THERE FOR YOUR USE. But if you don't want to use it—then it's just too bad—for YOU.

I assure you the God-Law will never shed any tears over your failure to use this Law for the accomplishment of whatever things you need. The attitude of God is that you can either accept the Power or refuse it. If you refuse it, ONLY ONE SUFFERS AND THAT IS YOU. If you accept it—YOU benefit—and not only you but everyone with whom you come in contact. You remember the old saying about "the mills of the Gods grinding slowly but grinding exceeding fine"? That is the truth of the God-Realm as it exists. Coupled to this unseen dynamic Spiritual Power there is nothing the human soul cannot have through this God-Power. But absent from it—nothing can happen. You have heard the story of the shipwrecked crew who were dying of thirst. There they were, out on the salty (as they thought) ocean. Nothing to drink except salt water. No fresh water in the ship's tanks at all. Finally a ship was sighted and hailed. Frantically the thirsty crew signaled the other ship "water—water—water; send us fresh water." Imagine their amazement when back came the answer: "Drop your bucket over the side."

And how like life that is. Men and women by the million, looking first here and then there for the things they need. They follow first this one and then that one, and ever the elusive "thing" eludes them. And yet—all the time—and at their very elbows, is enough of the Spiritual Power of the God-Law to enable them to get from life. "Water, water," they cry, and all they have to do is to drop the bucket overboard and draw to themselves all the pure fresh sparkling Spiritual Power they can ever need. Then again, life has many of another kind of folk. This kind, have a faint glimpse of knowledge concerning the Spiritual God-Law, but they never accept from this Law, all that they might accept and should accept.

Which reminds me of another story—this time about some sparrows. Many of these feathered creatures were out chasing for food one day when a bakery wagon drove past, and a loaf of bread fell from the wagon to the ground. Immediately there was a great fluttering of wings and the air was made noisy with the tiny shrieks of these foolish sparrows as they fought with each other over the crumbs which had broken from the loaf when it fell to the ground.

One would pick up a tiny crumb and another one would fight with him for possession of that crumb. And so they fought and fought until all the crumbs were gone. Then they flew away, leaving the loaf of bread lying there in the street. It was so big that they did not even recognize it for what it really was. And so again it is in life. Those of us who know some little of the Spiritual God-Law, have a great tendency to say "Oh yes—I believe God can do this or do that—but will he?" And so they go along, missing the very best and the very finest things of life, and all the while there is. at their very elbow so to speak, a wealth of the very things they need. But they cannot see them. They are fighting over the crumbs—and missing the loaf. I wonder if YOU PERSONALLY are one of that sort of folks. If you are then may I beg of you to recognize the existence and the presence of the greatest Spiritual Power this world has ever seen. And may I also implore you to put this POWER to work in your own life. If you will there is nothing you should have that you won't have. And I don't care whether it's a fine home or a million dollars or only domestic happiness. It is not possible for you to use the Power of the Great Spiritual God-Realm without receiving from it the things you need. If you can't do this—and this is not a fact—then THERE IS NO GOD. And this I cannot admit. And the reason I cannot admit that is because I KNOW BETTER. What was it, do you think, that took a life of absolute failure and made it an abundant success after every human effort had failed? Was it myself? Not at all, of course I had to WANT the good things of life and I had to follow the leadings when they came to me. But by no manner of means was the transformation done by me.

Had it been left to me I assure you there would never have been any transformation. But there was. And the transformation is due in its entirety to my recognition of the Power of the Spiritual God-Law, not so much in my life as in the complete universe around me. I knew that such must be a fact. I knew that no "god in the sky" could do anything for me. I knew that if there were no such a Spiritual Power as I am teaching you about here—then I was certainly a has-been. But I believed such a Power existed, and, I put it to the test. I believed in the existence of this unseen Spiritual Law. In other words—I believed God, the mighty Life Spirit that created this entire universe and every created thing in it. That is what I did. And did it pay? I think so. Millions of people see my picture every year now. Hundreds of thousands and perhaps millions have heard my voice over the radio. And best of all, my files are literally teeming with happy letters from my students all over the world telling me of their finding the same God-Law that I found and used. And that is evidence.

You might be able to fool just a few people—I admit that might be done. But it would not be possible to fool by far the great majority of my students and followers. They have followed me. as you have, and they know the Law exists. So do you. They have put it to work in their own lives—and so have you—or you will before you get through with these Lessons. For what a fool you would be to know of the existence of God for your edification and help and not use Him. A complete ass you would be if, with this overwhelming Spiritual Law of God WAITING TO HELP YOU. and you refused the help. All around you there exists this great God-Law. It exists FOR you. And all the Power of God you can ever need or use is here at your right hand awaiting your use of it. And that is not all. The manner in which you may obtain these things needed has also been put into your hands by me. What you do with this weapon is your lookout. Personally, I am using the God-Law every day and am going to continue to use it. And if you mean business and are not a trifler—so will you.

Let me run over once more the method to be used by you in the actual contacting of the God-Law. Follow me closely. The essence of YOU—is Life. Life is God. God is the mighty LIFE SPIRIT of the universe. There is no other life. Your thoughts are electrical connections running directly to the great Cosmic God-Realm. Also, your thoughts are A PART OF THE LIVING GOD-LAW. HENCE, YOU HAVE ABSOLUTELY WITHIN YOUR OWN HANDS. A CONNECTION WITH GOD, AND THAT CONNECTION IS A PART OF GOD. Do you see that? God is unseen Spiritual LIFE, or, as we saw LIFE—CAPABLE OF EXISTENCE WITHOUT PHYSICAL FORM. All right then. Here you are; a man, a woman. You have in your possession—LIFE. And LIFE is GOD. You can THINK. Your thoughts, being THINGS—LIVING THINGS—go direct to the whole of God. They get from that big whole the things that your little life needs. Now let's look back a little bit. Remember how I showed you the exercises in absolute relaxation. Remember how I asked you to concentrate at night on the "white spot" in your field of vision? You remember how I showed you the manner in which to let everything fade out of the picture at night, except YOUR THOUGHTS. And you will remember how I showed you the method of DIRECTING YOUR THOUGHTS, CHARGED WITH THE DESIRE OF YOUR HEART, INTO THE GREAT COMIC REALM OF THE LIVING GOD? You remember those things of course. NOW—how is the literal answer to come back to you from the God-Realm? How are you actually and literally going to get the things you want? I don't care what those things may be if they are for your own good and if it would be right for you to have them. How are they going to come to you? Now listen brother or sister, and I could not put it any plainer if you were sitting here with me in my study. If I knew how to make it plainer I surely would do so. The reaction to these Lessons though is that they are mighty plain and effective, so it must be that at this point I have been wonderfully able to make my students grasp this very important moment in their instructions. I must be making them see the point. And I know I am. And I know the God-Law works. But how are YOU to get these things from God?

Here is a woman writing to me, and she is very unhappy. She married one of another religious faith, and the poor dupes are letting that come between their own happiness. At any rate, this woman is very miserable. There is a man, and he writes to me stating that he is out of work and has nothing to eat. In a large city not so far from Moscow—Spokane, Washington, to be exact—a young lady writes me. She is broke. She can get no work. She is about to take her own life. Her friends cannot help her. She writes me in desperation. Away back east there is a bank manager whose bank has failed. In the middle west is a student who wrote me that his home was about to be attached and sold for notes. Then another writes me that he has had to sacrifice a $40,000 hotel for a mortgage of $6000.00. Many of such cases; thousands of them write me; and the invariable question is this: "CAN YOUR TEACHING HELP ME TO DO THIS OR TO DO THAT"? And my answer always is that the Great God-Law is abundantly able to do more than they can even ask or think if they will use it. But how? That is what we want to know here.

I have shown you the exercise in which you can contact God. I have told you in detail how to "wait upon God" until the promise is fulfilled. (And when it is fulfilled you will know it. By "promise" I mean the consciousness of the Spirit of God in your own life). Now—you have followed me closely. You have made the connection that has brought to you the assurance that God lives in your own life. You realize through personal contact that there is a great ocean of power at your disposal. You know that. But you ask me how you are to get your answers. All right—let me tell you by asking you this question: "HOW DID YOU MAKE YOUR DESIRES KNOWN TO GOD?"

Well, you will tell me that you sent your desires right out into the great Cosmic God-Realm through your concentrated thoughts. And I shall say "correct." You did exactly that. NOW—HOW CAN GOD MAKE KNOWN HIS THOUGHTS TO YOU? Now how do you think? How do you think the great Spiritual God-Intelligence and God Wisdom can communicate with you? Let me tell you. "IN EXACTLY THE SAME MANNER IN WHICH YOU COMMUNICATED YOUR DESIRES TO THIS GREAT LIFE-CREATING SPIRIT OF WISDOM AND INTELLIGENCE."

There is your answer, and get it well please—for after all it is simple and requires no great ability to grasp. The God-Law will communicate to you in the same identical manner in which you communicated with it. And through the same channels you used to make your request known will the answer come. The channel of your thoughts, through which channel you communicate with God, is a GOD-ORDAINED CHANNEL. The Life Spirit caused it to be that you can communicate with God through the realm of your own thoughts—which—don't forget—are living vital God-Things. You must use the channel the God-Law has provided for making your requests known, and the Law in return will use the very same channel in making the answer known to you. Simple, isn't it? And yet how scientific. How powerful. How dynamic. How sure. Herein lies the secret of the presence of the mighty Life Spirit—GOD. In the very closeness is He missed. We won't be quiet enough and we won't keep still enough to listen for the answer.

Now let us get down to a concrete case. You are all expert now in relaxation. You should all be expert in "contacting" the God-Spirit and in sending to this great Cosmic Realm, your heart's desires. Now to get the answers—I have just told you that they will come through the same channels—so what do you do? Why you keep still and LISTEN. JUST LISTEN—THAT IS ALL. BUT WHAT A POWER YOU ARE LISTENING TO. You are listening to the God of the universe. You are listening to the Creative Life Intelligence that gave you both LIFE and INTELLIGENCE. So you listen. You quiet every nerve. You stay still. YOU LISTEN. YOU WAIT ON GOD.

AND OUT OF THE STILLNESS WHERE GOD DWELLS WILL COME THE ANSWER TO YOUR NEEDS.

Let that statement burn itself into your soul to a depth that you never will get it out of there. Out of the stillness, where God is, will come the answer through your thought realm to you. In every case, of course, the answer will be different. In every case the answer will fit the need. In all of the above cases, if this method is followed out, the answer coming from the stillness where God lives will solve the problem—no matter what that problem may be. And another thing—when the living God-Spirit has given you the answer YOU WILL KNOW IT.

And until you DO know it—don't make a move. But when you KNOW that the "still small voice of God" has spoken, then follow that leading to the very ends of the earth if needs be. A man wrote to me the other day stating that in following this instruction the Spirit of God told him to go out and buy some oil stock, which he did. He lost his money and wrote to me asking why the Spirit of God told him to buy oil stock. You know what my reply was, of course. For the Life Spirit never tells anyone to buy oil stock. Nor does it ever tell anyone to do anything which will be followed by either loss or disaster. This good fellow probably mistook his own desire for the promptings of God—and of course, he lost. Let me repeat to you once more that when the voice of the Spirit of God tells you what to do—you will know it. You will never need to write to me and ask me if "this experience" or "that experience" was the voice of God. For there is never any mistaking those pure leads. Those spiritual leads.

Those silent leads. They are from the Spiritual Realm—hence you recognize them so easily. Just quietly waiting and listening to the stillness where God dwells. If the NEED is immediate—the ANSWER will also be immediate.

If you are constant in your moments of communion with this great Life Spirit, you will find that automatically you are doing what you should do. In other words, (listen well) it is entirely possible for a human life to live moment by moment in direct and full Spiritual communion with the mighty God-Law. And you will readily see that when this is done, life is an overwhelming life of victory. It cannot be anything else. This is the life that climbs over all sorts of obstacles and the public look at such a one and wonder why. They say he or she "has good breaks." They say "My— that man or woman knows where they are going." or course they do— because such a one is motivated every waking moment by the power of the mighty Life Spirit—and, of course, they WIN. It couldn't be otherwise. Every move they make is in tune with the Infinite Law of God, and in the Realm of God there is no failure. A good "Christian" educator said to me recently: "Dr. Robinson—I am not getting anywhere in life. My work seems to be just so-so, but as far as actually DOING THINGS and making a mark on the world goes—I am a failure." And he is—he doesn't know the reason why. I can tell him. This brother has a head full of knowledge ABOUT God. This man can probably give a lot of people cards and spades when it comes to church history or sociology, or Bible interpretation or the four gospels or any of the other allied studies. HE KNOWS ALL ABOUT GOD. But he knows mighty little OF God. There is the answer. A head full of knowledge. Teaching others. Trying to lead others into the LIGHT, but knowing very little of the actual Power of God.

And throughout this course of instruction, Brother or Sister, nothing that I have said to you will do you the slightest good, unless you use the methods I have given you for actually knowing God. But it's worth it, don't you think? I do. Just to know that moment by moment the overwhelming wisdom and power of the mighty Living God are all around you—over you—through you—below you. This fact alone takes all the sting out of life I promise you. It takes all the "chance" out of life. There is no guesswork where God is concerned, but a literal vital communion that may be had at any time and that may be the moment by moment experience of every soul studying these Lessons and of all the world for that matter. This is what I mean when I tell you that the Power of the Living God-Law is more than sufficient to make your life what it was meant to be. And another thing—there is NO LIMIT to where man may go with his God. None of us have gone very far I promise you—or if we had the world would know it. Jesus Christ probably knew more of the actual literal Power of the God-Law than most men know—but He did not know it to the full for He was a miserable failure on many occasions. That is but human though, and there is so much of God that this Carpenter man DID know that I don't ever think much of the mistakes and failures He made.

However—YOU—whoever you may be, get down to business from now on and never let a day's work begin until you have within you the sweet consciousness of the literal and actual presence of the Great Creative Power of the Universe—GOD. In the next Lesson we shall go a little farther into this subject of the presence of God and I want you to absorb this present Lesson to the very full. It's clothed in poor language, but through it all you will find the earnestness of the impulse which is driving me on to make the truths of the God-Law known to men and women. I write these Lessons while in communion with the mighty Life Spirit. Not a single word is ever changed. And so they win others by their Spiritual Power. It is useless to try and analyze this subtle power for it cannot be done. And never mind it—just get close to the mighty GOD-LAW NOW—and then stay there—listening for the answers to your problems, for such answers are somewhere in the Realm of God and that is the only place they are. And when the soul is "tuned in" to the God Realm, it isn't much of a job for God to tell you what to do to change the conditions in your life you don't like. Be earnest—be intensive—be dynamic in your communion with God and in your "listening" for Him. It will pay.

Sincerely your friend and teacher,
FRANK B. ROBINSON

LESSON 20

Dear friend and fellow student:

I am sorry that our journey together through this remarkable Spiritual Realm must come to an end. All things in this material world come to an end sooner or later, and I assure you that it is with a feeling of intense regret that I leave you for the time being. Our journey and our associations together have been pleasant. The thousands of students all over the world who have studied under me have been a source of continual joy. Many of them have helped me more than they realize and judging by the thousands of letters I have received, I perhaps have been able to be of a little assistance to them too.

No one realizes any more than I do the importance and the sacred responsibility of having thousands of people all over the world depending absolutely on me for proper guidance. The confidence displayed by these thousands of students will never be violated. I have never given them wrong information that I know of. I do not claim to be perfect, nor do I claim to be possessed of any supernatural power of any kind. All I do claim is that I might perhaps through years of earnest search have received a picture of Spiritual Truth which could not be obtained by anyone who would give less effort to their search than I gave, and yet I am more than ever convinced that Spiritual Law is natural law. I am more than ever convinced that only our ignorance of the great God Realm prevents our making use of the marvelous Spiritual Power this Realm contains. There is nothing supernatural in the universe nor is there anything miraculous in the universe. In my private study are files after files literally teeming with letters received from students, and these letters state in unmistakable language the actual material benefits which have been received through this course of study with me. Among those letters are to be found remarkable cures. There may be found in those files happenings which perhaps might be called miraculous to those who do not understand Spiritual Law. But I still contend that no matter how unusual many of these cases are, they still are but perfectly natural when viewed in the light of the Power lying inherent in the great Realm of God.

There is first of all essentially a Spiritual being, and the part of you that really matters is invisible. This invisible part of You is a very definite part of the great Life Principle which fills all space and without which no created thing could exist at all. Now being a part of the invisible Life Principle, you must see that this part of you which really is the true and the real part of you must of necessity have at its disposal all the power and wisdom of the Realm of God. Yes, and more than that—it must have, being a part of this Spiritual Realm, all of the power for actual manifestation that is contained in the completeness of this great God-Law itself.

Let me illustrate a little further if I can. Try and imagine a large reservoir filled with water. The reservoir supplies a large city with water.

Coming direct from the reservoir are the large mains, and these in turn feed smaller mains, which in turn feed the pipes into the thousands of houses. There is only one body of water and that is in the reservoir perhaps miles away. Now when you turn the faucet the water flows. This is the same identical water stored in the vast reservoir and more than that, there is a direct connection of water between your faucet and the great body of water in the reservoir miles away. If that connection is obstructed the water will not flow to you. You can safely see also that all the power of the water in the reservoir is directly connected with the water in your house. If someone colors the water in the reservoir miles away, the water coming to you in your home will be colored, proving, of course, that there exists a permanent water connection between the source of the water supply and the outlet of the water supply which is in your home. You will instantly grasp this illustration, and if you will also look beyond the Spiritual Realm in the same light you will see at what I am driving.

We know the Invisible, Creative, Cosmic Realm of God exists. We also know that you live as a direct evidence of, and through the power of this great, unseen Cosmic God-Law. Now then, this being a fact, do you not see that the unseen part of you which is the real part, must be in definite, permanent and living connection with the great reservoir of Spiritual Power from which you draw your life? If it be a fact and if it is a fact that the Power we call God is the Creative-Law which in some way, at some time or other first brought the Life Spirit to this earth, and which presence caused it to manifest on this earth, it must follow that you yourself, no matter who you may be, must be in definite presence and living connection with the greatest Power, with all the power the Spiritual Realm contains. This is a staggering thought and yet it is the truth of life as it exists. It is perfectly true that you cannot open the faucet in your house and receive as much water as can the fire hydrant on the next corner, but that is simply because your pipe is smaller, consequently the pressure is cut down. But the water in the hydrant and the water in your house both come from the same reservoir. One comes with force enough to throw it over the top of a building and the other comes with force enough to fill your bathtub. The size of the pipe, or, rather, the size of the outlet limits the volume of water and the volume of pressure passing through that pipe. The same identical thing applies in the Spiritual Realm. If you are practically impotent as far as Spiritual Power goes, then you may depend upon it that your pipe is too small. Your outlet is limited and before great Spiritual Power can manifest you must put in a bigger pipe. You must enlarge the outlet.

Usually we hear a man, whom thousands of people follow, called a tremendous Spiritual Power in the world, and we look at this man and say, "My, if I only had the power that he has." But do you not see that this man would have no Spiritual Power at all or very little unless the outlet were large, and as in the case of water, there can be no vacuum pipe? JUST

AS FAST AS THE WATER RUNS OUT, AN UNLIMITED SUPPLY IS DIRECTLY CONNECTED WITH IT AND THE FASTER IT RUNS OUT THE GREATER THE VOLUME OF SUPPLY.

You will see this illustration. I know, and I want you to live your life in the full recognition of the overwhelming and majestic power which can flow to you in unlimited measure and which will flow to you in the very moment you open the faucet and let it come. Many of your ideas, especially in regard to religion have been upset in your studies with me and the fundamental principle of so-called New Psychology has been exploded. All the New Psychology had to offer was passed on the "subconscious mind." We have seen, however, that there is no such thing as a "sub-conscious mind." We have also seen that there is throughout all space a far more potent and dynamic power, the manifestations of which have been erroneously credited to this "sub-conscious mind."

As we have traveled along on this little journey together. we have seen the great Cosmic God Presence through which every work has been done. I have brought to your attention instances of healing and other instances which have demonstrated the presence of a Power, which power is universal and which power must be from the very nature of it at the disposal of every normal man or woman in existence. Jesus, the prophet, used this Power if He ever used any power at all, for there can be no Power greater than the Power of the great God-Law. Certainly this Galilean Carpenter had no monopoly whatever on this Power, for if He did then you and I would not be able to use it today. Therefore, if the Power we have learned about is the very same Power this Nazarene used, then it must be a fact that if we understand this Spiritual Power as He understood it, we should be able to duplicate the works that He did. Many things were credited to Him, which things He never did, but I am talking here only about those things which He actually did. We have seen further that the theory of any power lying within is utterly at variance with the facts as they exist, and quite to the contrary we have discovered that instead of the Power coming from "within" it comes from WITHOUT.

THE GREAT WITHOUT

It is easily understood how the people of Christ's time utterly missed the directness of the message he brought, and it is easy for me to understand how the simplicity of the message went a thousand miles over their heads. We have seen that the mighty God-Law has ever been at the disposal of every created soul day and night. You could not remove the presence of the God-Law from this world for one instant without all life on it becoming immediately DEATH, and remember DEATH is but the absence of LIFE. All you have to do at any hour of the day or night is to turn to this great Spiritual Realm and there you find it, no matter what the hour may be, and if it be there then we may use it, for it would be foolishness to try and conceive of a universal God-Law which could not be found and used always and at any time. We have also seen that it is not possible to apply this wisdom and intelligence and Spiritual Power of the God-Realm to a human life and have things contrary to our highest desires manifest. We have seen that if this great Spiritual Power is needed to bring into manifestation in our lives either health, success or happiness, this Power being God, no one will question its ability to do those very things.

Now in this Lesson I am going to take you back into the realm of the Cosmic Ray. I am doing this because it would be very easy to underestimate the importance of this staggering discovery in its relationship to the great Spiritual God-Law this course of instruction attempts to disclose. From the very first moment I heard of the discovery of this marvelous interstellar ray or power, I thought I saw immediately a definite proof that my idea of the God-Law was correct. I might add in passing that long before cosmic rays were ever heard of, I had written concerning the existence of a Spiritual Power which filled all space and had no limitations whatsoever. The only criticism that I see at this time which might be directed at me would be the criticism that I am attempting to bring the Spiritual Realm of God down to the level of a material thing; but I have told you in this course of instruction that there is nothing supernatural in the entire universe. I have also told you that if this Spiritual Realm, with whatever God there might be, is so far removed from us that it cannot be contacted until after we die, then it cannot be of much use to us now. It is true that I am endeavoring to bring the unseen Spiritual Power of the God-Law within the grasp of every human being here and now and that certainly is as it should be, for that would entirely change the picture for every created soul. If you and I were convinced by unimpeachable evidence that there did exist throughout space the Intelligence and the Power and the Wisdom which was the All-Creative Intelligence that caused every created thing to be in the first place—if I can convince you of that—then I have brought down and put within your grasp the secret, not only of the universe, but of life itself.

This is exactly what I am doing. Furthermore, I am borne out in my contention by the findings of the world's greatest scientists who have experimented with this marvelous Cosmic Ray. Let me add here that too much is not yet known about this ray, and I am of the opinion that the scientists before they have finished their investigations will admit with me that this cosmic force, or energy is an intelligent, thinking force or energy. They admit now that it is the cause of every created thing and if that is not bearing me out in what I have written, then I do not know what it is doing.

I received a few days ago from Dr. Millikan's secretary at the California Institute of Technology, Pasadena, California, four of the latest bulletins on the cosmic ray. One of them is printed by the United States Government and is taken from the Smithsonian Report for 1928. This report was made by R. A. Millikan and G. H. Cameron. I shall refer to that report again a little later in this Lesson. By the way, the publication number of this booklet is No. 2986 and it may be obtained by writing to the United States Government Printing Office at Washington, D. C. I want to impress on my students here the absolute enormity of the possibilities tied up in the discovery of this world of cosmic energy. I see a lot in these discoveries; in fact, I see the solution to life's problems, and I see the startling fact that instead of the answer to these multitudinous problems of life lying in some so-called "Heaven" beyond the sky, they lie even at our very doors. No scientific discovery has been made for a long time instantly. We had such discoveries and experiences in Greek and other mythologies, but very few of them have ever sprung full grown out of a human brain. Usually these discoveries creep upon us unawares and the first thing we know we are using some marvelous power or discovery and at the same time are unable to state what it is or from where it came. I am just as convinced as I am dictating this to you that the world is on the threshold of the discovery of a perfectly natural Spiritual Power which. when fully understood and used, will put every natural thing on this earth into man's own hands. It has taken a long time to come to this period of scientific belief; but it is here and as the old, worn, tattered fragments of "supernaturally revealed" religion have been weighed in the balances and found wanting, men and women have turned their eyes to nature and to life and there they are surely, although slowly, finding the answer, and it is an answer that everyone can grasp. Instead of believing every old pagan religious teaching that comes along, men and women are turning their eyes not to the preachers and priests for spiritual enlightenment, but to the psychologists and the scientists and the thinkers. Many of them are willing to admit that everything these religionists tell us about the hereafter might be true, but in the absence of any proof of any kind we do not choose to believe them. Many there are who do not doubt these wonderful stories we are told, but at the same time there can be no possible objection to finding out what science has to say regarding this created scheme of things.

You cannot prove that any of the world's crucified saviors ever had a miraculous birth, supernatural conception, supernatural resurrection, or supernatural ascension into Heaven. If you believe that, you must do so by a stretch of the imagination, or by a blind faith, for certainly there never has been adduced the slightest scintilla of evidence that those stories are true. On the other hand. we do know that there does exist a cosmic energy of some sort or other which cosmic energy comes from the interstellar spaces, and when I say "interstellar spaces" I shall ask you to remember that the light from yon stars and yon Milky Way took many thousands of light years to reach this earth; so when I talk about interstellar spaces, I am not talking about a trip to Europe or anything on that order, but I am talking about millions and billions of light years away, and our little minds cannot even comprehend what a light year really is. We know that it is the distance traveled by light going at the rate of 186,300 miles a second in one year; but when we begin to multiply that by thousands and millions, it is slightly beyond the normal mental comprehension of man; but man is even mastering such distances as that. and it is conclusively proved that this cosmic energy does exist through all space and does come from the interstellar regions of space. The eyes of the scientific world are turned on this discovery, and well they might be, for if my theory should be borne out by these scientists—and it is being borne out—then can you not see that with a fuller understanding of this energy, thoughts of which stagger you, the solutions to all Creative Life processes might very easily be in our own hands? Remember it is only about ten years since German scientists discovered these cosmic rays, although prior to that "penetrating radiations" near the earth's surface were brought to light by McClennan, Rutherford, and their collaborators, who found that the rates of discharge of electroscopes could be very markedly reduced by surrounding them with successive screens of lead several centimeters thick, thereby showing that rays existed in the atmosphere capable of penetrating such thick screens and therefore these rays were appropriately named "penetrating radiations." Active credit for most of the research, however, belongs to Dr. Robert A. Millikan and Dr. Carl D. Anderson, his associate, who, supported by funds from the Carnegie Foundation, have relentlessly and tirelessly investigated these rays and given to us scientific, and therefore provable data concerning this invisible energy.

One might call cosmic rays "mysterious force rays" bombarding this world from the interstellar spaces. As Dr. Millikan recently stated at a lecture in the East "'They may be likened to infinitely small machine gun bullets traveling at enormously high rates of speed. Cosmic rays are something like light rays but of very much shorter wave length. For comparison we may regard the wave length of radio broadcasting as the longest in the scale. Next comes the rays of visible and invisible light, infra-red and red, getting shorter and shorter through the different spectrum colors to violet and ultra-violet. X-rays are still shorter in wave length and the gamma rays which are given off by radium have been thought up to a short time ago to be the shortest of all. But the cosmic rays have a wave length which is much shorter even than gamma rays and infinitely more powerful. The stupendous power of these newly discovered cosmic rays manifests itself in various ways. Some idea of the vast force of these visitor rays from outer cosmic space may be had by comparing them with the gamma rays of radium. Gamma ray particles leave the radium mass with such force and speed that sheet-lead armor several inches thick is required to stop them. Cosmic rays, however, require a lead armor plate sixteen feet thick to stop them. Expressed in volts of electrical energy the power of these new rays is even more startling. "Measurements made by

Dr. Millikan in his laboratory in Pasadena show cosmic rays to have an energy of one thousand million volts. I shall ask my students, if they can, to try to conceive of this interstellar energy bombarding this earth.

An energy of one thousand million volts. You must not try to tell me that there is no unseen, dynamic force in existence beside which all other forces fade into insignificance, for if you do I shall ask you to show me a more powerful force than this cosmic force which is known to have an energy of these one thousand million volts. I would like my students to lay this Lesson down here and try to realize this stupendous fact. There is just one argument, or one thought which will come into your mind at this point and that is that if this statement be a fact then why are we not conscious of such a dynamic power as that. And, in answer to that thought or question, let me state that being conscious of anything is merely a matter of having it called to your attention by some means or other. In this Advanced Course of "Psychiana" I have shown you specifically and definitely the existence of the greatest unseen Cosmic Power the world has ever known anything about. The little exercises I have given you to do have been designed to show you how to personally contact this force or power or spirit. You did not know perhaps when you were doing these exercises their extreme importance; but when you recognized the fact that you had been projecting your thoughts into an energy of one thousand million volts intensity, then you certainly were linking up with your thoughts an energy so dynamic that it has never been duplicated in the history of mankind. So, you see, after all there is a scientific explanation of the things I have said to you in my previous Lessons. The vast majority of my students have had implicit confidence in me and have believed me. As a result of this simple belief, my files are literally teeming with gratifying letters from my thousands of students all over the world. I will confess to you that no living soul has ever completely grasped the intensity of the ocean of power lying within the reach of everyone of us, for it will take some time before the greatness of this great God-Law is fully comprehended; but from different parts of the world telegrams and letters have come to me by the hundreds stating in no uncertain terms that some little connection has been made with this great, dynamic Cosmic Realm. And all the religious beliefs in existence are quite insufficient to shatter one little bit of evidence, and if I do not have that evidence, then certainly no man alive does have. No matter where you are, let me say to you that after two years' experience with this teaching I am in a position to state beyond the shadow of a doubt that this cosmic God-Realm does exist and can be used by you in the accomplishment of whatever proper and right things you desire.

Dr. Millikan states that probably these rays are the cause of the things manifested physically and materially upon this earth. If that be a fact, then once more I am borne out in my understanding of the great God-Law. Prior to the discovery of these rays with their energy of one thousand million volts, the highest voltage that had ever been measured was that of the gamma rays of radium which produced about eight million volts, and the highest voltage ever produced in the laboratory by artificial lightning has been around five million volts. In an Associated Press report released through the papers recently I find the following statements, headed by this caption:

"WORLD UTOPIA IF
COSMIC RAYS ARE HARNESSED"

"The source of this terrific power ray is believed to originate in the vast outer reaches of our star-filled universe and can, according to the scientists, be accounted for in only one way. It must be produced by atomic energy.

"What is atomic energy and how can it be produced? The atom, believed to be the smallest unit of matter, can be thought of as the building block of the universe. All gases such as nitrogen and oxygen which go to make up the air we breathe; all liquids of which water is the best example, and all solids such as iron, rock, wood are made up of different kinds of atoms differently arranged in a larger unit called the molecule. Different kinds of atoms have different weights, the same, for instance, as different kinds of animals. Atoms which go to make up gases weigh the least, atoms of liquid weigh more and atoms of the heavy metals, and silver, gold and platinum weigh the most. The atom itself is made up of a central heart or nucleus which has a positive charge of electricity surrounded by negatively charged particles called electrons. The heart or nucleus of the atom is made up of positively charged particles called protons, together with approximately one-half as many electrons.

"Scientists are already able to blast away the outer electrons of the atom with electricity. When this is done to neon atoms, the energy emitted by the negative electrons rushing back to their nuclei take the form of orange colored light which is a familiar sight now along most any city street in the form of Neon advertising signs.

"ONLY THE BEGINNING"

"This, however, is only the beginning. The real atomic energy is locked up in the heart or nucleus of the atom so tightly that enormously high voltages of electricity are required to tear it apart. When this heart of the atom is blasted open and reassembles itself again to form a new substance, so much energy is released that it makes our present-day sources of power seem like the brush of a butterfly's wing compared to a dynamite blast.

"Some idea of this tremendous explosive energy locked up in the heart of the atom may be gained by studying the high voltages which would be given off in the transformation of one substance to another. Twenty-seven million volts would be set free in the change of hydrogen gas atoms to atoms of helium gas. One hundred and sixteen million volts would be produced in the change from hydrogen to the still heavier oxygen atom. Two hundred and sixteen million volts would be given off in the change of hydrogen atoms to those of silicon, a metal. Five hundred million volts would be the result of changing hydrogen to iron and the 1,000,000,000 volts shown by the newly found cosmic rays would be the energy which would be generated in the change of hydrogen atoms to those of silver.

"Is there then a race of superbeings out in the depths of space somewhere that have evolved perhaps 1,000,000 years longer than we have, and have discovered secrets of making gold and silver from hydrogen gas or other substances? Are they perhaps trying to use these cosmic rays to signal to scientists on the earth? Are they wondering why we do not understand their signals and respond to them?

"IS UTOPIA OF POWER COMING?"

"One thing sure, if we do succeed in catching and harnessing these tremendously powerful cosmic rays, or through studying them learn how ourselves to release and control atomic energy, we may be sure that heat, power and light will then be as free as the air we breathe. Automobile engines that now weigh many hundreds of pounds will be replaced by engines which would need to be no heavier nor larger than a pocket tin of tobacco. If the atomic energy locked up in one cubic inch of coal could be released and controlled it would light, heat and turn the wheels of industry of New York City for a year. Warfare would be done away with, for beams of atomic energy could be used which would be powerful enough literally to blast a whole continent off the face of the earth, or split the earth itself wide open.

"With atomic energy made available, any substance could be used for what we now think of as fuel. Atomic disintegration of rocks or water would yield tremendous power, and very small quantities would suffice to create all the energy that could ever be used by all the people on the earth. Aviation and radio would take tremendous strides. A man could strap an atomic engine on his back weighing but a few ounces and fly through the air as fast as air friction would allow.

"NEUTRALIZE FORCE OF GRAVITY"

"With such power it would be possible to neutralize the force of gravity so that the air would be as safe or safer than the ground. The food question would be solved, since with unlimited electrical power crops could be grown as fast as desired with artificial ultra-violet light, perhaps from seed to matured plant in a few hours. Travel would be as simple and inexpensive as breathing and people could readily follow warm weather south in winter and be self-sustaining regardless of economic conditions.

"Dr. Millikan and his associates are already hard at work in research, and plans are to study the cosmic rays this summer in many different parts of the world and at all possible levels of altitude.

"Research so far at the California Institute of Technology in connection with cosmic rays has taken the one form in the study of photographing the paths of cosmic rays through what is called a 'cloud chamber', a large room made of glass and containing moisture-charged air or gas. The cosmic ray leaves a visible path of water droplets. Of 1,000 photographs taken and developed, 34 showed Cosmic ray tracks.

"During the experiment, the cloud chamber was in the sphere of influence of a powerful electro-magnetic field, and the cosmic ray paths showed curvatures dictating that the tiny particles were capable of being attracted by the electromagnetic force applied to them. This would indicate that cosmic rays are of similar nature to light and X-rays, and makes a good beginning for further study. It was also noticed in the experiment photographs that when a cosmic ray hit an atom in the cloud chamber both positive and negative particles were given off, showing clearly that the heart of the atom had been shattered by the impact, the first step in the release of atomic energy. What will be the next step?"

(Taken from Associated Press report.)

I think my students, after reading the above, will at least grant the possibility of this great cosmic energy's being a thinking or intelligent energy. Remember we do not know everything yet about what we have called "cosmic rays", and it might very easily be that these scientists are experimenting with the greatest Spiritual Power the world has ever known. It might very easily be, to repeat, that this old world is on the verge of finding a scientifically true explanation of the great God-Law I have taught you in this course of Lessons.

In a prior Lesson I called your attention to the penetrability of what was called a "neutrone." These neutrones are probably at the heart of this vast cosmic energy, and if this be a fact, then who can question the ability of these cosmic rays with their thousand million volts of energy to throw into play some unseen or spiritual force or power or energy which can and will and does in due time bring into existence material conditions necessary.

In 1925 Doctors Millikan and Cameron obtained indisputable evidence of a penetrating radiation which must be of cosmic origin. According to the booklet released by the United States Government, No. 2986, these experiments were conducted at Muir Lake, California. Without going into the technical end of these experiments, let me state that the electroscope used by these scientists showed with certainty the determinations of the absolute amount of the penetrating radiation. The statement is made in this booklet, "ALL THIS CONSTITUTES PRETTY UNAMBIGUOUS EVIDENCE THAT THE HIGH-ALTITUDE RAYS DO NOT ORIGINATE IN OUR ATMOSPHERE, VERY CERTAINLY NOT IN THE LOWER NINE-TENTHS OF IT, AND JUSTIFIES THE DESIGNATION 'COSMIC RAYS,' the most descriptive and the most appropriate name yet suggested for that portion of the penetrating rays which come in from above." In 1925 these scientists visited a small lake in Bolivia whose altitude was 15,000 feet. The most crucial tests were there used and readings, etc., were taken. Special attention was paid in these experiments to find out whether or not the mountain area is more or less effective than other portions of the country in sending these rays into the earth. On page 223 of this Government bulletin we find the statement that cosmic rays are produced by definite and continually recurring atomic transformations involving very much greater energy changes than any occurring in radio-active processes. On page 227 of this same bulletin we find this statement, "THIS WHOLE WORK CONSTITUTES, THEN, VERY POWERFUL EVIDENCE THAT THE SORT OF CREATIVE, OR ATOM-BUILDING PROCESSES DISCUSSED ABOVE, ARE CONTINUALLY GOING ON ALL ABOUT US, PROBABLY NOT AT ALL IN THE STARS, AND THAT EACH SUCH EVENT IS BROADCAST THROUGH THE HEAVENS IN THE FORM OF THE APPROPRIATE COSMIC RAY."

I am introducing this evidence here merely for the purpose of showing my students beyond a shadow of a doubt that this Cosmic Realm of creative energy does exist. You will notice that all through my Lessons I have consistently used the words "Life-Spirit." I have done this because I believe there to exist a God Spirit which was and is responsible for every created thing and for every material condition. I do not believe there is a thing, or there can be a thing in existence whether manmade or not, which did not have its origin in the great spiritual GOD REALM. Now, having proved beyond a shadow of a reasonable doubt that scientists have established the existence of a cosmic energy so powerful that it has a voltage of one thousand million, is it too much of a stretch of the imagination to ask you to believe that this realm of unseen spiritual or cosmic energy is the GOD REALM? I do not think so. Certain it is that there must be a reasonable and a natural explanation behind things as they exist. It would be foolish to accept the attitude of many religionists that we are not supposed to know these things, for their history and their origin is not such that it would inspire me to put much confidence in such a statement as that. That is a cowardly way of admitting ignorance. It is also a cowardly thing to do to tell the human race that it was born in sin, shaped in iniquity, and without the spilling of blood there can be no remission of sin. All one has to do is to study the great heavens above to know that there can be no truth in such statements as those. In the first place, they are not reasonable; in the second place, they cannot be proven; and in the third place, they are revolting to the mind of a normal human being. At the risk of being called an infidel and an atheist, I chose to purposely and deliberately throw into the discard such teachings as these; and in throwing over these teachings, I find a new realm opening up. I find there a realm that is illimitable. I find there a realm which my reason dictates to me might very easily answer the entire tangled problem of creation; and as I experiment in a spiritual way with this great Cosmic Realm, I find my theories are changing themselves into proved facts. With the discarding of the old allegorical stories of God, I find a new story and a new vision of God—not as some mystical, mythical, miracle-working individual seated in the sky, but I find a vision of an operating Spiritual Power which is creating every moment of the day and night and which sustains you and me moment by moment on this earth. More than that, I find the existence of a realm of Spiritual Power which, when fully understood, might very easily answer the question we would all like answered—that of life and death.

I do not think my students can do better for the next few weeks than to try to realize the fact that they are surrounded by a most dynamic, unseen Cosmic Realm, which realm is so powerful in itself that scientists in their cold-blooded manner of analyzing have definitely decided that its energy may be measured in terms of volts and have definitely established that this energy equals one thousand million volts. At this point let me go back to the question which will invariably arise in your mind until you understand it. That question is, "Why am I not conscious of this staggering volume of spiritual energy?" If you understood yourself as you are, you perhaps would be conscious of it. Take a brick, or a lead pencil, or some other inert mass. This mass was brought into existence primarily by the Cosmic Realm of God. Now, compare yourself and all your activities and your marvelous piece of physical mechanism with this inanimate object, and then ask yourself what kind of a Cosmic Power is it that caused you to be the marvelous thinking, intelligent being that you are. We know that in a piece of lead, or steel electrical bundles of energy are chasing themselves around with the speed of an express train. We know that we can reduce the physical body to a little water and a few lime salts; but would you attempt to tell me that an aggregation of water and lime salts creates the motivating power behind the human body? That power is an originating power; that power is a thinking power; that power is an invisible power which cannot be explained away by either water or lime salts.

There is, my friend, whoever you may be, a very definite connection between you and this great creative cosmic REALM OF GOD, for that is all it is. That connection is established and may be continued, as I explained in a previous Lesson, through your thought realm. What part of your brain do you think it is that thinks? Physicians will tell you that your mental activities are confined to only a very small portion of the outer layer of the brain; but if the brain itself be responsible for your actions, your thoughts, and your life, then what stops it? I have seen perfectly normal brains preserved for many years. I have seen the heart of a chicken pulsating in a glass jar entirely removed from the chicken it self. There was no brain there. It is foolish to think that life, or actions have their origin in anything physical, for that is not a fact; nor indeed can it be a fact. The great creative processes of life itself are conceived in and exist in an unseen REALM OF POWER. This is the realm I allude to as the "God-Realm," or as I often call it, the great "Spiritual Realm." Now, in our search for the finer things of life, you at least must admit to me that there certainly is enough power in this great COSMIC REALM to bring into existence for you here and now the things necessary to your happiness. If it were possible—and it was possible—that from a vaporous nebula whirling around in this COSMIC REALM OF GOD a planet was created; then would you say to me that no Spiritual Power exists capable of bringing to you the few things you need to make your life happy, healthy, and successful? You take the case of disease. What is that? There can be no disease when the perfect Cosmic Realm of God exists, for this great Power is a building power and not a destroying power. It is a life energy and not disease or death in any sense of the word. Then you ask me from whence comes this disease and this death; and I answer you—THROUGH AN IMPERFECT KNOWLEDGE OF THE POWER OF THE GREAT COSMIC LIFE-REALM. As the years go by and as we give this great Cosmic God-Realm a chance to work in our lives, we find that it does work. In other words, we find that by applying the law governing this great God-Realm, we achieve the results, and the only limitations that can be are the limitations we impose upon ourselves by our disbelief in the realm of the great Cosmic God-Law.

I want to say to you now that it is entirely impossible for you to call into play the Cosmic Realm of God with the desire for success and have failure manifest. Someone once said, "Think failure and failure will manifest." Little did the one who made this statement realize that he was stating one of the most profound of all Spiritual Truths. It is not possible for you to think success and have failure manifest if you really think SUCCESS. You may have to shake off a few old traditions in throwing the power of the Cosmic Realm into action for the attaining of the things you desire, but it is well worth while to do so. You are a lost sheep as it is now. There certainly is no relief for you in the religious teachings of the day; and if it be a fact that mansions are being prepared for you in the sky, you know very well that those mansions can be of no benefit to you here and now. You are thrown back, whether you like it or not, onto a natural power which must exist here and now for you. Now the question is—are you willing to be intense enough and earnest enough to actually spend time enough to release your thoughts into the great Cosmic Realm, never doubting until the desired things manifest? And here let me state that the degree of intensity and earnestness displayed is the measuring cup of the results to be achieved. This is a matter for you individually to decide. I can visualize ahead fifty or one hundred years and I can see men and women absolutely depending upon the Cosmic Realm and absolutely using this Realm for the instant manifestation of things which today would seem to be abnormal and beyond the wildest hope of possibility of obtaining; but we are moving rapidly these days and if you will but realize that this great God-Law can be instantly contacted by you at any hour of the day or night, then it is only a matter of time and of the intensity of your desires before you know better and have proved the existence of this marvelous realm.

I want to close this Lesson by stating that the Law of the Spiritual Realm is in a nutshell thus: "ACCORDING TO YOUR BELIEF, IT WILL BE DONE UNTO YOU." Now remember that I am not asking you to believe in a mythical God in the sky at all, for there can be no scientific belief in that kind of a being. I am asking you to manifest belief in a proven Cosmic Energy-Realm which your reason can easily grasp and which your common sense tells you might very easily be able to do for you the things you desire. You do not understand the processes whereby these results will be achieved, and neither do I; but if you really want to find out whether or not this great God-Realm exists, then let me urge you to put yourself and your thoughts where it can respond. If I would say to you, "I am going to take you to New York City next week with me," and you would say to me, "There is no such a place as New York City," certainly you would never get there. Instead of trying to argue with yourself that there is no such a realm as the great Spiritual God-Realm, why not take it as an accepted fact—and it is an accepted fact—and throw yourself unrestrainedly every moment of the day into this great Power-Realm. As you work, or no matter what you may be doing, do it with the consciousness that you are in definite contact with the great Cosmic God-Realm which created you and which created every other created thing. Do not make the mistake of thinking that you will contact this realm by physical means, because you will not so contact it. You will contact it by mental, or spiritual means and the only means of Spiritual Power you have in you is the power of your thought realm; so just be quiet and practice the existence of this mighty Realm and practice the consciousness of your union with it.

This Lesson has taken you farther, I think, and given you a better understanding of spiritual conditions than you have ever had before; so read it and reread it, and do not be afraid to openly commune with this great God-Realm, for, strange as it may seem, the spoken word is the motive power behind the spiritual thought; in other words, the thought is the bullet which penetrates the Spiritual Realm, but the spoken word is the dynamite, or the nitroglycerine which discharges the cartridge, so speak your desires into the great Cosmic Realm of God, and those desires will sooner or later come back to you in actual form.

So now I leave you with the future being held by you in your own hands. Where you go or what you do depends entirely upon you. Here is the great Realm of God. Here exists Spiritual Power enough to make you an overwhelming victor through life. Here in this great Realm exists a wisdom far superior to any manmade wisdom, for this wisdom is God. Here in this Realm exists a peace far deeper than any man made peace can be, for this peace is God. Here in this great Realm and in your own hands lies an infinite love far greater than any manmade love can be, for this great love is God. And there lies also achievement, success, wealth, and healing, and everything the human soul can desire at all lies in the great Realm of God. I have put into your hands the key that unlocks that door, if any key be needed, and am going to leave you with the knowledge you possess, which knowledge is more than sufficient to throw into play all the cosmic powers of the great God-Head, no matter what your circumstances may be and no matter what of life's gifts you desire. Standing behind you and over you, and all around you, and under you for your protection and benefit is the great Power of the God-Law. Can it be that you desire a personal God? Then to the extent that you change your own personality like that great personality of God will this God appear to you to be a personality but do you not see that you do not change God from a Creative Spirit into a little personality? All you really do is to change your little personality into the likeness of this great Spirit of God.

I should like to prolong this Lesson, in fact, I should like to talk to you about this great Realm for one solid month, or for a year, but that, of course, is impossible, so I am leaving you at this point and wishing for you the courage and the confidence necessary to take this great God-Power with you wherever you go and use it for the manifestation of whatever it is you need.

My thoughts run back this morning to the words of a very beautiful hymn which seemed to be quite appropriate in view of the fact that we are bringing our little journey together to a close. Regardless of the fact that the hymn was written by a Roman Catholic Priest and regardless of the fact that it may be found in some of our church hymn books, I am going to use that hymn in closing, for it conveys in no uncertain manner the thought I want to leave with you. This beautiful poem was written by Cardinal J. H. Newman, of the Roman Catholic Church. He was marooned on a vessel one night near his native city., not a breath of wind disturbed the smooth bosom of the ocean and the boat lay becalmed until such time as enough wind came up to carry it into port. Standing in the bows of that silent ship his mind being on things of God, as it should have been, this beautiful saint penned the following words which will live as long as time endures, and time has no end:

> Lead, kindly Light, amid th' encircling gloom,
> Lead Thou me on:

The night is dark, and I am far from home,
Lead Thou me on!
Keep Thou my feet! I do not ask to see
The distant scene; one step enough for me.

I was not ever thus, nor prayed that Thou
Shouldst lead me on;
I loved to choose and see my path; but now
Lead Thou me on!
I loved the garish day; and, spite of fears,
Pride ruled my will: remember not past years.

So long Thy power hath blest me, sure it still
Will lead me on
O'er moor and fen, o'er crag and torrent, till
The night is gone;
And with the morn those angel faces smile,
Which I have loved long since, and lost awhile.

The great probability is that I shall never meet even a small percentage of my students face to face. Many of them come to Moscow to see me and many of them I am unable to see. But whether I ever see you or not, I want you to forget all about this little life of mine with whatever little influence it may have, and I want you to place all your hopes and all your confidence and all your desires in the Power which so long has blest you and which Power surely will lead you on o'er moor and fen, o'er crag and torrent, till the night is gone; and with the morn we shall probably see many angel faces smiling, for what that morning will bring we do not know now, for we see as in a glass darkly, but you just depend upon one thing and that is this: when the morning of full knowledge breaks that knowledge will disclose just one thing, and that one thing will be the closeness and the reality of the presence of God. I bid you good-bye.

Ever your friend and teacher,
FRANK B. ROBINSON

EXAMINATION QUESTIONS
FOR LESSON NO. 20

These examination questions are for your benefit and you should know the answers to them all. If they are not clear to you, read your Lesson again and again until they are clear.

(1) You (the invisible part of you), being a part of the invisible Life Principle, must have at your disposal all of the power for actual manifes-

tation that is contained in the completeness of the great God Law itself. How is this truth illustrated in Lesson 20?

(2) What would be the consequence if the presence of the God-Law were to be, even for one instant, removed from this world?

(3) What is a light year?

(4) Compare the penetrating force of the Cosmic Ray with that of the Gamma Ray, which ranks next to the Cosmic?

(5) Compare them with reference to the voltage produced by each of these two rays?

(6) What is atomic energy and how can it be produced?

(7) Instead of the old allegorical stories of God, we have now an entirely different vision?

(8) In making use of the God-Law, what is the "measuring cup" of the results to be achieved?

(9) If you really want to find out whether or not this great God Realm exists, what course is recommended?

(10) One should not be afraid to openly commune with the God-Law. The spoken word, as well as the spiritual thought, has its function. How is this illustrated?

(11) Where stands the great power of the God-Law with reference to you? And for what purpose?

(12) With what well-known hymn is this final Lesson of the course brought to a close?

Made in the USA
Middletown, DE
29 July 2021